Something to Share

Our Enduring Love Story

Peggy & Al Schlorholtz

"A More Excellent Way"

1 Corinthians 12:31

All proceeds from this book will be donated to:

The Professor Alfred A. Schlorholtz Scholarship Fund
(For deserving and disadvantaged students in Pakistan)

www.something-to-share.com

Scholarship fund held and distributed by:

The Texas Presbyterian Foundation
6100 Colwell Blvd., Suite 250
Irving, Texas 75039
www.tpf.org

Something to Share

Dedicated to our children four:

Stan

Hope

Esther

John

To our grandchildren three:

Tanya

Erik

Arin

Cosmopolitans All !

_____

Note of appreciation: The author is most appreciative for the encouragement and assistance from the whole family. There has been a lively rapport, some criticism, but mostly positive help. Special thanks are recorded for John and Hope. John optimized and inserted photos with captions, designed the book, cover, and web page, and also oversaw printing and publishing. Hope did the long, painstaking hours of editing. Any typos that remain are fully the fault of the author and this computer.

For many years Peggy and I had hoped to share our life and actions as a record for our children. Finally, here it is.

PREFACE

This is an enduring love story which spans more than seventy years. Ours is a bonded relationship which provides more than a glimpse into the exhilarating reality of two persons made one. It is the beating of one heart, one mind, one spirit – a relationship founded on mutual affection and commitment molded and shaped by rapturous joys and glorious vistas. This was not easy. Life and love were tested and tempered by challenges so demanding and which so stretched us toward our potential that many times we found ourselves wondering whether we could make the next move, do the work before us, or adjust to yet another new culture and environment.

Join us as we, Peggy and Al, attempt to record the challenges and opportunities we have experienced during our lifetime. We intend to relate how a variety of people and cultures made possible a myriad of relationships, which not only enriched our lives but helped us face failures and successes. (A sorrowful note: On November 10, 2007, my loving Peggy died of complications from twelve years of Alzheimer's Disease/Dementia and other related causes. Her contribution to these pages is being gleaned from cherished memories as well as her faithfully recorded copious reports, journal entries, notes, and letters.)

Since the first time we met when Peggy was twelve and I a full thirteen, there has been a spark of affinity and endearment most difficult to explain but recognizable and traceable – even though we had to wait more than nine years to officially and publicly exchange our marriage vows. We were high school sweethearts, Peggy one class junior to me. This the Lord arranged so that we would not have to compete. Her IQ was higher than mine, and Peggy was competitive!

Little did we realize then that the grist for *Something To Share* would be milled in the U.S.A., Pakistan, and Nepal. Variety is indeed the spice of life, and there have been ample ever-changing, enriching, and expanding scenes, places, and situations that enabled us to survive a remarkable labyrinth of circumstances.

Note on 1 Corinthians12:31: "A more excellent way" is one of love, trust, integrity, and the building up of people, not tearing them down or using them for selfish ends. This passage sets out a powerful and inspiring vision that Peggy and I have sought to live by, a vision of a society based on respect for all equally, regardless of education, talents, or background.

Contents

Part III: Our Eleven Years With the United Mission to Nepal

Part IV: Retirement and Florida

Something to Share

Part I: How We Came to be in Iowa

Chapter 1

How Peggy Came to be in Iowa

We must caution our readers that we are about to share our description concerning that wonderful State of Iowa. As we describe the superb quality of Iowa's education system, the high yields of corn and soybeans, the succulent meats and produce, the caring openness of neighbors and friends, the wealth of diversity of peoples from many lands, some readers may gasp and suspect that we are bragging. Can you imagine that?

Peggy and I were both born and reared in Iowa.* Our parents' farms were five miles apart, hers three-and-a-half miles

The Hoft Farm: Now a "Heritage Farm"

south of Wall Lake and mine four miles west of Breda. Since we traded and shopped in different towns and attended different Presbyterian churches, we never met until she was twelve and I was thirteen. Both our families were dairy/livestock/crop farmers. Peggy's father, Henry C. Hoft, and his wife, Beulah, had a fine herd of

---

* Since this book, in part, is intended to document family history, some readers may find that sections of Part I contain a too detailed genealogy.

Holstein cattle, about two hundred pigs, a large flock of chickens, sheep, a number of strong Belgian draft horses, and a few beef animals for the family's food supply. On their fertile one hundred sixty acres, they spent many long grueling hours through good years and bad to exist and survive. Farming is a risky business. During the Depression years of the 1930s, we all were kept close to our farm work and the hard task of survival. Also many of the rural roads had not been improved, making for limited travel and almost impassable transport of produce and business.

Wall Lake, Iowa, with a population in those days of about five hundred people, was built on a rise of ground adjacent to what had been at one time the largest lake in Iowa. It stretched from what is now called Black Hawk Lake, near Lake View, all the way to Wall Lake and beyond, a distance of quite a few miles. But, with drought, dredging, and drain tiling, the lake shrank in size, leaving large sand pits exposed. These sand pits would become many acres of fertile farm land. You possibly know that Wall Lake is the birthplace of the popular singer, Andy Williams. His father was the Depot agent of the Sioux City branch of the Chicago and Northwestern Railway, Superintendent of the Presbyterian Sunday school, and Director of the choir. Peggy's mother invited the Williams family to an after-church lunch occasionally.

According to Peggy's great aunt Clara Willhoite, her great grandfather, Henry Christian Hoft, born in 1840, migrated from Schleswig-Holstein Province in Germany in the late 1850s, settling in Clinton, Iowa. His father, Jochin Hoeft, died in Germany at the age of fifty-six. His courageous wife, Catherine Hoeft, and the children came to America in 1861. They crossed the ocean in eight days in one of the first steamships. On arrival, the "e" was dropped and became Hoft. They settled near Clinton, Iowa. The Civil War began in 1861. In August of that year, Henry enlisted in the Union Army, being attached to the German Militia. By doing so he was given immediate citizenship in the United States of America. He served for the duration of the war, ending up in General Sherman's march to the sea, which we never mention to Southerners.

Henry Christian Hoft married Betty Giese. When Betty was a little girl of eight, her parents, Peter and Catherine Giese, with four sisters and a brother, crossed the Atlantic on a sailing ship. That crossing took three months. Imagine the hardships they endured. They made it to the Clinton, Iowa area and settled in the small town of

2

Camanche, famous for the terrible June 1860 tornado which took many lives, including one of the four sisters. They carried on.

After the war, Betty, having grown to be an attractive young lady, met that handsome ex-soldier Henry Christian Hoft, Sr. They fell in love and were married in 1866, making their home in the city of Clinton, Iowa. Betty was the homemaker, and Henry, a carpenter by trade, built houses in Clinton. After the Great Fire in Chicago in October 1872, he helped build houses there. Sometime after 1875, he and two brothers-in-law traveled by train to a small town called West Side, Iowa, which is fifteen miles straight south of Wall Lake. There they worked building spur railway tracks. They used pairs of oxen and dirt scoops to raise the level to the right height. This gave them a good income, which they prudently saved. After some time they each bought a one-hundred-twenty-acre farm of prairie land in Sac County, Viola Township for eight dollars an acre, which was the Railway's going rate for its landholdings. The down payment was two dollars per acre. They built simple one-story houses on each farm. The framework was cut and fitted in Clinton, shipped to West Side by train, and hauled by horse-driven wagons to the building site. At last they had a place in which to settle down and start farming.

To the Henry and Betty Hoft family were born four children: Elvina, Louisa, Louis Peter, and Amuel. Louis Peter Hoft was Peggy's grandfather. He married Ida Morgan from (guess where) – Clinton, Iowa! They had three children: Clifford, Henry Cecil, and Stephen. Henry Cecil Hoft and Beulah North from Cherokee, Iowa were wed in Sioux City. Beulah was one of three daughters born to Charles W. North and Ella Gibson (also from Clinton): Alma, Beulah, and Ella (Babe). They also had three sons: Norman Gibson, Grenville, and Charles, Jr. Mr. North was a train dispatcher for the Illinois Central Railway at Cherokee. Uncle Norman left home at fifteen to work in the railway. He rose through the ranks to serve the Canadian Pacific line as General Manager, with his own private rail car. He and Aunt Evelyn lived in Winnipeg, Canada. Uncle Grenville, who was an attorney-at-law, and his family lived in Omaha, Nebraska. Uncle Charles, Jr. and his wife Helen lived in South Dakota. They had two sons. Uncle Charles was an electrical engineer, a teacher. He made his first crystal radio at twelve years of age. Aunt Babe taught school in Omaha. She never married. Each summer, she would arrive in Wall Lake by train and amaze the Hoft children as she read stories and poems, and had the children invent their own stories by starting the first line and letting them improvise the rest. Peggy remembered her for the inspiring life and wealth of skills she so lovingly shared. How sad all were when their most loved Aunt Babe died of diphtheria and rheumatic fever at the young age of twenty-nine.

Henry and Beulah met in Manning, Iowa, quite a distance from Wall Lake in those days. Beulah had attended North Iowa College in Cedar Falls, Iowa, where she

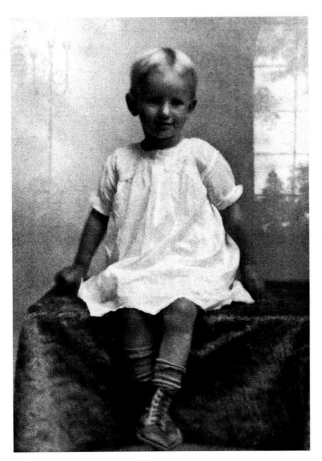

Peggy

received her degree in teaching. She taught for two years in Manning, boarding with Charley and Betty Schmidt. That is where Henry and Beulah met and attended barn dances, a common occasion because a new barn had smooth floors. Henry married Beulah North on December 21, 1918 in Sioux City, Iowa, where her sister Alma Salisbury lived. Their first son was named Henry Charles Hoft born on November 25, 1921. He died of bowel obstructions on December 26, 1921. Often I heard the grief-stricken mother say, "I cried for weeks, and then decided to have as many children as I could. I never did anything to prevent them from being born." On May 23, 1923, Norman North Hoft was born. On March 16, 1925, Peggy Joan (today it would be spelled Joanne) Hoft came into this world, born in the Carroll Hospital on the coldest day that winter. Imagine the hardship of traveling eighteen miles through high snowbanks on unimproved roads from the farm to Carroll! Two neighbors accompanied them along with their shovels to help clear the way through the drifts of snow. How did they ever do that? Later, I will tell about the five other children born to Henry and Beulah Hoft.

Chapter 2

How Alfred ("Al") came to Iowa

In the midst of an American-German community on a farm of one hundred forty acres just four miles west of Breda, Iowa, I was born one cold December 15, 1923 morning at the home of Abel and Emma Schlorholtz. I was to be the middle child of five. This helps to explain why I have such a gentle, compromising nature. My sister, Carrie, was nine years my senior, Bernard was two years older, the other two boys, Floyd and Wayne, were younger. My father was a dairy/crop farmer, with a superior herd of Brown Swiss Cattle, two hundred pigs, four hundred chickens, teams of horses, and fields of corn, soybeans, and alfalfa/red clover for the cattle. My parents worked long hard hours through thick and thin. As I said before, farming is a risky business.

Carrie, Al, and Bernard

Breda is located about thirteen miles from Carroll, the Carroll County seat. It actually took shape as a town in 1877, though was not incorporated until the Sioux City Branch of the Chicago and Northwestern Railway was built. That was the same Branch that was built through Wall Lake the same year.

According to the Breda Centennial book, the town's population grew to five hundred fifty-three people, and it is recorded that friendliness, honesty, and loyalty were the natural customary habits and qualities expected of its citizens. One distinction was that there were seven saloons in Breda – Wall Lake did not even rate! There were mostly farm homesteads and no roads, only trails, swamps, and deep ruts made by farmers on horseback or by wagons pulled by either oxen or horses. Any surplus livestock, potatoes, vegetables, and grains were hauled to Carroll, a larger population center and market.

After the Railway was built, a grain elevator and storage shops made it possible to ship things either to Carroll, to Sioux City, or to Chicago. Later, for the great convenience of the farmers and merchants, automobiles and trucks took on the burden of transporting goods. However, there was need of roads, not marshy trails. The farmers made crude roadbeds by plowing two furrows evenly spaced, clearing the tall grasses between the furrows, and then compacting layers of dirt by dragging heavy planks of wood over them. This was a community effort. These roads proved to be a great time and labor-saving improvement. Incidentally, Breda was named in honor of a city in Holland.

According to the genealogy book of the Schlorholtz family, the first arrivals were Jan Schlorholtz, born in Oldersum, Gottfried, Germany, on January 30, 1817. He married Auke Berends Riekena, born in Twixlum, Gottfried, Germany, April 25, 1820. They migrated to America with their five children: Jacob, Bernard, Lepke, Ockje, and Annie. They settled near Ackley, Iowa in the Webster City/Fort Dodge area. My grandfather, Bernard Schlorholtz, came to America with his parents at the age of fifteen, living with them in a log cabin until eight years later when he started out on his own.

In the spring of 1873, my grandfather Bernard and his brother Jacob, driving a set of four horses pulling a heavily loaded wagon, headed off through the unmarked, swampy way toward Breda, Iowa to buy and till a one-hundred-twenty-acre plot, bought from the Railway for eight dollars per acre. They had to pay two dollars as a deposit and the remainder later. How they ever found that homestead I will never understand. It was forty-five miles west of Ackley and three miles west of Breda and half a mile south in Wheatland township. The first year they built a simple frame house and a shed for the horses and the storing of the wagon and equipment. They also plowed the virgin prairie, often finding Indian arrows, and sowed the wheat seed. To their immense joy, the seeds sprouted and created a green carpet of thriving wheat. They planted vegetables, cut grasses for the horses, and dug a well for water. Then, to their utter horror, the weeds of morning glories, ragweed, and strange plants they had never seen before completely smothered the wheat crop. This left the fields tangled masses of vegetation which choked the wheat. It was a hopeless case. As the fall winds and changing weather approached, they had no alternative but to return to Ackley to survive the cruel blizzards of snow which were sure to come.

According to my father's telling of these events, not to be daunted by the seemingly hopeless challenge to fight the elements, his father and uncle once again made that long trek to their homestead in the spring of 1875. Again they ploughed the fields, harrowed them to make the soil smooth, and again planted the wheat seeds. Was there success? By no means was it to happen. Just about when they could begin harvesting their crops, hordes of grasshoppers from the Dakotas, Montana, and Canada (at that time a British possession) descended – often hiding the light of the sun. Those hungry, devouring insects ate everything except the prairie grasses. It was complete devastation. But, instead of retreating, my grandfather and his brother decided to tough out the winter on their homestead land. By the Grace of God, the next year they had a bumper crop!

My paternal grandfather Bernard married Haukea Catherine Middents, born March 20, 1861 in Liphausen-Gottfried, Germany. Her family had settled in Kamrar, Iowa (south of Webster City). Abel, born November 4, 1888, grew up on that homestead farm. Because of the need to help with the fieldwork and chores, my dad and his two brothers, John and Jacob, left their schooling after the fifth grade. My dad often reminded us that when only twelve years old he had to begin to do a man's work.

Abel married Emma Becker from Breda on February 11, 1914. My mother's parents were Otto Becker and Mattie Aden who were married in Carroll in 1877. Otto was born in Germany September 17, 1845. In 1867 he left the land of his birth and came to America, settling in Illinois. Hearing of the wonderful opportunity in Iowa, he moved there two years later. He bought land and began to farm two miles west of where Breda would be. At that time Breda was not on the map! One of the first settlers in that part of Carroll County, Otto experienced the loneliness of the prairie. The nearest town was Arcadia, ten miles to the southwest. After the C. and N.W.

Railway was established in Breda in 1877, Otto Becker shipped the first carload of barley out of Breda, being compelled by circumstance to shovel by himself the grain from his wagons to fill the rail car. To this pioneering couple my mother, Emma, was born September 25, 1889, one of four daughters and two sons. One of the sons died in 1893 at the age of eleven. To underscore how hard life was at that time, it is noted that Mattie, the mother, died in 1895, leaving those daughters in charge of much more toil.

Becker Family (Emma standing at left)

Chapter 3

Peggy's Childhood Memories amidst an Extended Family

One of the most cherished joys of Peggy's childhood was being part of an extended family. It was not quite like the extended families of India and Pakistan who live in

one large household. Peggy's extended family was the proximity of her uncles and aunts and her great aunt Clara Willhoite. Clifford and Elma Hoft lived a mile west and a half-mile north from the farm of Steve and Marie Hoft. Henry and Beulah Hoft, Peggy's dad and mom, lived across the road from Steve. Clara Willhoite, with her sons, Lee and Lyle, lived adjacent to Steve's farm. These families bonded to form an ideal milieu. Their active interrelationships created a sense of belonging and strong clues of identity and self-esteem. You always felt an integral part of the whole, and yet were free to be, to grow, and to work toward nurturing your potential. Peggy

Peggy (right) with Parents and Brother Norman

often shared throughout her life what a privilege it had been to be part of such a loving/caring/sharing extended family.

There was a good bit of sharing the work, like mutually helping in haymaking, harvesting the crops, butchering, and dealing with emergencies which sometimes cropped up. There were the monthly gatherings to celebrate anniversaries, birthdays, and national holidays, such as the Fourth of July, Thanksgiving, Christmas, and ringing in the New Year. They took turns in hosting such events – picnics in the summer months, sumptuous dinners the rest of the year in one of the homes.

The women always brought huge baskets filled with their specialties, cooked from scratch and baked/roasted/fried on the cast iron kitchen ranges, fired with corn cobs, wood, or coal. Aunt Elma's specialty was a white cake smothered with seven-minute white frosting. Aunt Marie's specialty was a chocolate cake topped with fudge frosting a quarter-inch thick. Aunt Clara brought dozens of cookies. Beulah's favorite was an angel food cake with rich caramel frosting. Those were the desserts. I have not mentioned the southern fried chicken, ham, mashed white potatoes, sweet

Hoft Hospitality: Stan, Steve, Marie, Peggy, Elma, Hope, Al, Cliff

potatoes, fresh breads and rolls, strawberry, peach, and apple jams/pies, corn casseroles, baked beans, green beans, carrots, beet root, pickles, gelatin, and a whole lot more. For Christmas and New Year's Day, Peggy's mom also made suet pudding, an oyster casserole, and roasted chickens with bread stuffing – gastronomical treats. The adults sat around the dining room table. Children sat at the kitchen table and at folding tables. You can imagine the loud babbling, competition for extra helpings, and not too subtle teasing of the girls. During the cold winter months, ice cream was a great hit. However, one had to be careful not to let the salt pollute the frozen cream by allowing the bung opening to get clogged and make it inedible. What a disappointment that was!

After the tables had been cleared, the dishes washed, and leftovers returned to the baskets, the adults played with gusto contract bridge, pitch, or cribbage. One evening after one of those fabulous dinners, a game of Scrabble was played. Aunt Elma, Aunt Marie, Lyle Willhoite, and Uncle Cliff became engrossed in the game of making letters into words on the board. Uncle Cliff had a problem – there didn't seem to be a place to play the X he held for several rounds of play. Suddenly, he had the perfect place. He added the E and the X on a triple letter score. There was a moment of commotion as Elma nudged his elbow, saying "Now Cliff!" Aunt Marie gave her loudest hoot of laughter. Lyle merely smiled. Everyone rushed to their table to see what had happened. What laughs, teasing, and cries of "Shame, shame!" Uncle Cliff had spelled SEX, a word in those early days that was not very proper for public use. Uncle Cliff just grinned and told himself, "I just had to play those letters. There was no other option. I guess I will just have to grin and bear their reproaches with as much dignity as I can muster."

The children took charge of the upstairs, playing their favorite games, that is, until the older boys began teasing the girls again. When this became too boisterous and loud, two of the uncles were delegated by their wives to quiet down the children. This they did with reprimands, threats of punishment, and a warning that next time they might be left at home! This worked for some time, but the noise always returned. During the summer months, after dinner, the children played games outside on the spacious lawn or in the farmyard. They had an immense number of games. To mention a few: hide and seek, pump pump pull away, annie annie over, kick the can, red light, mother, may I? There were more, but that gives you the idea. In the winter there were fox and goose, snow forts, snowball fights, making angels in the snow by lying on one's back and arcing your arms in that deep snow. There was also sleigh riding on sleds when the snow had hardened on Gerdes's hill. This was the highest hill in the neighborhood, about a mile from the Hoft farms. It took a lot of courage to slide down that hill because the sled accelerated as one descended. The worst part was climbing back up the hill!

Christmas Eve was a special event. The whole extended family gathered in the Wall Lake home of the widowed wife of Louis Hoft. He was born in 1871 and died in 1928, only fifty-seven years of age. His widow, Ida Morgan Hoft, was the grandmother of that generation of children about whom we have been writing. Louis Hoft had been quite an entrepreneur – a farmer and an officer in the Wall Lake bank.

Even at an early age, Peggy recalled that Grandpa Louis put her on his knee and called her his little lady. There was great excitement in anticipation of receiving gifts from Santa Claus. Impatiently the children waited behind the sliding doors separating the living room from the dining room and kitchen. They could hear Santa (and several helpers) arranging the gifts as they looked through the keyhole in their attempt to get a glimpse of Santa. Finally, the sliding doors opened and everyone rushed in to find a present or two under the decorated Christmas tree. What fun! To name the children of this extended family may be helpful. Cliff and Elma had four: Donald, Roma Jean, Clifford, Jr., and Patricia. Steve and Marie had one son named Morgan. Aunt Clara's son Lee married Hazel Kent of Auburn. Their children were Ila Mae, Ray, Kay, and Betty Willhoite. Lyle and Dorothy married late in life, having no children. Henry and Beulah had seven living children. They were Norman, Peggy, Richard, Willard, Harrison, Hope Abigail, and Cecil. These were the cousins who had a lot of fun together, and although at times they had their quarrels and tense moments of competition and conflict, they were a lively, close, and loyal gang. On most Sundays, all the cousins went to Sunday school and worship in their churches in Wall Lake. Morgan's family was Methodist. All the others attended the Presbyterian Church.

Peggy had a great time with her brothers and sister. In fact, she was called a "tomboy," which means anything the boys could do, she could do. These included boxing, walking on stilts, skiing down the steep roof of the machine shed on barrel staves in winter, swimming, racing on the lawn, playing softball in the calf pasture east of the lawn, riding the pony and their favorite horse Bill, using bow and arrows, and playing croquet. Peggy's mom often warned her, "Sissy, you'll ruin your health and be sorry someday!" She called Peggy "Sissy" when she wanted to get her attention and advise her to be more careful. Peggy was tall for her age and had long thin legs. Her brothers, when teasing her, called her "Legs!" Peggy's dad thought she would not make it in life because she didn't carry enough weight. Being born second in line, she thought it only natural to lead the gang and offer solutions to any problems they faced.

Each spring, Peggy would get on her cycle armed with a good supply of vegetable and flower seed envelopes, hoping to sell them to her relatives and neighbors. She was successful in this enterprise, winning a box camera, subscriptions to magazines, and other intriguing prizes. Peggy had the gifts of scrutiny and analysis, which served her well throughout her life. In adult life Peggy, having attended a seminar or conference, would relate to me the full character study and attitudes of all present! Most of the time she was dead center correct. When I asked her how she could do that, she replied, "In my early school days, I ordered a detective kit, sending in a few coupons from cereal boxes. That is where I learned the method of deduction. The basic questions are: who, what, when, where, and why?" That method she inculcated with finely tuned dexterity. I took note of this and watched my Ps and Qs!

Peggy never drank any liquor. I asked her why. It seems when she was seven a neighbor's daughter invited her to a party one evening. Since they were close neighbors, her mom thought it was okay. During the evening, they served a cold drink which tasted refreshing in that hot season. The next morning, however, Peggy was sick to her stomach and felt terrible. Her mom asked her a few questions, and she told her about that refreshing drink, which was in reality beer. Beulah warned her about the dangers of drink and drove over to the neighbors to straighten them out. That ruined a friendly relationship with Peggy's friend and her family.

One of the playful pastimes was for Peggy, Dick, and Willard to dress up in adult clothes and costume jewelry to visit Aunt Clara. They walked across the road and knocked on her door. She pretended to be shocked at seeing these strangers, inquiring who they were and from where they had come. When she could not keep from grinning, she invited them in for lemonade and cookies. Then she questioned them whether they had asked their mother's permission. Dick replied, "Oh, we asked her a whole mess of times, and she said No!" These examples give you only a sampling of the rich heritage of growing up in Iowa in the midst of an extended family.

Chapter 4

Al's Childhood Memories of Growing Up

Al's childhood memories are not as impressive as Peggy's. Our uncles, aunts, cousins, and grandparents lived at quite a distance from our farm. In my father's family line, his elder brother, Uncle John, wedded Mary (Bundt) Schlorholtz. Their children were: Mildred, Roy, Merle. Uncle John died young, January 22, 1926, at the age of thirty-four. Mary remarried; her second husband was Alfred Overhue. They had one daughter, Fay, and lived over two miles to the west. My father's younger brother, Uncle Jacob, was a veteran who had been drafted into the American army to fight in Germany from where the Schlorholtz family had migrated. He died on August 18, 1920 of complications from inhaling mustard gas and the wounds he suffered during World War I. He never married.

Grandparents Bernard and Haukea Schlorholtz, having retired, lived in Lake View (nine miles to the north). Their daughter, our Aunt Swanette, was their caregiver, never marrying. This was a heavy load of responsibility and caused her to suffer depression and mental anguish at times. The eldest daughter, Augusta, married Gottlieb von Glan. They were blessed with seven children (our cousins) and lived a mile west. We had a close relationship with this family. Their children's names were Julius, Helen, Benjamin, Edward, the twins Mabel and Marie, and Ruth. We had great fun at Aunt Aukie's, as she was called. I recall a New Year's party with the von Glans. Mabel gave me a kiss, saying that it was okay, because we were "kissing cousins." That was news to me! In the evening, we were served open-faced sandwiches, hot chocolate, delicious cookies, and a wide variety of nuts. One of the sons, Benjamin, wryly remarked that it was lucky for us that a cow had stuck her foot into a pail of milk that evening. That made it possible for us to have hot chocolate! I knew that Ben was joking – at least I hoped he was. Down in the basement, those boy cousins put on boxing gloves and showed us their skills. Of course, they egged us on to put on the gloves. My brother and I firmly resisted these challenges. They would have loved watching us beat our brains out for their entertainment. We were wising up.

My mother's line of sisters and a brother were scattered and distant from where we lived. The eldest sister, Mary Becker, was wedded to John Poen, who after farming four miles northwest of Breda for quite some years, retired to Lake View. Their son, William, took over the farm. Their daughter, Martha, married Claus Husinga. The next sister, Minnie Becker, married John O'Toole. They lived in Carnarvon which was six miles north and three miles east from where we lived. John O'Toole was an accomplished carpenter/cabinetmaker. The O'Tooles had two children: Harry and Evelyn. Anna Becker was the third sister in line. She married Mr. Luckow who lived in Algona, Iowa, a number of miles north of Fort Dodge. After his death, Anna married Albert Thielhorn. They had five children: Johanna, Viola, Millicent,

Bernard, Floyd, Wayne, Carrie, and Al at the Farm

Josephine, and Victor. Victor joined the Air Force during World War II and lost his life when his P-51 Mustang fighter plane flamed out. He is buried in Arlington National Cemetery, Washington, D.C. After Otto Becker, Sr. retired in 1900, his only surviving son, Otto Becker, Jr., took over the farm. He married Minnie Husinga. They had two boys: Donald and Darwin. Otto Becker, Sr. purchased property in Breda where he lived until he died April, 1918 at the age of seventy-two years, six months, and twenty-nine days according to his obituary. Otto's grave is in the

Wheatland Presbyterian Church cemetery four miles west of Breda. Emma Becker, the youngest daughter and my mother, married Abel Schlorholtz, as already noted. (Emma and Abel's children are pictured on the previous page).

We children played most of the games that Peggy's family did. Our favorites were annie annie over (throwing the ball over the machine shed), hide and seek, softball, riding Jack our Shetland pony, playing make believe on outlines of a ship which we laid out in the area south of the house next to the garden, tag, pitching horse shoes, and others. Inside games were checkers, flinch, risk, tinker toys, pick up sticks, Lincoln logs, dominoes, pitch, rummy, hearts, and old maid. After the day's work was done and supper eaten, we gathered round the Philco radio and listened to radio programs, especially the News, Jack Armstrong, the All American Boy, Little Orphan Annie, Jack Benny, George and Gracie Allen, Jimmy Durante, and the Hit Parade (the ten best songs of the week aired on Sunday evenings). Mom often made a great pile of buttered popcorn and delicious fudge, which we ate during the Sunday night entertainment. We boys made Carrie very peeved when we sang the words of those ten favorites. Especially boisterous was "Boo Hoo, You Have Me Crying For You." You can imagine the sorrowful tinge in our voices!

In the parlor, as the living room with two sliding doors was called in those days, Mom and Dad had put a piano, complete with paper rolls. These rolls were perforated by cutouts to sound the notes of a song with the air supplied by two foot pedals to fill the bellows. What a tremendous machine that was! One would sit in the middle of the piano bench and work the pedals as everyone else would join in the words of a song printed right onto the paper roll. Many hours were spent there with the whole family lustily joining in. Of course, that was during spring, summer, and fall. During the winter, the sliding doors were kept closed to lessen the number of rooms in the house that were heated by the coal-burning furnace in the basement. In the winter, the kitchen became the living/parlor room, which was warm and cozy, because Mom's cast iron cooking range was there. We had our meals in the kitchen the year round. There was a large table in the dining room, but that was used only when "company" came for a meal.

We visited our aunts and uncles for celebration of anniversaries, birthdays, and holiday events. Many times my mom would invite one of the relatives' families to have lunch after church at our house. On Saturday, she would make as full preparations as possible. We cousins always had a great time playing games, getting into trouble, and wearing down our energy levels. At our relatives' home, after a big potluck meal, the older men played poker, which my father did not care to play. Even at small stakes, he felt it was gambling and a waste of time. The rest of us played rummy, pitch, or pin the tail on the donkey, crossed scissors, I spy, and scaring each other in the dark.

Each mother brought loads of food for the potluck dinners. The menu was similar to Peggy's family, but not quite as elaborate. There were lots of home-cooked specialties, which were delicious. A good time was had by all. There was also, I surmise, whispered gossip among the women. The main source was Aunt Minnie O'Toole, who operated the Carnarvon telephone switchboard of party lines. When a call came in, she plugged the right cord into the connection. She forcefully maintained that she did not "rubber" (listen to conversations). Her alibi was that she had to make certain the call had gone through and that the connection was successful. Aunt Minnie was one aunt we respected and feared – she was the most informed person in the whole neighborhood. We knew for sure that if she heard anything we had confided to another of devious behavior on the party line, she would tell our mom! However, in times of emergencies, Aunt Minnie alerted the right people for help, which was timely and much appreciated.

We were all on party telephone lines connecting six to eight homes with their call numbers consisting of a series of long and short rings. Our phone was one long, four shorts, and one long. We all knew the number of every neighbor. If we thought it imperative, we would "rubber," listening to only what seemed important! If too many people were "rubbering," the voices would become fainter and fainter, because it drained the dry cells which powered the phone. Sometimes, when two of the women were conversing and there was ample evidence that there were too many listening, they would switch to High German, which we could not fully understand. At that point many of us promised ourselves to study High German. I have always maintained that I learned public speaking on those party telephone lines.

On Sunday mornings, all of us children attended Sunday school. Since the church was only a half mile away, adjoining our farm, we walked. An hour later, our parents would join in the worship hour. Until World War II, the worship service was in German once a month. There were that many people of German descent in our community to merit such an arrangement. According to tradition, the men sat west of the aisle; the women sat on the opposite side. At the back corner, there was a small room reserved for mothers nursing their child and for children who could not sit still and quietly during those long sermons. Mothers wisely brought a good supply of crackers to lessen the tension of having to keep the children quiet.

From Right: Al, Floyd, Carrie, Bernard

Chapter 5

Levey School, Number 7, Peggy's Early Elementary School Days

The State of Iowa insisted that provision be made in each county for rural schools to be built, maintained, and the teaching positions filled. A County Superintendent of Schools was appointed by the county officers. It was his responsibility to visit and inspect each school in the county at least once a year, hold teacher examinations to see whether applicants were qualified, and issue certificates to those who did. He also had the power to hire, or to fire a teacher with "good" cause. Teachers may not have feared God as much as they feared that Superintendent! The intent of such stringent measures was to ensure quality of teaching, integrity of character, and role model perfection. One had to be eighteen years old or older and have graduated from a Normal Institute (the center for teachers' training). Contracts for teachers were term by term: fall, winter, and spring. School attendance for children was mandatory until at least sixteen. All those who wanted to graduate and go on to high school had to pass the county examination conducted at the end of the spring session.

In rural Iowa Townships, subdivisions of the County, a one-room school was built on a square acre of land at a distance of two miles in each direction from another school. All eight classes were held in that one room. Since the land had been divided into sections of six hundred forty acres (one square mile), pupils had to travel to school a maximum of two miles. The teachers had to travel from their parents' home or board with a neighbor nearer the school. They were a highly dedicated lot, who braved all the elements of heat and cold, rain and drought on dirt roads often muddy or choked with snow in those frigid winter months.

The Hoft children attended Levey School, Number 7, a half-mile north and a mile west of the farm. Going to school meant walking, riding horseback, or horse and buggy. In severe weather conditions, Henry would pick them up in the family Ford Model A, or by a horse-pulled bobsled in winter. Most of the time, the parents were too busy with farm activities to "pamper their children." In the Great Depression of the 1930s, economic factors were making it tough for the rural schools. There were more teachers than schools. Consolidation of schools began, which proved a big problem for transport. The days for rural schools were coming to an end. This afforded Beulah the opportunity to make repeated entreaties for the children to study in Wall Lake town. However, the School Board members maintained that was not possible because tax monies were in short supply. All the Hoft children attended Levey School, Number 7 through the eighth grade except for Hope Abigail who went into the eighth grade in Wall Lake.

The school building had no electricity, telephone, screens, or storm windows. In winter, especially on Monday mornings, it was like an iceberg! The large stove in the center of the room had to be lighted, using wood, coal, or corncobs. It had a protective shield of galvanized tin, which saved those nearby from being singed. Nevertheless, one roasted on one side and froze on the other. Water was brought from a neighbor's farm and stored in a stone water cooler, or from a much prized well with a hand pump installed. There was a coal shed, outdoor toilets for girls and boys, a playground, and a tall flagpole. Mercifully, there were shade trees and a few flowers by the front steps planted and cared for by a "volunteer." In fact, there were lots of "duties" – sweeping the floor, taking out the ashes, washing the big blackboard on the wall behind the teacher's desk, and dusting the windowsills and row upon row of hard pine desks, two students to a desk. We always wished that they had been made using soft pine slats! Dusting the blackboard erasers was done by soundly pounding them against a hard surface outdoors.

All eight grades were in that one-room school. What a huge task that was for a teacher. Each class had its time to meet in front of the teacher's desk, where each pupil would report on an assignment, either reciting or writing on the blackboard in front of everyone the answers to arithmetic problems, sentences in correct English using cursive script, and various other proofs of diligent study. One great advantage was that pupils in the lower classes benefited from the exposure to correct as well as incorrect answers. The basic idea was to learn reading, writing, spelling, arithmetic, geography, art, music, physiology, and civil studies. A modest library was in evidence, mostly stocked by the teacher with her/his own funds, because he/she wanted the pupils to expand in knowledge and skills. We greatly enjoyed listening to records played on the phonograph, which was wound by hand.

One had to have an extraordinary sense of dedication, wisdom, and love for children to cope with the teaching/learning experience required to be a rural school teacher. He/she had to be single, not smoke, chew tobacco, or engage in any devious behavior. If you married, you lost your job. But, if anyone found the man/woman of their dreams, it was a relief and joy! The pay was low, the hours long, and the responsibilities were overwhelming.

Peggy loved to go to school. She and her brothers braved the elements, walking to school, or driving the buggy pulled by faithful Bill, and enjoying the occasional ride in the Ford Model A. She loved arithmetic, optional books from the library, and especially the recess period. A fast learner, mischievous at times, but a good, all-around pupil, she worked hard for those As and Bs. She and her brother Dick were close and engaged in friendly competition to see who had the highest grades on the monthly report card. These were sent to the parents and had to be signed by them to ensure they had scrutinized those marks. Woe to you when there were low marks! But, mostly there was praise for making the most of time spent in school. Also, there was a slot for deportment, a grade for a pupil's conduct and behavior. Whenever a low mark appeared, there was instant and rather severe punishment. Parents in those days were on the teacher's side. No excuses were allowed.

Most mornings, Peggy and her brothers walked to school, carrying their lunch buckets, wooden pencil and crayon boxes, and any books they wanted to study. To help her mother, Peggy prepared the lunches. There were sandwiches of home-baked bread with jam, peanut butter, or an occasional slice of meat, an apple, and a piece of hard candy to sweeten the day. The thermoses were filled with hot chocolate/tea, if that treat was possible. Mostly there was a cup of water from the water cooler. Pupils sat at their desks to eat lunch. They were careful not to spill anything, or drop crumbs onto the floor. That meant sweeping up!

All looked forward to the short recess of twelve minutes in the middle of the mornings and afternoons. This made possible outhouse visits, a quick game of tag, and giving the teacher a few moments to regain her equilibrium. One of the consequences of any misbehavior was to forfeit the recess time, having to remain at one's desk. An alternative was being directed to write on the blackboard at least a hundred lines: I will not again pull Mary's ponytail. The teacher had to keep a strict discipline, to be in control. With so many pupils in one room, it was imperative that no nonsense was allowed. At times, the older boys were a source of trouble, often kept after school to be punished for a serious infraction of the rules. They were taller and much stronger than the teacher. She had to rule with stern glances and a strong discipline. Three teachers are fondly remembered: Miss Crowe, Myrtle Ballard, and Josephine Lawler. At the fiftieth class reunion, Dick thanked Miss Crowe and told her she had taught him everything he had to know. However, he asked why she had been so strict. She replied, "Being eighteen and teaching my first year, I was forced to be tough to maintain control."

Peggy was an active girl to say the least. One time she jumped out of a high-flying swing and broke her arm at the elbow. That was very painful. When she was back at school, the teacher kindly excused Peggy from dusting-the-erasers duty. To his credit, Peggy's father massaged her elbow every evening for weeks with heated oils, gradually straightening her arm and getting that elbow to function well. This provided a warm bonding with her father. Later in life, Peggy always told how she had recovered due to his persistent loving care. She did not miss dusting the erasers. However, during one recess, the teacher saw her swing down the railing of the steps using that elbow. It was back to dusting the erasers again.

Chapter 6

Al's Elementary Schooling at Wheatland Number 4

Wheatland Township School Number 4, a one-room school, was at the far southwest corner of the section of land, a half-mile south and a mile west of our farm. Carrie and Bernard had also attended that school. Bernard was in a class two years my

The Student Body of No. 4; Al (standing, lower right)
Bernard (2ⁿᵈ row, 3ʳᵈ from left)

senior. We walked most of the time. I started school at the age of six. Miss Ethel Peters was my teacher for the first five years. She lived with her parents one mile east and three miles south of the school, on the way to Arcadia. She rode a horse until she bought a Model A Ford coupe, the envy of all walkers. There were other times during winter when the snow had drifted into such high piles that her father drove her to school on a bobsled. I have heard many teachers recalling frozen legs, face, and hands from wading snowdrifts. Facing blinding snow and bitter cold winds, they courageously fought their way to school to be there on time. In those early 1930s, the roads were actually muddy paths after a heavy shower of rain. All things considered, a teacher's job was not a happy one until spring arrived. It was easier to maneuver in the mud than those wintry blocked paths.

Thanks to my mother and sister Carrie, I could already recite my ABCs and simple numbers before starting school. I can honestly say I enjoyed going to school. The walk to school was long and tiring, but once at school one was part of a new family. I had quite an adjustment to make as from childhood I had spoken Platt (Low German). After a time, following some rather embarrassing experiences, I got the hang of English. Reading books became my favorite subject. We had good books at home, but the ones in the library were fascinating to me. Making new friends and enemies made life at school a challenge. Since I was a bit short, I learned early in life to be diplomatic. Being the middle child in our family began to serve me well. I must have have been very talkative and witty. In fact, sometimes my family sang a ditty following one of my "incessant jabbering" sessions: "Windy, windy Al moonshine" was one line. They meant well in an attempt to temper my talents. After crying a few times, I learned to be brave and strong. By the way, I was born as bald as an egg, but after several years I had grown a head of curls that made my mother very proud. Evidently, she must have had a secret desire to have another girl in the family. Thank goodness they cut off those long curly locks before I started school. Imagine the teasing I would have had to endure!

We boys wore overalls to school, the garment most suited to farming and schooling. They wore like iron, and needed to. Overalls had lots of pockets, one of which had a good number of marbles in the spring. I lost many a marble, shot out of the circle by a well-aimed shooter marble. The overalls had a front bib with a pocket into which one could slide pencils or a fountain pen. We carried our lunch buckets, complete with a thermos bottle in the upper curved lid. That hot sweetened tea was refreshing, and the sandwiches, cookies, and occasionally some fruit had to last until supper time. The school days were long and crammed full of studying assigned lessons, reciting as a class in front of the teacher's desk. There were three in my class, that is, until my classmates moved to another distant farm. This left me solitary in the class, allowing no slack. It had helped to have company while reciting what we were supposed to learn. However, to my great surprise, Miss Peters promoted me from the fourth grade to the fifth! I joined Merle Schlorholtz and Arlo Hinz. I never really knew why she had done that. Was it brains or a means to have one less class to teach? In deference to that wise teacher, I prefer the first reason!

At recess time, we played the usual games already mentioned above (similar to Peggy's school experience), so I won't repeat them here. It was a refreshing time. Our eyes kept an alert gaze at the clock in anticipation, cautiously, because the teacher didn't appreciate that. There was rough and tumble game time. I recall, however, the apprehension experienced during choosing up sides to divide into two groups. It wasn't too happy a time to be the last one chosen, as if one did not qualify to be a productive player, or one was finally selected a member of the team as if by mercy or reluctance.

A rural school played a big role in the neighborhood, serving as a Center for social and functional needs. Today, they would be called community centers. At the school elections were conducted, special issues were debated, and social events were held. A big event was the Box Social, to which each family connected to that school would bring a box filled with a lot of goodies. These were sold or auctioned off in order to raise funds needed to further equip the school with extra crayons, books for the library, construction paper for handicrafts and class projects, and the like. There was also enough food – cakes, cookies, and candies – to finish off the evening in fun and frolic. That was an excellent way to raise necessary funds without having to make an appeal or beg. At Christmas, just prior to a week's vacation, there was the Christmas program. For weeks we would rehearse a drama, practice carols, memorize our lines, and especially work on the poem one would recite. That was the highlight of the year, when all the parents and a few close relatives would attend with bated breath and high expectations for a perfect performance by their children.

Another big event was at the close of the school year. Of course, there had to be a special time of entertaining one's parents. When I was in the sixth class, Miss Louise Olberding had become our teacher. She had new ideas. All the students discussed what kind of program we should have. Several ideas were worked on. It was decided to form a Kitchen Band, a merciless noise-making assembly of kitchen utensils trying to play a tune. I was shocked! I told the teacher that we could not do anything like that. It would be too much noise for my father who had had an ear operation recently. Our family household had become a sanctuary of silence, and we talked in hushed tones. Miss Olberding asked me what we could do. In an inspired moment, I suggested we do a Western Night. I said that I would sing western songs and even yodel! And that is what we did in full cowboy regalia. It made a great hit with less noise than had we deafened the air with kitchen utensils. I had started my lifelong realm of entertainment – singing solos and telling jokes.

Walking to and from school also had its charms. One afternoon, our neighbors, Hans and Bertha Tjaden, and their daughter, Hilke, beckoned us to stop at their house. I recall it was Groundhog Day, because Bertha's birthday was on that day. They served Bernard and me a slice of angel food cake, with delicious caramel frosting. What a treat that was! In early spring one could see a robin pulling up a worm, a meadowlark serenading, red-winged black birds circling one's head while making their characteristic chatter. During the evening walk, we sometimes were startled by the rapid ascent of a pheasant from its nest or hiding place, heard the "bob white" of a quail, or watched a flock of geese seeking a warm refuge and food in some isolated lake or swamp. In spring and summer, wildflowers decked the sides of the road: daisies, wild roses, goldenrod, violets, and wild strawberry blossoms. Sometimes we picked a bouquet for Mom. She would tell us how she appreciated them and gave us a hug for being so thoughtful. During the fall weather, we saw leaves turn to deep reds and gold, fields of crops ready for harvesting, and patches of pumpkins ready to be turned into Halloween lanterns, or made into delicious pumpkin pies. It was almost time for the corn harvest two-week vacation to help pick the corn. That was hard work, but it helped our parents to gather in the fruit of their long months of labor.

It would be repetitive to record here what has already been written about Peggy's rural school experiences in the previous chapter. I will spare you that. However similar, they were distinct and unique in their own right. By now I hope you can picture in your minds the wealth of our common heritage, traditions, and rural settings. It all adds up to what we in the future would have as Something to Share!

Chapter 7

Our High School Days in Wall Lake

Already in 1893, the first class finished the course and graduated from the Wall Lake High School. That high school had resulted from a period of growth in the number of students and additional teachers. At the beginning of this educational enterprise, Wall Lake had been a small pioneer settlement. As mentioned above, Wall Lake as a town was platted in 1877 while the railway was constructed. The town was on the frontier edge of settlement with a population of six hundred fifty-nine. Early settlers had built their houses and ploughed the prairie sod. They had large families and had begun to think about how their children would get an education. The families who lived in town began by renting a simple one-story room and hiring a teacher. As the numbers increased, there was need of moving to larger rooms in order to cope with the ever increasing number of students. Eventually they constructed a large frame building. This, too, became overcrowded, and ever expanding facilities had to be provided. The subjects studied were basic reading, writing, and arithmetic, but there were also games, music, art, and other activities to help enrich the students' education. (I am indebted to the authors of *A Century of Living in Wall Lake 1877-1977*, a historical treatise compiled for the Centennial Celebration, for the facts and figures used.) By 1900, a tall two-story wooden building had been constructed. To this were built additions on an ever expanding schoolyard, needed for future development of facilities and playgrounds for the pupils during recess time. To make a long story short, the building that Peggy and I attended was of fired brick construction, consisting of eighteen classrooms, a gymnasium, and a large study hall with a stage and library. That was 1923, the year I was born! How thoughtful of them to get ready for my arrival in the fall of 1937. In the interim of 1923-37, great changes had taken place, especially in the extracurricular activities. These included physical training, musical training as an elective, group singing, manual and vocational training, basketball for girls and boys, baseball and football for the boys, and home economics for girls.

Competition matches raised the interest of students and school loyalty/spirit. Rival schools were Lake View, Auburn, and Odebolt. If you care to check on this, view the trophy case at the entrance to the school where many sports cups for champion feats are exhibited. Qualified teachers were "volunteered" until athletic coaches were hired as teachers/coaches on a full-time basis. Practices were held after school. That was fine for the children in town, but difficult for us rural people who had to hurry home to help with the evening chores of feeding animals, milking, and gathering eggs from the hen house.

To accommodate Carroll County, Wheatland township pupils, the Sac County School District was enlarged, because Breda had no public school. The Roman Catholic population of Breda was so dominant they had a Parochial School. Only a few Protestant families lived in Breda since they had businesses there: Dr. L. Jones, Walter Brandsma, Arthur Rickie, and Lottie Jones who owned the only drugstore in town. We had to drive in car pools eight miles from our farm to the Wall Lake High School. In the early 1930s, Jud von Glan drove a big car carrying his brothers and sisters, my sister Carrie, and Hilke Tjaden to Wall Lake. In my time, my brother Bernard drove the Model A with a load of fellow students. Roy and Merle Schlorholtz drove their Model A. Our first cousin, Don Becker, did the same. I will save you the description of the hardships we experienced on those unimproved graveled roads. You can well imagine!

Having graduated from the eighth grade, I enrolled in high school in the fall of 1937. My brother, Bernard, was one year ahead of me. Norman Hoft was in his class. This was like another world with so many pupils, new surroundings, and serious study. I did quite well. Peggy Hoft entered high school in 1938. We all had assigned desks, with a storage box under the desktop, convenient for storing textbooks, notepaper, and our lunch buckets. Members of each of the four grades sat in places assigned to them. The first-year students sat in their two long rows on the right-hand side of the Study Hall, the other classes accordingly filled their rows of desks. There was always a teacher seated behind us at a table (like a guard in a prison tower) to make sure we studied instead of making mischief. We all went to our assigned classroom at the sound of the bell. There our teacher would take up the lesson of the day, make assignments, test us, and try to impart some new knowledge into our heads!

For the first two years, Peggy and I had friendly exchanges. We did not date, because I was too shy and serious with studies. However, one noonday after the lunch break, things began to change. There I was, a third year student, seated at my desk hurriedly doing my Algebra assignment for the next day since there was a basketball game that evening. Suddenly, to my great amazement out of the corner of my eye, I saw something sailing through the air. I quickly caught an orange thrown way across the Study Hall by that grinning Peggy Hoft! She came over and we chatted. I asked to have a date with her that evening after the game. She agreed – that was our first date. She had gotten my attention! After that we dated occasionally, nothing really serious, because Bernard took the car to be with his dates, and he was handsome and popular.

Peggy became a star basketball forward. She had the height, stamina, and skills to make the team. In one game she scored twenty-nine points! Those days of being a

Peggy (4ᵗʰ from left) becomes President of Sac County 4-H Club

tomboy were paying off. I made the basketball second team playing point guard, a baseball left fielder, and in my senior year a guard in football on the starting eleven. My claim to fame was hitting a single to center field, with a man at second, who scored the winning run in the Sac County Baseball tournament. I still treasure those school letters W.L. in all three sports.

Both Peggy and I were active in the school programs. Peggy sang in the Girls' Glee Club as an alto. Both of us participated in the Mixed Chorus. This was coeducational singing in four part harmony. I took voice lessons, was the bass in Boys' Glee Club and the Quartet, and played the baritone euphonium in the Band until they needed a sousaphone player. Merle Schlorholtz was encircled with the other one. Bernard and Roy Schlorholtz played trumpets. We also did class plays, skits on national holiday themes, and musicals each year. Peggy starred in both her junior and senior year plays. In my senior year, I played the English butler, having mastered the accent! I had to learn one hundred sixty-eight lines. My mother coached me until late in the night to get those lines right.

We highly respected our teachers, who were well qualified and proficient in their subject(s). They became our role models. Dr. Underwood was Superintendent of the whole school. This included all grades from kindergarten on up. Our Principal was Mr. M. Edwards who also taught the Industrial Art classes. Ione Brown taught Math until she retired and Miss Huff took over her classes. Mr. Morris was the typing teacher. Mr. Roland Crandall was the Director of the Music Department (vocal as well as instrumental). Miss West taught Biology. Our revered Mr. Art Olsen was our history teacher and coached football, basketball, and baseball.

However, the most revered was Miss Wanda Sifford, the English/Languages teacher. She was a genius who made learning English a creative, captivating, and challenging subject. Every week there was a list of new vocabulary. Ask any student that took her classes, and they will affirm that at the top of the very first list was "alliteration." One had to not only spell the word, know its meaning, but also use it in a sentence. During my junior year, I took Latin in her class instead of Farm Shop. Miss Sifford taught in that same high school for forty-seven years! She was also active in the Presbyterian Church, teaching Sunday school classes, and as an Elder. To celebrate her twenty-fifth anniversary of teaching, the Women's Club of Wall Lake initiated the Wanda Sifford English Award which presented a twenty-five dollar scholarship to the senior student who had the highest grade point at graduation.

My graduation was in May of 1941. I stood third in my class. Viva Lee Marshall and Melvin Sommer topped me. It was with a sad heart that I left that dear high school, with strong intentions of going to college, although that was not to be until later. Peggy carried on in her senior year. We dated occasionally, but I found myself out of the loop, busily assisting my parents on the farm and very active in our Wheatland Presbyterian Church. Peggy graduated in 1942. The Valedictorian of her class, she made plans to attend Iowa State College in Ames, Iowa. Many of the girl graduates began nursing or secretarial training. Peggy's mom had gone to college; she was determined that all her children would get their college degree! And all of them did, except Cecil, the youngest son, who was born a Down's Syndrome child. Richard, Willard, Harrison, and Hope Abigail also attended Wall Lake High School and became college graduates. In the throes of the Great Depression, that was a sacrificial phenomenon by Henry and Beulah Hoft.

Peggy Graduates High School

Chapter 8

Some of Peggy's Experiences at Iowa State (College) University

Peggy at Iowa State University, Ames

In the fall of 1942, Peggy's two suitcases and bundles of other things were packed into the family car. Proud parents were taking their daughter to Ames, ninety miles to the east of Wall Lake. Affectionate goodbyes and parting kisses had been given by her brothers and sister, aunts and uncles, and a good number of the cousins. They made their way to US Highway 30, the Lincoln Highway, which was the first transnational road from the east to the west of the U.S.A. Heading past Boone, they soon arrived at the Iowa State College, now a University. They helped Peggy get settled into her dormitory, said their goodbyes, and drove back to the farm. There were a lot of heavy hearts that evening.

Peggy registered for classes the next day, paid the tuition, and started to explore the large campus. There were many buildings, graceful shade trees, and miles of sidewalks. Orientation was the following morning in the mammoth gymnasium filled with hundreds of students. Peggy told me that professors and administrators presented the rules and regulations, as printed in the small handbook. One of the orientation officials said, "Congratulations on becoming a student here at Iowa State College. Look to the ones seated on your right and left. Only one of you three will complete the requirements and graduate from I.S.C." (Not very encouraging or giving one confidence.) They meant business in that Land Grant College where the tuition costs were lower for residents of Iowa. The academic standards were high.

Classes began, and Peggy studied most diligently. She was majoring in Foods and Nutrition. Her mom had "suggested" that! "Sissy," she would say, "take practical courses that will serve you well in life!" Peggy made good marks. Gradually, she found friends and felt more at ease. She experienced the usual routines and challenges. In order to earn some extra cash, she found a part-time job serving meals, washing dishes, and doing a bit of cleaning at Mrs. Marty's boarding house near the campus. Peggy ate her meals there, which saved a lot of money. Mrs. Marty was from Scotland, rather short, but full of wit and firm in decisions.

Peggy made special friends – two of them, Virginia Lodge and Elva Ann Davies, remained lifelong communicators. The first year of study was one of basic subjects. The second year was more practical with labs and projects in addition to the advanced course work. They studied foods, planned menus, scientific buying, and preparing meals. One project was caring for a baby. Peggy had some practical knowledge of this from having been big sister in her home.

Occasionally, on a weekend or holiday break, she would take the train to Carroll where one of the family would meet her. What a relief that was! Mom's cooking was a treat. Everyone wanted to know what college life was like. What an enjoyable time they had! Sadly, on Sunday late afternoon it was back to Carroll, the train ride to Ames, and again resuming the daily grind of college work.

Al and Peggy (left) Double Dating

Peggy had an interest in Chemistry, taking enough academic hours to almost graduate with a Minor in the subject. This, of course, meant many afternoon laboratory periods. I recall her relating a scary experience. As she was busily conducting an experiment, out of the corner of her eye she noticed something moving. There, on top of one of the cages, was a large white rat! She gave out a shriek and started to move away. However, the graduate student in charge merely said, "Oh! Did Snookie scare you? That's my pet!" Peggy recovered, but she never had a liking for rats and mice on the farm, or anywhere else. Peggy tried golf, which she played quite well in a tournament. She excelled in archery, winning a medal at a tough national competition. Of course, Peggy was used to winning.

Peggy had dates with fellow students. (From 1942 to the summer of 1944, I was in no position to keep in touch with her. The next chapter will explain this.) She maintained close ties with her family, sending her soiled clothes home every two weeks for washing, pressing, and return by post. Her mom also wrote to her two times a week, sometimes enclosing a five dollar bill earned from the sale of eggs. That was when Peggy treated herself to a pint of ice cream which cost nineteen cents! Mom also had an arrangement with Lydia Thomas who worked in Ellerbrock's Ladies Wear in Carroll. She knew Peggy's size, style preference, and colors. At each sale when things were marked down, Lydia would set aside at least two dresses or skirts and blouses for Beulah to pick up to send to Peggy.

It is regretted that there is no list of studies and history of her experiences in detail. Peggy didn't have time to keep a personal diary. However, during the summer break of 1944, she arranged a party at the farm. I was invited to attend. We had a fun-filled evening with games, chatting, and much food. That is when I spent some time with Peggy after the party. It all seemed so natural, but it is quite possible that she had again "gotten my attention!" From that time on, we exchanged letters, two and three times a week. Also, I noticed much friendly attention from her parents when we met at meetings, dinners, and Farmers' Night School in Wall Lake. Peggy's dad encouraged me to join the Masonic Lodge, which I did. He even taught me to improve my cribbage game at the Lodge.

Occasionally, I would drive to Ames for a Saturday evening date with Peggy. We had much to share and wanted to get to know one another better. Her visits home seemed to be more frequent, which meant more dates. We often met at Evelyn Wolleson's home in Wall Lake to join school friends in singing and making small talk. There was a time when I arrived at Peggy's home for a date, to be told she was not yet ready. Her dad invited me in, and her mom coaxed me to play bridge rather than see a movie. We four really had a grand time playing cards. Peggy was always my partner. I was careful not to trump her Ace. At about 10:00 Beulah would ask me if I would like coffee and cake. We enjoyed her sandwiches, cake, or a slice of pie with the coffee. They say that the way to a man's heart is through the stomach. That is true! Discreetly the parents would then retire upstairs. Peggy and I had much to "talk" about.

On December 21, 1944, I asked Peggy to marry me. She accepted! This was her parents' wedding anniversary and a special time. For Christmas, I was invited to join the joint family for dinner at noon. Peggy and I exchanged gifts. There were also a few simple gifts for her parents from the "new" beau. I have already described those dinners. We really had a good time. After that special Christmas, I became a regular guest at all the holiday celebrations, even in the homes of the aunts and uncles. I recall one bitter cold New Year dinner. It was twenty below zero, with lots of snow. While assisting in the cleanup, I dried the dishes and sterling silverware. I took two at a time, until Aunt Elma instructed me to dry only one at a time to prevent scratching the silver. This was new to me, because at our home we only had Betty Crocker flatware. As the families were about to leave, Elma's husband, Clifford, went out to start the car so that the heater could take at least some of the cold air away. There stood Aunt Elma with her arms filled with a big basket, cake tins, a bag of leftovers, getting more and more exasperated with Cliff's delay. She turned to me and said, "Now, Alfred, I hope after you and Peggy are married you won't keep her waiting like I am!" "No," I replied, "I'll let Peggy warm the car!" You should have heard the roar of laughter, especially Aunt Marie's hoot! Aunt Elma also laughed. I always felt good about how I had saved Uncle Cliff that night from a scolding from his "wounded" wife.

The final two years of college, Peggy lived with her Aunt Verna Schmidt at 617 Northwest Avenue in Ames. She was the daughter of Charley and Betty Schmidt in Manning. Aunt Verna, the principal of an Ames junior high school, was reputed to be the strictest principal in the whole town. She was a Methodist. Peggy attended her church whenever she didn't attend the Presbyterian Calvary Chapel on campus. Aunt Verna had never married. She was highly educated, an excellent teacher, and had toured Europe quite extensively. England was her favorite. Peggy told her about this boyfriend of hers, Alfred Schlorholtz, from Breda. She was not impressed that as a student of a college where there were hundreds of eligible men from good families, Peggy should be interested in a farm boy with only a high school education! Of course, at that point she had not met me. That fall I was brave enough to meet Aunt Verna when picking up Peggy for our date. I became aware that she was scrutinizing and evaluating Peggy's farm boy. Eventually, she saw why Peggy and I would make a good couple. We were infatuated with one another. A growing love and devotion were much in evidence. I visited Peggy whenever possible. On one occasion Elmer Graber, a close neighbor of ours, asked me to join him in taking a truckload of flax seed to the I.S.C. farm. Peggy arranged for us to have supper with her at Aunt Verna's. We had a great time. Elmer was a close friend. He shared what an asset I was to the whole neighborhood. Aunt Verna's attitudes began to thaw a bit.

Peggy and I often discussed marriage. We heartily agreed that to make our marriage a lasting one there had to be at least four things: 1. First of all, there had to be commitment. Love is not just a warm sentiment, it involves a deeply heartfelt commitment to each other, which would never fade regardless of the most trying circumstances. 2. Being considerate of each other, putting the other's needs first instead of one's own desires, and ever guarding against selfishness. 3. Open communication and learning to share, not just one's major hurts and concerns, but also the minor details of our relationship. Listening to each other and making the right decisions were the keys to an eternal love. 4. A strong faith in God had to be the solid rock on which to build our lives, hopes, dreams, and future. We were learning that we had something to share.

Once we had set June 29, 1946 as our wedding date, the last few months prior to Peggy's graduation on June 15th seemed to drag. I attended Viesha, which was the grand finale of college days with skits, poems, inspiring orations, musical treats, and short dramas. It was staged in the athletic stadium. One student recited Lincoln's Gettysburg address in full regalia. Following this performance, there was dancing in Memorial Union. I recall giving Peggy a gardenia corsage to pin onto that evening gown she wore. It was a most memorable evening. Yes, Peggy did receive a kiss under the Campanile! At the end of the week Peggy's parents and I attended the Graduation ceremony. Peggy had made it with honors. She was among the select few – one in three – predicted to succeed at graduation. How proud we were of her!

The next two weeks were busy with preparation for our wedding. That is described in another chapter. Be patient – important occasions demand a lot of anticipation and joyous excitement.

Chapter 9

What Al Experienced from Graduation to the of Fall of 1944

That first summer following high school graduation was a busy one. Bernard, Floyd, and I worked long grueling hours to help Dad with the care and milking of twenty cows, disking, plowing, planting crops, cultivating, cutting weeds along fence lines, helping Mom to plant, hoe, pull weeds in that large garden, and mountains of other work. We also helped the neighbors when needed. To my surprise, Hans Tjaden asked me to assist Freddie Miller, a carpenter from Lake View, to build a new corncrib. Dad told me to go ahead and help. It was my first opportunity to put to work the skills I had learned in the Industrial Arts classes and to earn a little money. That was hard work in the heat of July and August, but we made it. The Great Depression's crippling effects were still affecting the economy. I couldn't afford to attend college even though I still wanted to.

That fall, we kept busy with harvesting the crops and getting ready for winter, in addition to the daily routine of morning and evening chores. The day started at five and ended late in the evenings. I began teaching a Sunday school class, sang in the church choir along with Carrie and Bernard, and attended Christian Endeavor meetings on Sunday evenings held in our nearby rural church. Each Saturday morning for two hours I attended Confirmation class to study and memorize the questions and answers in the Heidelberg Catechism. That course of study was two years. Then, it happened – returning from the Christmas program practice that Sunday afternoon we heard the startling news of the attack on Pearl Harbor December 7, 1941. Soon every boy of seventeen or older had to register for the Draft. It saddened the hearts of dads and moms to hear such foreboding news. They knew what war meant. We listened to F.D. Roosevelt's declaration of war. WW II had begun.

On hearing that defense workers could be deferred, my parents helped Bernard travel to California to seek work in a defense factory. He got a job, but in a matter of a few months, in 1942, that dreaded 1A classification arrived and Bernard was drafted into the army. He, Roy, and Merle did their training at Fort Hood in Texas. Both my mom and Mary visited them at their army base. Bernard was assigned to the 154th Tank Destroyer Battalion. Roy and Merle were in the infantry. Meanwhile, we carried on. There was more work and fewer to help. We put in fifteen-hour days. Now you realize why I was not free to date Peggy. I did watch her play basketball occasionally and attended a few football games, but no dating. Those were difficult days. This situation continued for the next two years. I also received my 1A notice and had my physical examination at Fort Leavenworth, but on an appeal by my parents, my induction was deferred so that I could continue helping on the farm. Agricultural production was also a patriotic service. We eagerly looked forward to Bernard's weekly letter, assuring us that though it was tough, so far everything was okay.

It was not only work on the farm that kept us busy, on Sundays we did no fieldwork, only daily chores caring for animals and the like. Almost every family in our neighborhood attended worship at the Wheatland Presbyterian Church. This church had its beginning in 1877 when a small wooden structure was built. On February 17, 1878, there was a dedication ceremony. The congregation invited Rev. Lubke Huendling, a graduate of Dubuque, Iowa and McCormick Theological Seminary in Chicago, to be its first pastor.

He served that church from 1878 to 1915! He was a Calvinist and was highly qualified to lead the church in the Reformed tradition. Rev. Huendling was also an innovator, buying the first automobile in Carroll County. He used that car to enlarge the membership, traveling to Lake View, Arcadia, Carnarvon, and to the west, Crawford County. After his retirement he started to print and publish a circular letter, which became a German newspaper: *Die Ostfriesische Nachrichten* (The Ostfriesland News). This had a large circulation of sixteen thousand in America and Germany before WW I. It was a family enterprise with all family members participating in its production every ten days.

Rev. Chris Walter was pastor from 1915 to 1941, over twenty-six years. Six daughters and one son were born to the Walters during their term of service at Wheatland Church. Following his resignation, Rev. Hensman Smidt from South Dakota was installed. In the first seventy-two years of the church's history, the pulpit was never left vacant. I mention this history to share with you the setting for my busy participation in its program. Since it adjoined our farm, we were always close to that church. I continued teaching a class in Sunday school, serving as its Superintendent, at times directing the choir, and was the Treasurer. What a busy schedule I had!

With the shortage of helping hands during the war, I also gave assistance to our neighbors. The Wheatland neighborhood was a closely knit community. In addition to our own farm work, we helped neighbors in haymaking, shelling corn, hauling manure to the fields, filling silos with chopped corn stalks, butchering, mending joint fences, shocking and threshing barley, oats, and flax. No money changed hands, except for threshing and shelling corn. There was a big investment in those machines. Hank Olberding, who had retired, pulled the thresher with a monster steam engine until Uncle Gottlieb bought a new machine and tractor. One consolation was the delicious lunches the woman of the house served (with plenty of help from other women who lived nearby). There was a close bonding of people who shared the burdens of hard work and effort. It was no fun to work in the heat of summer. We washed the grime from our hands and faces before lunch. Uncle Gottlieb had a noticeable bald spot (an elevated forehead) and often remarked that young men had an advantage. He had to start washing his face with a larger surface. Once in a while, a pint of cold beer was served to slake our thirst, especially at threshing time. I often did the straw-piling, which was a dirty job. A good amount of skill was demanded to shape that pile with such precision it would not topple over.

Bernard

I did not complain about this hand that had been dealt me. Everybody was doing their utmost to cope with rationing, bad news from the war, and the hard tasks of farming. Life became a humdrum of routine drudgery with long hours and little cash. But we carried on! There was still the desire and hope to attend college, but that was put on the back burner for the duration of the war.

Out of the blue, it happened. We were filling the silo with alternate rows of sorghum and corn, unloading those heavy loads into the blower. About three in the afternoon a car pulled up into our yard. It was the Breda postman. My heart sank as I greeted him. He said, "I have the worst job in the world. Here is a telegram from the War Department." I knew before I opened it what it contained. Bernard had been killed in action September 23, 1944, as his Tank Destroyer Battalion was crossing a river from France into Germany. He was in General Patton's army racing across Europe. My dad asked, "Is he wounded?" I gave him the telegram, and we began to weep. I had the heartbreaking task of telling Mom the sad news. Hilke Tjaden was there helping her with the lunch and tea. She said, "Oh! Don't tell her." But I knew Mom already knew that the worst had happened. I showed her the telegram. She sat down in the rocker, and we all wept. She said, "How I wish that I had rocked him more when he was my baby!" Leaving her with Hilke, I joined the men huddled around my dad. We agreed to stop work for the day and wait until Monday to finish filling the silo. After chores that evening, I drove to Breda to call long distance to tell Floyd, now in the Navy, the sad news. He got leave and headed home. In a few weeks, that flag-draped coffin with Bernard's remains arrived. He was buried with full military honors by the Breda American Legion in the Wheatland Presbyterian Cemetery close to the front gate. The neatly folded American flag was handed to Mom. Taps were sounded. Our dear Bernard had been laid to rest.

Somehow we stumbled on with heavy hearts and busy hands. Bernard's dream of taking over Abe Schlorholtz's prized herd of Brown Swiss cattle had vanished. We had all known that he would become the qualified successor of The Hillsdale Farm. It was he who had taken the Agricultural/Farm Shop courses in high school, was a member of the Future Farmers of America, and had exhibited the young heifer, Doris, his pride and joy as the Grand Champion of the National Dairy Cattle Congress at Waterloo, Iowa. "The heart went out of the business," as my dad said. The spirit was broken. Realizing that Alfred would not want to continue farming, the family sold the entire herd of forty animals at auction on Wednesday, February 27, 1946 at the West End Sale Pavilion in Carroll. A piece of history had ended.

In June 1946, my parents moved to Carroll to live near daughter Carrie (Mrs. James Cruchelow) and her family. Peggy and I promised to rent the farm for a couple of years to help in the process of closing down. After those two years the farm would be sold, which it was to the John Clausen family. Today, in 2010, if you drive by that stretch of land adjacent to Wheatland Cemetery, you will not see any buildings. All have been leveled and cleared for farmland by the new owners.

Schlorholtz Farmhouse with (from left) Carrie, Al, and Bernard

Chapter 10

Wedding Bells for Peggy and Al, June 29, 1946

Wedding Bells

That June morning was hot and humid. It had rained the previous night, a good omen. Carrie's husband, James, wryly remarked that it was lucky it had rained because Al would be freed from work, making it possible for him to attend his own wedding. The previous night, Peggy and I (after the rehearsal) had secretly hidden my car in Uncle Steve's garage. She drove me home in her car. You see, we had many "friends" who would really do a job of decorating the car with long streamers, tin cans, powdered windows, and cute remarks during the wedding ceremony. That morning, Peggy was getting ready for the great day. Too excited to sleep well, she had risen early and appeared for breakfast wearing mismatched shoes. You can well imagine how her brothers and sister teased her! The household was in disarray – there were last minute preparations to be made.

The wedding ceremony was held in the Wall Lake Presbyterian Church, with the Rev. Elijah James officiating. Promptly at 2:00, the two families, relatives, and friends from far and near arrived and were seated according to protocol. Our attendants were Peggy's sister, Hope Abigail, as bridesmaid of honor. My best man was Wayne, my younger brother. Young Jimmy Cruchelow was ring bearer. Judith Cruchelow was the flower girl. Judy was just four years old, but she did a marvelous job. The two mothers were seated. When the organist played the Wedding March, Wayne and I turned to see Peggy leaning on her dad's arm walking down the aisle wearing her wedding gown with a long train. She was radiant and beautiful. We stood together. Everyone was in proper rehearsed position.

We exchanged our vows, placed the wedding rings on the right (left) fingers, and the Pastor gave that ominous challenge: "If anyone has cause that these two should not be joined in marriage, let him now speak or forever hold his peace." No one raised a cause, and we were pronounced man and wife. Yes, I kissed the bride! We walked up the aisle to the vestry where we were greeted by all. It was an amazing gift to have such expressive people giving us their blessing for a happy wedded life. The photographer arrived, and we had a group photo of the wedding party and then just Peggy and me. What a beautiful bride! At last we were a married couple ready to face the future bliss of being "made one" in heart and spirit.

We then were to attend the Reception at the Wall Lake Community Building. As we walked down the church steps, we saw to our utter amazement a wheelbarrow! Lee and Lyle Willhoite had thought this up. They invited Peggy to sit on the decorated seat. I was to push her all the way to the Reception! This I did – the streets were lined with well-wishers enjoying the show. As we reached the center of town on Main Street, we were stopped by the upraised hand of the town Marshall, Ray Wright, and the Mayor of the town, Karl Ernie. The Mayor read a proclamation of a crime being committed. Our "crime" was that we had no permit to push a wheelbarrow on Main Street. Instead of paying a stiff fine or

I didn't Know I Needed a Permit

doing time in the local jail, it was so ordered that I continue pushing Peggy to the destination. You can imagine how this delighted the crowd. There may have been in that crowd some "friends" who had been the target of Peggy's and my practical jokes in the past years. We were paying the price of our popularity.

Huffing and puffing, I delivered Peggy to the Reception. She took it quite well, but I could see a faint glimmer of disagreement with the whole affair. The Reception room was tastefully decorated with an abundance of flowers, crepe streamers, tables with the wedding cake and another for gifts and hostess favors. There were several speeches and remarks made in celebration of this most joyful occasion. Then we cut the cake, shared it with each other, and sat in the place of honor while all were served from the bounty of food and goodies with their coffee. We opened the gifts and thanked everyone for their loving generosity. Later, Peggy slipped out saying she would change dresses. Uncle Steve unobtrusively left with her. I continued chatting with the guests, keeping a watchful eye on the door Uncle Steve would use to return. In due time there he came, nodding to me. I quietly exited to join Peggy at the wheel of my (our) car. I jumped in, and Peggy floored the accelerator on our way out of town. We headed to Route 71. After about ten miles, I took over the driving. No one was following us. They had been outwitted and denied any opportunity to spoil the new wax job. We heard from them later how disappointed and tricked they had felt.

We continued north for seventy miles toward Spencer, Iowa. We had made reservations at the Tangier Hotel, one of the best in town. After a bit of light shopping, we returned to the hotel and were served a delicious dinner. At the appropriate time we went to our room, ready to relax a bit after the day's strenuous activities. We were both eager to "take some rest." Peggy filled the bathtub with warm water and invited me to join her. That was a first for me! Later we embraced in our very first intimacy. (The remaining portion of the night has been censored.)

After breakfast the next morning, we drove farther north to Walker, Minnesota. We had rented a cabin on the shore of Leech Lake, an enormous body of water. It was twenty-two miles long and ten miles in width. Instead of fishing on the big lake, our guide, Orville Miller, rowed us onto a large inlet to the lake. It was seventy feet deep at the center. Orville was an accomplished fisherman, knowing where certain fish were. We had brought our rods and reels as both of us liked to fish. That week we caught one hundred sixty-eight fish: perch, walleyes, and northern pike. Orville shared with us his extensive knowledge of the lake, the people of the area, and, of course, how he had landed the largest fish in the lake. We were too polite to question our guide's transparent exaggeration. During the afternoons we visited various sites: Paul Bunyan and his blue ox, the source of the Mississippi River, a few State Parks, and several good restaurants. Every morning and evening we feasted on the fish we had caught. The cabin owners cleaned, filleted, and, thankfully, served us those succulent, fresh, coldwater fish. As that romantic week began to close, we packed a good number of fish in ice and started home. We made an overnight stop at one of the best hotels in Minneapolis, enjoying delicious food served at tables surrounding a skating rink with an ice show. That was fantastic!

Newlyweds

Chapter 11

We Kept Our Promise: Maintaining the Farm
1946-1947

Stopping at the Hoft farm to pick up our wedding gifts and cards, which Mom and Dad Hoft had so graciously gathered and carried to their home, we were in a hurry to start getting settled in our very own home-in-the-making, but Mom Hoft insisted we have supper and give a full report on our honeymoon in Minnesota. We shared many things but not all! Then we drove to our farm, unloaded all the bags, presents, and the ironing board Peggy had bought in Minneapolis. Years later she was to exclaim, "Now whatever made me do that?" My hope was that we would have a few easy days of light work before getting too serious about many time-consuming tasks. To my astonishment, Henry had mowed the mature alfalfa hay field on that Sunday of our return. There it lay needing to be racked into long rows early on Monday morning, a big job! There was no alternative; that fragrant hay would have to be baled on Tuesday and stored in the barn. Henry did come to help with the baling. This was my introduction to maintaining the farm.

Peggy had to prepare meals, not only for her husband but also for the crew that baled and stored the hay. Fortunately, my mom had left the refrigerator well stocked with the basic ingredients: milk, bread, eggs, meat, vegetables, and some ice cream. Peggy applied her cooking skills that she had learned from her mom and at College in Foods and Nutrition. She worked wonders and took this surprising challenge in her stride. The following morning we headed to Breda to replenish our food supply at Rickie's grocery store. We were young enough to laugh about the haying episode (a few days after it happened)!

For the next few months of summer, fieldwork kept me busy. There was cultivating the corn and soybean fields, cutting weeds, and daily chores. We bought several milk cows from Elmer Graber to increase our income, but that gave me extra chores to do. There were also the pigs and chickens to care for, the weeding and hoeing of the garden. Peggy helped me with the gardening and gathering the eggs. One day, I was cultivating corn, using our Farmall tractor, just north of the driveway in sight of the house. At 11:45 Peggy waved to me and shouted that lunch was ready. I finished the round and went directly to relax and enjoy dinner, as we called it, at noon. Supper was the evening meal. As I entered and washed my face and hands, Peggy announced that the dinner was not ready. I looked at her inquisitively. She said, "When we called my dad from the field for meals, he always worked at least fifteen to twenty minutes before arriving at the table." She had not realized we Schlorholtzes were always punctual and prompt to respond. My mom had never called us before the meal was ready. We laughed about this, and I helped in finishing preparations. That day, Peggy served a tall glass of tomato juice and had cooked fresh green beans from our garden. The problem was I had never really liked either of those. I couldn't admit this, so I ate the beans and quickly drained the glass of juice, forcing my mind to forget my prejudices. To my utter surprise, Peggy refilled the glass with more tomato juice thinking that I loved the stuff! A few weeks later I told her what had happened, and she laughed. It didn't really matter. By then I was reservedly enjoying green beans and tomato juice.

In July, we cut the oats, shocked the bundles into little huts of six, and did the rounds of threshing, neighbor by neighbor in our threshing "ring." Peggy thought I was spending too much effort and time with the neighbors. I explained that this was tradition in Wheatland Township. Neighbors liked and needed to join in the work of threshing, shelling corn, and even hay-making. In contrast to this, her dad had a combine, harvesting the oats/soybeans without the help of neighbors, with one of the boys hauling the loads to the granary where it was stored. Her consolation was visiting her mom more often. Inevitably, it became our time to feed the threshing crew. Peggy faced up to the challenge with typical skill and resolve. She had the help of her mom, Hilke, our neighbor, and several others. We men enjoyed the sumptuous meal they served us – fried chicken, mashed potatoes, rich gravy, vegetables, and freshly baked rolls, finished off with a generous slice of pie. We worked hard, ate well, and didn't gain weight.

Later that fall, it was corn-picking time. My dad had bought a one-row corn picker, which was attached to the tractor, sparing us the picking by hand. Our neighbor to the south, Hans Tjaden, helped me by hauling the loads to the corncrib. That was a great help. I also picked his corn crop. Sufficient rains during the summer had increased the yield per acre. We were thankful for an abundant harvest. However, I was increasingly becoming aware of the heavy load of responsibility that farming entails. I began to appreciate all my dad had done: planning, buying seeds to plant, caring for the animals and crops, and marketing surplus produce. I had helped him with the work, but taking on those tasks was different. These experiences would serve me well in the days ahead. Peggy was in need of treatment by Dr. Brown in Des Moines, a D and C. Her parents went with us. After the procedure, Peggy insisted she was well enough to have dinner together and to hear Fred Warring's Pennsylvanians in concert. We were thrilled by their music. Peggy endured the whole evening.

We were active members at my rural church, but I had to withdraw from the former load of participation. Occasionally, we attended Peggy's home church in Wall Lake to keep in touch. On alternate Saturdays, Peggy and I would drive to Carroll to do some shopping and to visit my parents, my sister Carrie, and her family. They were concerned how things were going on the farm and were pleased to hear the good reports. They appreciated our payment of the rent per acre of the farm. This helped their income to cope with the expense of retirement and living in town. We always took big baskets of vegetables from the garden my mom and I had planted that spring. They loved Peggy and had always endured me. We also visited Peggy's parents quite often since they were so near. What a great time we had playing bridge, chatting, and enjoying the goodies Beulah inevitably served. We were also included in those endearing Hoft family dinners and celebrations with Peggy's extended family.

That winter was severe, with a two-day blizzard which made doing chores exhausting. Shoveling snow is not an easy task. The roads were blocked. Extra care had to be given the animals, making sure the water pipes had not frozen. We had banked the lines with heavy straw, but sometimes the drop in temperature froze things anyway. After the storm, we wanted to see if everything was okay with Peggy's parents. I put a shovel in the car and we started out. To our great astonishment, the drifts across the roads were solid as a cement drive. We swooshed right over them. All was okay. We had a lot more snow all winter. There was no time for sledding down Gerdes's hill. On December 28, 1946, we drove Peggy's parents to Boone. Richard was marrying Merna Collis, the daughter of the dentist Peggy so greatly feared in her younger days. She thought he was too rough and touchy. On some occasions Peggy's dad stood guard during the drilling, threatening Dr. Collis to take it easy or else! During high school days, Peggy was close to her brother, Dick, and even drove him and Merna on their courting nights. It was bitterly cold. On returning to our farm late that night, I discovered that the young man we had hired to do the chores had left open the trapdoor to the hay maw, freezing the water pipes and causing much discomfort for the animals. In addition to that, the coal furnace had gone out, freezing the pipes in our house. Even the toilet bowl was frozen. It was fortunate we arrived home when we did.

To our great relief spring arrived. The snows melted and soon the ground was dry enough to disk, plow, and plant the oats, corn, soybeans, and vegetable and flower seeds in the garden. We again began the full cycle of farm work. Fortunately, we were blessed that sows each littered eight to ten piglets, the cows had heifer calves, and all the animals were healthy. I disked the oat fields. Peggy helped me by shoveling the oats into the seed spreader as I pulled the wagon with the tractor. I spent long hours plowing and preparing the ground for planting. Peggy's dad planted the corn and soybeans with his Ford tractor. That was a great help. One afternoon we were shocked while in the field planting soybeans to be buzzed by a Piper Cub plane which swooped over us a few times. It was Peggy taking her flying lesson and impressing us. She was about to solo, but got sick during practice of stalls and starts. We discovered the source of the trouble – she was pregnant! That put the kibosh to her flying training.

Again we had a bumper crop. The livestock increased in number and size. In the fall of 1947, we had to start planning how to dispose of everything, to get the best price, and to put the farm in the shape we had found it. You see, I was about to fulfill that dream of going to college. My parents rented the farm to Charles Lashier. He came from Schaller, Iowa and was the brother of cousin Ben's wife, Lucy. We went to Des Moines, Iowa's capital, to purchase a house trailer in which to live while attending college. We hooked it behind the car and brought it home, parking it next to the south porch of the house where we could load it with all our belongings, except the furniture and the kitchen sink.

On October 11, 1947, we bade farewell to our farm and drove nine miles north to Lake View. The Congregational Church there had heard we were moving, so they requested me to conduct the worship services, preach, and visit members. I was also asked to sing first tenor with a men's quartet one evening at the Ice Carnival. For our first appearance we simply sang songs. For our second appearance we dressed in pink ballet skirts and sang, "Glow little glowworm, glimmer, glimmer," while holding wands and blinking them in time to the music. The applause was deafening! It became even louder when Jim, the bass, popped out a grapefruit (his "breast") as we bowed in response to the audience's tumultuous cheering. That stopped the show!

It had been a gratifying experience to farm those two crop seasons. The work had been difficult and strenuous, but Peggy and I worked as a close team. Our love and devotion to each other were maturing and firm. We were ready for the next step forward.

Chapter 12

College Days for Al, 1948-50

After the Ice Carnival and bidding farewell to the Congregational members in Lake View, we moved the house trailer to the Hoft farm, after having pulled it loose from its embedded footing in the lot behind the Chevrolet Garage. We had hooked up water, electricity, and sewer fittings. Ice had formed around the tires. We had to hire a tow truck to pull it loose. This was early January 1948. Later in January, we pulled the house trailer to Indianola, a college town south of Des Moines. Parking in the Trailer Court was easy. We hooked up again and got settled. Peggy was pregnant, in the final month. We were concerned about her traveling, setting up in a new place, and making adjustments. Getting ready for the imminent advent of our first child, we drove to Des Moines to buy things we needed. The new baby buggy fit just right in the trailer, as did the small chest of drawers. Peggy bravely coped with the situation. We had immediately found an obstetrician and noted where the hospital was located, just six blocks away.

Stan's First Christmas

Registering as a student of Simpson College, a Liberal Arts institution, went well. I chose English, History, Psychology, Biology, Speech, and Music Appreciation. It was hard going – I had been out of high school for six years. I had read profusely, but academic pursuit was quite a challenge, especially the first ten days. I walked the four blocks to classes. There was a lot of snow on the ground. Then, one evening, Peggy said it was time to go! The labor pains were getting closer. However, dilation was slow and Peggy had to endure a lengthy process of labor. On a bitter cold morning, February 14, 1948, Stanley came into our world. What a joy that was – our first child. Peggy and I were thrilled! She and Stanley stayed at the hospital for five days. I saw them twice a day, brought flowers, answered the letters and cards of congratulations that were pouring in, and attended classes – studying late into the night.

Finally, they were allowed to come home. It was cozy in our warm trailer. Stan had his special crib. Peggy nursed him. He was okay except for severe bouts of colic. We took turns in trying to make him comfortable. Peggy's mom came to be with us for a week. She had the magic touch and experience to put Stan to sleep. It could have been that the new parents were too tired, tense, and anxious. Instructions are not included in such matters. Some evenings, we took Stan for a ride in the car – this quickly put him to sleep. After a few weeks, he settled into a routine of feeding, burping, sleeping, and being changed. I had to learn that art, which I did. Later in the spring term, I had Peggy bring Stan to Speech class where I demonstrated the art of changing a diaper. That made a great hit. We were a happy family. We also visited Aunt Verna Schmidt in Ames to show off our new baby. She was so proud of Peggy and loved Stan.

We then received sad news. Peggy's first cousin, Roma Jean (Uncle Cliff's and Aunt Elma's daughter), died February 27, 1948 of uremic poisoning after giving birth to her first child. We drove to Wall Lake to give condolences to her parents and to attend the funeral. It was a sorrowful time. However, on that occasion there was a timely meeting. Professor William "Bill" Grobe preached the sermon that day. He taught at Buena Vista College in Storm Lake, Iowa. His sermon theme was "Now is the time for faith in Christ, hope, and love." It moved me in spirit deeply. I decided to explore the possibility of transferring to that college. The week prior to the funeral, the Head of the Music Department had cautioned me, saying that while I had an excellent singing voice I had never taken piano lessons until joining college. He said it was not likely that I could teach music or make singing my career. This settled my mind. I had come to Simpson College because of its outstanding music department. Now I had to be realistic about a change in my life's goals and profession. It had been proven to me that I was being called to travel a different path. I had been conducting worship in two churches at Winterset, about thirty miles away, to augment our finances. Peggy and I discussed the situation and what was happening. We had reached another fork on the road of life.

After the close of summer school, we moved our trailer to Storm Lake and connected up to the Buena Vista College Gymnasium for facilities. There were many veterans using their GI grants, so one more space near the gym was not conspicuous. Peggy, Stan, and I made the transition well. Our parents were glad that we lived nearer now. We settled into BV College (now a university). In September I registered, choosing English Literature, Biology, Speech, and Biblical Studies. Finally, I was able to get into the swing of study, assignments, and class participation. Having been "through the mill," Peggy was a great encourager and counselor. She had met all our neighbors and soon made many friends. She enjoyed pushing Stan in the buggy, walking around the campus and to the shores of Storm Lake just south of the campus. That large body of water was famous for violent storms. When Stan was two, it was endearing to be greeted by him at lunch time and in the late afternoons after classes were over. He would stand on the sofa, watching for my approach from Old Main, the huge administration building in which most classes were held. Stan's "Hello Daddy" was music for my soul! Peggy always had nutritious meals ready for her weary husband. Over supper we would share our day's work and experiences.

There was a problem about finances. We had some savings, but tuition and books, etc. were draining our reserves. We attended Lakeside Presbyterian Church on Lake Street. The congregation had many members. Somehow, the minister, Dr. Richardson had heard about me and offered me the Youth Director's job. I taught a Sunday school class and participated in the Wednesday evening youth program – teaching, counseling, leading recreation, and assisting in the worship on Sundays. Also, it was my responsibility to proofread the Sunday Bulletin every Saturday morning at the local Printing Press. I would have preferred to sleep in instead.

Since I was in a hurry to graduate, I took, at times, twenty-two hours of course work each semester. It was fortunate that I was able to take German and Greek from Dr. Hirsch, who with Mrs. Hirsch had escaped Germany before WW II. What a scholar he was! Sociology really appealed to me and became my major, with a minor in Biblical Studies and Philosophy. Sociology was taught by the Dean of the College, Dr. L. Sampson. English Literature was taught by Prof. Bertha Supplee. She taught me well, and I opted for many of her classes. However, the best were the Biblical and Philosophy Studies taught by Prof. Bill Grobe. Having read the entire Bible several times and studied the Heidelberg Catechism in the past, I thought I knew quite a bit. But Prof. Grobe taught me how to dig deeper into the Scriptures and how to develop a wider perspective, adapted to life situations and problems. He also emphasized the imperative of personal faith in Christ.

There was an active Inter-Varsity Fellowship on campus, vital and challenging. Peggy and I both attended meetings: noon prayer meetings, bi-monthly evening studies of scripture, and recreational/social events. That was a group of dedicated Christians. We bonded well. However, we both thought there was something missing in our lives. It was then that Peggy and I made penitent surrender to Jesus Christ as Savior and Lord. We realized that prior to this encounter with God's Spirit, it was "head knowledge" not the quickening of the spirit. We now understood that one must be "born from above, by the Spirit" (John 3: 1-15). What a transformation that made in our lives. By Grace through faith in Christ, we entered into a vital relationship with our Creator, Redeemer, and Sustainer of Life Eternal.

For me it was a revolution, a crystallization of all I had intellectually believed. Christ became the center of my life, my actions, and life's perspective. From that point on, increasingly and exponentially, all that was read, heard in lectures, studied, reflected on, debated, added to the realization that both Peggy and I were beginning to live and cope with an ever expanding universe of truth, witness, and service in God's Kingdom. Through the lens of faith, the four gospels became vitalized and relevant. This was also true of the Epistles, especially the Book of Romans. For instance, Romans 8:28 now made sense: "For we know that in all things God is at work to bring good to all who love God, who are called according to His purpose." It was then that I realized why I had refused earlier at Wheatland Church, Mr. Ronald Myer's offer of a one thousand dollar scholarship if I went to Dubuque University and Seminary to become a pastor. At that point in my late teens I had nothing to share! In God's time and calling at BV College, the Light had dawned upon me. Peggy and I were more closely drawn together in faith, hope, and love. From time to time, Prof. Bill Grobe would inquire, "Have you ever considered the Christian Ministry?" I mused over this and finally told him that it was impossible for me. He agreed and said, "You are right in admitting that you can't do it, but you can let Christ continue His Ministry through you!" That did it. With Prof. Grobe's assistance, because it was his Alma Mater, I began to consider attending Princeton Theological Seminary of the Presbyterian Church, U.S.A. at Princeton, New Jersey after college graduation. I was beginning to have Something To Share! Peggy had been part of this decision and heartily agreed. We were about to embark on a new path, which we had never contemplated before.

Every two to three weeks we would visit our parents. On Friday evenings, we would spend time with them, often doing a load of washing. We always brought a bag or

Visiting Al's Family in Carroll; Stan is the Baby

two of groceries and some treats. My, how we did enjoy our mothers' freshly baked bread, cinnamon rolls, pies, and cakes. They spoiled us – we didn't get much opportunity to hold Stanley! He was passed around like a favorite toy. Occasionally, I would head back to Storm Lake Saturday evening for work at the church, study, and drive back to the farm for Peggy and Stan early afternoon on Sunday. Carroll was fifty-six miles from Storm Lake, so we spent more time with Mom and Dad Hoft. The farm was twenty-five miles from Storm Lake. Beulah and Henry brought an angel food cake for Stan's first birthday. In fact, that happened for all our birthdays. My parents also sent things.

Semester after semester passed, and we were kept busy. Peggy got a part-time job as accountant at a local lumberyard to earn some money. Whenever we had a free day, the three of us went fishing in Storm Lake. By then Stan could walk and was very energetic. To safeguard him, we tied a clothesline around his waist as we sat on the pier, so we had a chance to haul him out of the water if he tumbled in. I was fully applying myself in my studies, also singing first tenor in the church and college choirs, doing solos at college programs, and was elected President of the Inter-Varsity Fellowship my senior year. During the choir tour in the spring of 1950, I sang some solos and acted as chaplain. That meant prayer with the choir prior to a concert and making the pitch for funds at intermission. Dr. Olsen, the President of BVC, heralded me as a champion fundraiser.

In June of 1950, I graduated from college, cum laude. It had been a strenuous two and a half years, doing two semesters a year and summer school sessions without a break. Soon after graduation, I had a tonsillectomy to help clear up bouts of sore throats. I existed on sodas and ice cream for a week. Peggy and Stan commiserated with me, giving me first-class care. We moved the trailer to my parents' backyard in Carroll for sale. My mom sold it for a fair price. Peggy, Stan, and I were busily preparing to move to Princeton in late August. Our parents took it in stride, happy for us to carry on Al's education, but they had misgivings. Some thought we should attend Dubuque because it was closer. But Princeton Theological Seminary had accepted me for admission and to Princeton we must go! We would all miss each other and be separated by twelve hundred miles. There were the rounds of dinners and farewells to be made in the Wheatland area, at Wall Lake, and Carroll. We made the most of it.

Chapter 13

Our years at Princeton Theological Seminary
1950-53

Having stuffed everything we could into our Oldsmobile, we traveled from Carroll to Princeton on Route 20. Peggy, Stan, and I spent three tiring days making that trip. It was late August and still quite hot. We spent the first night at Princeton, Illinois. By the next evening we were in Ohio. We reached Princeton early the following evening and had to stay at a motel near Trenton, because it was too late to get the keys to our apartment. The next morning we found Mercer Street and South Hall. This building was reserved for married couples with children. We hauled our possessions to the third-floor furnished apartment. What a wonderful relief. We had made it! South Hall was two blocks from the main campus. There was a large Administration Building where most classes were held, Alexander Hall for single men, Brown Hall for married couples without children, Miller Chapel, spacious Erdman Library, and well cared for lawns, flowers, and shrubs. It was a beautiful campus. Most buildings had clinging ivy on external walls.

I wished the walls of those buildings could tell me the history and long-standing traditions. Six days later at orientation a good bit of that was shared by the President of Princeton Theological Seminary, Dr. John Alexander Mackay. He had come from Aberdeen, Scotland, bringing his lyrical gift of speech with him. He and Mrs. Mackay had been missionaries in Peru. He explained that Princeton was strategically located halfway between Philadelphia and New York City, halfway between Dr. Albert Einstein's School for Advanced Study and Westminster College of Music. This symbolized that PTS was at the center of things. He then told us to always be at the center of things – the truth in Christ. He challenged us to never have a balcony-view of life, but rather be involved in life's action. "Beware," he said, "we will not pamper you. Every possible theological and philosophical angle will be taught to prepare you for "life as it is!" He also emphasized that if we did not have a personal relationship to Christ by faith, he prayed we would find Him at PTS.

Courses for study were prescribed for juniors (first year recruits): study of Luke's gospel by inductive method by Dr. Kist, Introduction to New Testament Theology taught by Dr. Bruce Metzger, Greek taught by Dr. Thurman, Old Testament Survey taught by Dr. Gehman, Church History taught by Dr. Hope, Homiletics taught by Dr. McLeod, and Speech taught by Dr. Wheeler, who had been John Barrymore's voice coach. Those Professors were giants in their fields of study and always ready to guide and direct us in any needs we might have. A raw recruit from Iowa, I was awed by this new environment. Some of the students had already read Barth, Brunner, Reinhold Niebuhr, Charles Hodge, and others. There was a lot of hard work ahead of me, but I did not panic. I had been called to study at PTS and was determined to do my best. Classes began the next day.

Peggy and Stan were getting acquainted with our neighbors and enjoying the exploration of Princeton. A nursery during the morning hours for the younger children was arranged. Peggy would ultimately become chairperson and spend a week each month caring for the children. Paul and Esther Snyder, with their twins, lived below us on the second floor. The Ellisons lived on the first floor.

We learned that President Woodrow Wilson had conducted conferences on the League of Nations formation in the central rooms of South Hall. Dr. Einstein's house was just around the corner from us. It was a thrill to see him in his baggy pants and white sweater walking to his classes at precisely 10:00 am and returning at 2:00 pm. I joined Peggy and Stan for lunch, enjoying a very active boy, who was happy to be picked up from the playpen. He was walking all over the apartment, learning to pull himself up on the sofa, and keeping Peggy alert. What a fulfilling time we had. After a short nap, it was to the Library for study in the afternoons between classes. Evenings were special – a delicious supper, newspaper reading, playing with Stan, and sharing with Peggy what the day had wrought. After they had retired, I spent hours of study. The assignments were long and difficult. Peggy read a good bit and faithfully wrote letters to parents and siblings. She and her mother also arranged to have eggs sent to us. Every two weeks Beulah would send a large carton of eggs, which Peggy sold to South Hall families. They made a small profit. Occasionally, when we had a rare weekend, we would visit Dick, Merna, and family in Schenectady, New York, where Dick was working as Development Engineer at General Electric and studying for a Master's degree. They also visited us. We took them swimming in the Atlantic and had picnics. We also visited Willard, Betty, and their children in East Orange, New Jersey, where Will worked at an Edison Electric company. We always had a great time with quality family catch-ups and lots of fun getting to know our nephews and nieces. Hope Abigail, after a year at Iowa State College, transferred to Presbyterian Hospital in Philadelphia, Pennsylvania. She earned a Bachelor of Science degree in Nursing. That is where she met her future husband, Frank Arnold. She often visited us as we lived so close. We enjoyed her visits, and it was a great homecoming for all.

It was required that each student have a student pastorship in a church. The Pleasantdale Church in East Orange, a long drive to make every Sunday, selected me to serve. Since they were without a full-time pastor, I conducted the worship, preached the sermon, and also taught the adult church school class. Peggy and Stan went with me. We enjoyed many picnics in Eagle Rock Park. From there we could view New York City across the Hudson River. There was a weekly stipend which helped a great deal. I was gaining some practical skills and overcoming nervous moments of exertion. During my second year, I was assigned to a Reformed church at Pottersville, New Jersey. This was less distant and in a small-town environment. Families invited us to dinner after worship. We had some fabulous meals. The Herzogs served a sumptuous meal and three desserts, one of which was a venison mince pie. Church members would also send fresh fruit and vegetables with us. What a help that was! Peggy discovered that she was pregnant.

Following my junior year, I took the ten-week summer course of Hebrew. We were to meet at 8:00 and 10:00 five mornings a week. Dr. Weaver was the Professor. He lived near South Hall, so we met in a large room there. I will never forget the first day of class. Dr. Weaver had us write the Hebrew alphabet on the blackboard during the very first hour. We had an hour between class sessions. I labored hurriedly to learn those letters. Dr. Weaver began our second session by saying, "Pick up your Hebrew Bibles and turn to Genesis 1:1 and read the first paragraph." One by one we failed. He then called on Charles, who read proficiently. We were astonished, to say the least. Having relished our discomfort, with a broad smile, Dr. Weaver said, "Charles failed Hebrew last semester and is repeating the course." Studying eight hours a day/night, I passed the course, able to read, translate, and write Hebrew.

The next year, I studied Old Testament Prophets, Speech taught now by Dr. Beaners, World Religions taught by Dr. Christy Wilson, Ethics taught by Dr. Lehman, Advanced Theology taught by Drs. Hendry and Otto Piper, Christian Pattern of Life taught by Emile Cailliet, Comparative Religions taught by Dr. Jurji, and Cure of Souls taught by Dr. John Bonnell. It was another grueling year. There were too many term papers. I would write them in script as I researched, and Peggy would type them. I could never have done it without her help. Five mornings a week there was a half-hour break for prayer, scripture reading, and hymn singing in Miller Chapel. What an inspiration that was to hear two hundred students and staff singing at full volume. We were also required to preach a

The Scholar and his Support Staff

sermon in Miller Chapel in the presence of our Homiletics teacher and classmates each of our three years and to hear the critical evaluation by the professor. That was another rattling cliffhanger.

Stan and I drove to the Pottersville Church January 6th to celebrate Epiphany. Peggy didn't feel too well, so she stayed home. We had prayer for Peggy before we left. There was a good amount of snow on the ground. After the worship and goodbyes, Stan and I got into the car, and I suggested we pray for Mommy. Stan said, "Oh, we prayed for her before we left." But we prayed again. Arriving back at South Hall, we were met at the door by Jerry and Margretta Ellison who informed us that they had taken Peggy to the hospital. Delivery time had arrived, and Peggy had sought their help. Stan stayed with them while I made a wild dash for the maternity ward. I was ushered to the waiting room, where a young man was sitting with a mountain of cigarette butts in the ash tray. He had been there for six hours! After about twenty minutes, the nurse came in announcing the birth of a baby girl. The young man jumped to his feet, but the nurse pointed to me. By breech birth, Hope Ellen was here! Peggy and baby were fine. It was January 6, 1952. Peggy told me about her morning. We were thankful for such good neighbors and excellent care.

I visited Peggy and baby Hope each day for the five days they were there. Stan came with me to bring them home – he was as excited as I was. In Peggy's own words: "Our little Hope is unbelievable. She fussed a little last evening, but I fed her at 11:00, by 11:30 she was asleep…until 5:30 this morning and dropped off again after

eating…Al had promised Stan he could hold his new sister all the way home. He did tenderly hold her all the way home." He loved his sister and often held her. We were able to buy a black and white TV, which was a great addition to our apartment. To augment income, I worked at Mary Mason's kindergarten on Saturdays repairing equipment and painting. We did have a thrilling experience after Peggy wrote for tickets to the Bell Telephone Hour program live. On May 12 we hurried to hear Lily Pons sing in Carnegie

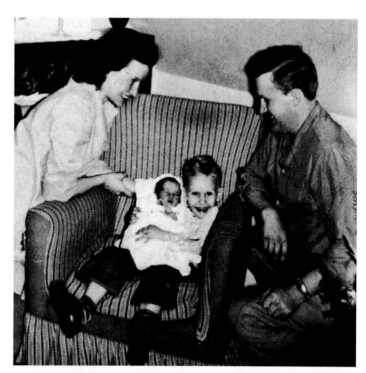

Welcoming Hope

Hall, New York City. Fig and Mary Newton stayed with Stan and Hope. Peggy and I had exchanged gifts for Mother's and Father's Day.

Peggy wrote:

> Esther Snyder and Margretta Ellison cared for Stan all week…When we brought Hope home, all of South Hall met us at the door and the fellows carried me all the way upstairs which at this point was not an easy task. They had pink and white ribbons decorating the apartment and a wonderful dinner on the stove…The next morning we opened our door – there were all the clothes that needed ironing. Margretta had taken them off the line in the basement and done the ironing for us…There was also a plate of cupcakes baked by Douglas, our neighbor across the hall…One evening Douglas had invited Al and Stan for venison steak while I was in the hospital. Stan was impressed, but told Doug,

"My dad is a good cook."…and when Doug asked, "What does he cook?" Stan told him, "He cooks Wheaties!"

On January 17th Peggy wrote to her mom:

> How we wish you could see our sweetest little girl in her new pink kimono. It is just lovely…she looks like a little dolly in it. Stan said, "Oh, look at our little kitten."…He checks her a million times a day and has only played outdoors one afternoon since Hope was brought home. One morning Stan took another look at Baby Hope and asked, "When is July so we can show our Grandmas and Grandpas our baby?" I could write a lot more, but there is not enough space.

Hope and Al

We did go to Iowa for a month in July. What a thrilling time we had with all our families. In August, my sister Carrie, James, Jimmy, and Judy spent a week with us. We showed them the sights of New York City and the Atlantic beach, etc. That was a special time together. In the fall quarter, I studied the required courses and opted to attend Dr. Mackay's Ecumenics and Dr. Cailliet's course on Blaise Pascal. Peggy audited Dr. Cailliet's course, A Christian Pattern of Life, which she found very helpful. I continued serving the Pottersville Church during my senior year. The studies were heavy going, but I made it. In June 1953, I graduated from Princeton Theological Seminary with a Bachelor of Divinity degree, now a Master of Divinity. The ceremony was held in Princeton University's mammoth Chapel to accommodate the many who attended. My mother came for my graduation. It was good to see her and share the joy we all had. After the festivities, I drove her to New York City to show her the sights. I recall how nervous she was as we drove through the Holland Tunnel. She had good cause to be uneasy. A large truck in front of us had a double blowout, bringing the heavy traffic to a full stop. They eventually cleared the lane and towed the truck away. We were both relieved to see daylight again. We visited the Statue of Liberty, NBC, and the Empire State Building, viewing the city from the observation deck on the seventy-ninth story. When I left for a few minutes to get sandwiches and coffee, I warned Mom not to talk too much to strangers. But when I returned she was busily engaged in conversation. I sat down, and she introduced me to a man who lived in Jefferson, Iowa, only twenty-seven miles from Carroll where she lived. It is indeed a small world. She stayed for a week – we had a great time. She really loved Stan and Hope. We were sorry to have her leave.

My study at PTS did not end at graduation. We had been challenged to rise to an even more demanding calling. Peggy's expression tensed as I shared one evening in the late spring of 1952 the explorative expression of what had been forming in my mind and spirit. "Peggy, it is becoming increasingly clear to me that God may be calling us to become missionaries overseas. All that I am studying and reflecting on is beginning to develop and gel. Lectures by Dr. Mackay, Dr. Emile Cailliet, Dr. Christy Wilson, and others point to a calling that is new and challenging to me." To this Peggy emphatically replied, "Well, that may be all right for you, but not for me. God hasn't called me and our children!" We agreed to pray about this matter and leave it for the present in God's Caring Grace. Peggy was not actually against such a calling; it was taking us both by surprise. Some time was needed for clarification and verification.

Imagine my surprise one Sunday afternoon on returning from Worship and calling on members at Pottersville Church to be greeted by Peggy sharing some exciting and inspiring news. She related that after lunch, as she was resting on the bed, she had distinctly heard her name and a voice that said, "Peggy, do you think I can care for your children only here in America? I only want you to be willing to go to the mission field." In affirmation, Peggy prayed, "Lord, I pray that you will make me willing and ready to do your Will!"

That was an amazing experience, and it left an indelible impression on both of us. In the following forty years and on into retirement, there has never been a doubt that God had called us to mission overseas and had inspired us to be willing to will God's Will.

We discovered afresh that when one catches a glimpse of God's Plan and Purpose for one's life, God reinforces and strengthens, fleshes out the design, makes plainer and clearer the fuller picture of divine intention.

I was ordained to the Christian Ministry of the Presbyterian Church on the evening of June 28, 1953 at the Wall Lake Presbyterian Church. It is a solemn event, marking the completion of years of preparation. Representatives of the Presbytery had earlier examined and approved my candidacy as to my intention, qualifications, dedication, and calling. Of course, our families, relatives, and members from many congregations attended. That was a culmination and also a new beginning. Peggy and I spent the whole month of July in Iowa showing off our son and daughter! Our parents, in fact all the extended families, neighbors, and close friends, made us feel right at home. I suppose that some of them wondered what was happening to the Alfred and Peggy they had known as kids.

Chapter 14

Further Preparation: Studying Islam at Princeton Theological Seminary 1953-54

The four of us continued living in South Hall. It felt good to have a few weeks free to enjoy a little leisure time. Peggy wrote in her notes: "On September 10, 1953, Stan started kindergarten, there are only morning classes. Hope Ellen sorely misses Stan, whom she loves to tease and bother. She is beginning to enjoy playing with dolls, her teddy bear, and other toys. She loves to rock her doll in the little rocker that Mom Hoft gave her in July…She likes to walk between Al's legs – she just fits through when he is standing. When Uncle Charles and Aunt Lillian were here, Hope put her head against his leg and before we knew it she was on his lap – and loved it! (I'll bet she thought he was Grandpa Hoft, don't you?)"

South Hall Entrance

One day, Peggy put together a picnic snack, and we headed to Washington Crossing. In a small chapel by the Delaware River there is a large mural of the adventurous General and his army crossing that river in the freezing waters filled with ice and snow as they went to surprise the Hessians. We explained to Stan and Hope what a feat that was. As we sat enjoying our picnic in the historic park, Peggy and I explained again what a difficult time General Washington had crossing that river during such a storm. Stan was quiet a moment and then asked, "Why didn't he use the

65

bridge?" Yes, there it was – the George Washington Bridge! We also had time for shopping in Trenton, visiting some parks and other sites in the area, and painting at Mary Mason's school.

September 30, 1953, I began to study Comparative Religions with Dr. Edward Jurji, who was a Syrian, born in Damascus. This included Islam, the religion of the Muslims. I had studied about that religion with Dr. Christy Wilson who with his wife had been missionaries to Persia (now Iran) for twenty-two years. Somehow I had been drawn to go deeper into the understanding of that faith. That is why I was doing a Master of Theology in Islamic research that year – to be better prepared before going overseas. During the spring of 1953, Peggy and I had filed applications to the Presbyterian Board of Foreign Mission Office in New York City. Whew! Those sixteen pages of questions were the real test of a call to mission. We did mention that we were open to the Muslim world, if there was an opening somewhere. We sent them in and waited for a reply. There had been three hundred applications. We were among the thirty accepted!

I discovered a wealth of study materials in the Erdman Library on the PTS campus and also at the Firestone Library on the Princeton University Campus. I had vital and comprehensive assistance from Dr. Jurji, who was my counselor and guide. He had known Islam firsthand in Syria and as a Christian scholar had firmly established himself in academic circles. I was most fortunate to attend his lectures, study books he had written, and have his wise guidance in my research. I also attended lectures by Professor Phillip K. Hitti, a renowned scholar of Islam at Princeton University. The books in my South Hall basement "office" kept piling up as I worked through the days and late into the nights. I had tackled a huge subject, which had to be focused on certain aspects of Islam, not the whole sum and substance.

As I progressed in my research, I was impressed by the contrasts between Islam and Christianity. They certainly seemed mutually exclusive. That is why the purpose of my study became an exploration of the historical and theological development of Islam. Since the Prophet Mohammad claimed to be the Apostle of Allah (the Arabic word for God), it was imperative for me to study his life and actions. I focused my study on the religious environment of Arabia, the milieu that had shaped his personality, factors which influenced his religious and political development, possible sources which contributed to the flowering of his thinking and his message, the Koran, and why there is such a contrast between Islam and Christianity. Each claims to be a revelation from God, each possesses a Holy Book – a guide to faith and practice – each believes in Divine creation of heaven and earth, each has a concept of the Hereafter, though the concepts may differ in the nature of future life, and each one arose in Southwest Asia. The basic question was: Is Islam unique, or were there possible borrowings from Christianity and Judaism? What about references in the Koran to the People of the Book (Jews and Christians) and the mention of the Prophets in our Old Testament, references to Jesus' virgin birth by Mary (whom he confused with Miriam, the sister of Aaron), a few of Jesus' miracles differing from the accounts recorded in the Gospels, the rejection of the crucifixion of Jesus, because Allah would not allow a Prophet to suffer that? Since God is One, Mohammad thought that the revelations he received had to be identical to the Scriptures of the Jews and Christians. Later, he would accuse the Jews and Christians of changing their sacred writings. He also claimed that his name would fulfill the predicted coming of the Holy Spirit, the promised Advocate, making him the Seal of the Apostles and the abrogation of the Christian faith. I pondered how Mohammad could argue that a Triune God would be impossible, because God is One! What were his sources for a base of disagreement? There are more points, but this gives you the gist of why I explored the possibility of his borrowing from Jewish and Christian sources. These are some of the questions I wrestled with in trying to be as objective and fair as possible. For more information on my studies, consult my thesis which I submitted in May of 1954!

Meanwhile, Peggy kept busy with our Stan and Hope. They were a handful now. Stan loved the sandbox near South Hall. But, there was a boy named Jimmy, Stan's age, who seemed to give him trouble. One day Peggy saw Jimmy hit Stan. Stan was about to retaliate when Peggy quickly took him aside and explained how Jesus had said to turn the other cheek instead of striking back. Stan thought for a moment and said, "I think Jesus should make a new plan!" Another time, there was an altercation that is best described in Stan's words: "Jimmy...stabbed me twice in the leg with a pencil. The pencil lead broke off in my leg both times and was visible through the skin for years. I retaliated by stabbing him between the eyes with a fork and hitting him on the top of his forehead with a shovel." After this incident, Peggy counseled Stan, "The Bible says that we are to love one another, not fight." His reply was, "I think they should tear that page out!" Margaret Dolman, just across the hall from us, complained to Peggy that Stan kept having Gary, her son, carry his cap and jacket up three flights of stairs to our apartment. Peggy had a talk with Stan about that issue, and he replied, "Gary likes to do things for me!" He was certainly a precocious child and at an early age demonstrated his leadership abilities. Hope was the petite little girl who loved her doll, the play tea set, and could occupy herself for hours just being a sweet girl with her toys. However, I recall an incident when the whole family went to the Pottersville Church with me. I had been convinced by my Homiletics professor to "preach without notes." I quote from Peggy's letter to her mom: "Hope kept up a constant giggle and a series of antics, such as hugging the little boy in the seat behind her, and while eating crackers to keep her quiet and inactive, she sneezed and blew the crumbs all over the floor, which made Stan laugh out loud, joined by the congregation!" This caused Peggy a great deal of care and worry throughout the rest of the service. How did the father react? Seeing this commotion caused by our dearly loved children, I completely lost all thought regarding that second point I was trying to make in the sermon. I went right to the third point, and no one seemed to notice. So much for preaching without notes!

Halloween was a fascination for Stan. He and Gary Dolman put on costumes and ventured down the nearby streets playing Trick or Treat. They knocked on several doors, one of which was the home of Albert Einstein! He invited them in for cookies and a chocolate drink. He told them he was glad they had come to visit him as not many children did. Somehow they didn't think he wanted company. After General Dwight Eisenhower was elected President, Stan announced he wanted to send a gift to him. To earn some money, he dusted his room and Peggy gave him six cents. She helped him send the coins in a letter to the President, thinking that was the end of it. But, to our utter amazement, a letter from the newly elected President returned the hard-earned money to him with thanks, saying since Stan had worked so hard to earn the money he was returning it. If you don't believe this, take a look at a framed exhibit in Stan's computer room. There it hangs today, a treasure!

On February 2, 1954, we received the news from the Board of Missions that we had been appointed to full-time missions overseas. We went to New York City later that month for our official commissioning, followed by a dinner of highly spiced foods in the home of Dr. Dodds, the Mission Field Secretary. That spicy food didn't agree with me – it was too hot! I wondered what they served overseas. Since we had indicated that we were willing to serve in the Muslim world, we were appointed to work in Pakistan. Frank and Eleanor Llewellyn in Pakistan were exuberant on hearing this news. They had been there thirty-seven years and had been praying that someone would come to replace them!

Suddenly, it dawned on Peggy and me what had to be done before we traveled to Pakistan. Since it was for a five-year term, we would have to purchase clothing, shoes, everything – in graduated sizes for the whole family. We ordered most things from catalogs and had them shipped to 156 Fifth Avenue, New York City, where the crates and fifty-gallon oil drums would be packed for unaccompanied baggage. It also meant traveling to New York City every two weeks to complete a series of eleven inoculations – shots in the arm! Before going for the third round, Stan inquired what those shots were for. When we told him, he said he would rather die of those diseases than get the shots! I will spare the reader from the mountain of details and history of preparation for the intended journey to Pakistan, set for November/December of 1954.

At the end of May 1954, the Master of Theology in Comparative Religions (Islam) degree was conferred on me by PTS. My thesis had been approved, examinations were completed, and I was free to leave. Hope Abigail, Peggy's younger sister, drove Mom and Dad Hoft from Iowa to Princeton for the graduation. Their only complaint was that

Henry and Beulah at Al's Graduation

Hope had not stopped often enough for coffee and snacks! The whole affair was impressive and inspiring. Again the graduation was held in the Princeton University Chapel. We took them to the usual sites of interest, and they were able to get acquainted with Princeton. But, as they were to leave, we all had a bad and sad time. Peggy and I had to attend a six-week Missionary orientation in Meadville, Pennsylvania, from June 20 to July 31. There was no accommodation for children. We had to send our dear Stan and Hope with Mom, Dad, and Hope Abigail to Iowa. They had graciously agreed to care for them. What a heartbreaker that was. We loaded their car with Stan's and Hope's suitcases, personal things, and our RCA Black and White TV. We all cried!

Peggy and I packed our belongings, and the truck from New York City was loaded with our things which the Mission Board office would crate. We thoroughly cleaned the apartment, working until 3:00 am, and said our farewells. Loading the car to the gills, we drove to Allegheny College in Meadville, Pennsylvania. It was a large conference with over a hundred newly appointed missionaries destined for many different countries. We settled into a dorm and joined the crowd. We were both heartbroken, missing Stan and Hope, wondering how they were faring. In the line for breakfast, we chatted with a couple, mentioning how much we missed our children. One dense woman remarked, "Oh, by now they will have forgotten us." That spoiled our breakfast.

The orientation was most helpful, with Cannon Max Warren from England leading daily Bible study, M.M. Thomas and his wife from Kerala, India, and Betty

With Rev. Inayat and Mr. and Mrs. M.M. Thomas

Cummings for language study. There were many more that lectured, sharing their experiences in overseas mission. There were discussion groups and a whole host of programs including outdoor games to keep us fit. We made new friends, wrote letters, and called our parents and children. Peggy was a bit uncomfortable in her pregnancy.

We especially enjoyed Urdu lessons, the language we would use in Pakistan. Miss Cummings drilled us as a Staff Sergeant would. I will spare you from further details except for the closing of the orientation. Miss Cummings had arranged for an Urdu lesson at 4:00 pm on Saturday, because on Monday the orientation would end. She knew people would begin to disappear. At 2:00 pm on Saturday, Peggy had labor pains; I rushed her to the hospital, where we had consulted Dr. Ewing in advance. Little baby Esther was born late that afternoon. Peggy was doing fine. After making sure all was well, I returned to the dorm to make long-distance calls to our parents.

My mother asked, "Where are you?" I explained what had happened. They were all very pleased to hear the good news and that Peggy and baby were doing well. All of a sudden I remembered that Urdu lesson. What to do? At breakfast the next morning, I saw Miss Cummings looking my way. I hurried over to her and said, "Miss Cummings, I'm sorry we missed that Urdu lesson yesterday, but Peggy had to go to the hospital to give birth to our new daughter, Esther!" She looked me in the eye and said, "Mr. Schlorholtz, that's the only excuse in the world that I would accept!!!"

After the fifth day in the hospital, Peggy felt well enough to leave for Iowa with baby Esther. She was in a hurry to get home. They discharged her with their blessings and "Take Care!" We started our trip home – Wall Lake, Iowa. We drove all day with that little bundle of joy sleeping on the back seat. I kept suggesting we stop for the night, but Peggy insisted she was okay and that we should drive farther. Finally, we found a motel near Indiana for the night. Peggy was absolutely drained with weariness. She didn't even care to have a meal. I brought her a tray of food, and we both survived. Peggy had emptied a drawer and laid baby Esther in it. She slept like a rock most of the night, except for feeding times and changes.

Grandma Schlorholtz Greets Esther

By the next late afternoon, we were in Carroll to see my parents and Carrie's family. Then, we drove to the Hoft farm, meeting Stan first standing by the mailbox down the lane where he had been looking for our arrival. What a thrilling, joyous reunion that was! After Grandma had held the new baby, both Stan and Hope took turns. Mom Hoft had prepared a feast – we thanked the Lord for all His blessings. The long separation had ended. It took several days to relate what had happened to us. It took the same time to hear how Stan and Hope had missed us and how glad they were that we had come home.

71

After Peggy and I had recovered, we had to resume preparation for moving to Pakistan. Continuing to order, purchase locally, and send things to New York City, we visited churches that had pledged funding and prayer support for our overseas work. We enjoyed the extended family's picnics, teas, and dinners and visited neighbors and friends to show off our three children. Of course, there was a foreboding of having to soon leave all these dear ones. We had discussed this many times in Princeton – there it seemed the thing to do. Foremost was concern for our children: how they would be cared for in a foreign land, educated, and a whole plethora of related issues and problems, like how would our parents take all this as we left for Pakistan? So far, they had rather reluctantly accepted our call to mission and were proud that we were doing so much and so well. Had we chosen to accept a call to a church nearby, it would have been something with which they could cope. Moving to where oceans and vast distances separated us would be hard to live with. The price for our next move would be having to relinquish closely knit celebrations of birthdays, anniversaries, and holidays. It was especially painful for Peggy, having to leave those dear ones – her mom and dad, uncles, aunts, cousins, and siblings. It was difficult for me also. When people think about the suffering of missionaries, the hardest is parting! Nevertheless, there was no turning back, no retreat. We had to go forward bravely, faithfully, and determinedly. God's Grace and Help would carry us on and through into the future. He had never let us down in the past. He certainly would go with us into the future!

Chapter 15

Retrospection and Gratitude

Inevitably, many asked the question, "Why are you going to the other side of the world?" We answered as well as we could, explaining our call, probable future work in Pakistan, and that we now had something to share. Reflecting on these and other issues, Peggy and I did a lot of retrospection. We marveled how we had arrived at this new stage in our lives. Wondering whether this was to become a pattern for our lives, we looked back at the small beginnings, which had grown to larger and more challenging opportunities. Peggy, who is smarter than I, exclaimed, "This is just like our family histories." Peggy's roots in America had begun when the North Family arrived in 1634 from Britain and the Hoft Family in the 1850s from Germany. Al's forebears had arrived in the 1860s from East Friesland, Germany. Those courageous people had launched out for a new land, not knowing where they would settle. They had escaped situations of poverty, suppression, lack of opportunity for themselves and for their children. They had dared to face the unforeseeable with a determined commitment and strong resolve. They would work at being, doing, and becoming the people on the frontier of untested waters and the wilderness of uncultivated land, putting into practice their faith, their skills, their dreams. We recognized they were the brave ones – we stood on their shoulders and were to carry on.

Our studies of Foods and Nutrition, Sociology, Psychology, Philosophy, Theology, and Biblical Studies had helped us have an enlightened perspective. We were part of a greater community, of a rich tradition. We recalled the people who had made a difference in our lives while growing up. There were our parents, our brothers and sisters, relatives near and far, neighbors, teachers, friends, preachers, church fellowships, 4-H Clubs, county fairs, schoolmates, and many more. We fondly recalled those who had helped shape us to what we were. There were bursts of laughter, fond remembrances, sorrowful hurts, and so much more. Peggy often thought of dear Aunt Marie who had insisted that she not slouch, but to stand straight and tall. Otherwise Peggy might have a curved spine like hers! There was Miss Wanda Sifford, our English teacher in high school, drilling us in English grammar, insisting that we write neat, correct, and imaginative essays. There was Art Olsen, the coach, who in the study hall at high school had sharply told Peggy and Verna Mae Johnson to "turn around and stop chatting!" There were many more, but let that suffice to make the point.

There were our dads. Both were experienced, hard-working dairymen, crop farmers, and heads of the household (they thought!). Henry was a Democrat, Abe a Republican. Henry had Holsteins, Abe had Brown Swiss. Henry contoured his farm, Abe did not. However, they had both struggled in the Great Depression to survive. They were in debt like everybody else, with prices so low for what they had produced by sweat, blood, and tears. They never had a surplus of cash any year, always mounting debts, mortgages, and ever spiraling costs. But they had carried on! My dad taught me honesty. In the Breda town hall, wrestlers would occasionally put on a show in the ring. Earl Wampler was one, I remember. My dad paid for the tickets for himself, Bernard, and me. To my utter amazement I heard my dad say, "You have given me too much change; I gave you a ten, not a twenty!" He also often quoted Benjamin Franklin, "If a job is once begun, never leave it 'til it's done!" Both had a hardness born of the drudgery and wearing effort as was often said to "make a living." As I have said, "Farming is a risky business!" Both knew the sorrow of losing a son, a relative, a close neighbor, a crop failure, or death of a valuable animal. But they carried on.

Peggy's mother was an extraordinary person. As I have mentioned before, Beulah North's home town was Cherokee, Iowa northwest of Wall Lake on the way to Sioux City. Her mother had died when Beulah was very young. Alma and Beulah had assumed the household duties and carried on. Beulah graduated from high school in 1916. Her photo is in the Yearbook, with this inscription: "Beulah North, A defender of women's rights." In those days, before women received the right to vote in 1920, she evidently took a vital, active part in debates, confrontations, and insistence on promoting a just cause.

It was not easy to be a wife and mother in the Great Depression. Beulah had the character and courageous persistence to meet the situation in which she found herself.

As I have noted, Beulah North's mother died too early for her to really know maternal care and a loving relationship with her mother. Probably that explains, in part, why Mom Hoft so strenuously poured out her life and energies in rearing her seven children, whom she fondly called "her seven!" In the midst of the Great Depression, those economic hard times, she unstintingly and most courageously struggled, not only to meet the needs of her brood but also to stretch the shoestring of poverty by always generously sharing whatever she had in hand.

At the same time, Mom Hoft managed to hold onto her passion for literature, learning, community, and keeping up with current events in spite of the tremendous demands and responsibilities. She loved to read books, poetry, Women's magazines, letters from the large circle with whom she corresponded, and the Des Moines Register. Of course, she always had to keep an eagle eye out for Henry, who sometimes burst into the kitchen to get a cup of hot – I mean hot – coffee! The kettle was always kept near to the boiling point on the back of the cooking range so that she could be ready to immediately oblige. She was always ready to jump up off the sofa and throw aside her book or whatever when she heard him approach. Woe to anyone, wife or child, who was not busily engaged in work – because when Henry worked, everybody worked!

How did Beulah manage to be an active member of the Wall Lake Garden Club, Eastern Star, Linger Longers (a social club where seven to eight close friends met to chat, share recipes, "brag" about their children, and enjoy simple refreshments)? She loved flowers and gardening. She enjoyed playing an annual April Fool's trick on Henry – calling him to the phone to answer a nonexistent long-distance call. He fell for it every year, because she waited for the right moment to make her move. Early on the morning of July Fourth, she would light a small firecracker under a tin can, which popped up and rattled step by step down the stairway. Peggy and the brood always got a bang out of that! I have already noted how she provided more than enough food for the extended family dinners and picnics.

Her sacrificial dedication to her family and the nurturing of each one flowed from a loving mother's heart, an avid reader's quest, a poet's wisdom and insights, a painter's vision, a teacher's aspirations, a homemaker's labors, a grandmother's joys, and a fountain of hospitality and concern for others. She painted over seventy oil paintings, distributing them among the family and close friends. She never sold a one. Once she sent one to Pakistan to a school that wanted the Good Shepherd's scene where Jesus reaches to rescue a lost lamb. It still serves as the worship center in the Kasur Girls' School. We have treasured the Nativity scene she copied from a small Christmas card painted by Asian artist Wesley Thomas that depicts the birth of Jesus in a typical Indian birth scene. It has dominated our living room wherever we have gone. How gratefully we reviewed the memories and actions of that role model who had influenced us to such an extent. And although we would dearly miss Mom Hoft as we

Our Treasured Nativity Scene, Painted by Beulah Hoft

prepared to leave for Pakistan, we thanked the Lord for her life and devotion. She had contributed the most to Peggy's preparation to live a similar life.

My mom, Emma (Becker) Schlorholtz, was also an extraordinary woman. She did not have the privilege of attending high school, because there was none in Breda, as far as I can understand. In that time and town, girls were not encouraged to get a lot of learning. The youngest of four sisters, she early on learned to be an excellent cook. Her mother died when my mom was only eight years old. One of her two brothers died at an early age. She, too, was acquainted with grief. In those early days, life was hard and demanding. She and Abe married and settled on our farm west of Breda. Exactly one year and one day later, my sister Carrie was born. We boys teased her that she had been born the day after the wedding. It always made her angry! We also accused her of having the traveling Watkin's Products man as her father. Naughty boys! Mom told us that she had suffered severe back trouble and pains after Carrie's birth. Bernard was born seven years later.

Mom was a leader in our church, serving three terms (1934-1936) as President of the Ladies Aid Society, which later became Presbyterian Women. Here is their purpose statement: "The purpose shall be to further Christian fellowship and by our humble services to aid in the upbuilding of the kingdom of God, both at home and abroad." They sent gifts to mission and worthy local causes. They had an annual Bazaar serving supper from 5:00 to 8:00 in café style. This effort brought in one hundred fifty-nine dollars, quite a sum in those days. One year, they served a second community meal, a special chicken dinner with all the trimmings, plus pumpkin pie. Those dedicated women donated the chickens, potatoes, milk, vegetables, and the pies. That year they earned six hundred dollars, half the Pastor's annual salary. What sacrificial giving in the throes of the Depression! I know these things firsthand, because I helped in the kitchen whipping the potatoes, a job which required a strong arm.

To relate all the hardships and trying circumstances Mom bravely faced would take a lot of space. The problems and challenges my mom contended with as a farmer's wife were similar to Mom Hoft's. I won't repeat them here. She helped with chores until we boys were old enough to help. Each spring, she would order about two hundred baby chicks from the Breda hatchery, put them into the brooder room of the chicken house, ensure they were warm by stoking a small coal-burning stove night and day, and give them feed and water. Fifty cockerels were also cared for to provide meat for the family. We all helped her process them, canning a few, and storing the larger amount in the new locker in town. She loved flowers and gardening, coaxing us to mow the lawn and to help in the seeding, hoeing, and weeding of the garden. Gathering the eggs, we put them into wooden crates with cardboard liners to sell them to one of the grocery stores in town. The egg money was hers to spend buying groceries, household supplies, and "pocket" money.

At times, whenever we children got "smart," she would ask us whether we could recite the sixteen townships in Carroll County. We could not, but she would recite them in order of their position! She taught us how to remember spelling Mississippi: "M i crooked letter crooked letter i, crooked letter crooked letter i, humpbacked humpbacked i." Many times her quick wit would amaze us. This must have been the source of my gift for witty remarks. Mom was realistically wise. Whenever we would hear a newly married couple had a baby too early, she would say, "The first child can be born any time, after that it takes about nine months!" Mom had a refined wit and used it well. Occasionally Aunt Annie would visit with her three daughters. We boys must have teased them, because they went and told their mother. She then told my mother, "If those boys were mine, I would spank them!" My mom replied, "Yes, I would spank them, too, if they were yours!" On another visit in the freezing cold of winter, Bernard and I, sick with the measles, were cared for on cots set up in the dining room where it was warm. That night, Aunt Annie had a splitting headache and moaned without pause. At breakfast, my mom thanked her for coming and was sorry she had to leave for home.

After retiring to Carroll, Mom helped all in need, baked cakes and cookies for the celebration of birthdays and anniversaries, and meals for all who would visit as she had done on the farm. One morning about 6:30 as she was sweeping the front sidewalks, Mrs. Olerick, her next door neighbor, came by. My mom inquired, "My, it is early, where are you off to?" The neighbor muttered, "Oh! To say another mass to get my departed husband out of Purgatory, and I wouldn't have him back for anything!" My mom replied, "Why don't you get even with him; leave him where he is!" The woman went off in a huff. When relating this, Mom would say with a sly grin, "I wonder why she didn't speak to me for weeks!" Larry and Stan planned a surprise for their Grandma. Carefully loading a box with a ribbon bow on top, they presented the gift to her on the front porch where we were all enjoying A&W root beer in the heat of the day. She cautiously opened the box to view hideous toads, snuggling together, getting ready to jump out. She was surprised! All laughed at this "terrible joke" on Grandma. Slamming the cover shut, she calmly said, "Just what I wanted to cook for supper tonight!" We all laughed even more heartily.

Peggy and I agreed we were all richer in character, spirit, and mind because our lives had been touched and nurtured by that host of gracious, compassionate, and loving people. Mirrored in us were the experiences of good times and bad. One uncle told us that firm, sharp edges enriched life, just like a knife held against a grindstone for sharpening. Looking back in retrospect, we were filled with gratitude overflowing. It had helped Peggy and me to more readily focus on the future, with the confidence and faith that we had been enriched by our community of noble, loving, great people.

Part II: How We Came to be in Pakistan

Chapter 16

Traveling From Iowa to Pakistan by Train, Ship, and Plane

Embarking on a New Life

On an early November 1954 evening, it was time to make our departure for Pakistan. A huge gathering at the Great Western Railway Station at Carroll came to see us off, including our parents, siblings, uncles and aunts, cousins, neighbors, and members of the Wall Lake, Wheatland, Auburn, Carnarvon, West Side, and Arcadia congregations. They brought flowers and fruit. Our baggage was on the platform ready to be loaded onto the Pullman Express from Carroll to New York City. We embraced, made our farewells, and wept together. Right on time the train arrived and we boarded, being helped with the baggage, and shown to our seats. Peggy had a berth for herself and four-month-old Esther; I had Stan and Hope with me.

After an all-night's journey, we arrived in the New York City Grand Central Station and somehow settled into a large room on the twelfth floor of the Edison Hotel. We spent several days buying some almost forgotten items, one of which was an Argus C-3 camera and film. Brother Dick had loaned us his car, which saved our lives in those hectic scrambles of preparation. We didn't have time for sightseeing. The children cooperated in a grand style. Stan and Hope had their own small carry on bags. Our accompanied freight was taken to the pier at Hoboken, New Jersey. This time members of Grace Church of Montclair and the Arlington Second Presbyterian Church came with a large bouquet of flowers and a huge basket of fruit for the voyage. Dick and Merna, Willard and Betty, and Hope Abigail, also came to say farewells. After prayer by one of the Pastors, we boarded the passenger/freight ship Excambion. However, no one saw us leave because it was so foggy, the ship's departure was delayed from 4:00 to about 6:30. We were traveling by ship since Esther was not yet six months old and there had to be a doctor on board. Peggy settled into our cabin with Esther. Stan, Hope, and I stood on deck to experience our departure. I was holding Hope so she could see what was happening. Stan was duly impressed! Suddenly just above us there were loud blasts of the ship's horn. Hope threw her arms around my neck and exclaimed, "Help! They are blowing me out of my skin!" We were all thrilled as the ship plowed through the Hudson River. Saying goodbye to the Statue of Liberty, we entered the Atlantic Ocean. We settled in as a family in the large stateroom and enjoyed our first dinner on board. The children were good sailors! Baby Esther seemed to enjoy the rhythmic, rocking waves. However, the first day out to sea most passengers, including us, were seasick. We spent that day resting and eating sandwiches and having tea in our cabin room. One afternoon while Stan and Hope were at a party given for youngsters and Esther was playing in her bed (able to turn herself over from her back to her tummy, she was a strong one at less than four months old), Peggy and I sat looking out the portholes hardly able to believe we could be so far from home. Peggy was an efficient Deputy Captain. She somehow kept us all comfortable and healthy.

Our first stopover was Gibraltar, where we saw two submarines at the dock. We were not there long enough to disembark. The next stop was Barcelona, Spain, where hundreds of oil barrels were unloaded. We sailed on to Marseilles, France, where more cargo was placed onto the dock. Since there was time, we hired a taxi to help us tour the city. We began to learn how to use foreign currency, which was a new experience for us. Naples was to be the next port of call. En route, on a gloriously clear morning, we saw the snow-capped Mt. Etna in the distance on the island of

Sicily. Its base was shrouded in fog and low-lying clouds, but we could see the summit with a thin wisp of smoke erupting from its volcanic cone.

Having docked at Naples, Peggy insisted I take a tour – Pompeii, Mt. Vesuvius volcano and the lava flow catastrophe – and do a triangular tour of Amalfi, Isle of Capri, and Sorrento. As we stopped for lunch, a young girl accompanied by stringed instruments sang Santa Lucia as it should be sung! We were off again. Rounding the island of Crete our ship was caught in a terrible storm, reminding us of the Apostle Paul's shipwreck experiences. We kept to our cabin for safety and because we were a little seasick. Suddenly the heavily weighted crib with Esther in it tipped over. I stopped its tumble by catching it on my shins. What a blessing that I was sitting on the bunk in just the right place. The room steward came in to clean the bathroom. Peggy asked him, "Where are we?" "Lady, we ain't nowhere," he replied. Very comforting! We survived the storm and continued on to Alexandria, Egypt, arriving on a Sunday in time to worship with Christians, who also took us to see the famous library. The worship was in Arabic, but we could follow what was happening. Continuing on, we safely docked in Beirut, ending our sea journey there.

We had four glorious days in which to see that beautiful city, taking many side trips. We slept soundly. What a blessing solid ground is. Most enjoyed was the American University of Beirut, where we chatted with students and faculty from many Middle East countries. It was an appropriate introduction to a different culture than our own. The students were very intelligent and openly friendly. We were meeting the future leaders of that whole area of the world. (How sad it is that there is such a divisive situation in the Middle East today.) The weather was ideal in the winter season. It was good to have some days of rest, to explore and meet people who made us most welcome. We appreciated the generosity of our Board of Missions for providing that informative orientation and relaxation.

Our freight was shipped unaccompanied to Karachi. We boarded an ancient DC-3 plane fully loaded with a detachment of Dutch soldiers headed for Indonesia. It would be an eight-hour flight. All of us had a seat except for Esther who was placed in a basket where Peggy could care for her needs. To our great astonishment, she slept all the way! What an introduction that was to the art of loud droning engines soothing a baby to sleep. Getting quite weary as we approached Karachi, the major seaport of Pakistan, we were eager to disembark, but were all kept in our seats. Presently two officially dressed men boarded the plane and sprayed insecticide everywhere, under and over the passengers; they feared we might bring Yellow Fever and mosquitoes into Pakistan. That was our welcome committee! After clearing customs, we took something like a tram to the Metropole Hotel. A man talked to Stan seated opposite Peggy and me. I heard him ask why we were in Pakistan. Stan replied, "We have come to tell you about Jesus." The man looked at us as if to say, "More missionaries!" Peggy and I glanced at each other in amazement. How proud we were that Stan had quietly testified as a witness for Christ to a Pakistani. He must have been listening to some of our discussions! Our overnight stay at the Metropole Hotel was eventful and educational. We had arrived in a new culture, heard language we did not understand, ate food that was delicious but highly spiced. The hotel personnel, however, spoke English for which we were most grateful.

The next day, December 10, 1954, we took a plane to Lahore. As we departed from the air terminal, we were met by a crowd of people. About twenty missionaries and fifty people from Kasur came out to greet us. Frank and Eleanor Llewellyn, the senior missionaries in Kasur, had arranged two busloads of the Kasur Church members to welcome their new missionaries. They gave us their salaams in greeting. There we stood, Stan wearing a red fez from Egypt, Peggy holding baby Esther, and I holding Hope Ellen. They placed garlands of marigolds around our necks, read a long welcome speech, and applauded our every move. It was our first meeting with Christians in Pakistan. What a memorable day that was! The Forman Christian College van took us to the FCC campus where we would stay with the Don and Doris Bell family until our freight was cleared and reached Lahore. How we appreciated the generosity of the Bells to make us "feel right at home!" We celebrated Christmas in their home, attended the FCC worship in one of the rooms where English was taught, and exchanged the few gifts we had brought in our hand luggage. On January 6, Peggy and Doris arranged a birthday party for Hope, inviting other FCC children. On February 14, Peggy and I celebrated Stan's birthday. He was enrolled in the Anglican Cathedral School in downtown Lahore. It was English medium; he quickly made friends. On December 15, Al had reached the advanced age of thirty-one, which was duly celebrated. In March we celebrated Peggy's birthday.

About three weeks after arriving in Lahore, we received notice that our unaccompanied baggage had reached Karachi and was to be held in Customs until it was cleared. The Mission Treasurer and I took a plane ride there and began the eight-day clearance process. What a challenge that was! One example of trouble was that they would not allow a slide projector to enter Pakistan. It was not on The List. However, we learned from a Pakistani gentleman to call it a magic lantern and it was cleared! Finally, having cleared each and every item, paid the custom fees, and received the Discharge, we got the entire lot loaded on a goods (freight) train and flew back to Lahore. It had taken ten days!

Meanwhile Peggy entertained the children. They had lots of fun with new playmates, had ridden in horse-drawn carts (called tongas), were thrilled to see a couple of camel trains, and went shopping with Auntie Doris. They had also missed their daddy, and I received a great welcome home. I told them what had happened in Karachi and that our baggage would soon be coming to Lahore by goods train. When our things arrived from Karachi, we had them transported from the Lahore Railway Station by ox cart, which Stan was allowed to drive, to House #12 on the FCC campus, our home until going to Murree Hills for further Urdu language study in May.

The Monday following Christmas we started Urdu lessons taught by a young Pakistani. It was hard work. The Urdu Book text was a great help. Learning to hear Urdu rather than English sounds was difficult. Bravely and persistently the teacher carried on. How happy we were when we could make sentences out of the single words we memorized. It meant long hours of study and recitation. Senior missionaries, Margaret Ewing and Marge Velte, helped us to hire household helpers. Imagine Peggy and me needing help! But learning Urdu was the priority for the first six months, then half-time for a year. We learned that the cook, the gardener, the sweeper to clean the floors, and the ayah (who cared for the children) were indispensable to our new situation. We did not have the free time to do what those helpers did so faithfully. Once a week the dhobi (washer man) would pick up our laundry and take it to the river where he would pound it on a flat stone. What a wonderful method of losing buttons. This was really difficult to accept until we realized that we were helping those helpers make a livelihood. We were getting acquainted with the stark reality of mass poverty, which we would soon have to address in our future work.

Peggy shared with me that while I was in Karachi, she took the children for a walk on the campus, pushing little Esther in the stroller. There she saw a destitute scantily dressed woman with a dirty, sickly child – both were skin and bones. The woman had the look of despair in her eyes. This made Peggy weep and resolve to minister to the wretched poor and needy in Pakistan whenever possible. Everywhere we looked there were people in need. We saw a "new world" – new only to the newcomers – with so many in the grip of mass poverty of mind, body, and spirit. We were beginning to see in vivid reality some of the reasons why the Lord had called us to Pakistan. Peggy and I began to wonder whether we had the ability, capacity, and love in Christ to continue "Christ's ministry." We were not doubting, but becoming even more deeply committed to the tasks before us. We had to quickly master Urdu so that we could study this new culture, the needs of these people, and become enabled to do the best we could to have something to share.

Chapter 17

Murree Hills, Rosenheim Cottage, Urdu Schooling, Family Life

Toward the end of April we began packing things we would need, storing the rest, and getting ready to travel to Murree Hills where we would attend Urdu Language School. It was becoming hot on the plains with temperatures in the low hundreds. We looked forward to being in a cooler place. Renting the Mission Van, we loaded our family and the family of Bill and Ruby Ella Price and their two sons, and with all our luggage started out from Lahore at 4:00 am because we wanted to escape the heat of the day. We were on the famous Grand Trunk Road, engineered by the British. Since it was early, we met only ox carts loaded with things to sell, bicycles carrying wares, men carrying carefully balanced goods on their head, trucks, and buses. Eventually we passed Gujranwala and Jehlum and arrived in Rawalpindi. We stopped for a cool drink and a snack at the Silver Grill. Frank Llewellyn had suggested we hire a driver to maneuver those steep winding mountain roads, but I decided to see how dangerous it was. We made good time and stopped at the halfway mark – a village with the strong scent of pines, cool air, and magnificent vistas – to stretch our legs. Then we continued onward and upward until there was Murree! Dropping the Prices off at the Methodist home, we drove to the Presbyterian retreat named Rosenheim (Home of Roses), which had been purchased from a German couple. There were four cottages on the property completely furnished. Marge Velte had told us why they had made the cottages comfortable and ready for our personnel. In the early days there had been no screens, no throw rugs, no stove, etc. They made sure that the next generation of missionaries would not have to start from zero! We soon looked for our sweaters, though we were only one hundred eighty miles north of Lahore. A seven-thousand-four-hundred-foot elevation makes a great deal of difference! The cook had preceded us and had a delicious hot meal ready for us. This was a blessing as we were weary and starving. In the next few days we settled in. What a change from Lahore. Peggy wrote to her mother, "We are literally living and walking in the clouds these days. But is it ever cold! We are all bundled up with sweaters and coats. The monsoon rains have begun, dousing our tin roof with deafening rain. We burned pine logs in the fireplace to keep us warm and to dry the hand-washed clothes." The next day I drove the van back to Lahore and returned by bus to Murree. That bus ride helped me get closer to the people of Pakistan!

Murree had been a garrison retreat for British soldiers and their families, plus administrators from the Plains. Tradition was that the Virgin Mary had settled there after the crucifixion of Jesus; a corruption of Mary became Murree. Peggy wrote of Murree in a letter: "I don't know how to describe Murree and its shopping center. The little shops are lined up along three streets. The shopkeepers sleep on the floor until you really look interested. For Americans they ask four times the price they would charge their own people. All the men chew betel nut – they spit a red liquid anywhere. Frequently seen are men taking a bath or going to the toilet in the gutter. One sees very few women. They, in accordance with Muslim law, must stay out of sight. In public they wear heavy veils that nearly cover them from head to foot. It is really funny to be introduced to someone like that, as you wouldn't know them again for anything." We had great fun exploring. There were mountain trails, heavy forests of pine trees, look-out-point picnics when the sun illuminated the place, and teas at Lintott's complete with pastries and cookies. Stan attended Sandes Home School just beyond the Jhika Galli bazaar. This was run by the United Presbyterian Mission for missionary children. Hope and Esther kept us amused and active.

It was Language School time for Peggy and me. The School was held in the Murree Union Church, a worship center a little over a mile from Rosenheim, where we attended Sunday worship. There were sixty-eight students from all denominations and missions in Pakistan. We began to enjoy school even though we had not looked forward to it very much. We left home by 7:00 am five mornings a week. There were classes for beginners, for second-year students, and for the advanced third-year experts. We started from scratch. Classes were limited to six to seven students, taught by a Pakistani. There was a chapel break with tea at midmorning. We began to hear short meditations and learn to sing hymns in Urdu. It was inspiring to begin to understand Urdu words, phrases, and sentences. We had textbooks to study, model sentences and word lists to memorize, and thorough recitation of conjugations and writing the Urdu script. Our teachers were friendly, but they put us through the paces! We enjoyed meeting and getting to know fellow missionaries from many countries. Everyone had a distinct story-of-my-life. We returned home by 12:30 for lunch, checking on Hope and Esther who had been cared for by Rani, the ayah from Lahore. She was middle-aged but really did a great job in our absence. We rested a bit, then had to prepare for two additional hours of study in the afternoon with a teacher who gave us personal attention and help with our lessons. It was a daily eight-hour grind.

Using Urdu words had its surprises and difficulties. It made even our teacher, always the formal and all-business instructor, laugh. For example, when we substituted the word for camel with the word for brick, when we used soap for the word soup, and as I did wanting to say that in America I had been a farmer (*kissan*), told them I had been a field (*khet*). But, there was an all-time moment when Ruth, a quiet, unassuming young woman, misused a word. She wanted to say, "I never drink liquor (*sharab*)," instead she used (*peshab*) urine! I had never seen such a brilliant blush in my life, or since! Even that stony-faced teacher had to laugh. Of course, Peggy used Urdu better than I did. She worked hard at it and practiced speaking Urdu with the helpers in the home and in the bazaar haggling with shopkeepers. She used it with gusto, hoping that it was correct, not seeming to mind if it was not. I, however, had to get it right or I wouldn't try. I had studied four languages by reading the script (Latin, German, Greek, and Hebrew) but not in conversation. I always seemed to form the script in my mind before speaking. It took some time for me to think in Urdu and use it with gusto. However, I gave a meditation in chapel, not using one word of English. This encouraged me to realistically hope that sometime in the future I would be able to preach in Urdu. Each Friday there was a quiz over what we had studied that week. Peggy and I both passed and moved on. However, we students arranged a picnic on our verandah for the Urdu teachers just to get to know them and make them feel ashamed if they had to fail us! I wrote a poem for the occasion. We had daily rains, and it poured as I recited: "Rain, rain, rain. Irritation Irrigation. Rain, rain, rain. Learning Urdu is fun. It has us on the run. But with teachers like George, Bashir, and Good we will surely give it the gun!" At the end of term, both Peggy and I passed the exams. We had made the most of our full-time study. We hired George to come to Kasur in the autumn to continue our studies.

Each summer a Missionary conference was held in the Anglican Church across from Lintott's. They invited me to give one of the four lectures. With full-time Urdu study,

88

I found it difficult to find time to research and write in longhand what I wanted to present. I called it "The Nature and Mission of the Church," based on II Corinthians Chapter Four. The main thrust was that missionaries had to be a part of the Church but not dominate it. We were to preach the gospel, assist, and supplement a growing community of faith, hope, and love as new creations in Christ. We were to help enable the Church to become the mission to shed abroad the Light in Jesus Christ. It went quite well. Dr. Rhea (Principal of FC College) and Margaret Ewing and Dr. Mowbry (English Professor) and Marge Velte told me that "I was a courageous preacher and well informed." Yea, Princeton! Peggy agreed that I did the best of the four, but that I had gestured too often and vigorously.

Stan and Hope enjoyed the hillside near our cottage. They pushed Esther in her stroller. There were loads of daises, dandelions, white clover, and buttercups. There were tall pine trees and one mammoth Cedar of Lebanon on the hill near Yusaf's house. He was the night

Hope Plays in Murree (2ⁿᵈ from Left)

watchman. A former missionary, many years prior, had brought a sapling from Lebanon and planted it. What an inspiring champion of nature! Often both Stan and Hope would bring bouquets to their mom. Other members of the Mission came to Rosenheim on vacation. Dr. Mowbry Velte and his wife, Marge, arrived from Lahore. Peggy invited them for supper the first evening. We had a grand time joking and playing Scrabble. The next week Hope went to their cottage and asked, "Does your thansama make tookies?" She meant, "Does your khansama (cook) make cookies?" They were so charmed with her brave request that they had her repeat it several times before inviting her in to have cookies! Hope made friends easily and chatted away on many subjects. She had a fertile imagination and often set up a "hospital ward" on the lawn for her "sick" dolls and teddy bear! Stan also made friends easily. He had a special friend, Jim Knudson, who had been adopted on the condition that his parents also adopt Jim's three younger sisters. The children were Native American. What a lovely family they were! Stan and Jim made bows and arrows and tree houses and roamed the hillside and trails. Esther was thriving in the mountain air and enjoying her baths in the family's tin tub. They were splashing affairs! All three had good appetites and enjoyed Pakistani food.

We often invited families to join a picnic on our front lawn under the shade tree. Peggy was following her Mother's tradition of hospitality and plentiful goodies. She loved inviting families to supper, good conversation, games, and singing. We felt privileged to have friends from so many different countries. We were also invited to

Esther Acclimates Joyously to Pakistan

their picnics and dinners. All were part of a close community of faith, hope, and love. On July 30 we celebrated Esther's first birthday. Peggy's mom sent a little necklace gift for her. She wore it proudly! Peggy baked a big birthday cake with one candle lighted. Stan and Hope helped Esther blow it out. She then grabbed a portion of frosting and succeeded in smearing her face more than getting a good bite of cake. To my amazement, Peggy let her

get her hands into the cake itself! We had a chicken dinner with all the trimmings, including ice cream. Borrowing a hand-cranked freezer and buying ice and rock salt in the bazaar, we produced a winner with Stan and Hope taking turns to "rest" my arm and baby Esther looking on. What a treat! It reminded us of other picnics and birthday parties we had enjoyed on the other side of the world. Peggy had worried about our baby's health in new settings. She wrote to her mother with relief, "Our little Esther is such a good eater. She loves mashed potatoes, carrots, is the biggest milk drinker, and loves Jello too...I hope that when we get to Kasur, and in the heat, she will be as healthy as she is now."

One lazy Sunday afternoon ten days before we would be leaving this wonderful retreat to make the move to Kasur, Peggy and I reviewed all that had happened during our first summer in Murree. We reclined in our chairs on that sunny verandah and watched Stan and Hope on the rope swing which we had tied to a strong branch of a pine tree. How they had grown to love being in Pakistan! Of course, we often thought about our parents and families in the U.S.A. and missed them. But we were beginning to get the feel of missionary life. We were so glad the Urdu language study here was drawing to a close. It had been a grueling experience. We had only one final exam to take before finishing the course. Esther was walking strongly now and well-balanced, laughing as she maneuvered so expertly. We thanked the Lord for the many blessings He had showered upon us that summer of 1955. Stan had done so well in school and made so many new friends. He had led in prayer at the beginning of the Parent-Teachers program, had written a hymn, and had been more demonstrative in showing how much he loved us. How proud we were! Hope had become an unstoppable chatterbox. She played so well with baby Esther and Stan, she was open and friendly with everyone, she was efficient in using Urdu, and was adored by everyone. Peggy and I loved one another more deeply and were becoming confident that we had made the right decisions so far.

However, in five days I would be traveling to Lahore, packing our belongings onto a truck, and getting things settled in Kasur. Then I would drive up to Murree for the family and down into the heat and on to Kasur.

Chapter 18

Settling in Kasur from September 5, 1955
Complications/Adjustments

According to plan we loaded everything into the jeep and headed toward Kasur via Lahore. We stopped in Lahore for lunch and to buy provisions we would need. Traveling on the same Grand Trunk Highway, we drove the thirty miles southeast to finally arrive in Kasur, a town of seventy-five thousand, not a village as we had been told. Since Frank and Eleanor had moved to Llewellynabad, where the Boys' Boarding School was located a half-mile from the Mission Compound, we unloaded our things into the Mission Bungalow. Finally, we were to settle in and begin our work. The bungalow was a two-story, fired brick construction with ample room for our family and guests. (There were no hotels in Kasur.) Rooms with attached bathrooms were for our guests. Local Christians welcomed us and made us feel a part of our new community. Among them were Gail Asel, the Principal of the Girls' Boarding School across the driveway in an almost duplicate bungalow, and James Iqbal, who was to be the co-administrator of Kasur District mission work, and his wife Alice. Having graduated from Dubuque Seminary, he had recently returned. Evidently Frank had thought we needed help and teamwork. It was the first time there was such an arrangement. James was busy in evangelistic preaching and nurturing the twelve pastors, each with their twenty to twenty-five village congregations. We welcomed their friendly greetings.

Peggy and I got busy arranging the sparse furnishings: the refrigerator (which we were glad we had brought out with our baggage), cleaning the kerosene cooking stove, spreading the coconut fiber throw rugs, arranging the tables and chairs, and placing cotton-stuffed mattresses which I had bought in Lahore on the charpoys (rope-woven beds). We had also bought mosquito nets to protect us at night from being eaten by those hungry insects. We thought we had done a rather good job of setting up the kitchen, but by the next morning the helpers who had worked for the Llewellyn's changed back everything to the very same positions that had previously been in place. We were learning what tradition and order meant! In time there would be a cook, Teju, the handyman who went to town for the mail and did errands, Harnama, the chokidar (night watchman), and a young girl Peggy hired to clean, hand-wash clothes, and babysit the children. The next week our Urdu teacher, George Sadiq, arrived from Sialkot. There was a room reserved for him among the helpers, but he told us that being a college graduate and teacher, he was not too happy with that arrangement. We solved the problem by having him move into one of the small rooms with bath at the corner of our bungalow, which had an outer door. He was very pleased, but you should have heard what senior missionaries had to say about that! We insisted, saying George would be part of the family, sharing meals, and readily available for teaching us Urdu. What radicals we were!

We were fascinated with Kasur town. Peggy and I shopped in the rustic bazaars, learned where the stores/stalls were, and realized how strenuous shopping was for our helpers with vegetables in one, fruit in another, meats in another, brassware, carpets –

you name it. Since most people had no refrigeration, they shopped daily for fresh produce. We also learned firsthand how to deal with the many beggars who stretched out their hands. One had to be very discerning. If you gave to one the crowd would multiply! Fresh milk was delivered each morning to the kitchen door by a dudh walla (the milkman). We were warned to discern how much water had been added. It was rich buffalo milk. We all loved it.

Stan and Friends, Kasur

Stan, Hope, and Esther were thrilled with their new home and surroundings; there was much to learn and do. Hope and Esther had limited areas of the Compound being

93

cared for by the Girl. She pushed Esther in the tram or stroller. Hope trudged along carrying her doll and talking to everybody. They were more homebound. On the contrary, Stan was able to roam about with the three Harnama sons, Dr. Young's sons, and Kenneth, son of James and Alice. Soon there was an upstairs room that served as a menagerie for pigeons, hawks, rabbits, etc. Peggy began teaching Stan, using the Calvert System of graded books which thankfully had arrived from the New York City Mission Board. He learned quickly and studied with concentration. At one point while doing arithmetic, Stan paused and asked Peggy, "Why do you think pigeons have different colored eyes?" He was also learning from his playmates the Punjabi dialect. At times while the family was taking an evening walk, someone would ask us a question. Peggy and I tried answering in Urdu, but Stan made it correct and plain by replying in Punjabi (the dialect). We were textbook people – Stan had the direct method of language study!

A.P. Gill with (from left) Shaista, Azam, Wife Sosan, Muazzam

One of the families we met was the A.P. Gill family. He was the District Magistrate located in Kasur. He and his wife, Sosan, and their three children, Muazzam, Shaista, and Azam, lived nearby the Compound. Peggy invited them to tea and they came. We had a great time, especially because they spoke English. During the ensuing years we became fast friends and learned so much from them about Pakistan and its culture.

As they were leaving, Stan asked, "Do you want to see my bunnies?" The children bonded over his menagerie. A lasting relationship was firmly established! A.P. was a Christian from Gujranwala who had overcome many obstacles to rise to the level of District Magistrate and had a sterling reputation as a man of integrity and firm rulings. Space limits me from elaborating here, but there will be more added in the future.

We discovered that Kasur had a long history of development, with two rail lines intersecting the town. One ran from Lahore to Ferozepur, fifteen miles farther east on the Sutlej River, now in India. There were also canals running east to west, bringing irrigation water to a big area. Mission work in Kasur District was begun by two women of the Zenana (Women's) Bible and Medical Mission in 1893. They were denied housing by the Muslim community, so they commuted daily from Ferozepur by train! After some months, they did find lodging and brought with them Nathe Khan, a convert from Islam. He became a catechist supported by the Sunday school of the Naulakha Church in Lahore. His faithful and effective witness and service initiated much of the growth of the church then being formed. There followed a series of dedicated missionaries. To list some of them is necessary: Mr. Morrison, Dr. and Mrs. C.W. Forman, Dr. and Mrs. McCuskey, Miss Wherry, Mr. and Mrs. Duff, Mr. and Mrs. Zoerner, and Mr. and Mrs. Ross. During the period from 1908 to 1921 there was a large ingathering called the Mass Movement. In 1921 the Indian Census states that there were thirteen thousand one hundred fifty-four Christians in Kasur District. How did this happen? Frank Llewellyn told me, "We preached to the educated and elite and they did not respond so well, but around the edges of the crowds were many Untouchables – *Chuhras* (Sweepers and Sanitation), *Chamars* (Leather Workers), and lowly scavengers. These people were the serfs of landowners: Muslim, Hindu, and Sikh. They were the dregs of society, knowing they were outcasts, but in the gospel message they heard hope and a new identity, "a royal Priesthood" as it is written in the Epistle of First Peter 2:9-12. At last they could be fully human and free from slavery. They continued their lowly work but had within themselves and as a group risen above the stigma of a suppressed people. By the hard labor of Dr. C.W. Forman there were nine Village Day Schools.

There had been early beginnings, a period of large ingatherings; now began the period of consolidation and strengthening, which is the most difficult of all. Quoting from the Survey of the Evangelistic Work of the Punjab Mission of the Presbyterian Church in the U.S.A., 1929, it is noted: "In Dr. and Mrs. Llewellyn, Kasur had found the right people for this important task, and they built well and strong upon the foundations laid by those who preceded them... It was realized that the Llewellyns could not be left to do the work alone. Accordingly in 1925 Mr. and Mrs. Duff were stationed in Kasur, followed by Mr. and Mrs. Zoerner in 1928, Miss Boyd worked among women from 1923-28, and Miss Hesse succeeded her in 1928." The Llewellyns labored there for thirty-seven years! Their goal was to assist the churches in Kasur City and in the District to become self-propagating, self-governing, and self-supporting. The Rev. P.D. Paul became the pastor of the Kasur City church – he did a remarkable job! Peggy and I as newcomers were to continue that challenging work of enabling the Christians of Kasur City and the District to a higher stage of maturity and independence. What a formidable task was before us!

Frank Gives Al Orientation

In the Mission jeep over many dusty trails and roads, Frank L. introduced James and me to the twelve church Pastors and pointed out their circuits of village congregations and most of the twenty-four Primary Day Schools. He encouraged James and me to give short messages – James in Urdu or Punjabi and I in faltering Urdu. That was my introduction to Mass Poverty, to the have-nots, the illiterate, a suppressed people, living in mud-brick houses plastered with the mud from the bottom of the village pond which the sun turned into adobe firmness. Dependent, they wondered what these new people would give them and how they would help them survive. It looked hopeless to me as a newcomer. The people referred to Frank as *Bap* (father) and to Eleanor as *Ma* (mother). These needy people saw the missionaries as their parents! The title *Ma/Bap* is the designated term for Paternalist. This really shocked me. I sensed a strong inner resistance to that being my status and role someday soon. Peggy and I

96

had come to Pakistan to be evangelists and minister to the needs of the people, whether mental, physical, or spiritual, but this was a situation and complexity I had never been exposed to in preparation and orientation. Today we would say I had experienced Virtual Reality! I shared this with Peggy, and we often thought and prayed about this seemingly insurmountable problem.

We as a family worshiped in the Kasur City church whenever we could. It was constructed with fired bricks and had a bell suspended in the belfry which called the congregation to worship, much to the displeasure of the Muslims. Urdu was used, and we learned to sing the *Zaburs* (Psalms), which were accompanied by the playing of the tabla (two drums), harmonium (a small hand pumped organ), and chimpta (the tongs to tend the fire). It was rhythmic and lively. How thankful we were that indigenous instruments were used. Urdu lessons continued, and we diligently tried to use it.

While I was being oriented to the District work, Peggy was bravely trying to cope with her situation. She wrote to her mom, "All day long there are people all over both verandahs. Many are just curious because of the children, many want to greet and welcome us, and then there are those who are looking for a handout. Just now, as I try to type this letter, there are five grown boys asking for books. Another old man, who begs all the time, was just groaning at the door. I find it very disconcerting to see the lack of pride. They don't mind asking for anything, never a qualm. Of course, a lot of it is due to the old missionaries…handing out all the time. What to do? Al and I feel this is a new day in missions, but do these people know that? A people that want everything for nothing never become independent. Consequently, the church will never become a strong national church unless they become self-supporting. (In the midst of Mass Poverty, is there any hope that this will happen?)

And yet, we feel very selfish especially when we have so very much, but the principle of the whole thing is at stake. We pray that we can be unselfish with ourselves in doing things with and for them rather than giving out only material things. In a country where there is so much poverty, one has to help the poor and needy, but I wonder if that only makes it worse somehow, if done in the wrong way." I was amazed that Peggy was being confronted with the same problems that were down the line for me in outreach, witness, and service. And yet, there was George in the early morning singing loudly as he showered. Education and opportunity were imperative, but how to do that on the wide horizon of Kasur District?

To make things worse, on the night of October 8, 1955, a major flood bore down on the whole District, water six to seven feet deep rushing and destroying whole villages where there were no fired brick structures. The more prosperous had built on higher ground. Our Christians were in the low-lying areas. This was to be a new chapter in our lives and work. In Chapter Nineteen, I will share how we tried to cope with such a catastrophe.

Chapter 19

A Major Flood, Direct Relief Work, Rehabilitation
A Bleak Winter

Suddenly, without warning a major flood attacked our whole area. The raging overflow of the Sutlej River that forms the border between India and Pakistan became a six to seven-foot wall of water. It devastated our whole District where there was low-lying land. Those on higher ground and with fired brick buildings were spared to a great degree, but the damage was tremendous!

Peggy wrote to her parents the following aerogram:

> You can't imagine the kind of week we have had! And we are afraid it is only the beginning. No doubt you have seen far more than we have on your TV, but we had an experience that we dread to think will happen many more times in our lifetime. Today we have no telephone, no way of getting anywhere, even into Kasur City where the shops are. Providentially we are on a high spot which is at the most two square miles in area. For some unknown reason we still have electricity, and Al with great foresight had filled our cupboards with supplies.
>
> However, we are down to eggs, which we can get here, a few at a time, and we still get milk, but we exist as kings compared to the tragic plight of so many around us. Whole villages have literally been swept away. Many people have the clothing they were wearing and usually some bedding. After that they have nothing but the few things they could snatch up. Some of them could escape that muddy torrent and get out of their mud houses and villages. They may have brought a little food with them, but in a few days that will be gone. We

have a barrel of relief milk powder and some tins of cheese sent by Church World Service of the Presbyterian Church in the USA here on our verandah, ready for distribution. At this point, refugees of the flood cannot reach Kasur. This is reported to be the worst flood they have ever had though many others have been serious. Since the level of land is so low and the water so deep, it will take months to drain and dry up the excess water. In the meantime the bugs and disease will multiply. Even our children now understand why they had to have multiple shots before they could come here.

"The Railway Bridge has Gone Down"

There are three roads into Kasur City, and bridges for the railway and Grand Trunk Road. They are all undermined or gone! People say this is the first time in history that the railway bridge has gone down. The only way to Lahore is to cross the main river by boat and take a bus from the other side. The way the boat has to cross the river is a sight. They take the loaded boat about an eighth of a mile upstream beyond the terrible swift current and let it take them downstream again to the place that juts out, the landing spot. The force of the river is still tremendous. It will probably be a couple of months before we can again drive to Lahore.

In the meantime we are praying that everyone stays well. We do have lots of penicillin, aspirin, sulfa, and almost everything we need. We certainly are

100

disappointed that India opened the floodgates to take pressure off Ferozepur and other villages downstream. This control of water has been the cause of bitter contention for a long time. In dry weather, they don't send enough water for irrigation; in times of flooding they divert the excess Pakistan's way.

Now, a few days later, Al is ready to go out in the jeep as far as he can go taking bags of wheat, rice, and other supplies to the villagers he can reach. Padre Latif, pastor of the Kasur City church, will drive because he knows the routes. Yesterday, three men came in from thirteen miles away. They said that on the way they saw many people and animals that had died. They themselves had to swim and walk all that way. Early this morning three other men

The Trees were Refuges During the Floods

from near the border came and said no losses there. But another pastor's wife sent a note that they were sitting on a rooftop because their own house was covered with five feet of water! The Muslims were after them to move off this high spot! I haven't time to write Al's mom just now. Please call her as it may be some time before we can get mail out again.

[Note: Peggy's mom sent a copy of this letter to Secretary J.L. Dodds in the New York City Board office. He replied to her that this was the first report they had received directly from the flood area.]

We learned that for days and nights people had clung together in trees while all about them everything crumbled and was carried away. With little or no food to eat, no clean water, and no place to rest, they had a most difficult and trying time. Even the snakes took refuge in the trees. One young woman gave birth to her child on the branch of a tree! There were heroic young men who risked their lives to save people beginning to float away. Barkat, one strong young man, had rescued over thirty people! When I met him later, I gave him a cash prize.

After the water had receded from the roads many villagers came for help. We set up tents, distributed wheat flour, rice, powdered milk, tins of cheese, vegetable oil, and medicines to many, many people. George Sadiq, our Urdu language teacher, was a gem to help translate requests in Punjabi into English or simple Urdu. He also diplomatically dealt with those who demanded more than their share, or of what we did not have. After returning from an exhausting day taking supplies to villages, I was reminded that I had not taken my Urdu lessons that day. It was hard to concentrate those evenings, after supper. James and I alternated going out to the villages. This took some of the pressures off, but whether one was in the villages or in our mission compound it was wearying. How thankful we were that those bales of used clothing from American churches and Church World Service were there to be distributed. But it wasn't easy. There always seemed to be more people in dire need!

Hitching a Ride on the Bags of Supplies

In the mission compound we set up a quilt-making program, hiring local people to stitch those quilts (*rezais*) blue on one side, orange on the other. Esther, Hope, and Stan were fascinated with all the commotion! Several hundred quilts were made and distributed. This wasn't easy. I recall one day when villages were finally drying out, going in the jeep with attached trailer filled with bags of wheat, rice, and twenty quilts. Eleanor, Peggy, Stan, and Hope accompanied us. The local villagers welcomed us! However, when we tried to distribute the quilts there were more families than the number of our quilts. Eleanor tried her best to give them to the poorest of the poor; that didn't work. Give them to the widows? "No," the village leaders said, "give one to each of us or none at all!" And that's what we had to do – take those twenty quilts back to Kasur. What a heartbreak that was. Eleanor was furious! We were glad she, as an experienced trooper, had witnessed that debacle. Otherwise rumor would have it that those "newcomers" didn't know how to do things!

Even Padre Latif had problems distributing used clothing to needy members. He solved it by placing a small pile of clothes on the ground with numbers on each pile. In a turban he had slips of paper with numbers corresponding to the piles. He had each family draw a number and made sure that each received according to plan. It worked! He was saved from partiality.

Part of the rehabilitation work was to assess the number of church and school buildings that had been damaged or swept away. I will spare you the haggling: it was decided the Mission would build or repair each school and the congregations would restore the church buildings by using mud bricks to the roof level. The Mission would pay for the beams, roofing materials, iron bars for the window space, and a heavy door with padlock. That took a lot of effort and time. We learned that rehabilitation is almost a hopeless task. At what point does direct relief stop and rehab begin? Where is the dividing line between dependence on the Mission and self-help independence? Some people demanded more and increased handouts. Sadly we learned that those to whom we had given much were the most vehement complainers. We did our best to be fair and to err on the "spoiler" side. Gradually the situation was improving; we were thankful that no heavy rains occurred as things were drying out. At this stage the villagers were hard at work rebuilding the mud walls of their houses. Those who could make and use mud bricks did so. Others added a foot of wet mud, let the sun bake it, and then added more layers to reach roof level.

Soon cold weather would arrive – the winter season. Our concern was that because the walls were wet and soggy there would be much pneumonia. It was to be a difficult winter. The crops and gardens had vanished in the rushing waters. It takes a long time to plant, care for, and harvest the staples of life. But the people carried on! They had suffered like this before. When asked why they did not move to higher ground, they replied that where they were was all they had. They were trapped where they were in the strangling grip of Mass Poverty! We discussed all these issues in our local Monthly Pastor's/Teacher's Conference to begin planning how to do something positive to solve these problems. We decided that prayer, preaching, and programs were needed: education for the children, adult literacy, and possibly community development programs such as cooperative loan cells, mobile clinics from United Christian Hospital (UCH) to screen for TB, visitation by trained nurses to teach mothers in homemaking and child care, and the like.

Mud Bricks, Dung Cakes, Quilts, Straw: Starting Over Once Again

Education was the key for change and development. To illustrate this allow me to share the story of Arnold Naseem, the name given him at Raiwind Christian Institute where he studied for his Matriculation after completing the first eight years in one of our village schools. One day in the summer of 1956, he appeared at our door almost demanding we pay for his typing course at the Lahore YMCA. (His parents had often been regular beggars at our door.) We asked ourselves: was this another youngster of sixteen "too good to do manual labor," as many Matric students thought of themselves? It was the wheat harvest time so Peggy and I promised Arnold that if he worked in the harvest for two months we would give him a full scholarship. He went off in a huff and some anger. After two months when he did not appear, we felt badly, thinking we had been too hard on him. However, the day before his typing course was to begin, there was a bronzed Arnold, beaming and confident. He told us how he had helped in the harvest and had earned enough wheat for his parents to last a year! His whole attitude had changed. We gave him the full scholarship with a "shabash" (Well done!). To make a long story short, Arnold graduated, got a job, and began earning his way. In the meantime, he took courses in Radiology which he also passed. He worked at United Christian Hospital in Lahore.

Having gained experience and the necessary skills, he traveled to Algeria to work in a Government Hospital. He did well and returned to Lahore on paid vacation, with enough earnings to build a house for his parents in Lahore. He also married a talented young teacher from Sialkot. Returning to Algeria, where both were employed full-time, they began sending money home to help a sister and family get some education. Years later they were guests in our FCC home, with their five bright children. Peggy had invited them to a tasty Pakistani lunch, and she also got to hold their baby girl! A couple with great faith in Jesus Christ, they had started a house church in Algiers where Pakistani and Indian Christians worshiped and praised the Lord for their many blessings. What a confirmation that was of our efforts to positively help those in the dregs of poverty!

Another example is Elder Mangal (literally Tuesday for the day of the week which marked the day of his birth) from the Harihar village five miles east of Kasur. He came to visit us and show us his site plan for moving his village of farmers to higher ground. Highly respected and persistent, he had gotten Government Permission to build a new village above the flood line. Those twenty-six farmers pooled their funds from the sale of their lands to settle in the new village. This gave us assurances that things were changing and that the Lord was raising up His people to overcome great odds, to build a promising future. Elder Mangal proudly showed us that in the new village common ground there would be a church building, a school, and even a clinic visited by government and Mission nurses. What a saint!

Chapter 20

Family, Farewell, Conflict, Summer in Murree

The spring of 1956 was a busy time, following the flood and its aftermath. We were overwhelmed by the hordes of people at the door, the visits to the villages, and the seemingly endless rehabilitation challenges. It was wearisome and yet, this is to what we had been called – and to persist. We were a family of troopers. Peggy did an excellent work with the needy people and caring for the family. Thankfully we kept quite well, except for bouts of tummy upsets, fevers, and colds. Peggy and I often consulted Doctor Spock and medical manuals. Near the compound a Pakistani Christian, Dr. Young, a medically trained clinician, lived with his family. He helped us immensely. Mrs. Young took joy in baking a chappati (wheat flat bread) for Stan while he sat on a moora (low cane stool). Mooni and Zahir, their sons, were some of Stan's compound playmates. He was doing well in his home studies and managing his zoo. One morning he excitedly called us to see what he had found; there in a pigeon nest were three naked baby rabbits! They became exhibit number one for all his friends. Hope was her sweet self, tending to her dolls, talking to everyone, and playing with Stan and Esther. Esther was walking all over the house and exerting her independent spirit. One morning, when I was studying Urdu in the study, Esther came saying urgently, "Come! Candy!" I didn't understand what she meant. She repeated it, took my hand, and led me to a guest room where Stan was surprised. He had found our cache of hard candy which was being saved for special occasions. Peggy and I both laughed, distributed a few pieces to each, and hid it in a new secret place! Peggy hired a young man to help with the cooking; he wanted to learn. With her instructions and training, he became quite a khansama (cook).

One day George, our Urdu teacher, shared with the family that the previous night he had truly accepted Jesus Christ as his personal Savior and Lord. He thanked us for our family's "living in Christ." We invited our Bible Medical Mission Fellowship

(BMMF) friends, Theo Williams and Ruth Carter, for tea to join in the celebration and joy of George's conversion. It was a thrill to hear George singing God's praises as he showered in the mornings. With gratitude we thanked the Lord for being a Christian family with strong faith and love. We weren't perfect, but George had seen the difference between being a nominal Christian and one born of the Spirit in the fellowship of our family.

In the meantime, Frank and Eleanor were busily preparing for their retirement after thirty-seven years in Kasur District, packing and saying their farewells. They were also greeting villagers who came in vast numbers to say sad and sorrowful goodbyes.

They made visits to the twelve Pastors and their congregations and to most of the forty-eight teachers in the rural schools. There was a Mission dinner for them in Lahore which we attended. They were given a silver cream and sugar set. We noted that this was farewell to close friends and family! With the able assistance of James, Alice, and Gail, we arranged a Farewell lunch on the compound. There were three hundred served. Peggy said there were at least that many present when it was time to eat! The City church also held a celebration and garlanded Frank and Eleanor with many many strings of marigolds and roses. There was a mixture of sadness and joy – sadness for their leaving, but joy for what they meant to them. What a huge job it was for them to sort out the accumulation after so many years.

*Completing 37 Years
of Service*

About ten days prior to their departure, Frank called me to their house for final instructions and helpful hints on how to continue the work. He had been sharing lots of that while we worked together, but this was different. Frank gave me nine large account books. Since he had to hand them over to a missionary according to Mission Rules, I was the one! There were accounts of stipends to the Pastors, Cycle Fund, Salaries for the teachers, Maintenance of all buildings including the Compound, Travel, Work Programs, and contingencies.

There they were in a huge pile ready to be placed in the jeep. Frank informed me they had not been audited but were correct. I hauled them home to my "office" wondering how I could deal with this heavy responsibility. Added to everything else, I was to "keep" the books!

That night I wept! I shared my feelings with Peggy who commiserated with me, shaking her head in disbelief. What struck me so hard was that Frank had placed the mantle of Paternalism on me, making me de facto a *Ma Bap* in a Mother/Father relationship with the whole Kasur District. The villagers had an inborn attitude in their culture that they had the right to demand care and things from the Head of the Family! And he had the obligation to comply and provide! Having no alternative, I buckled down to do my best.

Peggy Prepares to Drive the Llewellyns to the Border

In March 1956, Frank and Eleanor were to make their way to Ferozepur on the Sutlej River marking the border between Pakistan and India, fifteen miles east of Kasur. They had many friends in India. Since there had been border clashes between the police and armies, it was a dangerous crossing place. The flood had created new islands which were fought over. They had a permit to cross the border, but were restricted to only three vehicles, with men drivers. James had his car, I had our jeep, and there was the Mission jeep. Not wanting to miss this exciting adventure, Peggy insisted on driving the Mission jeep and convinced the police let her do it, even though the permit authorized only men to drive. James took Frank, Eleanor, and Padre Latif. Gail went with Peggy, and I was loaded with most of the baggage. The children were cared for by our helpers, sorry they couldn't also go. Without incident we arrived, said our farewells, prayed for their safety, and returned to Kasur. We were witnessing the end of an era and the beginning of another. Frank and Eleanor had crossed the border just in time; a week later there were bullets flying. In fact, after two days the Police officials borrowed our large worship tent as a temporary hospital.

Unfortunately a conflict between James and me began to develop. The Llwellyns had kept the peace by their presence and Frank's refereeing among James, the pastors, and teachers. But with his departure differences began to openly appear. Prior to their leaving, at meetings and conferences I had noted friction between James and Pastor Samuel Rashid, Rev. Jamal ud Din, and others. I had taken James' side out of loyalty, giving him a chance to right himself again. To make matters worse some villagers gave James a hurtful time; they preferred missionaries to a Pakistani administrator. James had always expressed his enmity for paternalistic domination, with which I had always agreed. But now, beyond my control or liking, people were taking sides. The same thing often happened in hospital/clinic situations where nationals demanded treatment by a missionary doctor! From their point of view missionaries, as foreigners, had superior skills. This was eating away in James' mind and heart. Even before Frank left, James had terminated a teacher couple in one of our boarding schools without the knowledge and consent of Frank. He reinstated the couple!

The nub of the conflict was as co-administrators, how could James and I share and use the power, when I was in charge of the accounts and official reports. I tried my best to share with James our new status and role, but there was a cultural difference. With an idealistic individualism and democratic bent of teaching/training Pastors to assume more and more responsibility and freedom from authoritarianism, I was working to decrease my role as District Superintendent while James, with his cultural values, measured success of achievement in becoming the Head/Authority in Charge. In truth, Pakistani culture was paternalistic with the man the head of the family. Public officials lorded it over the people, demanding not only unquestioned loyalty but also that they knew and accepted their place! This approach was imprinted in James' mind. We spent long hours discussing these things and sharing the work visiting villages

Pastors and Elders, Kasur District; Al (left), James Iqbal (upper rt. corner)
Padre Latif (lower rt. corner)

together. He was included in the payday for Pastors and Teachers at the Monthly Workers' Conference as it was called, and other financial matters in the District. It became apparent that James actually desired to be the District Missionary in Charge, not a co-administrator. He must have thought I was actively thwarting his advance in status. I noted an increasing resentment toward James by the Pastors and Teachers. I often took the counsel of Magistrate A.P. Gill who had a wealth of knowledge and wisdom in these matters. A highlight of our last week in Kasur was a conference led by Dr. and Mrs. Thomas. He was a Professor of Rural Sociology at Cornell University. Great people, they shared how to encourage and enable villagers to lead, cope, and share even in poverty.

It was time to take the family to Murree for the summer. I would return to Kasur for the summer except for a month's vacation back at Rosenheim in cool weather with family and friends. After two days I returned to Kasur and the intense heat. This meant that everything was on Peggy's shoulders, a heavy responsibility! Stan entered the Jikha Gali School, and Hope began kindergarten. They both loved being with those whom they had met the year before. Esther made the most of it playing with the dolls and toys. She was talking nonstop now. There was a round of mumps and chicken pox. Stan was ill with high fevers. The doctors thought he was having a bout with polio. This was later confirmed. He recovered from polio except for a slight limp, which he outgrew. The cuckoos put on a grand performance, their calls echoing on the hillside. Esther was quite fascinated. It was good that Peggy could escape the heat – she was pregnant. The family discussed the wonder of having a baby. Hope told Stan that we ought to have two hundred babies. We had ice cream again before Daddy had to leave. Now we had to correspond by letters. Peggy wrote that Hope really loved school. Esther kept

Stan (with Bow) and Friends at Rosenheim

busy playing with her toys and dolls, and she enjoyed taking walks on the hillside trails and flowering meadows with the ayah. All of us carried on, although it was tough going. It would be September before we could be together again – that is, all but Stan who wanted to enter the boarding and attend school in Murree until December. It was wonderful to have another summer in Murree.

Chapter 21

Fall Program, New Recruit, District Touring, Finale

Peggy and I both passed our second year Urdu exam. We had stuck at it and cleared a big hurdle. Since it was September, we were back in Kasur picking up where we had

A New Jeep from the Churches in the U.S.

left off. We missed Stan, but weekly letters informed us he was fine and enjoying school. Hope studied the Calvert books; she loved to read and even shared stories with Esther. It was still hot, though the ceiling fans kept us comfortable inside the house. Even so the Fall Program of work had to begin. Without flood waters it was easier to reach the villages. Elder

Mangal wanted us to visit his village to have meetings of worship, witnessing, health, stewardship, and cooperatives. We set up our tents and equipment. In the evening we showed films, one of which was "The King Of Kings," the whole account of Jesus' life and ministry. Even the Muslims came to view that. They were greatly impressed when they saw the crucifixion scenes. During the evening meeting I heard a child crying loudly. I wondered why. Afterwards I asked Mangal, and he said that it was his grandson – he must have stones in the bladder.

The very next morning I drove them into Lahore to United Christian Hospital. Since I was preaching at FC College that morning, I could not stay with them. I dropped them off and explained what to do. When I returned to check up on the operation, I was told that Mangal had left for his village. I drove there to inquire what had happened. Mangal apologized and explained that he couldn't figure out where the Lab and X-Ray Room were. It was his first time there. We all headed back to the Hospital, informing Peggy on the way what had happened. It took several days, but I stayed there and helped them find their way. The operation was successful. Mangal's grandson was free to go after several days of recuperation. As the costs were too much for Mangal, I paid them in full, saying, "This is the Lord's money. You don't have to repay me. Sometime you may be able to help someone in need." Punjabi hospitality is the ultimate as I was to experience after an evening meeting. Mangal invited me to his house for chicken curry, chappatis, and highly spiced vegetables. Delicious! Hot tea was served in a small bowl. During the meal a young man kept filling my bowl. In the darkness of that lantern-lighted room, I began to wonder how he knew when to refill. I discovered that he slid his big thumb inside the bowl; when he felt no tea he refilled. At this point in time I figured that his thumb had been thoroughly sanitized. Why not proceed!

This series of programs was repeated in many villages. The Pastors welcomed the visits because the congregation turned out in great numbers and saw and heard helpful things. We added adult literacy lessons. We checked the Session Meeting Minutes, the Baptismal Record, and the Births/Deceased list. On occasion Peggy and the children joined us. What an impression they made! There was more Pakistani cuisine. Peggy conducted special meetings for the women and girls: nutrition, hygiene, simple cures, and daily worship. We had learned that when one teaches a mother, the whole family is mightily influenced. Of course, they also shared their problems – Peggy was almost a match for King Solomon!

I was again invited to preach at FC College in Lahore. Since Peggy was drawing close to delivery, she and the girls accompanied us. We stayed overnight with the Ewings in #11. As the worship center was directly opposite #11, it was decided that during the service Peggy and Margaret would sit outside on the front verandah of the house while Dr. Ewing would sit in the doorway of the worship center, where they could see him and signal to him if Peggy needed to be taken to the hospital. I was the preacher and watched Dr. Ewing. It was the first Sunday in Advent, December 2, 1956. To my astonishment the responsive reading included, "To us a son is born." I wondered at that! Following a delicious lunch, I cared for Hope and Esther while Peggy took some rest. About 2:30, Peggy said it was time to go to the UCH. Dr.

Esther Morris was her doctor, and in the evening there was a new recruit: John Alexander Schlorholtz. Peggy and John were fine. I proudly spread the good news

John Arrives in Kasur

and sent telegrams to our parents. With the time changes, they were informed before the birth! Five days later we as a proud family drove to Kasur with John. What an impression he made on everyone with his blue eyes and reddish fuzz on top! Word went around that there was a white baby at our house. There were lots of visitors. Pastor Latif and his wife gave

John a wooden swinging cradle made in the Kasur bazaar. How Hope and Esther loved to keep John swinging! The next week Stan came for a four months' holiday. It was too cold in Murree! He would hold his very own brother and marvel at how little he was.

We had a great merry Christmas. From our barrels and shops in Lahore gifts for all the family appeared. Peggy's forethought had paid off! We had many carol groups at the door; they treasured the cookies Peggy had baked. There was even a band playing Pakistani tunes. What excitement we had. But there were visits to village churches to be made for Christmas and the New Year. James and I were kept busy. Village Christians love their Barda Din (Big Day) as Christmas was called by the Christians of Pakistan. In late December Elder Mangal came to see that new child of ours. Removing his turban, he led in prayer for John. In Punjabi he opened the gates of heaven thanking God for this newborn child, and he included, from memory, the entire genealogy of Jesus as recorded in Luke 3:23-37, ending with "the Son of God and my God!" We stood in awe of this Punjabi farmer who had learned to read the Bible given him by Eleanor twenty years before in his village. The only one in that village who had promised to read God's Word, he had kept his promise. I have never in my life heard someone pray as he did. Try reading that genealogy and try to pronounce those names!

In early January we loaded the jeep and trailer with the tents, generator, projector, and all the equipment we would need and visited more Pastors and their congregations. We also engaged the UCH mobile clinic van with its x-ray to screen whole villages for tuberculosis. Most effective were the Adult Literacy booklets we distributed. It was Dr. Laubach's method of Each One Teach One. We encouraged each church elder to teach adults to read and to write. People got excited by this. Some of their children had learned to read in one of our village schools, now it was their turn! One woman told Peggy, "You have given me the dignity and self-esteem I always thought impossible to receive!" That for her was a beam of light and help in the cruel life of women. They were too often mere chattel in a man's world. When it became too hot and dusty to continue touring, we had conferences and retreats at the compound for men and women to reinforce what we had taught. At one women's retreat Peggy personally bathed ten children, scabies and all, at the hand pump. Thus the work done in village tours continued.

One late afternoon there was a knock at the door. It was Elder Mangal and an older woman. We invited them in for tea and wondered what this was all about. We had a good chat. As he was leaving, Mangal gave me a subtle smile and said, "This village woman needed medical attention; I took her on the bus to UCH. I had to show her where the Lab, X-ray Room, and nursing stations were. She as a villager had never seen such a place – now we are even!" That is why we Christians believe in the Fellowship of the Saints!

The conflict between James and me widened and deepened. He continued to assert his authoritative search for how he could attain power and influence in the District work. By now I understood his suffering. We requested that the Lahore Church Council grant us permission to divide the District which was to give him a sense of being fully in charge. This was granted. We had joint Pastors and Teachers monthly meetings, but the work in the District was divided between two Subdistricts. For awhile it seemed to work. But then things began to fester between the Pastors and Elders in his area. He transferred teachers for reasons known only to him. They wanted their missionary back; James was playing politics (*partibazi*). It says in Scripture that a house divided is bound to fall. I made a point of keeping open communication with James and Alice. We candidly exchanged our views and what to do. It didn't help too much. I realized this was not all James' fault. The history of Missions, the differing cultural variables, the prestige of the missionary, the paternalistic ministry of Frank and Eleanor and others, the demands of the oppressed villagers, the disparity, the hurt feelings, the despair of succeeding, and the time factor – all were contrary to a solution to our problems. I had hoped that James would overcome all this and become the man in charge who knew how to minister to the needs of his people. I was the outsider who would go on furlough, be transferred to other work; I was to decrease and James to increase. One night I was thinking about these things and stumbled onto a quote from Abraham Lincoln: "Nearly all men can stand adversity, but if you want to test a man's character, give him power." Was I seeking power and influence? No, I had inherited it from the Mission. Peggy and I did not plan on building a little kingdom of our own. We had come to witness, act, and continue Christ's ministry.

I requested the Lahore Church Council to choose which one of us would assume responsibility for the work in Kasur District. I was ready to withdraw to have James be fully in charge. We waited for a decision. Finally, after a long delay, it was decided that both of us would be withdrawn and George and Ann Tewksbury would take over. The Council did not want to be partial in their decision. What a strange turn of events. James was transferred to teach at Rang Mahal High School in Lahore, I was appointed a Church Worker at large to develop a new group of churches along the Ravi River near Lahore. (By the spring of 1958 we were given the assignment as evangelists in charge of teaching stewardship, Bible study methods, lay leadership training, and preaching in our whole church area.) We were particularly happy about an assignment as Fraternal Workers rather than District administrators. This is where we should have started. In this position we were not in competition with the national leaders who could and must assume responsibility for church administration. We were now in a position to work with such leaders, encourage them, and assist them in having a greater and more productive ministry to their own people.

We toured Kasur District for two months. The children loved camping out in the villages, and though it was a bit cold we had a productive time. Esther discovered that there was nothing so lovely as watching the sunrise, as she stood in the door of our tent, and again the glorious sunsets. Stanley had had jaundice September 1957, but after four weeks of rest was once again in school. Both Stan and Hope had been in the Jikha Gali Boarding School until early December. That was to be the last winter tour of Kasur District. The final curtain had fallen after just two and a half years. Peggy and I were tempted to resign from the mission, but we still felt called to minister in

Pakistan. We packed, rented a house in Lahore, and made the move, leaving without the fanfare that Frank and Eleanor had received.

We moved to a house on Ferozepur Road in Lahore near to Aziz and Portia Akram and their family. Their children were Alice, Johnny, Mariana, and Susan. Our four and their four became fast friends and playmates. There was a protected area where all could roller skate, ride their bicycles, and enjoy playing tag and other games. Life was more settled in Lahore, the provincial capital of the Punjab. During the summer holiday in Murree we did further language study and happily met our dear friends. I was invited by Dr. Christy Wilson, the son of my Professor at Princeton, to conduct worship services in Kabul, Afghanistan, giving him a month's vacation. In July 1958 our whole family, with our dear friends Merle and Gloria Inniger, headed for Kabul. We drove through Peshawar, the Khyber Pass, Jalalabad, and on to Kabul over the bumpy cobblestone road, which was adjacent to the rivers. How impressive were the bare mountains and hills, with very few trees except in an occasional oasis in valleys. In Kabul we were the guests of an American AID family, who were members in the only church building in Afghanistan! I preached four times during the month and had fascinating discussions with the personnel working there. We visited Babur's tomb and other scenic sites, shopped, and enjoyed the spicy foods. What a fascinating place! We visited a factory outlet with many onyx lamps, carpets, and art treasures. Peggy was especially impressed with a twin set of onyx bedside lamps inlaid with lapis lazuli. When she asked the price, the salesman replied, "Madam, you have good taste. Sorry, they are on order by the King." Stan bought an antique flintlock pistol and powder horn, which he treasures to this day. Peggy and the children spent the rest of the summer in Murree and school for Stan and Hope. I returned to Lahore to resume working at Naulakha Church in Lahore. The next chapter relates how that happened.

Chapter 22

Our Ministry at the Naulakha Church, Lahore 1958-60

We were busily engaged in our new assignment; it was demanding but most fulfilling. The celebration of Christmas and the New Year was a blessing to the whole family. In

Peggy has Settled into Pakistan: Vegetable Shopping

Lahore we could buy special foods like Hunter's Beef (salted and cured), Punjabi sweets, basmati rice, fresh curry powders, and gifts to be shared. The whole family was together and we were thankful that all kept well and active. The churches in which we were working conducted their own worship and celebration. This gave us a breather and some rest. We were included in many holiday parties in the homes of

Lahori Christians. Our dear friend, Magistrate Paul Gill, invited us all to a forest reserve, Changa Manga. What a thrilling time we had! Paul took Stan and Hope and his own three children the day before. Peggy and I took the train the next day with Sosan accompanying us. My what a different world. We rode a small electric trolley all through the wooded area and saw many wild deer, nilgai (blue bull), jackals, but the peacocks were in hiding. Then we all came home on the train and were served tea and pastries by special police servers. What respect was given Magistrate A.P. Gill; we got a glimpse of how well he was guarded and honored. How grateful we were that the Gills had been transferred to Lahore! On Epiphany, January 6, 1958, we celebrated Hope's birthday. It was a big party. Joan Mitchel, Hope's teacher in Murree, was there for a short time. She told us how our little girl was too good to be true. At times they marveled at the things this little girl of six came out with. We, of course, absolutely agreed with her. One evening Hope called us to the roof of our house, saying, "Come, I will show you the gates of heaven!" There it was – vast shafts of sunshine shining through the darkened clouds. What a glorious sight!

However, things were about to change. One evening in January three elders from the Naulakha Church came calling. We had worshiped there a few times. It was a congregation of nearly four thousand members. They made a request that I become the Pastor of that large congregation! Their Pastor, Dr. Andrew Thakur Das, after forty years of presiding there, had been recruited by the Ecumenical Mission and Relations of the Presbyterian Church to become the Staff Secretary in New York City of the Cameroon Church in Africa. This was to implement the newly adopted Integration of Church and Mission, appointing qualified Nationals to posts formerly held by missionaries. It was a great honor for him; the term would be for two years. The congregation was in need of an Interim Pastor. They explained that since I was a Missionary they were certain I would relinquish that position in two years. This, they suspected, would not be true of Pakistani Pastors, "who would hang onto the pulpit and not leave at the due time." Wow! I confided in them that my Urdu was not up to the standard of preaching to people who had M.A.'s in both Urdu and English! They said they would help me. After telling them that Peggy and I had to think this through and pray for God's Will and Way to cope with such a challenging task, they allowed us a few days to make a decision. Peggy and I were floored by this request. (I recalled how Moses had said he couldn't speak so well!) In consultation with senior missionaries and nationals, I was urged to accept the call.

By the Grace of God and the Spirit's leading, we accepted the call to Naulakha. We were still trembling and awed, but with the Lord's help we would give it a try. We moved the family to 8 Empress Road, the Pastor's manse, a spacious fired brick structure with plenty of room for all. While settling in, there was almost a fatal tragedy. Unobserved by anyone John had climbed into the refrigerator which was empty because it was being cleaned. It was the type with a latching door that couldn't be opened from the inside. We searched everywhere – in open wells, behind the shrubs, and all over the church compound. Finally, our cook, Barkat Masih, called out that he had come home early from shopping and had heard a noise. He had found a blue-lipped John in the refrigerator. We were all greatly relieved! (Yes, we learned that one must place the fridge so the door is next to the wall.) Otherwise we were getting settled and acquainted with so many. It was difficult to remember so many new names and faces, but soon we would have to.

Peggy writes, "In mid-February, Al preached for the first time in the church. He really worked on that sermon. He writes them in English, translates them into Urdu, reads the sermon to our retired Murree language teacher, Mr. Rafiq, who makes corrections and suggestions. Then Al studies the sermon until it is time to preach. It went quite well. Afterwards Magistrate Gill told Al that it was so good, he felt like running up and kissing him!" (I'm glad he didn't!) Sermons became a weekly drill of preparation and delivery. Often Mr. Rafiq would laugh and ask where I had gotten that word or phrase; he knew I had

With Magistrate Gill (center) and Family

consulted the dictionary. He would explain that Pakistanis did not use such philosophical words in that context! During the two years I prepared over a hundred sermons, meditations, and prayers. Occasionally we invited guest preachers to relieve the tension and to again present the congregation to a normal forty-minute sermon, not my twenty-minute ones. Prof. Cornelius from FCC kindly remarked, "At first I thought they were too short, but then I realized you condensed them after a painstaking effort to give us the meat of the message, unlike many Pakistani Pastors who did their preparation while delivering the sermon." That was comforting! The Elders took turns reading the Scripture lessons, leading responsive readings and prayers. We had lots of hymn singing and a highly trained choir. This helped to extend the service to over an hour. Everyone seemed to fully and enthusiastically participate in the worship experience.

One morning, however, Bill Zoerner, the Executive Secretary of the Lahore Church Council, came to see me. He had received from the New York City Mission Office a copy of a letter sent from the Kasur District Pastors. Twelve Pastors had signed a petition that I be removed from missionary work and sent home because they maintained I was a paternalist, that I had been too authoritative and had not allowed the Pastors to make their own programs! They said they were making their case now because even at the present moment I had forced my way into becoming the Pastor of the Naulakha Church! I stood in utter disbelief. Bill jokingly remarked that the fruits of my labors were being heaped on my head. Having served in Kasur District, he understood what was going on. He said that the petition would be dealt with in the Executive Committee of the Lahore Church Council, but said not to worry because the home office in New York City was fully aware of what was happening and had full confidence in me. Bill told me he was sending a cable to New York City seeking more information. (It would inform them of the situation and possibly assist in any decisions to be made.) To make a long story short, the situation was resolved and I continued at Naulakha. Everyone knew who was behind the scheme. Peggy and I marveled at this turn of events and kept going.

Our four were making the transition well. Stan couldn't find enough to do, being bound by the walls of the church compound, not able to roam the area as he had in Kasur. He did find time to tease Hope and Esther who were entranced with their new dolls sent by Grandma Hoft. Peggy wrote, "Our little John looks so sweet walking around. He is such a little joy to all, but you know with four I do feel that I have my hands full. Guess I will give up the idea of six...anyway for a few years. Hope and

Esther played nicely with each other and with John. Al says, 'Four and no more! We have to seriously consider the cost of their college expenses.' I suppose he's right."

We had begun to visit some of Lahore's famous sites and especially enjoyed the Lahore Fort built by the Mughals in the 1600s. The Gills showed us around that place; it is huge with forty-foot walls and impressive fortifications. While shopping in Anarkali we saw the Zamzama, Kim's cannon, in front of the Lahore Museum as described by Kipling. What an inspirational city! We were duly impressed to learn that the first missionaries of our Mission arrived in November 1849. They were Rev. John Newton and Rev. C.W. Forman, evangelists for forty years of the first order in Lahore. Almost daily they preached the gospel and opened a school in the city, with an enrollment of three students, to each of whom a pice (the lowest coin in value) was given every day. This was not bribery; it compensated for the loss of what these boys could earn in a day! Their parents were Kashmiris. This was the first and, for many years, the only English-medium school in Lahore. Out of this humble beginning the Rang Mahal High School and Forman Christian College would emerge.

"Four and No More"

Naulakha was organized into a church in 1853, not with a National pastor and session, but with missionaries conducting the worship and pastoral duties. The church offered a model where local Christians learned what it meant to be a Christian, not in name only, but in faith and practice. This continued for about thirty years until a theologically trained Pakistani pastor was called in 1889; he was Rev. Talib-ud-Din (literally "Student of Religion"). Under his leadership and loyal service, that congregation became self-propagating, self-governing, and began to become self-supporting. He served with great faithfulness and devotion until his death in December 1919. Rev. Andrew Thakur Das was then installed, continuing to strengthen the congregation and ministering there until January 1958 when I was called to succeed him! He had been inspired to send his seven elders into Lahore city to preach on Sunday afternoons. Eventually seven new congregations were formed and nurtured toward maturity and further outreach! You can imagine how awed I was to be called to follow those two extraordinary leaders.

The ten-member Session did help me greatly in administration, planning, and the programs of the congregation. So did Peggy! In addition to caring for our four, she was hostess, counselor, and teacher of a Bible Study group for women. She attended the Women's Fellowship and made a lasting contribution in helping them to grow in faith, hope, and love. These women were educated, competent homemakers, with a zeal to serve the Lord. Many of their children were in the Youth Group and the Choir and also taught Sunday school classes. There were over forty boys and girls in the Youth Group. Besides their meetings and study, Stan, Peggy and I added something new – we taught them how to play softball. We had a large open section of the church compound, which was just the right size. How they enjoyed this new sport. Having

Boxing Day Book Stall

played some cricket, their batting and catching were quite good. After a few years they won the national tournament of Pakistan and got the trophy. Stan was exuberant to be a part of that! Thirty-one of those young people were in our first Confirmation Class, making commitments to Christ and becoming communicant members.

Pastoral visitation to families of the congregation, conducting baptisms and funerals, hospital visits, counseling, and worship preparation kept us busy. There was a vibrant unity of spirit and cooperation, with few really difficult issues. Peggy did stay with the children in Murree during part of the summer. I joined them for a vacation (when we went to Kabul). The Elders kept things going. That fall both Stan and Hope were in Boarding School and loving it. They returned in early December. What a blessing it was to be together as a family again! Then it was time to prepare for the Christmas Program. Mrs. A.P. Gill (Sosan) wrote a marvelous drama of the Christmas Story. After many hours of rehearsal, it was enacted in the church on Christmas Eve. Stan was a shepherd, Hope and Esther were angels, and John wiggled in the pew! Peggy, Sosan, and others produced a masterpiece, greatly appreciated by all! Also included was a competition of writing and performing original Carols. There were many entries, winners, and prizes given. The choir and tabla/harmonium players showed much stamina during that rather lengthy program. The day after Christmas was Boxing Day, when many members gathered in the church compound to have a lot of fun. There were games, food stalls, music, loud speakers, and good fellowship. Peggy and our four sold and distributed religious literature.

As the Lenten season progressed, Sosan was requested to write an Easter Drama. This, too, was an effective and inspiring means of worship and witness. Many non-Christians attended. One morning Joyce came with her sister to request a wedding ceremony. I had never performed one in Urdu, but agreed to do it. The wedding of Joyce and Victor Faiz was held in the church with loads of people present for a beautiful event. (Years later after they had moved to Toronto, Canada, he called their three children and pointing to me said, "Peter, Irene, and Andrew, there is the man who is responsible!") I recall their names because I had associated the first letter of their names as PIA (Pakistan International Airlines).

What a blessing it was to have the Gills living so close to us. Many Sunday evenings they invited us for a delicious meal. It was good to relax and enjoy their loving hospitality. The children put on dramas of their own making, sang for us, and even recited poetry. Just prior to Stan's leaving for Murrree, Uncle Paul arranged for both families to spend a night in tents on the banks of the Ravi River. The next morning he announced that everyone had to bathe in the river! We all hesitated. Then he asked Shaista, "When will you bathe?" "I will not bathe, Daddy-ji," she replied. With a twinkle, he excused all of us! He gave Stan a special prize for being the best kite flier in all of Pakistan. Stan loved the sport of flying kites with strings that were coated with powdered glass to cut the strings of others in contests called *pechas*. He could certainly skillfully maneuver those kites in many shapes and colors, and had the cut fingers to prove it.

Paul Gill's Ravi Picnic

Sosan Gill and Peggy on the Ravi River

Chapter 23

Continuing Work at Naulakha and Welcoming the New Pastor

With the help of the Session and the enthusiasm of the faithful members of the church, great progress was made. The attendance increased, more of the members assumed heavy responsibilities, and there was unity in faith and outreach. We were working as a team. Where I was weak they were strong; we all depended on the Grace of God to a greater degree. Members in trouble with a problem came to the manse for help. On the verandah was a large bench on which they had sat waiting in earlier days. Peggy and I invited them into our home, serving them tea and whatever we had handy. Many said they had never seen the interior of the manse before! These new missionaries believed in meeting people on a level playing field. There were issues discussed by the Session, but they had the wisdom of the ages. I learned that they had overcome the attitude of a suppressed people and were confident citizens of Pakistan, even though as Christians they were still regarded by the Muslim majority as second-rate citizens (*dhimmi*, a controlled minority). Education and tenacity to attain their potential had made possible a healthy, vital Christian community. Peggy and I prayed for the time when even those living in the rural areas would attain that goal. One evening the Session and their family members joined Peggy and me at Shalimar Gardens, built by the Mughals of white marble with fountains evenly spaced in large pools of water. We had arranged a Pakistani dinner to be served and enjoyed a great evening of fellowship. Visitation of members kept me busy. One Sunday Elder Channan Khan, a nationally qualified soccer referee, kidded me about getting all the refreshments families served me while calling. I invited him to accompany me. After the third Coca Cola he said, "Let's go to my house for tea!" That famous soft drink had recently come to Lahore, and everyone thought it was the ultimate treat. He called John "Johnny Beenda" (a bark beetle that makes a high pitched, continuous sound) because he chattered constantly.

Dr. Thakur Das had initiated a Festival of Light held annually in the church compound. This was the occasion of evangelistic preaching and witnessing to Jesus the Light of the world. Open evangelistic preaching in the bazaars was now dangerous and nearly impossible. Since the Partition in 1947 when Pakistan and India divided to become two distinct nations, Muslims were highly nationalistic and fervent about defending their religion. The Session decided that the crowds attending the Festival had become increasingly too large for that limited space. We made a plan to hold a Christian Convention at the Anglican Cathedral which had ample space for at least eight thousand. We enlisted the cooperation of all the churches in Lahore and worked long hours in preparation. Since I was Pastor of Naulakha, I was given the privilege to take leadership. We invited the renowned Dr. Abdul Haq to be the prime preacher. He was the champion of Interfaith debates held in previous years. He always won those exchanges with Hindus, Muslim, and Sikhs in Pre-Partition days. Overflowing crowds came to hear the gospel; many Muslims requested prayers for their sick family members; many nominal Christians became new creations in Christ. It became an annual Conference on the Anglican church yard.

Hurrying back from a meeting, with twenty minutes before the next one, I rushed home for lunch. Near the verandah was a man who asked me for some money to help care for his family. Wishing to quickly deal with this problem, I put five rupees into his shirt pocket. To my utter astonishment Peggy rushed out and adeptly snatched out the bill with the explanation: "Don't give him any money. He is a regular beggar, and he will only spend it for cigarettes! Drive him to the YMCA and Percy Din who is the director for helping such people." Skipping lunch, that is what I did. Percy gave him a bar of soap, a razor, and two rupees, saying, "Go home, shave, bathe, and wash your clothes! Return here on Monday morning. I will give you a list of names to contact for a job!" Leaving this situation in Percy's capable hands, I attended my meeting, a little late. Peggy had the finesse of community development; I had the theory but didn't put it to work. I had learned a great lesson. Of course Peggy dealt with such needs daily while I was busy with many tasks! About two months later following Sunday worship, Peggy called me over and introduced a couple with their three children. She asked if I remembered them. I had no idea who they were. She said, "This is the man you gave five rupees to and introduced to Percy. He and his family are here to express their gratitude for helping them turn their lives around. He is now working full-time as a cook, earning enough to provide food for the family, put the children into school, and quit smoking!" The man thanked us for giving him back his dignity and helping him to break his bad habits. Peggy got the full credit for that one!

During March of each year the women from many of the churches in Lahore celebrated World Day of Prayer. Peggy gathered as many as our new VW van would hold and drove them to the meeting. That evening, after delivering everyone to their homes, she had such an excruciating pain in her right side she had to crawl into the manse. I immediately called Dr. Joe Carter who lived next door to examine her. He said she had better get to UCH immediately. He would alert them that Peggy needed an emergency appendectomy. I drove like mad. They were ready to receive her and rushed her in for the operation. It was critical; her appendix had almost burst. Dr. Orville Hamm from Sialkot sat with her all night with me. Our helpers were caring for our four. Her condition developed into perineuritis. She was in the hospital for a full month. Dr. Chris Martin from Scotland nursed her back to health. It had been touch and go. I took our four to visit her often. That was a sad month. To complicate matters further, it was time for Stan and Hope to return to boarding school by train to Rawalpindi and by bus to Murree. This time I had to buy or have made multiple items of clothing and toiletries and pack them into their trunks. The morning they were to leave, I discovered their rubber boots which I hurriedly placed on top of everything. Stan and Hope said everyone laughed to see what an amateur packer I had been.

Dr. Thakur Das sent word that the New York City office had requested him to stay an extra year. He said he would be too old by that time to continue at Naulakha and that the congregation should call a young qualified Pakistani Pastor to fill the pulpit. The Session began to search. They considered many candidates, but nothing clicked. We were much in prayer. Then three Elders and I were invited to attend special stewardship meetings held by Dr. Paul Lindholm in Sialkot. We drove there and listened attentively. Since the speaker was from the USA, a translator was needed. Rev. Edgar Khan did a superb job; his English and Urdu were top quality. At lunch break, the Elders asked me whether they could ask him to become Pastor of Naulakha. I encouraged them to speak to him about our need of a Pastor and would he consider moving to Lahore. He answered he would have to pray about this and seek permission from his Presbytery of the United Presbyterian Church. We presented this to the Elders at a special meeting. They were impressed and prayed that this young man would favorably agree. By the Grace of God ten days later, Edgar accepted the Call pending the approval of both Sessions involved, both the Lahore Church Council and his Presbytery, and ratification by each congregation. In due time Rev. Edgar Khan and his wife, Lois, moved to 8 Empress Road, Lahore. We moved next door to 6 Empress Road, to Dr. Joe and Nancy Carter's apartment since they were on furlough. Our prayers had been answered; there was a highly qualified Pakistani Pastor installed and warmly greeted by the whole Naulakha congregation! (The only exceptions were his church in Wah north of Rawalpindi, some irate UP missionaries, and the Pastors of the Kasur District.)

Edgar shared with us his life's story. His Muslim parents had been killed during the Partition riots leaving four children, a boy and three sisters. Their aunt, a Christian Nurse in Rawalpindi, reared them until they were of knowledgeable age when she gave them a choice whether they would be Muslim or Christian. Two of the sisters remained Muslim; Edgar and his sister became Christians. He had graduated from Gordon College in Rawalpindi and the Theological Seminary in Gujranwala. His Urdu and English were impeccable. How we all rejoiced that Edgar and Lois were broadminded evangelicals, showing great promise for a fruitful ministry. (Edgar and Lois ministered in the Naulakha Church for forty-one years!) Peggy and I had been part of the best appointment by the Lord in our whole twenty-four years in Pakistan.

The congregation requested me to stay on for an additional six months to help Edgar get acquainted, master the administration, plan out a lively program, and support him in any way needed. As he increased, I decreased. We four became the best of friends. What a relief not having to prepare and give those sermons! Edgar preached, I assisted. Mrs. Ghose exclaimed, "Seeing those two Pastors walk down the aisle after the worship to greet the congregation was like seeing two angels." That was a high compliment!

At the end of April Peggy went to Murree to care for the children during the summer months. They enjoyed school and their friends, the cool air, and the beauty of the Himalayan foothills. I was to have a much needed rest and relaxation for a whole month. Edgar was fully in charge! But that was soon to change. On May 28 a cable arrived informing us that my mother had passed away. Circumstances made it impossible for me to travel to the USA. I returned to Lahore in grief and deeply felt sorrow. It had been five and a half years since we said goodbye in Carroll. We had been eagerly looking forward to seeing my mother and everyone in December of 1960. A note was waiting my arrival in Lahore. The Gills had invited me to dinner at their home. They embraced me as a younger brother and comforted me. Peggy and John came to Lahore for a few days to be with me. Stan, Hope, and Esther were in school, and the school opened a temporary hostel for them. Everyone was so kind and considerate.

In late November I drove up to bring the family to Lahore. Peggy and I packed everything into the 6 Empress godown (storage room) except for what we would take on furlough. The curtain was falling on an exciting epoch of our lives, but we had the comfort and encouragement of knowing that God in His mysterious Way had given us His blessings and care throughout our first term in Pakistan. We did not have a future assignment, but we knew that was also in our Lord's hand. You see, we live by faith not by sight and our own abilities, weak though they be.

Chapter 24

Our First Furlough, Iowa, Cornell U., Travels to Pakistan

Hope and John Ride a Camel Named "Whiskey"

On John's fourth birthday we took a plane to Karachi. They served a birthday cake and gave Wings to John. The send-off by our many friends had been terrific. It had been a long six years. We were starting our first furlough, which was to be fifteen months instead of twelve because we had served a six-year instead of the normal five-year term. I was granted permission to do a Master's Degree in Sociology at Cornell University at Ithaca, New York. We flew from Karachi to Amman, Jordan, transferred to another plane and arrived in Jerusalem for a two-day stopover. We felt happy and fortunate to be in the Holy Land. The first day we visited many sites in Jerusalem. The next day we toured Jericho, where John filled his pockets with stones until his

On the Way Home

shorts began to slip down, we swam in the Dead Sea, filling a 7 Up bottle with the salty water as a souvenir, and drove past the Good Samaritan Inn. When he saw the inn Stan exclaimed, "If they show me the hoofprints of the Good Samaritan's donkey I won't believe it!" (The previous day our guide had pointed out two or three possible sites which strained our credibility.) Too soon we had to leave for Cairo, Egypt. We toured the Pyramids where I carried Esther on my back and John in my arms up a long, dark ramp toward the center tomb. Stan, Hope, and John enjoyed camel rides. We were impressed by the exhibits in the fascinating museums, saw a large mosque, and many crowded streets where Peggy added a few more items to give as Christmas presents in Iowa. Through Menno Travel Service Peggy had arranged a stopover in Vienna, Austria. What a beautiful city in full Christmas decorated splendor! Especially thrilling was the Carol singing in a nearby church – it was in Austrian but we knew what they meant. Then we touched down at Frankfurt, flew on to New York, on to Des Moines, and to Carroll by car. We had made it home!

Of course, meeting my dad and Carrie's family was sad; we consoled one another as best we could. Then we drove to the Hoft farm. What a joyous reunion that was! They were astonished how the children had grown and met John for the first time. At last Esther and John, having only heard us talking about Grandma and Grandpa Hoft,

132

Harry, Hope Abigail, and Cecil, could shift from imagining to reality. We celebrated Christmas in great style, dividing our time between our two families. Everyone was too generous with gifts. Now we didn't have to ship packages by Post. Our Pakistani gifts seemed exotic to everyone. We had much talking to do, sharing our Pakistani experience, and catching up with the changes in our dear families and neighborhood. Mom Hoft had made tons of goodies. She spoiled us with fresh home-baked

In Spite of the Smiles a Sombre Homecoming

breads, buns, cinnamon rolls, and cakes. We ate with relish the candies, cookies, and the feasts of Christmas time! How good it was to be back in Iowa with family, relatives, and dear friends. I especially enjoyed sitting back to hear sermons preached by another Pastor. Peggy reveled in showing off our four and helping her mom in every way she could.

Hoft Relatives and Friends; Grandma Holds Hope

However, in mid January we drove to Ithaca to begin study. We had rented a church house on Court Street next to the First Presbyterian Church. It was spacious, fully furnished, and had a good furnace for that cold weather. Stan, Hope, and Esther attended the public school quite close by. How relieved we were that they were up to standard in their classes. In fact, their reading skills were advanced! Hope and Esther, when asked while registering to what denomination they belonged, had answered Christian. They were asked which church and didn't know. We told them we were Presbyterian. This had to be explained to them – in Pakistan we only referred to Christian! It snowed heavily and temperatures fell below zero my day of registration. I walked up the hill almost freezing my face, to be told registration had been postponed, but they let me fill out all those papers and choose my subjects and classes. I was assigned a study room in Warren Hall in which most of the rural sociology classes were held. That week, I met with Dr. Thomas, my advisor, laying out the full course of study and requirements. It looked formidable to me. I bought my books and dug in, attending classes, and getting acquainted. It was shocking to see such young kids in those classes! Or, had I aged that much? Yes, I had. They were smart and grounded in their studies. I had a lot of catching up to do, but my Pakistani experience compensated a great deal. Meanwhile, Peggy was enjoying supermarkets, fresh produce and meats, ice cream, and the work of American home-making. We were greatly pleased with this new situation. No more Urdu lessons! I won't go into detail about my studies which included a whole range of subjects, long hours of study, exams, and written papers. My main interests were community development and social research methodology. Dr. Thomas helped me a lot. The immense library was a gold mine of books and other materials.

At the close of that first semester, we drove to Iowa for the summer. Peggy, not wishing to give her mom so much extra work, rented a cabin on Black Hawk Lake. Mom Hoft didn't like the idea; she wanted the whole family to stay at home. We promised to visit daily and spend lots of time together, which we did. The children thoroughly enjoyed swimming, boating, fishing, and on-the-lawn picnics. How everyone enjoyed hot dogs, burgers, potato salad or chips, and ice cream! Stan became an expert fisherman. One misty morning he kept catching large carp. Two men fishing near by were amazed; they were catching nothing. They asked Stan how he did it. He replied, "Concentrate on the nibble and be quick on the hooking." He gave them his catch of eight! We also took long hikes and visited local sites.

On the farm, the children had free reign. They ran about exploring and admiring the big garden and rows of flowers. Rolling on the lawn in clean grass was a treat. We taught them many of the games we had played in our younger days. But the highlight was when Harry attached the play wagon to the garden plow and gave them all rides. He taught Stan how to operate it and Stan became the driver, round and round the yard. Hope, Esther, and John took turns riding in the wagon. Fetching the cows at

Getting Acquainted with the Farm

milking time was another wild adventure. They eagerly watched Grandpa Hoft do fieldwork, milk the cows, and feed the pigs and chickens. They all helped gather eggs from the nests. One noon while Grandpa was taking a short nap, Stan and one of Norman's boys stuck a live minnow from the big water tank into Grandpa's gaping mouth. How he did spit and shout but afterwards laughed with them as a big joke. Another time he came in from the field really thirsty. He went to the fridge and took out what he thought was a cold 7 Up. After one swallow that tasted horrible, he spit it out, poured the remainder of the bottle down the drain, and asked who was playing a trick on him. That was the water from the Dead Sea we had so carefully protected! So the summer went on with many visits to the uncles and aunts, cousins, and neighborhood friends – with picnics galore! We alternated worship at Wall Lake, Wheatland, and Carroll. We visited James, Carrie, Jimmy, Larry, and Ruth, but in the town there was not as much our four could do. The spark of my mom was gone.

Too soon we had to return to Ithaca. It was back to school for our three, lots of work for Peggy, and back to the grind for me. We did visit delightful parks in the area on Sunday afternoons and loved Cayuga Lake. The fall colors of the trees were magnificent! Then came the cold and snows. On one occasion, Peggy's brother Dick stayed overnight as he returned from a conference. It was so good to be with him. The plan was that Merna and their three sons would arrive the next morning to stay with us a day or two before returning to Schenectady, New York. What a surprise we had. During the night thirty inches of snow had fallen. The lake effect had worked; we were literally snowbound! Merna called from Utica, saying she was marooned. Her bus could not make it through the storm. A day later she arrived after a harrowing ordeal. We made the most of it, but the children had fun cleaning the sidewalks and making snowmen.

The final semester went fast and furiously. I had read, taken voluminous notes, and categorized my findings on the giant computer there. The research was finished, but the writing of the thesis remained. Peggy wanted us to drive to Iowa for Christmas. I had a lot of typing to do so she drove our four to Iowa! All went well until a blizzard hit them near Cedar Rapids. Anxiously looking for a motel sign, they finally saw one. Stan had to walk on the edge of the road to guide Peggy to the turn. They settled into the last room available! Putting on car chains the next noon, they safely arrived at the farm. They had another joyful Christmas celebration, and returned to Ithaca in time for school to begin. I had in the meantime finished my thesis and was preparing for final exams. What a time we had!

In early March we boarded the SS United States, seventeen stories high and the world's fastest super liner. We had said our farewells to Dick and Merna, Will and Betty, and to Hope Abigail. It had been bad weather with lots of snow, ice, and cold. They bravely came to see us off. A Northeaster was blowing in. The Hudson River was not too bad, but as we turned to the Atlantic the full force of that hurricane hit us. The water was so rough the harbor pilot could not board the tug boat; he sailed to France and South Hampton with us! Everyone got seasick except Stan who loved to walk the enclosed decks and watch those huge waves fifty feet high. It was tea and sandwiches in our cabin the first two days. Esther claims she threw up seventeen times, a record in our family, but she didn't win by much! Even though the ship had broken all records for speed, we were a day and a half late in our crossing. It was a mercy to dock at South Hampton with good weather. As our freight was being transferred to Liverpool, we spent four glorious days in England. We toured Trafalgar Square, shopped at Harrow's, saw the changing of the guard at Buckingham Palace (Stan thought it was too formal and time-wasting; he said he could organize it a lot better!), Windsor Castle, and Shakespeare's Stratford-upon-Avon. It was good to boast we had been through Oxford and Cambridge – they thought we meant to get a degree! We then took the Boat train to Liverpool to board the Circassius for a nineteen-day cruise touching Port Said, the Suez Canal, and Port of Yemen. We hit another storm off the coast of France. Stan and I shared a cabin. That night the ship rocked from side to side, causing our large steamer trunk to slide across the floor. We could hear glass falling and tinkling; Stan laughed at the pandemonium. It was one class and filled with friendly, open minded people like ourselves! There were games and activities for the children, table tennis (Peggy emerged as the champion!), and the most delicious food prepared by chefs from Goa. Stan loved the food and went to eat before we did. He informed us which was the best main course and best of five desserts. Hope and Esther enjoyed their dolls and new friends. Many families were aboard. An Indian woman, wife of a high-ranking officer in the UK Indian Embassy with her two children, was most charming.

FC College Chapel where Al Served for 15 Years

The stopover in Port of Aden had an added surprise. A cable was awaiting our arrival in which FC College requested me to consider becoming the College Chaplain. Since we had no other assignment and considered it a great privilege, we cabled our approval. Now we had something to think and pray about! It is said that when one door closes another door of opportunity and challenge opens. This was something we had never even thought about. Peggy and I started wondering what this new development would be like.

Entering the Indian Ocean we were entertained by porpoises racing our ship and leaping through the waves in graceful harmonious ballet. We docked at Karachi and saw our freight unloaded. According to plan, Magistrate A.P. Gill was there to help us clear customs. To the delight of our children, he had brought his son, Azam, with him. We had bought a fridge for the family, which we would "sell" them. With Magistrate Gill's status and clout, our freight was quickly cleared and loaded onto a goods train. We all spent the night at the Metropole Hotel, enjoying the Pakistani food, the floor show of Spanish Flamenco dancers, and, of course, our friends' company. Following Paul's lead, we exited when a belly dancer began an explicit performance. The children entertained themselves by riding the elevators up and down – those latticed sliding doors were enticing. The next morning we boarded the Tez Gam (a fast passenger train) for the long trip to Lahore. It was a hot and dusty ride. But now we knew the language, the customs, how to order hot tea at the stations along the way, and to enjoy the curries and flat bread served by railway waiters who were most agile in moving from car to car, sometimes through the windows! At last we reached the Lahore Railway Station, built like a fortress by the British as a place to protect people in times of riots and war.

In the next week we moved our things from 6 Empress Road to 44 Forman Christian College – settling in was a big job. This two-story, fired brick house, with two open verandahs upstairs and one off the living room, a large backyard, nicely spaced Sheeshem trees, flower gardens, and a privet hedge around the borders, was to be our home for fifteen years. It had been built by a physics teacher as an experimental air-conditioned house with cool air blown in through a series of conduits from an underground rectangular tunnel about ten feet deep under the lawn. This made a twelve-degree difference in temperature throughout the house. All these features also lent themselves well to imaginative play by the children. Periodically, Peggy would allow them to crawl through the large, dusty cooling ducts and, during Halloween, to set up haunted houses in the underground tunnel. Esther, along with John and other children, created a pirate ship on the verandah outside her bedroom, complete with sticks that were used as swords and also as mops for swabbing the deck. A convenient metal-rung ladder led up to the flat roof which doubled as both a crow's nest and a place to plant flags after winning imaginary battles. We were fortunate to have such good housing. There was also brick housing for the helpers. The College staff and our neighbors bid us welcome. Thus, a new era in our lives had begun. We were grateful for our safe return to Lahore.

Chapter 25

Murree, FC College History, Learning, Teaching, Preaching

Toward the end of April it was time to escape the heat of the Punjab and settle the family into Rosenheim and schooling. Peggy and John, now five, were busy with cleaning the cottage, shopping, and picking up the threads of living in the clouds of monsoon rains. Stan, Hope, and Esther resumed their studies in the Murree Christian School. Esther was in Kindergarten – she loved it! Stan and Hope found their stance and did very well in their studies. The year in the USA had broadened their scope and perspective. It was good to be back with friends and their teachers. Walking to and from school along the Forest Path was exciting and hard going especially when raincoats and boots were a necessity, which was most of the time. Peggy was kept very busy caring for our four, helping the newly hired Cook and Ayah to do their best, and making sure all were warm and healthy in that cool environment. During the brief time I was able to spend with the family before returning to the plains it was a great joy to watch the children play in that beautiful setting. Our dear, innovative Esther discovered an elaborate Enchanted Forest on the hill where she could have adventures. To the ordinary, untrained eye it looked like just a a few trees, rocks, grassy swatches, and flying bugs. But in Esther's vision these were magic realms to visit, and she created magic rooms, each named after a flower. She made tiny drawings of those flowers and pinned them to the trees. Magic keys made of hairy vines that opened magic locks were required to enter the forest. Esther also enjoyed making things. Under the Cedar of Lebanon, using bark, sticks, and leaves, she led little John in building elaborate, tiny villages, complete with barter systems. She was particularly adept at making "mud bread" for barter using clay and grass seed. At night, the children liked to camp out with pillows and blankets in our Volkswagen bus until the calls of jackals made them retreat to the house. It was difficult for me to return to Lahore, leaving the family yet another time.

Lahore was hot, but it was imperative that I get started with the chaplain's work, learning what my duties would be, and making preparation for teaching English classes in the fall. Gradually I became acquainted with the Principal, the Dean, Staff members, and the lay of the land. I researched in Ewing Memorial Library the history of the relatively young Pakistan, its culture, its people, and its ethos. I had much to learn. Living in the large city of Lahore was a sharp contrast to Kasur District and rural settings. I would be teaching students from all corners of Pakistan. Discovering the diversity was astounding. I wish I had space to trace the whole history of how the Islamic Republic of Pakistan was founded in the 1947 Partitioning from India. Allow me to briefly summarize that point of history.

The Subcontinent has a multiplicity of people and religions: Hindus, Muslims, Sikhs, Jains, Buddhists, Christian, Jews, Parsees, and others. They trace their history back at least five thousand years to the Indus Valley Civilization. Then followed waves of immigrants and conquerors: Macedonians with Alexander, Scythians, Persians, Mongols, the first Muslim traders in Baluchistan and Sind, the Turkish and Afghan invaders, the Mughals, the East India Company with its British trade and colonial rule, the rule of Ranjit Singh (Sikh). These were followed by the struggle for independence from British rule. During World War II, both Hindus and Muslims pressed Britain for independence with increasingly overt agitation. They were promised independence on condition that Indian armed forces would fight for the Allies, which they did. The original intent was to form a united India, but Muhammad Ali Jinnah, a distinguished barrister from Bombay (now Mumbai), pressed for a separation from India. As leader of the Muslim League, he formally endorsed the Lahore Resolution of 1940, which called for the creation of an independent nation in regions where Muslims were in a majority, including Kashmir. Most Muslims perceived the Hindu-controlled National Congress as a bad portent for an improved future and chafed under the apparent domination by the Hindu majority. Unable to agree on a formula ensuring the protection of Muslim religious, economic, and political rights, Jinnah pushed for Partition. On August 14, 1947, Pakistan as a State was born.

The Partition of 1947 was a tragic occurrence. Over fourteen million people were relocated: seven million Hindus and Sikhs leaving West Pakistan and Bengal, and seven million Muslims leaving India. Over two million lost their lives in that mass movement. Whole train loads of people were slaughtered. I recalled how Frank Llewellyn had helped save the lives of Muslims, Hindus, and Sikhs by transporting in his jeep and trailer hundreds of refugees. He would take the people leaving what is now Pakistan to the Sutlej River and bring another load back on the Grand Trunk highway. Once challenged by border guards to show his permit, he searched his billfold and found a "permit" – a doctor's prescription! How wonderful their signatures are illegible. He related that over one hundred fifty mothers gave birth in the Serai (a guest house on the Kasur compound). Local Christians brought water to the refugees on the run. Later, Frank got an official permit to cross the border signed by Lord Mountbatten. During the Partition FC College converted two of its dormitories into emergency hospital wards. These eventually became the United Christian Hospital.

As I have written, FCC grew out of the labors of Charles W. Forman. His early work at Rang Mahal strengthened over the years. To accommodate the growing number of students, the Lahore Mission College was founded. Buildings were erected in Nila Gumbad (near Anarkali), the main center of Lahore in 1915. Enrollment grew from eighteen students in 1896 to six hundred by 1915. In honor of Dr. Charles W. Forman the name was changed to Forman Christian College in 1894. Graduate degrees were awarded through Calcutta University until the University of the Punjab was in operation. Today FCC has nearly four thousand enrolled students. Dr. Forman continued his Sunday evening evangelistic preaching in Lahore City. One evening a young man struck him down. The crowd violently reacted by beating the young man and threatening to kill him. Dr. Forman got to his feet, embraced his attacker, and forgave him. He said, "We are to love one another." On his demise, his funeral procession winding through Lahore City to the cemetery was estimated to be three miles of weeping people of all faiths! No wonder the FCC motto is, "By love serve one another." Growth continued and in 1933 FCC moved to its present site on the Lahore canal four miles out of the city. It soon became known as one of the best colleges in the Subcontinent.

What does a chaplain do? I was informed that in addition to teaching college English classes, he conducted services four times a week in the chapel. On Sundays he led the worship for English-speaking members and, due to a misfortune, also led the Urdu congregation. Prior to our arrival the local pastor had been discovered in bed with a female member, which wrecked the congregation, now down to nine attending members. For three years beginning in April 1962 I became the Urdu congregation's Pastor. Within eighteen months the attendance increased to two hundred fifty. The congregation included servants, students, local families near the college, doctors and nurses from UCH, members of staff, and faculty of FCC. Elders of the church were invited to share in leading in prayer, reading Scriptures, and preaching. When the congregation reached a competent maturity, I encouraged them to call Rev. J.D. Arthur from Sialkot to become the full-time Pastor. He and his wife Munir faithfully and effectively served that church for many years. For a few months I assisted him and then placed full responsibility in his hands.

Peggy and Munir became fast friends. As a young pastor's wife, Munir sought Peggy's help and counsel. Both were active in the Sunday School, Youth Group, Women's Association, aiding the poor and disadvantaged, and Hospital calling on the sick. Peggy taught Bible Studies for all ages. One afternoon Munir asked Peggy to accompany her to UCH. There was a young Muslim woman in a coma. She had been lying there inert for three weeks. Her mother sat by the bedside in despair. Munir asked Peggy to pray for that young woman. This was an unsuspected challenge. Peggy said a humble simple prayer in Urdu for the Lord's healing and restoration, for His praise and Glory to be demonstrated. Three days later that young woman opened her eyes, began to move her fingers, and in a few more days sat up, restored! Her mother had witnessed the Lord's healing power – she was amazed and thankful.

The English-speaking congregation was another big challenge. At this time, there were many USAID engineers and technical support people, American Consulate personnel, relief organizations such as CARE, WHO, United Nations people and their families, in addition to the English-speaking FCC staff, UCH staff, students, and others. In fact, there were more than a dozen nations and ten to twelve denominations represented. What to call such a large group? I made a suggestion which was accepted: we formed the International Christian Fellowship. This was a way to include everyone, but to have all of us leave our denomination at home! We had no bishops, synods, presbyteries, superintendents, and the like over us – we were under God only! Sunday school classes for all ages were conducted. There was much appreciation that an overseas church was available. Bible studies were in the homes of members who took turns in leading them.

Peggy and the children returned in early September. Stan, Hope, and Esther had ten days of holiday before returning to boarding at MCS. John was enrolled in a local school which he enjoyed very much. It was good to have family back! College had opened, and I was busy teaching three periods of English: grammar, literature, and poetry, with lots of assigned essays to give students an opportunity to express themselves in the English medium. We teachers read, corrected, and helped them with remedial exercises. One could see the influence of the British. I had to learn how to use British accents and spell the Queen's English. I recall a visit by Mrs. Pat Young, wife of the British Officer for Education. Dr. Sinclair, the Principal, introduced the entire staff, leaving me to last. I was introduced as an American English Teacher, to which she firmly stated, "That is impossible!" I responded with a brilliant flow of British English much to her astonishment. On Sunday, October 28, 1962 we had an influential visitor in the ICF. The Dutch embassy contacted us to arrange for a "small, quiet, and secure worship service" for Crown Princess Beatrix of the Netherlands. What a flurry of preparation that entailed. Since it was Reformation Sunday, I prepared the sermon very carefully to instruct what that Reformation was all about. Every Dutch missionary in Pakistan joined us. The chapel was packed, with the exception of the first three rows reserved for our Royal Visitor and her entourage. Everything went well as scheduled: proper hymns, special anthem by the choir, appropriate readings, and my sermon, which included a reference to Erasmus' contribution to the Renaissance and freedom of reason for the satisfaction of our Dutch visitors. I requested the congregation to stand at the close of the worship to allow our guests to exit. In the vestry, the Crown Princess thanked me, and then she asked, "Do you have such a full congregation each Sunday?" I replied, "Not quite as many." I suggested she attend each Sunday to make sure the Chapel would be filled! She left the campus to meet the Dutch citizens who were in Pakistan on assignment. What a memorable occasion that had been.

But of course, in the midst of all this there were three English classes five days a week, four morning chapel services, and lots of counseling of students, both Christian and Muslim. The one hundred seventy-five Christian students were members of the Fellowship which met in our backyard each Thursday afternoon following classes. Peggy arranged tea and biscuits (cookies for you Americans). It helped increase the attendance and aided the students in forgetting their weariness and being away from home. We also played volleyball and badminton. For them I prepared Bible studies and lectures on "The Place of a Christian Minority in an Islamic Society" and encouraged discussion, which helped them to better cope as a minority in FCC and the nation. We used Urdu hymns in chapel which gave them a sense of continuity with their church and families who spoke only Urdu or Punjabi. They enjoyed taking turns

143

playing the tabla and small organ (harmonium). There were also foreign students from Saudi Arabia and the Middle East to counsel and assist. Added to these activities were frequent committee meetings related to the administration and instructional programs of the college. Most Saturday evenings and late into the night, I finished preparation for my sermons on Sunday.

In an attempt to make learning English more palatable and interesting, I mixed in witty remarks and jokes. When they laughed at puns I knew they understood the meanings of those words and idioms. Many students were pleased and receptive. However, two of the Christian students went to Dr. Sinclair and complained that Prof. Schlorholtz was not serious enough as a teacher and preferred telling jokes! Fortunately, the Principal told them that I was trying to make learning and using

FC College Sports Day

English more pleasant rather than boring and discouraging. I was impressed to learn that many students memorized the materials and recited them in tests and exams. It was, however, rote learning rather than mastering the usage of the English language. To help them overcome this weakness I assigned essay topics that demanded thought and correct expressions. One assignment was to describe their experience of Riding the Lahore Omnibus to College. I had stressed that the leading sentence should get my attention. Parvez received the highest marks in the class. His leading sentence was, "Entering a Lahore bus is like entering into the gates of Hell!" I thought that was quite descriptive and used it as a model of what could get my attention. I was learning, teaching, preaching, and during a rare holiday relaxing with the family at one of Lahore's many historic sites, enjoying picnics which Peggy prepared with loving care.

Chapter 26

Peggy's Experience: Working With and Relating to
Pakistani Women

Peggy maintained a vital ministry to the women of Lahore and Pakistan. She joined a variety of groups and actively participated in them. Since we had combined appointments as missionaries, Peggy did not have a specific assignment. In addition

Planning over Tea to Better Society

to being a homemaker for six, the Chaplain's wife, the Pastor's wife, and a good friend and neighbor to all, she was busily engaged in numerous organizations. This will not be chronological, but rather topical/thematic. For instance, she was a member of the Soroptimist Club of Lahore. This was an excellent means for Peggy to relate and participate in a

cause dear to her heart with the educated and professional women of Lahore. She shared enthusiastically with me the discussions, debates, and commiseration of caring and concerned women, mainly Muslims. I had to ask Peggy what Soroptimist meant. She informed me that in 1921, Soroptimist ("best for women") was founded as an international volunteer organization of business and professional women who worked to improve the lives of women and girls in locally oriented community service projects, as well as on national and international levels.

This was a movement and cause close to Peggy's heart. She learned that these Lahori women did not really favor multiple marriages, where a husband could take up to four wives, even though Muslim law allowed it. They discussed many issues: a wife's right to divorce, inheritance, changing the legal age at which girls could be married from fourteen to sixteen, the woman's choice of wearing a veil (purdah) not her husband's, the right to family planning and the technology, and recognition of the woman's role in the home and being a mother. There were many more issues. Peggy not only listened but shared from her experience of what she had observed in the villages of Kasur. She appreciated the bonds of friendship that developed, many of them for many years. In later years many of these concerns were incorporated in the Muslim Family Laws when General Ayub Khan was President.

One of the Soroptimist members was Editor of the women's page for "The Pakistan Times." Peggy read her columns regularly, which were a mixture of social events and news from a woman's point of view. Peggy telephoned to arrange a meeting in her office and paid her a visit. At first, the Editor was quite reserved and cautious. What were this foreign woman's intentions? What did she hope to gain? Can a missionary be

Peggy Entertaining Tooni Sher Khan
at our Home

like this smiling, confident woman who kept asking searching questions regarding so many issues? Peggy put her at ease by telling her of her concern for women, their home life, their children's future, how she had been impressed with how charming, hospitable, and generous Pakistani women were. And she meant that! Over the years Peggy and Miriam became fast friends. On one occasion Peggy invited Miriam and her husband to join in one of her large tea parties on our 44 FCC back lawn with up to one hundred twenty guests. Peggy felt that there should be a diversity of guests – Muslims/Christians, rich/poor, highly educated/not so highly educated, staff/strangers

– as an opportunity to become acquainted. There came the day when Miriam thanked Peggy for her hospitality and for the introduction to people of all levels of life and especially educated Christians! Peggy had many tea parties with lots of new people. She made our home a bridge, helping those with doubts and fears to adopt new attitudes and tolerant acceptance.

Another "project" was Peggy's concern about the FCC Campus School for the Pakistani children on campus. It had kindergarten and grades one to five. Joined by Trudy Foster, they often visited and took note of where there were needs to be filled. The teachers greatly appreciated their interest. In special meetings, Peggy and Trudy sat with the teachers to have them list their needs, problems, and plans. Armed with this information they spoke to the ICF and Urdu congregations about how they could become informed, help meet the needs, and encourage those dedicated teachers. The response was great, and soon constructive assistance was given. The school was whitewashed and cleaned. New slates, quill pens, ink, construction paper, books for the library, and other supplies were made available. The teachers thanked them and related how encouraged they were that at last someone had taken interest in the welfare of the children and the school. On another visit by Peggy and Trudy the children sang a welcome/thank you song in appreciation. To ensure continuity for help and guidance, Peggy and Trudy promoted the idea that a School Managing committee of local parents and representatives from the FCC staff and the Urdu congregation be formed. It was accepted and implemented!

Quite a bit of time and effort were devoted by Peggy to the YWCA of Lahore. Located on Queen's Road, the YWCA was a vital center for enabling young women and girls in their search for identity, self-esteem, and technical training leading to skills needed in seeking employment. Typing, English tutoring, shorthand, ethics, Bible studies, and evening discussion groups were offered. To encourage parents to get their children educated there was a kindergarten. The Boarding arrangement complete with kitchen, library, and social rooms made it possible for students from rural areas and towns to live in and get acquainted with other students and city life in Lahore. In charge of all this was the ably proficient Ms. Jane Subha Khan, the Administrative Secretary. A jovial soul with a hearty laugh and quick wit, she served in that capacity for many years. Jane did not need a hand calculus; she could add a list of numbers faster than anyone! There were heavy responsibilities and yet it was a strategic position for effective assistance to many young women.

Peggy met Jane at a high tea held in the Anglican Cathedral mini garden. It was a fundraising event – Peggy was always ready to help out on such things. Stalls with knickknacks, handiworks, delicious pastries, pakoras, and Punjabi sweets were on sale. Jane and her close friend, Margaret Phailbus, were operating one of those stalls. Jane's hearty laugh and jolly retorts got Peggy's attention. She not only enjoyed the tea and pastries but was introduced to that pair of super saleladies. They invited Peggy to the YWCA at her leisure to become acquainted and to see the good work that was being done. Duly impressed, she offered her services when needed. Jane called her on occasion when there was a problem. This eventually meant that Peggy was elected to the Management Board! She soon became aware of the cliques and factions that Jane had to deal with. Two prominent women were at loggerheads with Jane (and many others). They seemed to take opposite sides on any issue or problem. Peggy was to experience many opportunities for "suggesting" the correct solutions! She learned a lot about human nature at its worst. How glad she was that she came from a large family.

On many happy occasions, Peggy and I were invited by Jane for delicious Pakistani dinners. What grand times we had! I paid the price for this by being Santa at their Christmas party, arriving on a horse-drawn tonga in full regalia, shouting my "Ho Ho Ho!" Another time, for the seventieth-year celebration of the

Another Skit by Bill and Al

YWCA's founding, Captain Bill Ratcliff of the Salvation Army and I were requested to put on a skit. The venue was the large front lawn with a small stage and a large audience. Both of us wore saris and wigs – I was Jane, and he was Mira Phailbus, Principal of Kinnaird College for Women (Margaret's sister-in-law). Pretending "seventieth" referred to Jane's age, we dramatized our jokes and witticisms by relating to the crowd a "typical day" in the YWCA. I told how the cook had dropped some dishes that morning (dropping several cheap dishes from the Anarkali market). Ratcliff responded by saying, "You mean like this?" He threw more dishes to the floor! The audience loved it. Our closing remark was, "It's a good thing the cook didn't drop the fridge!" Jane affectionately called us *Badmash*," the Urdu word for bad characters, which we considered a compliment. However, there were serious times also: the need for prayer, consolation, counsel, and encouragement. Peggy and I were most impressed by the dedication and loving service of Jane's concern and care for those young women now competent and skilled to more successfully cope with the increasing opportunities for women in Pakistani society.

Another valuable contribution of Peggy's was her Bible Study Groups for Christian women. These were held in our home with ten to twelve attending these monthly scheduled studies. Favorites were the gospel of John, Ephesians, Romans, and John's Epistles. It was not lecturing, but rather inductive search by the whole group wrestling to find the true meaning and intent of God's Word and Will for their life. Many nominal in faith discovered the reality of personal faith in Jesus Christ. Peggy assigned questions to be answered in the next session. These were shared and discussed by the whole group. It was an experienced teacher's means to encourage personal study of the Bible, not relying on what the leader said. A few of the ICF members joined, making it a diverse fellowship.

The fall of 1963, we enrolled our four in the Lahore American School (LAS), sponsored by the American State Department. Stan had not been well, suffering from lack of energy and loss of weight. It was good to have them home with us. We had reluctantly agreed to let Stan have a motorcycle so he could spend time with his friends, many of whom were from elite Pakistani families. Hope and Esther enjoyed riding their bikes around the campus. John also was free to play and read the books he enjoyed so much. Esther, a voracious reader, too, found that her library books often disappeared because John "borrowed" them to read without telling her. His excuse was the she chose the most interesting books! All were impressed with the numerous chipkalis (lizards) clinging to the ceiling of the front entrance to our house and on the bedroom ceilings. When it was "lights out" our children declared they could still see their staring eyes. They all were happy in LAS. A car pool was formed with Wynn and Carol Mumby's three: Lynn, Ted, and Kim. Wynn had finished teaching the children of the Mir of Hunza, far to the north in Pakistan. We took alternative weekly turns driving. The children got along very well, especially after I bought a small TV, which broadcast three hours each day from three to six in the evening. The three English programs were "I Love Lucy," "Bewitched," and one other. Soon they were joined by the Wheeless and Ritze children whose parents complained that I should not have gotten a TV. My answer was that they could prohibit their children from coming to watch! In the midst of this Peggy was volunteering to plan UCH monthly menus. She also helped Kinnaird College for Women when they could not find enough clerical staff to cope. This gave Peggy more contacts with Pakistani women and girls. She also initiated meetings for the FCC Staff wives to enable Muslim and Christians to relate and get acquainted. On Saturdays Peggy took our and the Mumby children to visit the Fort, Shalimar Gardens, Hiran Minar, boating on the canal, shopping, and the Gymkhana Gardens. I was teaching English even on Saturdays. Peggy combined immense responsibilities with fun.

Then came an amazing request from Mira Phailbus, the Principal of Kinnaird College. She asked Peggy to teach a seminar class of twenty to thirty students on the subject of A Guide to Marriage and Family Living (Creative Marriage). When Peggy asked her why she was offered this challenge, Mira replied, "Peggy, you are the most broadminded conservative I know!" No one had done this before. Peggy had to develop the course, duplicate it on stencils, and teach the class. It is regrettable that I can't print the entire material, but here is a condensed table of contents:

I. Know yourself.
    A. Heredity
    B. Personality
        1. Courtesy
        2. Show yourself friendly

II. Growing into Maturity.
    A. Physical Development (Structural)
    B. Functional Development (Behavior)
        1. The story of life and reproduction
        2. The role of sex

III. Marriage.
    A. Emotional considerations
    B. What is love? (Discussion)
    C. Some cultural differences concerning love
        1. Western 'way'
        2. Eastern 'way' Pakistan
            (a) Practical considerations
            (b) Common difficulties
            (c) Some positive helps

IV. Preparation for Parenthood.
    A. Parent-Child Interaction
    B. The importance of a happy home environment on the physical and
        mental development of the child
    C. Common difficulties

    Summary and Final Comments. Written assignments included
    Personality Profiles, My Values and Attitudes, My Expectations.

Peggy's Marriage and Family Living Class Kinnaird College

What a notable contribution Peggy made sharing insights and perspectives to the
women and girls of all faiths in emancipation and opportunity! Peggy's course at
Kinnaird was a tribute and recognition of the understanding, knowledge, and wisdom
she showed in her rapport with the women and girls of Pakistan. Few had the courage
and cross-cultural experience to be able to portray so ably the universal quest for
womanhood at is best.

Chapter 27

Family, Holiday in Kashmir, The Pakistan-Indian War of 1965

During the years 1963-64, we continued to maintain a close relationship with the Gills and enjoyed picnics near the Ravi River and rowing boats, taking turns. Of course, we joined in dinners at the Gill's and in our home. The children had a grand time. Life at FCC was pleasant during the winter season but torrid in summer. We slept on charpoys upstairs on the verandah. Each of us had one with crossed cane sticks holding the mosquito nets in place. One learned at his/her peril not to lean against the net – fair game for attack! The routine was to soak the brick floor with plenty of water, soak the nets and sheets, and hope you were soundly asleep before they dried!

Peggy with Edna and Patrick Joshua

An added attraction on occasion was to suddenly become aware of a severe dust/sand storm at 4:00 am. Rising to go inside, the mattress and net would rise with you. That was uncontrolled pandemonium!

At Mrs. Sinclair's tea party, Peggy met an interesting person named Mrs. Edna Joshua, also called Annie, whose husband was a Sessions Judge. Patrick had retired and was presently serving as the Administrative Secretary of the Pakistan Bible Society. They had a family of five children: Ivor, Ronald and Donald (twins), and Roy and Joy (twins). Edna invited Peggy to visit her sometime, which Peggy soon did, as was her custom when meeting someone new. They had great times sharing their life's adventures and family histories. It was our privilege to meet and eat at their home, at the entrance to Anarkali market. Peggy, of course, invited them to teas and dinners at FCC. Our four read English stories to the grandchildren; they "taught" ours Urdu, they claimed. En route to the the campus in the van for a visit, all sang among others "Make new friends, but keep the old. One is silver and the other gold."

During our short stay at Rosenheim the Joshua family joined us and we met Joy, with her three daughters: Koruna, Onila, and Benita Biswas. Joy's husband, Benoy, was on army duty. Edna and Donald livened the party! Blossom, Roy's wife, and their children also came to the picnics and fun. Like Benoy, Roy was on army duty. That

fall Peggy arranged a big tea party in honor of Edna's birthday. We decided to play a joke on her. Peggy had the cook decorate a dekshi (aluminum cooking pan) with frosting and decorations. Edna was so pleased – until she tried to cut the "cake." She glared at me in mock horror and asked, "Al, how did you ever become a Padre?" There were similar good

Peggy Hosting a Party with Joy Biswas

times we shared, too numerous to record. One hot summer evening, we arranged a "wedding" for Donald. He was working in Rawalpindi. We invited him to attend; we would furnish the cake and bride. To his surprise, the "bride" was one of his close friends – Emmanuel Daniel – dressed in a glorious wedding gown and wig! During Holy Week, Joy stayed at 44 FCC to study for her B.A. exam. She had had to postpone her finals in college because of a severe case of shingles. She and Peggy discussed many things, including the need for personal faith in Jesus Christ. On Good Friday the Light dawned, and Joy was a radiant Christian that Easter morning at the Chapel. She passed her exams also!

In June of 1965, Dr. Jim Brown, the overseas Commission Representative of our New York City Mission office, requested me to fill in for him for three months. His wife was Virginia; they had three boys. He said that in the summer months the hotter it got the lighter the work. I should have known better! Stan had been diagnosed with Tropical Sprue. Our Doctor, Bob Dunlap at UCH, advised folic acid and home leave for him. Stan was also allergic to gluten and suffered from anemia. Stan would be a senior in the fall and would stay with my sister Carrie and family in Carroll. Dr. Brown volunteered to have him join them on the flight to the USA. We gratefully agreed and gave Stan his farewell parties. It was a sad parting. We were heartened to learn that the Browns took him to the New York World's Fair! To our relief, he did recover quite soon with American food.

It was time for our month's holiday in August. Rev. Bill Zoerner agreed to do the Commission Rep job and Bill Price the pastorate at ICF. Our passports, van permit, visas to India and Kashmir, and reservations were approved. Despite rumblings of Freedom Fighters from Pakistan making trouble in Kashmir, we drove along the

The Cherry Stone Houseboat: Proudly Advertised as
"First Class and Sanitary Fitted"

northern tip of India, stopping at Pathankot for the night, to Srinagar, the capital. What a a terrifying mountain road, with signs noting the deaths of twelve construction men falling two thousand feet into the river below! Hope moved farther and farther from the front window toward me. But even with a disabled horn we made it. Entering the Kashmir Valley, we were amazed at the beauty: snow-clad mountain ranges, green valleys, lush meadows, raging streams. We settled into the Cherry

Stone houseboat on Dal Lake. By water taxi (shikara), past floating lotus gardens, floating vegetable gardens, and boats loaded with Kashmiri handicrafts, we arrived at our home on the water, complete with a cook who treated us to meal after meal of Kashmiri cuisine. What a paradise for relaxation! Shopping in the Srinagar city bazaar was fascinating. There were stalls filled with walnut wood knickknacks, papier mache articles, jewelry, nests of small tables, embroidered pillows, tablecloths and napkins, mirrored vests and Kashmiri outfits, and much more. Peggy was in her element! Our favorite houseboat "store" was called Suffering Moses, floating on the Jhelum River. We asked the owner which country Kashmiris desired to join: Pakistan or India? He replied, "Neither! We are like the young maiden who wants to be independent!" The Mughal Gardens were spectacular. Touring Nishat Bagh (garden) and Shalimar's flowing waters was a once-in-a-lifetime experience.

The Game Warden (left) Helped Us Catch Our Limit

The trip to Kokarnag, forty miles from Srinagar, where there was excellent trout fishing, was for us a rare treat. Having obtained a license for a limit of sixteen trout, we drove by meandering roads to this famous spot. We were met by two men who were to show us the art of fishing. In two hour's time we had caught fourteen. It was getting late. With a tight curfew imposed from sunset to sunrise, I suggested we leave for Srinagar. Those men would not allow this until we had caught our limit. Moving to another spot one man told me where to cast; a trout was landed! A little farther the same thing happened! As we prepared to leave, I asked whether I should tip. The deputy informed me that was not necessary – our guide was the game warden! We made it back to the houseboat just in time. The cook served us a delicious trout dinner, with all the trimmings. For our final week we moved to Pahalgam, seven thousand feet above sea level, in the picturesque Liddar Valley sixty miles east of the Capital. A large tent was our new place of relaxation.

Everything was provided to make us most comfortable. Peggy, however, was suffering from a dry socket, a painful condition resulting from having a tooth removed in Lahore. She was in misery. As she rested, Hope, Esther, John, and I climbed to the top of Green Mountain, meeting a quaint shepherd on the way. Many pilgrims arrived for their ascent to Amarnath, a cave sacred to Hindus. We did not join them; the sacred cave was at eighteen thousand feet!

The departure time arrived and we made our way back to Lahore, stopped three times by Indian soldiers who searched our van for "Freedom Fighters!" Things were getting serious. We crossed back into Pakistan and home. Everyone was shocked to see us return safely. "The Pakistan Times" had reported nineteen bridges destroyed along our route! The following Saturday, Peggy, not wanting to waste the last ten days of our Indian visas and never one to be afraid, decided to take the children and Dr. Martin back across the border to Amritsar to purchase food items not available in Pakistan. They had a grand time and safely returned.

On Monday, September 6, 1965, we took our three and the Mumby's three to LAS to start the new school year. At 10:30 we were called to take the children home – India had invaded Pakistan's eastern border (thirteen miles from our home)! We heard the rumblings of heavy armor moving toward the Ferozepur border. Radio Pakistan warned everyone to blackout every window and glass door to guard against guiding Indian pilots in their bombings and strafing. We were to be attentive to the sirens and stay away from windows and open spaces outside. I was appointed Air Raid Warden of FCC by Principal Sinclair. My job was mainly to keep the watchmen awake and to enforce a strict and complete blackout. To our surprise no one would sell us flashlights or batteries. They feared we would signal incoming Indian fighter planes! Suddenly we had become "hostile foreigners." Even close Muslim friends became distant and wary. We were greatly disappointed by this sudden change of attitude.

In the evenings we listened to Radio Pakistan, Voice of America, and the BBC. The BBC was the best source of objective reporting. There were fighter plane dogfights during the day. Bombers dropped their devastation during the night. They mainly aimed at airfields and train stations with thousand-pound bombs. The danger was they were missing their intended targets, which increased the odds of hitting civilians. I kept checking with mission personnel who were not in the danger zones. Many moved to Murree Christian School and to hospitals that were safe from bombings. All were accounted for. I was able to send a confidential letter relating this and the whole situation to the New York City Mission Office by one of the families leaving for Tehran. I mentioned that this classified information was to be safeguarded and answered by cable, not to be referred to in correspondence. Imagine my shock on receiving a reply letter, which included a copy of the classified letter I had sent! How thankful I was that the censor did not read that one.

The war was something of an adventure for the children. One afternoon Peggy noticed they had gone outside on the lawn during an attack. When she rushed to bring them in, they protested that they were safe because they were standing under our shady trees. Pieces of shrapnel were later found in our yard. The children laboriously dug a trench on the back lawn, just in case the bombs got too close. One evening there was a rumor that India would parachute troops over Lahore. To my utter amazement, Mr. A.P. Gill brought me a .303 heavy rifle, saying how proud he would be to see in "The Pakistan Times" a headline about how an American sharpshooter had defended Lahore! I am most grateful that the attack did not materialize. It did cause a stir in the Cantonment when soldiers shot local people in the dark of night. We had heard the firing on rounds of the Campus.

We organized a crew of refugee women to sew quilts and sort used clothing in our backyard. Then came the order for all foreigners to evacuate to Tehran in Iran. Long caravans of cars, vans, and buses streamed toward Quetta and on to Iran. All the USAID people, non-essential Consulate personnel, and missionaries in Lahore evacuated – that is, all except our family. Peggy and the children decided not to leave me. I could not leave, because I was the Mission Representative and had the General Attorney Power for all of the Mission property, plus blank checks for all the Mission's funds. Literally the only American family in Lahore, we were criticized for staying. But we stood our ground. (After the war, Benoy and Joy presented us with a brass artillery shell inscribed "To the only American family in Lahore during the Indo-Pakistan War of 1965.") We still treasure that commendation. One blessing of our staying in Lahore was the encouragement to the Christian Community. They had taken heart that we had not deserted them in a time of peril. Many had complained that "those missionaries are fair weather friends who can leave us and return home, deserting us to our fate." Then they heard that the Schlorholtz family was still in FCC. That made a great difference!

For nine weeks Peggy taught our three on the upstairs verandah in that warm pleasant sunshine. We were together when we heard the planes overhead. John, our nine-year-old, said, "Nothing this time; when you hear the sound of the engines getting fainter, you know that the plane is going away from you." Peggy gave them much material to study, wondering how far behind our three would be when this was over. (John's class never did catch up to him!) It was a sad time, however, for those who had loved ones in the thick of battle. We helped arrange prayer sessions and united worship services by all the churches of Lahore. After three weeks, a tenuous cease-fire was agreed upon. But clashes persisted. Things got really tense, and we knew if the cease-fire failed the intensity of fighting would explode. Thank God it held and at last we could remove the blackout curtains. This was literally a breath of fresh air! The government did not allow the foreign refugees to return until it was "safe." That meant a long delay. Some of the LAS teachers and AID families never did return; they had had it!

College classes were five weeks late in opening. Staff and students were on edge. Many of the students violently demonstrated on the streets of Lahore against India and the USA. It was rumored that cases of ammunition had been discovered in India marked USA. In fact, Pakistan would have suffered a worse fate had not President Nixon intervened and helped arrange the cease-fire. One morning we discovered in crude letters on the canal bridge: "Missionary, Go Home!" That fazed us a bit until the next morning. Someone had added, "Fly PIA!" (Pakistan International Airlines). We were under a lot of pressure to finish the course work – the college year was extended a month to provide extra time for personal review and teachers' assistance. That would mean Closure on the Fourth of July, in the midst of burning hot weather. It had been a difficult experience, but we survived and had been able to help lots of people through a dangerous time.

Chapter 28

A Scattered Family, FCC, Furlough, Sorrow,
Carrying On

Meanwhile in Iowa there were many changes. The closely knit neighborhoods were breaking up. Family members were moving and doing their own thing. This trend closely followed the prevalent demographic patterns in the USA following World War II. In 1963 Henry and Beulah sold their farm to the Willhoite family. Ray and Kathy started farming there and have continued to the present. Doctors blamed arteriosclerosis for Henry's loss of memory; today we know it was Alzheimer's Disease. They moved to a modern brick house in Carroll. Beulah cared for Henry and Cecil. She also continued her oil painting and generous hospitality. They became members of the Carroll Presbyterian church.

To appreciate the changes, the locations of the children should be noted. The Cliff and Elma children made these moves: Donald and Marcella moved to Rembrandt, Iowa, Patricia to Grand Island, Nebraska. Steve and Marie's son Morgan moved to Florida. The Henry Hoft families scattered far and wide: Norman and Dorothy to Fort Dodge; Peggy and I were in Pakistan; Richard and Merna were in Columbia, Missouri; Willard and Betty were in Huntsville, Alabama; Harrison and Helyn were in Virginia; and Hope and Frank Arnold were Presbyterian missionaries in Brazil. This was extremely difficult for Beulah to deal with. She wrote weekly letters to all and sent packages for birthdays and holidays, but she suffered from having her children so distant and scattered. Of course, we also missed them!

Peggy and I were enjoying having the children so close. They did well in LAS, made many friends, and were free to roam the FCC campus. That winter we visited the Gills who had moved to Sargodha. Magistrate Gill had been assigned a murder case involving a highly placed head of an elite family. That was a dangerous assignment.

We stayed the week, pampered with gourmet Pakistani foods, kinoo oranges, chicken curries, and roasted leftovers eaten by the fireplace or on the sunny verandah. It was good to be with those we considered family. Back in Lahore we also kept in touch with faculty members, the Urdu congregation, the ICF, the Joshuas and Biswases, friends at Naulakha Church, our Muslim friends, and countless others.

In the summer of 1966, the Joshuas and Biswases made a big decision. As Christians in Pakistan, they felt they were treated as second-rate citizens, suspected in the war of being pro-India. Having become convinced that they and their children had no worthwhile future in the country, they decided to emigrate to Canada, open to receive qualified people ready to help Canada make progress. Since brother Ivor had settled there, he was able to sponsor their moving to Toronto. They had sought our counsel, and we agreed that all things considered, it was the right move, except that we would miss them dearly. This called for a round of dinners and teas. Peggy and I invited them to a dinner on our back lawn. We illuminated the trees and shrubs, garlanded them, and honored them not only with food with all the trimmings but also a drama put on by Captain Ratcliff, Peggy, me, and our three. It was a grand party! Bill Ratcliff exposed Peggy's secret for determining who and how many guests to invite. He told how she consulted the Lahore telephone directory, choosing every tenth name. It was a successful and great send-off! Even our friends John and Mavis Sequeira with their children moved to Alexandria, Virginia. They were concerned about crime, drugs, and discrimination in the USA – they had heard the worst! We assured them it was not that bad. They wrote how they loved the USA.

Things were going well at the college. There were heavy loads of teaching, counseling, and relating to many of the twenty-five hundred students. The Forman Centenary, 1864-1964, was celebrated in appropriate fashion. Colorful tents, border screens, hundreds of rented chairs, and loads of food, tea, and sweets made for a grand festival. Many prominent guests were in attendance: President Ayub Khan, who gave a moving speech and donated two lakhs of rupees toward the construction of the College Hall, Governor of the Punjab, Amir M. Khan of Khalibad, Bishop Woolmer of the Anglican Church, Lt. General Nasir Ali Khan, distinguished alumni and guests, staff, students, and crowds of visitors and well-wishers. The Vice-Chancellor of the University of the Punjab, Dr. Hamid Ahmad Khan, sent his greeting. Among other remarks, he wrote, "I should like to refer to an important aspect of the educational ideals of Forman College. As a Christan institution in a Muslim country, it is a symbol of human fellowship, and represents a fusion of cultural values cutting across the frontiers of religious dogma...May I express the hope that Forman Christian College...may generate spiritual impulses which soothe the old strain of acrimony and heal the scars of centuries long past. All honor to the educational institution that helps us catch a glimpse of this larger vision of the brotherhood of man." That was well said!

In May 1967, we went on our second furlough, making stops at Athens and Istanbul. Visiting most of the important sites and enjoying the people of Turkey and Greece, we continued on to the USA. It was good to be back in Iowa among families and friends. We stayed with Henry and Beulah, who insisted we make that our home base for visiting the more than twenty churches that were supporting us with prayers and funds, and spending some time with relatives and friends. Much of this I did on my own to give Peggy and the children more quality time together. However, they accompanied me on many of those visits where we showed slides of our Pakistani work and shared our experiences. After a while the children knew that program by heart. In fact, one evening as we drove back to Carroll after a long day, they asked why we had changed the order of two of the slides!

In early July, as Peggy and I entered the Hoft house with arms loaded with groceries, Beulah fell to the floor of the living room with a groan. Peggy immediately called for an ambulance, which came within five minutes and took her to St. Anthony Hospital. We followed in our car – breaking a few speed limits. Beulah was diagnosed as having suffered a stroke. Thankfully, she recovered in a few days with no paralyzing effects. How providential we were there to help in that emergency. We all joined in to do all the work of housekeeping, meals, and caring for Peggy's mom. Daily she grew stronger, but we were very concerned about her welfare. Quite unexpectedly a problem arose. In September we had planned to move to Princeton where I had been invited to become Dr. Jurji's Teaching Fellow in Islamics. Hope, Esther, and John were to attend the Public Schools there. We had reserved a Seminary apartment. Peggy, of course, wanted to be near her mom and be her caregiver, and we all agreed with her on this. We changed our plans. Our three were enrolled in the Carroll Public School. We rented a house near the school, set up housekeeping there, and I drove all alone to Princeton. That was tough going to say the least. I dove into a busy routine of research and lecture preparation. The classes went well because I could speak

162

firsthand about Islam and Pakistan. Dr. Jurji and I became fast friends and colleagues. I also began to write about Pakistan and its relation to Christians.

Then Peggy telephoned me the afternoon of November 26, 1967 that her mom had suffered a fatal stroke in the hospital and passed away. I tried to say the right things and immediately made plane reservations to fly from Newark to Des Moines where Jimmy Cruchelow would drive me to Carroll. I drove the next morning to Newark, parked the car in the lot, and boarded the plane. It was a sorrowful time. Peggy, Norman, and Dick had made the arrangements with the Funeral Home, requested Rev. Peterson to officiate at the funeral, and informed all concerned. Many people came to the viewing. The church was packed with grieving relatives, neighbors, church members from many towns, friends of long standing, and the whole Hoft and Schlorholtz families. Beulah was buried in the Town Wall Lake Cemetery next to the grave of her infant son. A dearly beloved person had entered Glory! She had wholeheartedly cared for Henry with Alzheimer's and Cecil with Down's Syndrome. As sometimes happens, the caregiver is the first to die. She had loved and cared for her family with unstinted devotion and compassion.

Three days later I flew to Newark to find my car smothered with snow. Borrowing a shovel I dug it out. To my great surprise the car started, and I returned to Princeton to consult with Dr. Jurji and the Seminary administration. They consoled me and accepted my resignation with regrets. I drove back to Iowa to help Peggy and the family. There were many important decisions to be made. Who would care for Henry and Cecil? Where could they live? Who would close down the house and pack and dispose of the household furnishings? The answer was Peggy and me. After long discussions it was decided to move Henry and Cecil to Twilight Acres Nursing Home in Wall Lake. Many people knew them there, could visit them, and keep in touch with us. Dick was appointed as Executor of the Will and to visit them each month to pay the bills, check on how they were doing, and make adjustments as needed. This necessitated driving from Columbia, Missouri, a seven-hour drive, but he faithfully did that.

We tried to celebrate Christmas and the New Year. There was not much enthusiasm. I helped Peggy sort and pack, sending to each brother or sister what they would most like to remember Mom Hoft by. It was a mammoth job. The children went back to school, Stan attended Boone Community College, and I visited all the churches I could. Hope, Esther, and John finished the year with excellent marks. They fully appreciated how friendly and open their fellow classmates had been. In the closing of the school year, Hope took part in the school's drama program, which included performing the Can Can. This brought down the house! Peggy and I could only grin and bear it. Our four were getting well-adjusted to American ways. And how!

However, the furlough was about to end – time to return to LAS. Peggy wanted more time to finish the details and recuperate. She and John moved to Des Moines for five months. John loved the school there and started learning how to play the cornet. Hope, Esther, and I made our way to Pakistan, stopping over in Copenhagen, visiting the sites, including Tivoli Gardens and London where we saw "Fiddler On the Roof" in Her Majesty's Theater, and two other plays. We got back in time to brave the heat and to pick up with studies, my teaching, preaching, and everything else.

In January, Peggy and John returned to Pakistan via Toronto, London, and Moscow. She had bought airline tickets, made reservations, paid the In-Tourist fees, but in each city she was told that the Russian visas had not been finalized, though she was assured that the visas would certainly be in one of the cities en route. No luck even in London. Peggy and John decided to go anyway by flying to Geneva and then on to Moscow by Aeroflot, the Russian airline. They boarded the plane in Geneva without trouble. During the flight, Peggy met a teacher who taught American students in Moscow. When Peggy disclosed they had no visas, she exclaimed, "My God, you'll never make it!" She said she would watch to see if Peggy and John were cleared while she waited for a ride to the Embassy. Peggy waited to be last in line, walked up to the counter, and placed her documents on the desk. There was a pause, then the Officer said, " Oh, I see your visas were not signed!" Peggy explained how that had happened. And the Officer signed them! They spent a whole day in Moscow, visiting the Kremlin, Tolstoy's favorite chapel, and the like. When they visited a large Russian Orthodox church, John snapped a flash picture of the Epiphany service, creating a minor consternation in the congregation. Who would do such a thing! The friendly guide (really a security person), who had earlier warmed to John when he asked her to teach him the Russian alphabet, explained that he was an American boy who didn't know the customs. Peggy took advantage of the diversion to quietly place three Russian language Bibles she had brought with her in the Church's library (against the law!). Their accommodation was at the airport hotel and was strictly guarded. At breakfast the next morning Peggy wanted some tea. The server did not understand.

An Indian gentleman at the next table said, "Ask for chai." To Peggy's great astonishment the Russian word for tea was the same as in Urdu! They made it back to Geneva and on to Pakistan. What a great reunion we had! It took a long time for each of us to share what had happened in the last seven months.

It was difficult for Peggy with those sad memories. She missed her mom and her letters and communications. It takes time for grief to heal. But, we had to carry on and Peggy knew that. Patrick and Edna Joshua agreed to the pleas of their children in Canada to join them. They packed their things and moved to the 3 Mission Road hostel. We gave them many teas and dinners. One dinner in particular was complete with entertainment – yes by Bill, Peggy, and Al. It was a "roast par excellence!" Even Bishop Woolmer laughed and applauded our extravaganza. Again a great loss, but we had learned that one has to carry on.

Chapter 29

Family, Teamwork, 1971 War, A New Friend

Except for Stan, who was continuing college studies, we as a family united again dove into the heavily loaded activities of College, LAS, and Peggy maintaining our home's Christian radiance with her personal touch of creative faith and devotion. She again resumed driving our three to school, began coaching basketball for the LAS girls, and arranged trips to the Zoo, Fort, swimming pool at the German Vocational Institute (the FCC pool was without water), while continuing her teaching at Kinnaird College, Bible studies, and seminars. One special event was a three-day Retreat for Christan Lay People – living, working, worshiping, witnessing. It was designed to be an orientation for newcomers and a refresher for those who had been in Pakistan for some time.

The program outlined aids in overcoming culture shock, being an active Christian in a foreign land, appreciating the minority status of Pakistani Christians, staying informed of mission projects, and studying one's work attitude and habits/ethics. In the home situation, the program offered help in being open and friendly, aware of the living standard gap, handling domestic help problems, respecting cultural diversity, proper social behavior, and entertaining in the home. Peggy, with the committee, put in long hours of preparation and presentation. I was invited to speak between English classes – no use sitting around! The discussions were vital and illuminating. Christians from eight countries related to Pakistanis and vice versa. Many stated that the discussion of tolerance and intolerance had been most helpful. Another time this same group met to study "The Key to a Successful Marriage." I was asked to assist Peggy in sharing our marital experience. There were some embarrassing questions from the floor. Peggy shared how I was too lax with our children, leaving the discipline problems for her. I countered that too often I only saw our three at breakfast and supper. My days were too full to assist in discipline matters at the occurrence – she was possibly too quick in making decisions and taking action! We were also asked whether we had been excited about getting married. Peggy replied, "I could hardly wait to get in bed with Al!" Not anticipating such topics, I surely must have blushed!

In the summer of 1969, Peggy took Hope, Esther, and Lynn Mumby to Nepal by train from Amritsar to Varanasi where they saw burning funeral ghats, many temples, and thousands of pilgrims bathing in the Ganges River. By bus they ascended to Nepal. In Kathmandu, the capital, they lodged with Tom and Betty Mendies, who had organized an orphanage for fifty-five Tibetan refugee children. Their parents had been killed as China occupied Tibet. Tom and Betty drove the four to the Tibetan border to show them the Himalayas of Nepal. What a contrast with Pakistan! There were Hindus, Buddhists, and animists in a cultural setting much in contrast to the Islamic Republic of Pakistan, with its rigid monotheism. Wherever one looked there were temples, what we call idols, fervent pilgrims, and loads of tourists.

Back in Lahore, Hope and Esther continued their sitar and Kathak dancing lessons at the YWCA and piano lessons from Mavis Sequeira and Janet Barrett. Peggy met Mrs. Murat Khan and her five daughters. Mesme and Hope joined in a piano duet, Hope declaring she had finished first! We had many discussions about the issues percolating in Pakistan. We also met Maryam and Meral. Another time Hope, Esther, and Mesme performed an impressionist dance under Anese Majid Khan's direction at her home and school called the Esena Foundation. John also took piano lessons from Janet who was an accomplished soprano. She and her husband, David, taught English at FCC. Hope and Esther joined us in singing the Christmas and Easter portions of the Messiah.

It was time for Hope to complete college admissions, advised by Bob and Anita Bingham from Ipswich, Massachusetts. He was helping Bob Stanton, our treasurer, with legal work. Anita was a volunteer teacher at LAS. Hope had difficulty selecting the right college for her. Anita noted that Hope had not applied to Radcliffe/Harvard. We thought that was out of our league. Anita insisted that those colleges needed students like Hope, so she decided to go for it! (Note: She was accepted by Radcliffe/Harvard!) While we were in Lahore, busy with many things, Stan and Jo Ann Harmeyer decided to marry. They had fallen in love at the Starlight Ballroom in Carroll while Stan was in college and Jo Ann still in high school. How sad we were not able to be present and celebrate with them. This was one of the difficulties of being so far away from loved ones.

In the summer of 1970, we began a three-month furlough. We visited Hong Kong on our way to Japan. Peggy had carefully planned our travels. We visited Kyoto and the Osaka World's Fair, with its amazing exhibits from many countries, and flew on to Tokyo. Approaching the airport, the control tower put us into a long holding pattern, during which our three experienced severe ear pains and queasy stomachs. We spent several days there before continuing to the USA via Hawaii. Especially pleasant was relaxing on the beach and shopping at the Ala Moana open-air mall. Pointing to a plane overhead, John said, "Those poor people up there." We bought a car in Los Angeles and drove to Iowa, making stops at the Grand Canyon and the Painted Desert

Hoft Relatives and Friends, Black Hawk Lake

of Arizona. We made my sister Carrie's home our base. How grateful we were that she had invited us and how we enjoyed being with family again. We visited Henry and Cecil often and as many relatives, friends, and supporting churches as we could.

The summer was suddenly over. Peggy stayed on to assist Hope get started in college. Esther, John, and I headed toward Pakistan via Paris where we visited the famous Louvre Art Gallery, the Eiffel Tower, and other sites. Then on to Athens and an eventful time there, except by the second day both Esther and John had had their fill of museums and sites, preferring to feed the swans in a park near the Olympia Stadium! We needed that restful interlude before returning to LAS for them and for me resuming a busy schedule of teaching, preaching, and loads of committee meetings, conferences, and seminars. Peggy joined us later, after making sure that Hope was settled and going full steam. Soon all four were busily engaged in the daily round.

The next summer we took our month's vacation by visiting Patna in India and Kathmandu, Nepal. We stayed at Shanta Bhawan Hospital, one of the first established by the United Mission to Nepal. It had been a Rana Palace previously. We trekked to nearby villages and through the winding streets, admiring the exotic sites of that famous city. Someone told us we could view Mt. Everest from Kathmandu on a clear day, but that is not true. Checked in with the Mendies, we toured the UMN Headquarters and many intriguing museums, temples, and countless shops.

During the 1971 fall, there were rumblings of trouble brewing in West and East Pakistan. At the Partition in 1947 these two portions of Pakistan were distantly separated by India. It was difficult for the two to relate and govern. Following the 1970 national election, a power struggle developed between Zulfikar Ali Bhutto of West Pakistan and Sheikh Mujibur Rahman of East Pakistan. To make a long story short, the Bengalis declared independence, started a program of resistance, and sought to break the stranglehold of West Pakistan's colonial control imposed by the military. The Pakistan army conducted a "get tough" suppression. India increased its military adjacent to East Pakistan, fully aware that it was a dangerous situation. Then on December 3, 1971, West Pakistan fighter planes began pre-emptive strikes on airfields in northwestern India. The conflict exploded into a full-scale war with Indian forces opening strike fronts into East Pakistan and along the borders of West Pakistan. I mention all this because again I was appointed Air Raid Warden of FCC. This time we were more efficient during air raids and wailing sirens. We pulled the main power switch, causing a one hundred percent blackout! Park Johnson was block captain in the Empress Road section, I had the same designation. Some dear misinformed Pakistanis referred to us as "Block Heads," unaware of what that implied, I hope. Again we resisted the evacuation of all foreigners – we had a hunch that the war would be a short one.

Peggy was concerned about Captain Tajik who had been sent with his military contingent to East Pakistan, leaving his wife Promila and three children to cope as well as possible. Their home was nine miles from the Indian border. The shriek of fighters and heavy artillery caused them alarm. We took them into our home for the duration. The war ended on December 16, 1971, but Captain Tajik and ninety-seven thousand soldiers and civilians became prisoners of war. I wrote him a long letter of consolation, sharing that his family was well and safe. However, the Post Office refused to send it to India! There I stood explaining the need to help a POW in northern India. What to do? A "hippie couple" approached me, having heard my plea, offering to post the letter in India the next day after they had crossed the border. I gave them the letter with profound thanks and more than the required postage! Two years later when Tajik returned to Lahore, he embraced and thanked me for that letter. In the POW camp he had been threatened with cruel actions for "pretending" to be a Christian. He related that what saved his life was proof provided by my letter signed, "Your brother in Christ, Al Schlorholtz." That humbled me!

In the summer of 1972, we had another short home leave. We were proud that Esther, too, had been admitted to Radcliffe/Harvard! I shall never forget going through customs at Boston Terminal. There we were with all our luggage plus Esther's sitar, which was promptly searched because others had hidden many things in that big gourd! They pulled out every one of Peggy's saris used to protect the gourd from being broken. Just ahead of us was a young man with a wrist zip bag. To our surprise he was whisked away by security. We asked why? The custom officer replied, "He tried smuggling one hundred ten wrist watches into Boston." Dear reader, you have been warned! Esther settled in, we met Hope, visited Bob and Anita Bingham in Ipswich, and as many supporting churches as possible. Peggy stayed on to ensure that Esther was going to be okay. Really I think she hated to say goodbye so soon. John and I headed directly back to Lahore.

Peggy joined us a month later and again we got busy. During the summer of 1973, Peggy got a call from Begum Bilquis Sheikh, who said that Marie Old from Gujranwala had called her and given her our telephone number. Bilquis had recently moved to Lahore from Wah, north of Rawalpindi. She had become a Christian. Being a member of one of the three most prominent Muslim families in Pakistan, this courageous woman had caused quite an uproar. Bilquis and Peggy introduced each other on the phone and a few hours later Peggy visited Bilquis, living with her son,

Khalid. They hit it off as if they had known each other for years. Peggy did not waste time. She asked if it was true that Bilquis had met Jesus in a dream, then point-blank asked, "How did you come to know the Lord?" Bilquis related how six years previously God had made Himself known to her through first a dream in which she saw Jesus and John the Baptist, then another dream in which she had smelled an exquisite perfume. She dared to visit local missionaries to obtain a Bible and was given a Phillips' translation of the New Testament by the Mitchells who also explained references in the New Testament pertaining to Jesus, John the Baptist, and that the perfume reference was in II Corinthians 2:14, where it is recorded "...makes our knowledge of Him spread throughout the world like a lovely perfume." Bilquis had experienced an intense struggle over how she as a devout Muslim could find the reality and Presence of God. She knew her Koran, now she read the entire New Testament. Briefly, here is a summation of her search. Bilquis's grandson, Mahmud, suffered from severe earaches. She took him to the Holy Family Hospital in Rawalpindi. There Dr. Santiago, from the Philippines, saw a Bible on the bedside table. She asked Bilquis how that could be? Bilquis told her about her struggle and quest. The doctor gently asked, "Have you ever made your prayers personal? Pray to Him as you would relate to your own father." In the morning, Mahmud had fully recovered. They returned to Wah. Bilquis questioned how a Muslim could call God Father, but when in prayer she did, the Presence of God filled her being. She worshiped Jesus as her Lord and Savior. (For a firsthand account of Bilquis's quest, forbidding consequences, the Reality of her faith and Christian journey, read *I Dared to Call Him Father*, the book which she wrote with the help of Richard H. Schneider.)

Peggy had listened with rapt attention. Taking this beloved Christian's hand she said, "Oh how I wish you would come to America with me! Soon I am traveling there to get my son John admitted into Northfield Mt. Hermon School. How the churches would love your testimony! I'll be there for four months. Let me arrange for you to speak in many churches there." This flabbergasted Bilquis who promised to pray about it. The next morning, a note was delivered to Bilquis: "Have you prayed yet?" signed Peggy. Bilquis knew that she would have to bid farewell to her dearly loved Pakistan, but was this how God was planning for her future since she had been totally boycotted by her Muslim relatives? How could she find the money for fares? The law was she could only take five hundred dollars out of the country and Mahmud two hundred fifty dollars. Peggy invited her to our home for a visit. During their conversation, Dr. Christy Wilson's name was mentioned. The Afghanistan

Government had dismantled the church built for foreign Christians and commanded that Christy leave! At that moment the phone rang and Peggy answered the call. Returning to Bilquis she asked, "Would you believe that was Dr. Wilson who is in Lahore!" The next day he came to celebrate a great reunion and to hear about her conversion. Peggy explained the problem about funds. Dr. Wilson said that he would consider this and telephone in a few days. He called with some great news – he had contacted Dr. Bob Pierce of Samaritan's Purse, who would sponsor her and her grandson. Wow! Only seven days remained before the flight. Khalid helped her sell her house, get an Income Certificate, and make travel plans.

Peggy and John flew to New Delhi to shop, enplaned, and picked up Bilquis and Mahmud at the Karachi Airport. They were on their way to America. Bilquis related to Peggy and John that years ago she had had a strange dream of floating over a country filled with churches. She could not identify which country, but had visited London and seen churches there. Peggy surmised that soon she would see those churches in the USA! They made a safe flight and helped John get settled into his school in the Berkshires of Massachusetts. For four months they toured many churches in the East, including those that were supporting our mission in Pakistan. What a pair of evangelists they were! The congregations heard and were amazed how God had called to faith, hope, and love this remarkable woman from a different world. They thanked God the Father for His blessing and mercies.

In the ensuing years, we became acquainted with some of Bilquis's family: daughter, Dr. Manawar (Tooni), and her husband, Sher Khan, their two children, Omar and Tanya, who lived in Rawalpindi, and Khalidah, Tooni's sister, who lived in Nairobi, Kenya. We invited them to Lahore and our FCC home and visited them when we were in Murree. They were staunch Muslims. This did not matter; they had acquiesced to their mother's conversion knowing that it was about personal faith and devotion to God. Bilquis had fully shared with all of them her testimony. There was nothing for them to do but accept reality. After Bilquis's tour of the eastern part of the USA, Dr. Pierce invited her to speak in California, where his World Vision organization was located. In fact, since she was so cordially invited to speak in many places on the West Coast, she made her home in Thousand Oaks, California. Peggy and I often visited her and Mahmud there while on furloughs. She missed her garden in Wah, but created a hillock in the backyard filled with fruit trees, flowers, and shrubs.

Peggy and I thanked God for such a rare experience. We learned that following her conversion the Pakistan government sent Magistrate A.P. Gill to investigate whether Begum Sheikh had done this for political reasons. He reported that she had not. President Ayub Khan then visited her to hear firsthand the conversion experience. He warned everyone not to harm her, wishing that all could be as close to God as she!

Chapter 30

Focus, Loads of Responsibilities, A Changed Situation, Farewells

During the spring of 1977, Dr. Pritchard conducted our PDIs (Personnel Development Interviews), which George Tewksbury called Pretty Darned Personal Interviews. However, this gave Peggy and me an opportunity to scrutinize and evaluate all our previous work in Pakistan. Twenty-three fascinating, gloriously inspiring years had raced on since Peggy and I, with our children – born and unborn – arrived in Pakistan to begin a new life as witnesses and servants of our Lord. Where had the years gone? It seemed as if we had arrived a few months earlier in this exciting land of contrasts with its heat and cold, its droughts and floods, its affluent elite and countless poor, its generous hospitality and suspiciousness of missionaries, its desire for development and those who guarded the past, its fervent faith in Allah and those who used it as a weapon of hateful actions, its magnificent edifices and the humble mud huts with plastered roofs, its innumerable hopeful children with flashing eyes from being educated and those with dull despairing globes grown sickly and lackluster from malnourishment and lack of opportunity, its modern water towers and village women and girls so straight and graceful wending their way home with two and even three water pots balanced on their heads, its honest shopkeepers and those who adulterated products, its students who loudly chanted the lesson as they memorized the content and the privileged few who learned to use those highly qualified intellects, its women and girls behind screened windows, veils, and walled-in houses and the chic, flowing elegance of those allowed to become educated and who enjoyed a measure of freedom to become efficient modern mothers and careerists...the list could go on and on, but it is hoped you grasp the contrasts and are able to read between the lines.

The PDI summarized that "People who know and relate to Peggy gladly acknowledge her devotion to her family and the evidence of this is in the character and personality of their children, her vital commitment to Christ, her thoughtfulness, friendliness, and capacity for arduous work in teaching and helping so many in need. She is a most gifted teammate with her husband." My report was "Al is an extraordinarily thorough and diligent worker. Although he may accept too many routine tasks, he works efficiently and dependably. He is notably friendly. With the variety of tensions under which he has been working his sense of humor is particularly valuable. He remains stable under trying circumstance. He is persistent. He is usually optimistic, but sometimes in recent months this attitude has been very difficult to maintain. He is friendly and enthusiastic in his personal relationships." Peggy and I could have added many more qualities, but modesty prevails! We loved Pakistan and its people, its culture, and the friends who tolerated us. We missed our four and prayed they were well and excelling in their studies. Hope and Esther wowed Harvard friends with sitar music and Kathak dancing. John had gone out for track, learning to pole vault. He certainly was getting up in the world!

For the record, I will share here, if I may, what those heavy responsibilities were: Chaplain of FCC; a teacher of English, Sociology, and Biblical studies; Pastor of the International Christian Fellowship; Secretary of the Technical Services Association (to provide continuity after Elsa and Friedel Peter retired to Switzerland), a social welfare enterprise that employed and trained over one thousand women and girls in shadow-work embroidery and knitting in thirty village centers; Chairman of Planning and Development at the Christian Technical Training Center in Gujranwala assisting Director Ken Old in thoroughly redefining, rebuilding, and newly equipping a center for two hundred underprivileged young men learning vocational skills, upgrading the staff, creating new courses of instruction, establishing a hostel complex for staff and students, and shaping future plans for the initiation of light industrial enterprises by graduates; Convener of the Administrative Council of Presbyterian Property in Pakistan to form a Trust to protect properties from being nationalized; Executive Secretary of the Association of Christian Colleges in Pakistan; Co-Rep in Dr. Bob Tebbe's absence to diplomatically reconcile and calm factions and "parties" in the National Church; and helping to form a Society for Community Development encouraging Christians to initiate self-help and development programs, necessitating many conferences, seminars, and training sessions, sometimes giving five lectures in one day to the group forming a self-help organization and setting long-terms goals and short-term objectives relating to development. There were also many committees with the West Pakistan Christian Council, as a consultant with wide-ranging skills.

But, the situation in Pakistan was changing. In 1972 Prime Minister Zulfikar Ali Bhutto nationalized all Christian Colleges and Schools in Pakistan, including staff and properties, and made Urdu the medium of instruction rather than English. Things began to deteriorate; the standards were lowered. Staff rosters had to be sent to the Education Department, and many teachers were more interested in their pay than teaching. I was listed as Prof. A.A. Schlorholtz the first three months, but then came the revised list: I had become Abdul Aziz Schlorholtz! (The name Abdul Aziz translates as Beloved Servant.) There followed many student strikes and protest demonstrations related to the political unrest. One surprise was our FCC hostel students demanding a mosque in every hostel. This rattled the Principal who sent cables to our New York City Board for advice – they had little to offer. Fortunately, a much respected Staff Muslim, Prof. Mazzur Ali Khan, said he would solve the problem. The very next morning the students withdrew their demand! When asked what he had done, he replied, "I merely asked the students, who like to carouse at night and sleep in late, how they would like being awakened by the call to prayer before sunrise and four other times during the day?" Problem solved! A later demand was that the study of English should be in Urdu. That is when I began having misgivings about continuing at FCC.

That summer Peggy was attacked by malaria and paratyphoid. We went to Murree where I discovered the only food she liked was roasted chicken. Daily, I brought one from the bazaar. Slowly she was responding to medicines and my expert care, following the doctor's orders. Then we received a telegram from Lahore. After ten inches of rain in one night, our #44 house had been flooded, the tunnel and basement room filled with water. A tree root had punctured the tunnel. I immediately returned to Lahore and tried to salvage what I could, but everything stored downstairs had been destroyed. The verandah foundation opposite the living room gave way, cracking the floors in the house. We had to move to #20 FCC, leaving the house we had come to think of as our own and those beautiful chrysanthemums and fruit trees so loyally cared for by Sadiq and Barkat. The children were devastated on hearing this bad news; now #44 would only be a memory.

That summer Peggy and I decided to apply for transfer to another country in Asia. Things were not working out so well with the newly appointed Principal, the low morale of the Staff, merely coaching students to learn what would be on the final exam, changed attitudes – the whole situation did not bode well for continuation.

176

Also we had worked ourselves out of a job by preparing Pakistanis to replace us, giving them an opportunity to serve in our place. We had to decide whether to continue and write long exaggerated reports to the New York City Board, or to make a clean break. Having consulted our superiors near and far, it became clear that we should move on. With the help of Dr. Pritchard, letters of application and our resumes were sent to ten Asian countries. After about a month word came that we were needed in all ten! There were openings in Iran, Botswana, Hong Kong, Indonesia, Korea, Nepal, India, UNICEF, and Japan.

We received a letter from Odd and Tulis Hoftun from Norway, requesting hospitality on their long drive from Norway to Nepal. They were to pass through Lahore. One afternoon they arrived in their van; their sons Erik and Martin were with them. Peggy had made full preparation with fresh sheets, hot showers, and loads of Pakistani foods. We had a great time sharing our life stories. They asked us many questions about our work in Pakistan, our views on many subjects, and how much we loved Pakistan. The next morning we guided them to the road leading to Amritsar and sent them on their way. We commented what a great family they were and so dedicated to mission work. Peggy and I continued working at FCC and Kinnaird and planning our move when the time would come. The big mystery was which country we should choose to work in. Where was the Lord leading us and opening the door to further witness and service in Christ's Kingdom? We gave those issues lots of prayer and serious thought.

Predictably, there were many who questioned our leaving – we had a lot of explaining to do. We tried not to be negative and spoke of how many opportunities had opened up and how qualified Pakistanis could replace us, etc. Imagine our surprise when we received a letter from Gordon Ruff, Executive Director of the United Mission to Nepal, informing us that we had been accepted by the UMN Executive Committee to join the work in Nepal. We were to move to Kathmandu as soon as we could. What a relief! Now we would be able to really start packing and make preparations to shift to Nepal. Have you ever fully listed all items and their value as we were required to do, including absolutely every last one? The paperwork was exhausting! In "The Pakistan Times" we found an ad stating that a new Moving Company had been cleared to transport things from Pakistan to India and Nepal. They were located in Kabul! We telephoned them and started negotiations on costs, security, and the like. When they assured us they could do the job, we made a deal. We were to pack our possessions and have them moved to Rawalpindi for transport preparation at their branch office there. This we did; it had taken a great deal of effort. While our things were being made ready, I went to Islamabad to the Indian Embassy for visas, instructions, and reassurance that our plan and method of transfer were in order. They assured me that at the border, our truck would be inspected, approved, and sealed. There would be no trouble. (Famous last words!)

Peggy and I stayed at the guest house at Kinnaird College. Jane Subha Khan was there as a hostel warden. Everyone made us feel welcome and comfortable. We visited our many friends. There was a seemingly endless round of teas, lunches, and dinners. Our fellow missionaries arranged an all-morning farewell at the FCC Educational Building which we had built in 1966-67, complete with air conditioners. It was a two-story fired brick construction with a large hall on the top floor and classrooms on the lower. In the heat of summer we had used it for ICF and the Urdu congregation. About thirty attended the farewell with lots of roasting, shared experiences, and questions as to why we were leaving Pakistan. Some made us feel as if we had given up on Pakistan and the National Church. We again explained the reasons we had for transfer and reminded people that Jim Tebbe was already Pastor of ICF. We described UMN and its work in Nepal. To sum things up, Ken Old shared how we had worked together at the Christian Technical Training Center and how successful it was now that the whole place had been upgraded. He related how the Planning committee of five members were to do the planning and to implement the plans but that many times only Al and he attended the meetings. That was when things really got accomplished! He shared the example of needing the permission of the New York City Board to build the new Staff housing. We waited and waited for word to come. Our committee finally cabled the Board saying, "With confidence that permission would arrive by October 1, we would begin to build the housing on that date!" When permission finally came much later than October 1, we were already making good progress on the construction. Then Ken said something I will forever remember. He said that Al was the best committee member he had ever worked with and that Al had the gift of bringing out the best from everyone in any group, bar none! That was very kind of him.

The large van from Kabul was to pick up our things, including me, by the middle of January. Day after day passed and no truck. I telephoned Kabul, and they assured me it was only a matter of a few days. Peggy, not planning to ride in the van, had gone on ahead to Kathmandu where she waited for word that I was on the way. She stayed at the UMN guest house, making many new friends and learning about the different projects at work in Nepal. She waited and waited, as did I. Because of the long uncertain delay she finally returned to the USA. One day, as I was chatting with Mira Phailbus, telling her about my problem of the truck not arriving, she advised me to call her brother, a Brigadier General in the Army. He would surely be able to help. I phoned him in Rawalpindi and told him how I was being kept waiting for the van to come for our things. He asked for the number to call and said he would soon get back to me. Within a half hour he called to report that the next Monday morning at 8:00 am sharp the truck would be in Lahore with all our freight on board. He then said, "They may not fear God, but they do fear the Pakistan Martial Law Army!"

I hurriedly said farewell to close friends and to Esther who had recently taken leave from Radcliffe/Harvard to spend a term of Urdu study in Lahore sponsored by the University of California at Berkeley. Early Monday morning, Bob Tebbe drove me to the meeting place where we found the large truck waiting for me right on schedule! After picking up the checks from the Treasurer's office on Empress Road, we headed to Wagah to clear Pakistani Customs and cross for the Indian border. The next chapter relates what happened on the way from Lahore, through the northern tip of India, and on to Nepal.

Part III: Our Eleven Years with the United Mission to Nepal

Chapter 31

From Pakistan to Nepal Via India by Truck, and Home Leave

The moving van was in reality a huge, twenty-five-foot-long semitrailer, the kind used to transport large households from Afghanistan to the Middle East and much larger than the ornately painted open-bed trucks commonly seen on the roads of Pakistan in those days. One had to grasp a handle and pull oneself up two steps to the cabin seat. It was an impressive rig. We were sitting on top of the world! Nearing the Wagah border, I felt apprehensive never having liked custom inspections in our travels. Upon arrival, I climbed down, briefcase in hand, with that fat list of items on board. I showed it to the Custom Officer on the Pakistan side, and he ushered me to his office. Now what? Offering me a seat, he casually said, "Let them do the inspection and paperwork. Have some tea and biscuits." We chatted. Half an hour later, they brought the documents for his signature. He said that I could go on my way. I thanked him for his courtesy and the prompt inspection. He smiled and said, "Thank you for getting my son through FC College in First Division. You were his English teacher weren't you?" I was awed to say the least, admitting that it had been a pleasure to teach such a fine student. As I boarded the truck again, I wondered which of those hundreds of students had been his son. At that moment I could not recall which one, but I had taught English!

We lumbered across no-man's-land and reached the Indian customs. Officials there were not happy to see us. They inquired what was in the truck. Showing them the fat list and also a letter from the Indian Embassy, I related how embassy personnel had said there would be no problem. After a close inspection of our things, they had assured me, the truck's doorways and any openings would be sealed and we could be on our way. Custom officials did not agree and impounded the truck, saying this was not the route to take to Nepal. You send the things to Karachi, transport them by ship to Bombay (now Mumbai), and then ship them by train and trucks to the Nepal border. What could I do? The driver, his buddy, and I took a taxi to town and booked into a small hotel. I made a long-distance call to the American Embassy in New Delhi, explained what had happened, and implored their help. Since it was Saturday afternoon, they could not deal with my problem until Monday morning when the India Foreign Affairs Office would open. I took a fast train to New Delhi and a motor rickshaw to the Methodist Guest House, where Peggy and I had stayed. Sunday morning, I called the Embassy. It was fortunate that an emergency officer was on duty who listened to my story and commiserated with me. He said he would call the Indian Office at 8:00 am Monday morning and that I should stay where I was by the telephone.

Monday morning at 8:30, the officer called and said they had gotten permission for me to free the truck and travel to Nepal – on condition I agree that this was a once in a lifetime exception, never to be repeated! Thanking him and the embassy staff, I hurried to the Air India Office. The ticket desk person informed me that without a reservation it was impossible to fly to Amritsar. No seat was available! I explained my predicament and pleaded for a seat. She sent me to her superior in Management, an attractive woman dressed in a sari behind an awesome desk. Again I related my story. She listened attentively and agreed with me that something had to be done, because I had suffered enough. She phoned Air Flight Center, but was told there was not one empty seat available. All were sold out. I heard her explain that the plane was too small for extra passengers who needed transport. Then, smiling, she thanked the person for agreeing to send a larger plane. Turning to me she said that I could buy the ticket and board the plane, which would leave in an hour. I profusely thanked her and assured her that I would always warmly remember India due to her gracious, efficient heart of compassion and expertise. I was on my way.

Arriving at the Amritsar terminal, I took the fastest taxi I could find to Customs. The official in charge had been informed by Foreign Affairs and said that we were free to take the truck. Then he hesitated a moment before saying, "However, the truck keys are locked in a file cabinet and the man with the key has gone home. We open at

10:00 am." This meant another night in the hotel. The driver was getting impatient, but I paid for the hotel rooms and food. He felt a little better. The next morning, we picked up the keys to the truck and headed toward New Delhi, where we checked into a hotel for the night, because two friends of the driver wanted to travel with us to Nepal. We spent the next day and night in New Delhi while they obtained their visas for Nepal.

The next morning, we were on our way to Agra and points beyond. It was a fascinating trip. Everyone swerved out of the way to let that monster pass! We did not stop to view the Taj Mahal. About a hundred kilometers beyond Agra, we were ordered to stop by the Police. A long line of trucks was parked there. The trucks in front of us were departing in groups of ten, with an armed guard in every other vehicle. We asked what was going on. An officer told us that two days earlier, a loaded truck had been highjacked. The driver and his helper had been killed, the truck emptied and smashed in the dangerous area ahead of us, famous for its bandits. I recalled that we had been delayed in New Delhi for two days. If events had unfolded differently, we might have been the ones who were robbed. I thanked the Lord for His gracious timing and care.

We proceeded in the convoy of trucks, with a Policeman holding his .303 rifle between his legs, until we reached a point where we were stopped so that a relief Policeman could join us. This was repeated four times, or every twenty kilometers. We noted that similar groups of trucks were passing us in the opposite direction going toward Agra. We arrived at Kanpur, a large steel factory center, then drove on through Lucknow, Gonda, and to Gorakhpur, where the driver discovered a burst tire, the inner one of the two. Since it was late, we ate our curry, rice, and spiced veggies. We slept in the truck, with a window slightly open to have enough oxygen. I thought it a good idea until the next morning when I discovered quite a number of mosquitoes had found a picnic table on my arms and forehead! The men labored for two hours to change that tire. Finally, we arrived in Nautanway, the Indian border town between India and Nepal.

At Indian Customs, I got down from the truck and showed the officials the letter from the Indian Embassy in Islamabad and the fat file containing the contents list. They insisted that they would have to break the seals to see whether all the items were "intact and present." This is when I began to argue, trying to convince them that since the truck was sealed, all the items were there. If the seals were to be broken, the Nepal Customs would accuse me of opening the seals and disposing of the items so securely protected. This debate went on for some time, but finally they saw my point and permitted us to move on to Nepal Customs. Officials there were duly impressed by the size of the truck and proceeded to break the seals and check the contents according to the fat list. Finally, they were satisfied. Learning that I was with the United Mission to Nepal, they gave us permission to proceed to Butwal.

We made an impressive entrance into the Development Central Services (DCS). They had never seen such a large truck! I introduced myself and the driver, shared with them who I was, and related how glad I was to become the newest member of the UMN. They told us where to place the truck and hired a crew, mostly women, to unload our things into the receiving freight room. Informed that no one had ever brought so many personal belongings into Nepal, I explained that Peggy and I had worked in Pakistan for twenty-four years. I had not realized how simple life in Nepal was. Since the Nepali roads and trails could not accommodate that large truck, our things would have to be stored in Butwal until further notice. I had the local treasurer pay the workers and reimbursed him. We said farewell to the driver and truck. The two men with visas were disappointed not to see Kathmandu. I was escorted up the hill to the Butwal Guest House, where I would lodge for two days before taking an Express Bus to Kathmandu (KTM).

My stay afforded an opportunity to learn that Butwal was the center for technical, industrial, and business sectors, a series of seven factories where young Nepali men were trained on the production line. After they had passed basic training, they were paid for their work. This center had been established by a man and his wife from Norway, Odd and Tulis Hoftun. Were they ever impressed when I told them that I had met the family in Lahore! Briefly stated, the Hoftuns had been recruited to build the Mission Hospital in Tansen. He had recruited and trained many young men to help in the construction. Many of them from the Hills of Nepal had never seen a pliers or screwdriver! After that work was completed, the question arose what these young men could do in the future. Odd put his ideas on paper and presented them to the Mission. They studied and approved his proposal and named it a Technical School. The Government rejected this saying, "No more Mission schools." Odd did not give up. He rewrote the Plan calling it an Institute of Technology and Industrial Development. With his creative genius and farsighted vision, he had conceived and devised a Plan never before initiated in Nepal by UMN or the Government for technical/industrial/business and economic development! It took a long time to convince the Government to accept this innovation, but finally permission was granted and the green light was given by UMN. More will be shared about the Hoftuns and Butwal in later chapters. Let this suffice for now.

Two days later I took the Express Bus headed for KTM on the recently finished paved road between the Border and Pokhara to the north. We passed Tansen and many villages on that mountainous, winding, narrow road. The rivers ran close to the road and sped down the gorges. From Pokhara, we headed east to KTM. It had been an education for me to become acquainted with this newly adopted land where Peggy and I were to begin an exciting challenge. In KTM, I found the UMN Headquarters and registered at the Guest House. I introduced myself as Peggy's husband; everyone had met her and had been duly impressed! Having made reservations to fly from KTM to Delhi to London to New York to Boston, I was homeward bound after two days.

Peggy had been awaiting my arrival. She had arranged for us to stay at the Salvation Army Lighthouse. Since the General was on a tour, we enjoyed his comfortable apartment. They even requested me to preach at the worship service! It was great to visit Hope who was completing her senior year at Radcliffe/Harvard. She had spent two years visiting India for "cultural exposure" and doing Sanskrit study. I think her future husband had something to do with her introduction to India. Stephen had studied Sanskrit and Indian Studies as an undergraduate at Harvard. As a graduate, he was working on his Ph.D. in Philosophy. He had noticed Hope in a class they shared and was determined to meet her. One day, thinking he saw Hope in the distance, he called out, "Hope! Hope!" When she didn't respond, he hurried to catch up with her while still calling out her name. She still didn't respond. Finally, when he reached her he asked why she wasn't responding. She replied emphatically, "Because I'm not Hope!" It was Esther. When he suggested that she must be Hope's twin, she did allow that she had a sister named Hope. Mindful of admonitions by her sister, she refused to give him Hope's address or phone number but did say that she would tell Hope he wanted to see her. And, of course, Hope and Stephen did eventually get together. We were proud that Esther had graduated the year before (1977). We were sorry to miss out on her graduation, but you know the circumstances of our 1977. We also visited John at Hamilton College in New York State. He was in his junior year and doing very well in his studies and activities. He especially appreciated Professor

Williams and his family. John was leading the class in creative writing. He humbly told us that it was a little unfair as all he had to do was describe the sights, sounds, smells, and culture of Pakistan. We were impressed how he had grown and matured. It had not been easy to finish his last two years of high school and go on to college, with his parents on the other side of the world. Esther applied for a job in Nashville at Vanderbilt University. Needing a character reference, she gave the name of the jeweler/clock repairman in Boston for whom she and Hope had worked to earn what was not covered by scholarships. Traveling the subways, they had delivered repaired items and brought things that needed repair to his shop. When the prospective employer called him, he initially inquired what Esther was being hired to do but then quickly said, "Whatever it is, make her president!"

Peggy and I also visited our supporting churches in the eastern U.S., sharing what their prayers and funds had made possible. Peggy always wore a sari, which evoked a lot of questions as to how one puts on a six-yard-long piece of cloth! We had lots to share about Pakistan and our new assignment in Nepal. Of course, we visited Bob and Anita Bingham in Ipswich. They were so kind to our three, slipping a bill into their hands just in case it was needed!

At the end of May we attended Hope's graduation from Harvard. It was a rainy, misty day for commencement on Harvard's spacious Yard. The main speaker was Alexander Solzhenitsyn who delivered his profound address in Russian. The spontaneous translator did a marvelous job, I surmise, not knowing any Russian! Hope graduated cum laude; we were very proud of her. Anita Bingham sat with us, and we recalled filling in those college applications years before in Pakistan. That seemed a long time ago. How thankful we were that Anita had encouraged Hope to apply to such a revered University. Too soon the time arrived for Peggy and me to return to Nepal – there was much to do including Language School again! I have to admit that at fifty-five years of age that would be difficult and demanding for me. Peggy being two years younger would adapt more readily.

Chapter 32

Language Study, Orientation, Assignment, Vacation in Pakistan

Peggy and I returned to Nepal in early July 1978. We booked into the UMN Guest House, Asha Niketan (the Abode of Hope), which was down the street from the UMN Headquarters. This guest house was one among many to accommodate personnel visiting on official business, doing language study, and the like. Each Project had one because there were no hotels in the villages or small towns. The hostess was in charge of the whole establishment, including a cook, housekeepers, and other help. What a relief it was not to have to set up our home at this point! We were registered for the Language School session to study Nepali, a six-month program. On our first morning, we were joined by a young bachelor from the UK who got our attention by saying, "Al and Peggy, did you ever think at your age you would be studying Nepali?" That didn't make us feel any younger, but we were getting acquainted with newly appointed UMN people. In our class of seven, there were a German couple, a couple from England, and a single woman from Germany. The Nepali teacher began by teaching us the alphabet written in the Devanagari script. It was entirely new to us, nothing like Urdu at all.

It took some time and effort to master the script and to read the phrases and sentences. Urdu is read from right to left, Nepali is read left to right as with English. It was an entirely new form of communication with only a few Urdu equivalents. Pronunciation was another hurdle with hard Ds and Ts, aspirated and non-aspirated letters. Word lists and model sentences were a challenge. We had four class hours in the mornings and two hours of tutoring in the afternoon. Slowly, we made progress and began to use our new form of expression at local shops, while making excursions to the city, and at worship services at Gyneshwar Church, which were conducted each Saturday morning according to the Nepal custom. It was a great blessing to sing the Psalms and

Hymns in Nepali. There were no pews or chairs. We sat cross-legged for almost two hours on the carpeted floor. Early arrivals braced their backs against the wall which afforded some comfort. The men sat on the left side of the room, the women on the right. The large meeting room was packed with enthusiastic worshipers. Pastor Robert was a gifted preacher. Once in a while, he would make the point in English, knowing he had some illiterates in the audience.

Since Nepal at that time was the only Hindu Kingdom in the world, many references were made to Sanskrit-derived vocabulary and Hinduism in language class. One day, our teacher remarked that Nepal had thirty million gods. This I accepted as an example of the multiplicity of gods and spirits in Hinduism. However, Cliff, an engineer from the UK, began questioning that number, wondering if it was exactly that number, or an approximation. Things began to get complicated until Cliff was informed that he would understand this after he had been in Nepal for some time. There were weekly/monthly exams to check our progress, or the lack of it. Peggy and I did quite well. We had learned that one had to concentrate on hearing, inculcating, and using what one had studied. It wasn't easy, but with determination and effort we would do our best to understand the culture and people of Nepal.

To increase our understanding and appreciation of Nepal and the UMN, orientation lectures were presented by senior missionaries in the conference room at Headquarters. These were most informative. They shared that Nepal was a small country squeezed between Tibet and China to the north and India to the east, south, and west. About eighty-eight percent of the population was Hindu, nine percent Buddhist, two percent Muslim, and there were about fifteen hundred Nepali Christians. Until 1951, Nepal had been closed to the outside world, and no Nepali Christians or missionaries were allowed to be in the country. For over a hundred years there had been despotic rule by the Rana Prime Ministers and feudal landlords, resulting in Mass Poverty and painful living conditions for the people. There were no hospitals or schools – not even a radio was allowed! That explains why until 1951 Nepal was in isolation from the world and extremely underdeveloped. There was severe agitation and unrest in the country, probably influenced by the Independence movement in India and other nations of the world. Pressure kept building until King Tribhuvan was brought back from exile in India to establish His Majesty's Government which would democratically govern Nepal and manage the public works. Many appointed Councils attempted to run the country but failed. The King died in

1954. His son, King Mahendra, established a structured absolute monarchical government with non-political participation of local leadership. He continued opening Nepal to the world.

In other sessions of orientation, we learned how God opened Nepal to the Good News in Christ. For many years, the Missions working in India had prayed for the Nepali people and the opportunity to engage in mission work. That is all they could do until there was an open door. During the years 1948 to 1952, Dr. Bob Fleming made visits to Nepal on behalf of the University of Chicago and the National Geographic Society to study the birds there. He had noted the poverty and the need for medical help. To make a long story short, Dr. Bob, his wife Dr. Beth, and their two children planned a trip into the Butwal/Tansen area – he to watch birds and she to do what she could in medicine. They were joined by Dr. Carl Friedericks, his wife, Betty Ann, who was a nurse, and their three children. They were well received in Tansen and were able to rent a large house. In six weeks they treated fifteen hundred patients! Before leaving, some of the town leaders implored them to return to start a new hospital there. Even the Governor urged them to open a permanent hospital. He also began to influence government officials to aid him in getting the Nepal Government to grant permission. It took about three years before actual work was begun on a hospital in Tansen and on a small clinic in KTM. This was how the door to Nepal had finally opened.

The final month of language study was done in the village setting. Peggy and I took a bus to Pokhara where we settled into one room of a Nepali woman's house. She had a small son. This was primitive living. The bore hole latrine was at the edge of a nearby millet field, the outside cold shower which we used after dark was adjacent to the kitchen, there was no electricity, and the floor was packed dirt. The first night as we lay in our sleeping bags, I became aware that we were not alone. Rats kept climbing over our bags. I made sure Peggy was covered and safe, but did not wake her because as you may remember from an earlier chapter, rats were not her favorite animals. The next morning I gathered some stones "to make our room more attractive," and covered all those holes. Having successfully coped with the situation, I never saw another rat. Only after returning to KTM did I tell Peggy.

During that month, we ate thirty-eight consecutive meals of boiled rice, lentil soup, and seasoned veggies. For a real treat, our hostess one evening treated us to a curry of minnows complete with heads and everything else from the rice field channels. When she inquired whether we liked them, we politely nodded our heads. The next evening, we were served the same, but the minnows were even larger! We then had to admit the curry was not our favorite. Our teacher was a young Nepali woman who helped us a lot in the local setting. Dr. Park and Alice Johnson visited us. They thought we were courageous. The final weekend was a three-day holiday. Peggy and I loaded up our backpacks and made it appear we were trekking to nearby sights and sounds. However, we walked to Pokhara town and to a large hotel adjacent to the air tarmac. We took five hot showers the first day, enjoyed the meals, and rested our weary bones. On Sunday afternoon, we sat in the courtyard sipping hot tea and savoring the pastries, when who should should drop in for tea but our German classmates. They greeted us with glee, agreeing that our "trek" was a good way to celebrate the end of village language study. To their credit they never told anyone. The Anhorns are still our friends today. We exchange Christmas letters even now. We headed back to KTM and prepared to settle down into our own home.

Dr. Gordon Ruff, the UMN Executive Secretary, conversed with us and sent the following appointment letter dated October 7, 1978:

> Following our recent conversation, I am happy to ask you to accept the assignment initially of consultant, Rural Sociology, under the Economic Development Board. You will be responsible directly to the EDB Secretary, Odd Hoftun. He will work with you on your job description.
>
> Al, this has been a position that we have greatly longed to fill and are grateful that God has brought you and Peggy here for such a time as this. We look forward to you, with your creativity and initiative and all around maturity, to be a pioneer in developing the many possibilities for such a position.
>
> Peggy, we know you have your own gifts and skills and are sure that you will find a way to put them to good use in due course. Please feel free at any time to discuss any ideas you may have as you see something which interests you.
>
> Your home base of operation will be in KTM...I suggest that you begin now looking for a place to live in KTM...I am sure that Stephen Bull, Chairman of the KTM Valley Housing committee, will be happy to help you and make suggestions...

We began our search, looking at various apartments. Peggy recalled where Betty Mendies had lived in an old Rana Palace. Sure enough it was available, and we got permission to move our things there. The rent was lower than most apartments. So the next week, I took the bus to Butwal, loaded everything onto a truck, and we moved into our new ground floor home. It had a living room twenty by thirty feet, an attached kitchen, two bedrooms, and two bathrooms complete with stools and cold showers. Colonel Rana and his family lived above us. Peggy did her usual art of interior decoration, including drapes for those long windows, carpets for the floors, and her mother's paintings on the walls. How grateful we were that we had brought our household things with us. There were propane gas cylinders to fuel the cooking stove. We breathed a sigh of relief. I began to study the rural development situation and to get acquainted with the EDB Staff.

In 1979, we had a month's vacation due. Where and how should we spend it? We decided that since Esther was in Lucknow, India, working in a Village Development Project, we would visit her by bus and continue on to Pakistan by train. We had a good time with Esther who showed us the sights of Lucknow and her research survey of disadvantaged rural people. We were impressed during our visit to a Village Project by how sensitively and with what dedication Esther was relating to and working with the villagers. That was a difficult and challenging enterprise for her. The experience would serve her well during a career dedicated to creating opportunities and housing for low and moderate income people.

As we were going through customs at Amritsar, an Indian Officer informed us that it was dangerous to be in Pakistan. The day before, November 21, 1979, students had tried to burn the American Embassy in Islamabad, forcing the personnel to take refuge in a steel-coated room until the Army freed them the next day. We thanked and assured him that we had lived in Pakistan for twenty-four years, knew Urdu, and were to stay at Kinnaird College for Women. Taking a taxi to Lahore, we found Kinnaird College barricaded with the gates firmly locked. We climbed over a gate and went to the guest house. Thankfully, employees there helped us settle in, fed us, and assured us all was okay. After a few days, when things began to quiet down, we cautiously explored the city, met our dear friends, and phoned those at a distance. We had a great homecoming!

Dr. Tooni, Begum Bilquis's daughter, called us from Rawalpindi and invited us to take a flight to visit them, which we did. Arriving on the tarmac, we headed toward the terminal but were stopped three times by young officials. Tooni and her husband, Brigadier General Sher Khan, became anxious, wondering what was happening. After we had greeted them, they asked why we had been stopped. We laughed – those three young men were my former students at FC College! Staying at their home for a week, we had an endearing time sharing all that was happening to us in Nepal. Tooni and Sher Khan shared how things were in Pakistan. They explained the students had heard a rumor that Americans had facilitated the attack on pilgrims in Mecca where many had been killed or wounded. That is why they had attacked the Embassy. We all recalled how rumors of actions against Islam had caused many riotous demonstrations. Americans were always the first to be suspected and attacked. We learned that Bilquis had bought a home in Thousand Oaks, California and was actively sharing her testimony. She greatly missed Pakistan and her family, but it would not be wise to return to her homeland, knowing the adverse feelings and resentments.

Too soon, we had to leave and return to KTM. There was an immense amount of work to be done. Tired, but still refreshed, we arrived at our new home, and I resumed work at the EDB office in the old part of KTM.

Chapter 33

Family, Mountains, New Friends, Rural Development Consultancy

Soon after our return to Kathmandu, we made preparation for our first family visitors who would be arriving to celebrate Christmas in Nepal. We had been fortunate to

Al in the Himalayas

purchase a VW sedan from a couple retiring from their stay in UMN. Petrol was expensive at nearly four dollars per litre, but it was certainly a convenience. A few eyebrows were lifted by our colleagues who maintained that one should walk and approximate the standards of Nepalis, instead of riding around like lords. We tried to balance our use

of time and our efforts at conformity. Soon, our dear complainers were accepting transport in our VW. Attitudes do change. Peggy and I were innovators, aiding the introduction of modern technology into Nepal. (Our rationale!) Actually there were quite a few cars and buses in KTM, all driving on the left side of the road as we had done in Pakistan, staying at a distance from the sacred cows. The law was eight years in prison for ending a cow's life in an accident.

Hope and Stephen arrived first from Varanasi. They had married in July 1979. Peggy and I had felt badly about missing out on their wedding, but what could we do? Esther arrived from Lucknow to complete the gathering. We had scrounged up a pine branch and decorated it for the occasion. With the ornaments and trimmings, our living room became a festive and cheerful home. What a time we had recalling other Christmases in Iowa, in Boston, in Pakistan. Peggy prepared sumptuous meals. In a KTM store, we had found an electric rice cooker, which helped produce that fluffy delicacy on which curries were served. Peggy had even made chocolate fudge and brownies. There was an ample supply of oranges and bananas. Another guest was added, Lilli Amman. An unmarried nurse recovering from surgery, she had gratefully accepted Peggy's invitation to recuperate at our house. Lilli was one of the early pioneer UMN missionaries in Nepal. She had experienced the rigors of living in remote villages and helping many needy Nepalis. Coming from Switzerland, her English, she said, was called Swenglish. She had a hearty laugh and a great sense of humor. We were in stitches when she told about falling headlong into a watery field from a narrow path. And we laughed when she related a visit by bus to see some friends who had a bicycle for sale. She forgot to ask them about it until she had boarded the returning bus. Suddenly, she remembered and called out to them through the open window, " Oh, Henry I wanted to see your seat!" To our children's surprise, she won most of the Scrabble games, because she had special words and spellings in her Swiss dictionary! Our Harvard graduates had a hard time accepting that. We showed our "guests" the sights of KTM: the King's Palace, Singha Durbar (now the eight-hundred-room National Secretariat), the old Palace at Hanuman Dhoka, Taleju Temple and many more Hindu temples, the Buddhist stupa at Boudhanath with its all seeing eyes, and Durbar Square in Patan with its ancient palaces, exquisitely carved wooden windows, its many temples and shrines, and its crowded bazaars. We took them to UMN Headquarters, Shanta Bhawan Hospital, and Freak Street filled with hippies and souvenirs and many Nepali nationals who crowded the streets wherever we went.

But, the dessert of all sights was to the north – the grand Himalayas. In our VW we traveled twenty-three kilometers of winding roads to Nagarkot. On that clear day, the splendor of those snowy mountains was at its best. Stretched out before us was the full panorama of those famous mountains. In fact, there are in Nepal fifty peaks which are more than twenty-five thousand feet in elevation, the highest being Mt. Everest (called Sagarmatha by the local Nepalis). Imagine the vast expanse of that range, beginning in Burma (now Myanmar) and extending all the way to Afghanistan fifteen hundred miles to the west! Peggy had brought along a picnic lunch, with thermoses of hot tea, which we enjoyed lounging on the grassy plot near the yellow twenty-foot tower we all climbed. An arrow marker pointed to Mt. Everest, which was clearly discernible that day. We have many photos to prove it. For over two hours the view was clear and bright, then mist started creeping up from the hills and valleys below the mountains, like a stage curtain rising from the floor instead of the ceiling. At last, we could see only the white-gold summits before they also disappeared from sight. It was time to return to KTM, satisfied we had seen the top of the world. As Hope and Stephen were about to depart, we gave them a dragon motif carpet made by Tibetan refugees. As she had in Pakistan, Peggy was getting acquainted with Nepali carpet wallas. The end of the week's visit arrived, and we had to say our farewells.

On Sunday evenings, there was a hymn sing at UMN Headquarters, each Wednesday evening a prayer circle at the Niketan guest house. We often attended because it was an opportunity to worship and sing in English, and to become acquainted with our fellow UMN-ers. There we met close neighbors of ours, Dr. Walter and Florence Bond, who had transferred from India. He was the pathologist at Shanta Bhawan. She was a hostess with the most delicious meals. We were instant friends. They shared their work experiences and expertise of living in Nepal. All four of us exchanged puns, but Walt's wry humor was contagious. Besides that, they were fellow Presbyterians. In the midst of a different culture, it was relaxing and inspiring to be together. On the mission field colleagues become family.

One evening, Peggy shared with me how she had met a Buddhist woman who lived just around the corner from us. In the bazaar, Peggy saw Angdoma bargaining with the shopkeeper, something dear to Peggy's heart. Peggy gave her a winning smile and greeted her in Nepali. Angdoma replied but soon switched to English. She explained that she did not have too many opportunities to use her English. During their chat Angdoma related how she and her husband had lived in France and in Baltimore. She invited Peggy to see where they lived, and served some Tibetan tea and biscuits. This newly found friend related that her husband was the nephew of Tenzing Norgay, who with Sir Edmund Hillary, had been the first to reach the summit of Mt. Everest in 1953. Nima, her husband, had climbed eighty of the major peaks with various groups, including assisting the first American team to conquer the twenty-nine-thousand-twenty-eight foot mountain in 1962. As a young man, Nima had been with the Survey of India Team that mapped the borders of Nepal, India, and China. The cook was inexperienced. When told to serve roasted chicken, he served it with the crop not removed. He was fired. Nima was asked to take over that job and succeeded by serving foods he had helped cook in his Sherpa mountain district of Thame Khola, high in the Himalayas. After their marriage, Angdoma absolutely forbade Nima to climb any more mountains, because it was too dangerous. Twenty-six of Nima's relatives and friends had died on those treacherous slopes. A Swiss woman living in KTM hired Nima to become her cook. She loved his cooking and took Nima, Angdoma, and their small daughter, Pasang, to Paris where she entered him into a school for chefs. After a while that Swiss lady moved to Baltimore, making possible more chef's training for Nima. It was there that Angdoma learned to speak English from TV commercials. She was illiterate in Nepali, could neither read nor write, but could converse very well in English. In Baltimore, Nima, Jr. was born. He often teased his sister by saying, "You are Nepali, I am USA!" That was the beginning of a friendship that has lasted forty years! There were many more new friends, but we must hurry on.

In late October 1978, I began to implement my assignment as Consultant, Rural Sociology. That meant going to Jaytatole in the old KTM city, where the Economic Development Board (EDB) had office staff upstairs and, downstairs, exhibition sales showrooms filled with furniture made at the Butwal Wood Factory. At UMN Headquarters where Odd had the Economic Development Secretary's (EDS) office, I discussed my work with him. He explained what my assignment entailed. He had it all written down and gave me a copy. My heart sank a bit by the enormity of my job description. Odd assured me that when I had become acquainted with Nepal, its need for industrial and economic development, and finding my niche in EDB, I would be able to meet the challenge. "You have the experience of an Iowa farmer," he told me, "for the practical side, exposure to the theoretical aspects, and experience in Pakistan for community development. You do not have to pioneer new dimensions, we have a Five Year Plan. Study that and the actual work being done to see what can be added to what we call appropriate technology, making improvements to what rural people already have, helping them to meet their needs."

And that is what I did. Sharing office space with Stephen Bull in charge of the Maintenance Training Program, I studied the Five Year Plan, reviewed the Project work in progress, and its personnel. Was I impressed! I had been joined to a dedicated work force of sixty to seventy individuals from many different countries, all highly skilled in engineering, technical, and vocational expertise.

I made bus trips to Butwal to attend committee meetings. These not only informed me of what was being done but also attuned me to rural conditions and needs. Many items were being manufactured in Butwal, transported to villages, and installed. These included water turbines to supply electrical power; grinders/hullers for rice and wheat; irrigation weirs; suspension bridges; methane-producing tanks and fittings; design and consulting services on a self-cost basis for UMN Projects and on a commercial basis for others; a Management Consultancy Program to provide skills in

Farmers can Break Bones Falling Out of Their Terraced Fields

management, accounts, sales, and marketing; a Design Office offering services related to survey, design and/or supervision of building projects; and a Plywood Factory which produced a third of Nepal's needs. There was much more, but what impressed me was the number of students from the Hills and Plains of Nepal being trained on the production/managerial lines in the factories and offices. Upon graduation, they would return to their home village and start up work and business on their own. They would be bringing new ideas, new skills, and new attitudes to the less developed areas of Nepal. Above all, they would help to break the chains of rampant poverty that were binding their families in despair.

What is Mass Poverty? Here is an example. The Community Health nurses conducted a survey, inquiring what UMN could do to help people rise above the poverty level. Some said better seeds and crops, others said clean drinking water, and the like. But one family summed it up by saying, "Save our buffalo. It gives us milk and manure. We have invested all our savings, wedding jewelry, and borrowed money to buy that animal. If it dies, we are done for." The surveyor asked, "But isn't the care of your children the priority?" The answer shocked them, "We can produce a child in nine months, but lose that animal and we are lost forever!"

Reforestation (upper left) and Appropriate Technology

Chapter 34

A Nation of Contrasts, Goals, Objectives, Survey

It was an exciting time to be in Nepal. Peggy and I were not innovators of pioneer work. We arrived to help consolidate the gains made in the previous thirty years by the UMN and other groups. That does not mean to say we defended the status quo. No, we became involved in the aspirations of a nation that was determined to overcome the debilitating consequences of over a hundred years of isolation from the modern world, the ravages of Mass Poverty, the paucity of education and opportunity to reach the highest level of one's potential. The lack of an adequate infrastructure on every level of administration, services, and production was painfully noted. The list could go on and on. Nepal's Royal leadership and the active support and efforts of the elected Ministers, Government Officers, and a rapidly growing number of professionals capable of establishing schools, institutes, businesses, factories, hospitals, social services, and a University in KTM proved that there was a press for development. A new national spirit was in evidence. Openness to the outer world was full of promise. King Tribhuvan in 1951/52 said it well, "We must do in our generation what has not been done in the last hundred years." His challenge was working toward a new socioeconomic system, a bold renunciation of the old outmoded era under the Rana Kings and Prime Ministers. The contrasts between the haves and the have-nots had become glaringly apparent – something had to be done.

Sadly, there were remnants of the old Nepal: the underdeveloped remote areas, the uneducated, the underprivileged, those needing medical attention, the unrepresented. To better facilitate and communicate, the nation was divided into a new system of administrative/political and development regions: 1) The Northern Himalayan mountain ranges, 2) the Central Hills, consisting mostly of hills and valleys with sixty-two percent of the Nepali population and thirty-seven percent of cultivated land, and 3) The Southern Tropical Plains, or Terai, which means marshy, low-lying land.

In the Terai, which is only fifteen to thirty kilometers wide, sixty-two percent of the land is cultivated by thirty-eight percent of the total population of Nepal on seventeen percent of the land. These three "belts" run East to West. Nepal is also divided into five economic development regions, fourteen zones, seventy-five districts, forty-five Councils (Panchayats), and nine wards in each Panchayat. A Panchayat is a traditional institution for administration at the local/grassroots level. This structure provided opportunity for the local people to elect their leaders and hold them accountable. To counteract the "medievalism" of powerful landlords and deprived, poverty-stricken feudal serfs, the Land Reform Act was launched in 1965. It was a massive reshuffling of land ownership, reorganizing agriculture production and marketing, allocating capital for new programs, and emphasizing the development of industry.

Contrasts were also noted in the mixtures of ethnic groups, languages, religions, and distinctive cultural traits. Over centuries, various migrations had been made from Tibet, Burma, and India. This created distinct contrasts, as ethnic groups settled into remote mountain areas, valleys, hills, and the tropical plain, the Terai. These people differed not only in their lifestyles, but also their building, dress, work, farming practices, and traditions. I mention all these factors to illustrate the complex situation Nepal faced in its development process.

It was into this situation that UMN made its timely entrance to assist the nation in attaining its goals. At first, Nepal had to endure "foreigners" to enter their land, evaluate the proposed assistance, and cautiously permit the initiation of Projects and Programs. This was the beginning of a joint effort. How providential was the match of Nepal's needs and UMN's expertise. His Majesty, King Birendra, the grandson of King Tribhuvan, was by now the absolute ruler of Nepal. He ordered his Council of Ministers to reach out into the numerous ministries, departments, and sectors to urgently administer the affairs of government throughout the whole nation of Nepal. Achievement goals were set in successive Five Year Plans, each to be revised and updated. However, there were reservations regarding a missionary presence.

As noted above, Christian missions were not permitted to enter Nepal until late 1951 and then only under specific conditions and restrictions. In summary: Missionaries were to serve in nation building, follow the rules of the department to which they were related, travel and live only as visas stated, and not to propagate their religion or convert Nepalis. UMN negotiated an agreement with His Majesty's Government of Nepal (HMGN) every five years. There were precise stipulations in those agreements where His Majesty's Government insisted that the UMN and its members not engage in any proselytizing and other activities which were outside the scope of their assigned work. UMN took this seriously and avoided evangelistic work as such. Individuals, however, both expatriate and national Christians, were free to share their faith, vision, and expertise, because HMGN had agreed to the UMN constitution which stated its purpose: "to minister to the needs of people in Nepal in the Name and Spirit of Jesus Christ, and to make Christ known by word and life." We were making our top priority to do our best in the work assigned and to let our light shine in the midst of what we were doing, whether a Doctor, Nurse, Teacher, Engineer, or Maintenance Worker. There would be ample opportunity to live lives worthy of the gospel.

I recall some of the questions Nepalis put to me: "Why have you come to Nepal? Couldn't you get a job in your own country? What do you believe as Christians? What is your Caste? We Nepalis have thirty million gods, why do you have only one?" I tried to answer as fully and truthfully as I could, because on such occasions God's Spirit opens the mind and questing spirit in asking the right questions and in giving straight answers. It was right to affirm that God loves everybody and wants to bless all who desire the best in life. I affirmed that, "Where the Spirit of the Lord is, there is freedom." If a Nepali wanted to go deeper into the meaning of faith in Christ, I referred him to a Nepali Christian who would be able to explain it more clearly in his own language. Nepal had joined the United Nations and had signed the Human Rights document guaranteeing religious freedom. I often referred to that. Within the freedom of religion framework, members of the UMN were able individually to share in the life and worship of the indigenous Christian Church in Nepal, but not to dominate it or be an officer in the congregation.

The goals being set, how were these to be implemented? In brief, the objectives (the actions to be undertaken to reach those goals) were being met by the efforts of the Medical, Educational, and Economic Development Projects and Programs. In following chapters, this will be described and put into perspective. All of the above is stated to share with you the enormity of the task assigned to me. There were UMN traditions, rules, and regulations. There were the values and rich heritage of the Nepali nation. How could I contribute to the ongoing work in the technical, industrial, economic projects and programs? I decided that my priority at this stage was to get to know my colleagues, who were experienced and masters of their skills. My previous orientation had been the paternalistic setting in Pakistan. It had been in a Muslim context – this was entirely different. As I conversed with the EDB staff and visiting members of UMN, engineers and technical personnel shared that they had to concentrate on the mechanical/physical aspects of their Project work. They could not deal with rural development issues and opportunities, even though they were concerned and interested in helping village people. I discussed this with Odd Hoftun, and he sympathized with the technical people in their heavy responsibilities to complete the work they had in hand. Rural development was being done in the Projects and Programs of EDB, but there was need to work more closely with the rural population on a social level in a way that allowed and invited people's participation. I wondered how we could deal with this issue and what could be done to direct more emphasis and assistance to rural development in a practical and realistic way. This had to be "put on the back burner" for awhile because of Odd Hoftun's request to conduct a Gobar Gas Plant Survey during January 1979. The actual Survey would take a whole month in the Terai. Andrew Bulmer and I worked in KTM and Butwal during October 1978 on the survey questionnaire, which we revised six times, finely honing it to ensure we would gather the correct information. The Biogas Research and Development staff at Butwal – John Finlay, David Fulford, and Dick Peters – gave invaluable insights and practical assistance. They were the specialists; we were to gather the statistics.

Having gained the permission of the Chief District Officer, we were to tour the districts of Rupandehi, Kapilbastu, and Nawalparasi. We planned to interview fifty Gobar Gas owners and twenty-five non-users. To make sure we understood the farmers, we employed two Nepali young men, Sarab Bahadur Thapa and Prakash Chandra Shrestha. They were fluent in English. We cycled many miles on dust, dirt tracks, compacted surfaces, waded through rivers, and even found a paved road. I had bought an English Raleigh bike at the border with India. It had to be rugged. We had decided to use cycles rather than Land Rovers or jeeps. They were more appropriate, and we would not be branded as "foreigners" by the farmers. You may be wondering what a Gobar Gas Plant is. Let me explain. It is basically a masonry-lined pit full of cow dung slurry with a painted steel drum floating upside down on top to collect the methane gas as it is given off by bacteria in the slurry. The gas is piped to the house in plastic tubing and used for cooking and lighting. (Very few farmers had electricity.) Cow dung mixed with water in a one-to-one ratio was deposited daily through a mixing box. After fifty days, a continuous flow of gas was delivered to the kitchen and lamps. The slurry was collected in a pit and used as top-grade fertilizer on the fields. The purpose of the plant was to "make available to as many Nepali people as possible, an alternative, renewable energy source in the form of methane to replace wood and kerosene." Firewood was getting scarce, and the kerosene imported from India was expensive.

Our assignment was to study the social, cultural, and economic effects of installed Gobar Gas Plants. We began by visiting those fairly close to Butwal, revising yet again the questions to be asked. Gradually, the circle enlarged. We stayed overnight in tea stalls, having our evening dal bhat (boiled rice and lentils) and veggies. We enjoyed the hot tea served. After they closed for the night, we rolled out our sleeping bags on tabletops. A thin rubber mat for cushioning did not quite provide posturepedic comfort. At least no rats ever bothered us! January has some cold weather, so mosquitoes were not in evidence. In the morning, we had hot tea, chapatis, and halva (a fried cream of wheat with raisins and nuts). Then, it was off for

Appropriate Official Transport Vehicle

another busy day. Often a farmer would hesitate about giving so much time for an interview until he learned that we had cycled all the way from Butwal to learn how his plant was working. Some farmers candidly discussed problems and possible improvements. Most of them proudly showed us the plant itself, the slurry ready for the fields, and the kitchen with its burners. Quite a few women offered their insights and gratitude by giving us a demonstration of how they used the gas burner to prepare tea, which was graciously served. Some farmers thought the price of a plant was too high, each large plant costing six to seven thousand rupees. They appreciated that the Nepal Agricultural Bank had loaned them the funds needed. We explained that the cost would decrease as more plants were installed and Butwal could start mass production. We noted sociocultural change. The farmers were being exposed to other development efforts and planned the construction of improved wells, better roads, bridges, the coming of electricity, and possible other improvements for which the community could request help from HMGN. We were finding an openness in people from different countries, status, and caste to meet and discuss technology, economics, business, farming, use of slurry rather than expensive fertilizer, reforestation, and the future development of Nepal.

Even non-users were considering the merits of this amazing sustainable alternative to their fuel problems. I record an excerpt from our Report:

As we stepped into those gobar washed kitchens so ceremonially and ritualistically clean, I wondered whether we were violating some norms and values. The hearth was considered sacred, non-family members were not to intrude! What a social change to be greeted by the woman standing in her kitchen, proudly lighting a gas burner and showing us how easily, efficiently, and cleanly water could be boiled. The kitchens of non-users were a stark contrast with blackened walls, utensils, and clothing. Those were dangerous settings for damage to eyes and lungs. A few women shared how much time was saved by not having to scrounge for wood, grasses, and corn stalks. Now, they had more time for their children and their education. They could prepare better foods in less time, learn to knit, and have a small garden. There were signs that rural people could dream of a new world, hope for a better life. Yes, our data showed that Biogas was making a difference. On our final evening heading toward Butwal some children beside the road shouted, "Namaste (a greeting) Gobar Gas!" Word had gotten around who we were and what we were doing. It was recognition that EDB and its projects and programs were making a significant contribution in Rural Development.

Chapter 35

Teaching English, Hospitality, Carpets, Festivals

During my absence doing the survey, Peggy had busily begun to help people in need. Through a mutual friend, she contacted an unmarried Nepali woman named Shanti who lived near us. She was doing some training and was in need of improving her English skills, both conversational and script. Peggy invited her to our place and conversed with her to gauge her level of fluency. Shanti admitted that her writing in English was better than her speaking, because in school she had done a few years of English study. What she needed was more practice in conversation. This had been the status of many Pakistani students Peggy taught. She had Shanti read a paragraph from the "Kathmandu Times," and they discussed the contents in English. This led to direct questions about Nepal, her family, favorite foods, her schooling, friends, and hobbies. In a few weeks, Shanti was making great progress; her confidence was improving. She dared to launch out on many new subjects and sentence structures. Peggy was having the time of her life learning more about Nepali customs and daily routines of Nepali families.

Peggy loved candles and always had them generously displayed in the living room. In one assigned essay, Shanti expressed her appreciation that Peggy was such a religious person because she worshiped the same gods as Nepalis do! Illumination displays were important in their ceremonies of worship (*pujas*). Peggy, of course, was a little shocked by this and had to explain subtly that, while she used candles for effect and beauty, her religion was not involved. This initiated discussions on religion and ethics. From that day on, Peggy was more cautious in her display of candles – she was thankful she had taken down the Christmas Tree with all its colored bulbs! Eventually, Shanti took her exams, which included an interview in English. She passed with high marks and was recruited. Occasionally, Shanti sent gifts to Peggy, especially on Festival days.

Another girl needed help with her English to pass the Matric exam (high school), the requirement to enter college. She was Monica, a Nepali Christian. Peggy found her bright and alert, a fast learner. She went through the same drills she had used with Shanti, but this was in a different context. Peggy inquired how she had become a Christian, whether her parents were believers, her ambitions, and the like. Monica, too, passed with high honors and joined the University. After our retirement, we received an email from her in flawless English, again thanking Auntie Peggy for her help with English. She had done her MBA and was now employed in a large business firm. You can imagine how that pleased her teacher of English as a second language.

Rameshvori and Peggy met at the Patan church. She and her two sons sat nearby. Peggy inquired who she was and complimented the boys. After the worship they chatted. Peggy learned that Rameshvori had recently become a Christian. Wanting to hear the details and to get acquainted, Peggy invited the family to dinner. She and the boys came, but her husband, a contractor overseeing some construction at a distance from KTM, could not. Rameshvori shared her story. In her infancy, she had become severely ill. Her mother, a Hindu, fervently prayed for her recovery, promising her god that she would dedicate this young girl to divine service after she recovered. Rameshvori recovered and grew up, married, and had a son. He also became severely ill. Her mother came to her and told her to pray for the child. In her anxiety, she had recalled her prayerful dedication of her daughter years before. Never having told Rameshvori what had happened, she now told her how she had recovered and had been dedicated to god. Rameshvori prayed for her son with the same promise, and he, too, fully recovered. But there was a difference – Rameshvori had been reading the Gospel of John. She opened herself to God and was soundly converted to Christ.

Rameshvori explained to Peggy that she was planning on doing her B.A. exam but felt weak in English. Right! Peggy became her teacher. After several months, she sat for her exam and passed well up in her class. Her Professors praised her excellent use of the English language. Rameshvori went on to become a lawyer, and used her degree not to make money, but to represent women who had been falsely thrust into prison by a husband who wanted to take another wife to have a son. This was frequently done in Nepal, which outraged Peggy. What a witness Rameshvori became. She led first her sister, then two brothers, and finally her own mother to faith in Christ. Her second son was born and did not suffer illness. How thankful we were. We again affirmed that God in His mysterious ways performs His Will and Way!

Peggy, throughout our eleven years in Nepal, continued to use her Gift of Hospitality. Our home again became a meeting place for friends, a recuperating haven, a center for Bible studies, dinners and teas, and a safe haven for an overworked husband. Many UMN colleagues from Europe and Asia and Nepalis were introduced to an authentic American Thanksgiving, July Fourth, and to the delights of Peggy's magic as Chef Number One. Tom Wilson from Scotland learned that the gelatin salad was not a dessert – there was more to come. It was open house for any of the Project people who resided at a distance from KTM, living in primitive conditions and working under trying circumstances. We recalled many times our month's language study at Pokhara and could empathize with these couples with their children. We had lived in a village for one month, they throughout the years! Peggy really enjoyed doing this, even though it meant a lot of effort. As in Pakistan she carefully invited a varied group of guests. The after dinner visits were priceless and inspiring. However, there were moments of panic. After inviting a Newari Caste family, we learned that they could not eat some foods – meat was forbidden. Most Nepalis were vegetarians. Many had to refrain from food not cooked by a high caste priest. Peggy solved that one by serving potato pancakes, lentil gravy, and several vegetables, followed by local sweets. Dietary restrictions divide many people, but she overcame even this challenge.

Carpets had always been fascinating to Peggy, who was an expert on the number of knots to the square inch, the designs, the quality of the wool, and production. She knew many of the carpet dealers by name and had bargained with each one. What glorious displays of colorful carpets were hanging from the front of shops throughout the city. Many were the products of Tibetan refugees who had fled the Chinese invasion of 1949/50. One day, Peggy directed me to Jawalakhel, a center for Tibetan carpet-making. We toured the whole production area from the combing of the wool, dying the wool, and spinning the wool into long threads to the ten looms side by side. Seated at the looms were boys and girls, men and women, threading the knots to the melodious chant of the Carpet Master informing the workers which colored thread to use to create the design. We regretted the use of child labor, but they said this was part of their survival, having lost everything as they were forced out of their country.

There was rhythm to the chant, the whack of the looms, and the melodious singing of folk tunes which reminded them of their homeland. The motifs woven into the carpets are numerous: a lotus, one or two coins, dragons, good luck charms, a phoenix, even Himalayan peaks with clouds, and many others. Outside the factory was a ring of piled stones, around which Tibetan pilgrims were circling, chanting as prayer flags fluttered in the breeze. We felt that we had visited Tibet and had a glance at its rich culture. Yes, we purchased a carpet!

A visitor to Nepal called it a home of the gods and a land of festivals. Some of these were locally celebrated, but others were city-wide or national. All work stopped so that devotees could fulfill their ceremonial/ritualistic worship. Temples and shrines were colorfully decorated, holy men were in abundance, and crowds of people streamed the streets, especially with the images of Hindu

Tibetan Refugees Circumambulating a Sacred Site

divinities. According to their traditions, most festivals are observed in the name of honored gods and goddesses. Others are related to the names of the departed ancestral souls. Still others commemorate the beginning or ending of the agricultural cycle of the land in gratitude for a bountiful harvest, blessing the planted seeds or rice shoots. Vast numbers of celebrants take ritual baths in rivers or lakes, visit temples, enjoy feasting or undergo ritual fasting.

A popular national festival is the Birth Anniversary, celebrated each January, of the highly renowned King Prithvi Narayan Shah, who had unified Nepal with Kathmandu as its capital by 1769. (The people of Kathmandu were celebrating the festival of Indrajatra when Prithvi Narayan Shah marched into the city, sat on the throne, and was accepted as King.) It was quite a sight to view the processions in KTM of musical bands and horse-drawn carriages carrying a life-sized portrait of their revered King. There were many other festivals in the spring, too numerous to mention. In May/June the Machchendranath Rath Jata festival is held. A fifty-foot-high wheeled chariot is assembled and pulled by a corps of strong men throughout the city of Patan. Ropes are attached at the four corners of the top-heavy structure to keep it in balance. One year the chariot traveled through our street. We were surprised that our power was off. Peggy and I went into panic worrying about the foods packed in the refrigerator freezer. We informed Colonel Rana. He calmly explained that the chariot was to pass our house, necessitating temporary removal of the power lines to make room for the passage. We blinked in astonishment, until he comforted us by saying it would be for only three days! What a crowd assembled that evening hour to view the chariot's passing. The massive structure did tip, but they righted it and proceeded to Jawalakhel.

In August, the Gaijatra festival is a big event. Teenaged boys dress up in the attire of a cow and parade through the streets. This tradition springs from the belief that cows help the members of the family who have died that year to travel to heaven. Peggy told me she had learned from the hospital that many patients fearing they were about to expire went home. The family carried them to a riverbank where, holding the tail of a cow, they died. Some patients dreaded going to the hospital, because they thought it was the cause of death.

The truly national festival of Nepal, Desai, is held in October when the weather is cool and balmy with the mountains in full view. It lasts for ten days. The first nine days are devoted to the worship of the goddess Durga Bhavani. To satiate her thirst, a myriad of buffaloes, goats, and chickens are sacrificed at temples, public grounds, and households. On the final day of the festival, elders of the family place a tika mark (colored paste of rice) on the foreheads of younger family members and relatives who come for a blessing. Feasting is sumptuous and most enjoyable. All work stops, and it is a good time to take a holiday.

Chapter 36

Integrated Rural Development, Hoftun's Furlough, Dash to USA

It took several days to recuperate from that strenuous Survey. But, having brought my cycle to KTM on top of the bus, I began cycling to the Jaytatole Office of EDB. It was back to work as the IRD (Integrated Rural Development) director. The hands-on survey experience had provided a better understanding of development needs and of rural Nepal. The first order of business was to tabulate the statistical findings, write the narrative sections, and share an overall evaluation. Odd Hoftun was pleased with the information gathered and the description of the Biogas Project's success. He had planned the initiation of that work (among many others) as the EDS (Economic Development Secretary). He elaborated on the process and how that service to farmers could be expanded. Odd was a man who knew all the details and activities of every EDB Project. He commended the statistical method used – a first for UMN. (Thanks, Cornell!) However, it was time to concentrate on my job as IRD director.

In consultation with many colleagues engaged in Project work, gradually a plan had begun to form in my mind. There must be a way to assist farmers in their development needs. What could be done practically to improve their situations and give them not only the information needed but also a center providing motivation? Rural development activities had been added to various UMN projects under the Medical and Education Boards by assigning agriculturalists to do something to help in a positive way. At that time, ninety-one percent of Nepal's population were in agriculture or related activities, so the need was great. Visitors to the Amp Pipal Hospital or School were able to see demonstrations of vegetable gardens, fruit trees, fodder grasses, selection and care of buffaloes, pigs, chickens, and milk goats imported from Israel, while discussing business connections. However, the effort eventually failed because of lack of staff and for other reasons. This I heard from

Jonathan Lindell who had helped initiate and promote those models adjacent to Amp Pipal's large Boarding School and smaller branch schools as well as at the Amp Pipal Hospital.

Should a new approach be taken by establishing a Rural Development Center to deal with these matters? We began to envision a Center which would prioritize and concentrate on improving the effectiveness of the IRD-related Projects. What was

Rural Development around Pokhara
(Annapurna Range)

needed were the <u>means</u> to promote animal health, agronomy, horticulture, tree-planting and forestry, rural industries, and project studies. A five-acre farm was needed to demonstrate new/improved varieties of plants and animals, evaluations, and a resource library that could collect and distribute relevant materials toward reaching the <u>goal</u> of aiding rural individuals, families, and communities to a better future. Having drafted the document, I shared it with Odd Hoftun, the EDB Staff, and Agriculturalists. There was surprising agreement and enthusiasm for such a Project! The question arose: where should such a Center be located? I favored Butwal, because it was located in the Terai and EDB activities were in place. We agreed to think about it. I had a heart to-heart-talk with the EDS, Odd Hoftun, about this location question. He did not favor Butwal. There was enough going on there, and he did not want a Center that would not quite fit the Technical/Industrial work in progress. Then he smiled and suggested Pokhara. That seemed to be far enough removed from Butwal. What visionary wisdom he had! Odd suggested that we carefully estimate the number of Staff needed, the cost, the criteria for choosing suitable personnel, an administrative office, and a whole host of other items. Having made the necessary adjustments in the document, I forwarded it to the UMN Executive Committee for its approval. In due time the plan was accepted, and we were given permission to forward it to the appropriate Ministry or Department for His Majesty's Government of Nepal (HMGN).

It was then that I got acquainted with Mr. Joshi, the Nepali Liaison Officer, whose job was to make a presentation of any Project Plan, praise its worth to Government Officers, follow it through the circles of HMGN bureaucracies, and encourage a positive decision. A man with encyclopedic knowledge of Nepal and how government works, he was amply qualified for the job. He also had a deeply felt loyalty to UMN/EDB and was a master of reading our characters and manners as non-Nepalis. With the solid sense of independence and honesty of Nepalis, he did not hesitate to give his opinion and evaluation. Confiding that the IRD Plan would be approved by HMGN in about two years, he comforted me by saying, "No use trying to hurry this. You know such things take time." Odd suggested we start discussing this at all levels of UMN on a personal basis to acquaint them with a new Project in the making and to give hints of this innovation to financial donors who might be looking for such mission work.

It was time for Odd and Tulis Hoftun to take a furlough from July 1979 to January 1980. They certainly had earned time to return to Norway, enjoy family and friends, and speak in churches that supported them and their work with UMN by prayer and funding. Two months earlier, Odd had hinted/requested that I be the Acting EDS during his furlough. I blinked! "Were there not more experienced personnel in EDB to take on such an awesome job?" I asked. Odd explained that in April the UMN Board Meetings were finished, so the Project Directors could effectively carry on their work. The next year's work and plans had been completed, leaving me only to answer correspondence, attend the UMN Executive Committee meetings (and others), while working closely with his fellow Norwegian, Tor Mogadal, as Assistant EDS, and

Stephen Bull, who would help if anything suddenly came up. He made it sound easy. I knew better, but reluctantly agreed to take on the job. This would also mean visits to EDB Projects every six weeks, dealing with administrative business and problem solving, reading a mountain of reports, corresponding with donor organizations, and dealing with personnel. In UMN at that time there were over four hundred expatriates sent by thirty-nine mission/church agencies from twenty different countries. It took all my diplomatic skills to motivate the seventy EDB men and women from so many different cultures to cooperate and participate as a united team in every Project and Program. In addition to all this, there was something very important that had to be done. Peggy had insisted that I spend two weeks in the USA to attend our son John's graduation from Hamilton College and to visit Stan and Jo Ann, who were expecting a baby in mid May. She also wanted to go, but finances were tight. What was there to do but make a dash to the USA?

I flew (as a passenger) to London, JFK, Utica, New York, and on to Clinton where the college was located. It was good to see John again and to join in the celebration of his graduation. John had taken a wide selection of subjects, including Japanese. His top subjects were Literature and Creative Writing, and he won awards in these subjects and graduated with Honors. John explained to me that he had an advantage. Writing essays about Pakistan – its people, customs, foods, the stench of open latrines, exquisite sitar music, martial bands of pipes and drums, and the struggle against mosquitoes, bed bugs, and the scorching heat – was merely recalling what he had experienced. He introduced me to his professors and classmates. We attended many receptions. The campus was beautiful with its trees and flowers. Graduation ceremonies were impressive. John, in his cap and gown, received his diploma. How proud that made me! John confided that he was hoping to be accepted to teach English in Japan for a two-year term. I thought that was terrific. Too soon it was time for farewells and another parting. How I wished that Peggy could have been there.

I traveled on to Omaha, Nebraska, where Stan met me to drive us to Papillion, the town in which they lived. Waiting to greet me were Jo Ann, Tanya, and two-week-old baby Erik. What a thrill it was to hold our first grandson! In complexion, he favored Jo Ann's family, with a good growth of dark hair. We rejoiced together. What fabulous meals Jo Ann prepared, excelling any Midwestern cooking, which is still true today. Stan shared that he had completed his Securities training at A.G. Edwards and was now busy with his new skills and expertise. Jo Ann, a registered nurse, was on maternity leave. Tanya, now ten, introduced me to her many friends, both her age and older. She loved swimming, swinging on swings, riding her cycle, talking to anyone she met, teaching games new to me, and holding Erik. Big sister had waited a long time for a brother to appear. She was a good organizer. Stan and Jo Ann were surprised when a large number of guests for Tanya's birthday arrived – she had invited most of their neighbors. What a tremendous time we had! I bored them with talk about our work in Nepal, describing how high the mountains were, and what Grandma Peggy was doing. I gave them the gifts she had sent with me. Their novelty as Nepali artifacts made them special.

Then it was time to be on my way to KTM and Peggy. I did not make any stopovers, as I was in a hurry to get home, to catch up on my work, and to get acquainted with what faced me in the immediate future. Peggy and I marveled how good the Lord is. We could never have imagined where we were, what we were trying to do, and the challenges that were ahead. I think Peggy had some doubts that a teacher and preacher could be an administrator of such a magnitude. She was, all things considered, most of the time the "driving force" in our home and activities. I shared how sometimes a person is talented enough to take on heavy responsibilities, but there were also times when seemingly insurmountable circumstances made the man or woman! We were still convinced that what was needed were faith, hope, and love. After all, "I" didn't have to do it alone. Christ was completing His life and ministry in the midst of our efforts to fulfill His Will and Way. Confronting me as Acting EDS for six months were a plethora of challenges and hurdles, but this was not Pakistan and the Paternalistic setting. In Nepal, the goal was to enable Nepalis, through every development effort, to deal with their own needs. With grass-roots participation where they identified their basic problems and needs, we cooperatively planned how to solve them, and to actually implement these plans, with UMN and HMGN giving help and resources, as requested by the people. This was not doing something for those in need; this was rather, doing something with people in what they were attempting to do for themselves.

Chapter 37

Butwal Conference, Surprise, Balancing Act

The Economic Development Board (EDB) arranged for a conference in Butwal, February 22, 1980, to hear a full presentation of the Projects and Programs in which the UMN personnel were engaged. Odd Hoftun, Tor Mogadal, and I outlined the agenda. The theme was "We Share because we Care, because we have Something to Give, because Development brings HOPE." Dr. Carl Johannson, the Executive Director of UMN, was the Chairperson. I was to take notes and compile the findings. The purpose of the conference was to record the highlights and summarized presentations by thirty speakers during an eight-hour time frame. We knew that with so many speakers there were ample opportunities for tangents and boredom, but quite the opposite happened. Lively presentations, searching questions, and competent answers helped each one to concentrate and participate at a high level of effort throughout the day. Dr. Johannson's winsome and humorous encouragement, plus the encyclopedic store of background and direction from Odd Hoftun made the time pass quickly and most profitably. (At this writing, the compiler for the meeting is tempted to attach the seventeen pages of the Report, but let me summarize instead.)

To get started, Odd reviewed the Functions of EDB as it relates to the UMN as part of its organization and composed of UMN personnel recruited from many lands. EDB is to be a tool for handling economic development projects. Administratively, EDB deals with Projects in planning, funding, recruitment, assigning positions, receiving reports, evaluating, seeking to fulfill UMN's aims and purposes relating to the policies and philosophy consistent with Nepal's development needs and objectives. It also seconds builders, maintenance men, agriculture resource persons, and other experts into UMN work under the Health Services and Education Boards. The three Boards – Health Services, Education, and Economic – combine their input and leadership in reviewing plans, assigning responsibilities to various Boards/Programs, and evaluating results through the Integrated Rural Development Committee. I wish there were space here to record all that happened that day, but it would be too long and boring for readers. I presented three reports: Rural Development Division, Gobar Gas and the Farmer, and Working with People. Dinner for the whole group was served by the Butwal Guest House, during which the room buzzed with discussions on matters that had arisen during our sharing time. It was good to get to know each other better and to commend/challenge even small details which enriched this or that work. To close the Butwal conference, Dr. Johannson summed it all up with the concept of Unity in Diversity. It had been a most productive day. Open and candid insights reverberated in the Economic Development Board meeting held in Butwal later that month, where the whole report became Appendix One.

The UMN Board of Directors had their annual meeting in May 1980 in the KTM Headquarters. Member Bodies from many countries were in attendance. They met for three days to do all the business on the docket, scrutinizing all the reports from the three Boards, Projects, and Programs. I think they looked even under the carpet! They made all the final decisions, having heard and evaluated everything being done. Odd Hoftun had completed his term of office as Economic Development Secretary and requested not to be re-elected to another term. The question of who would replace this untiring, creative, and dedicated leader was considered. Finally, they voted and announced that the new EDS would be (you guessed it) Al Schlorholtz! Wow! I was glad not to have been in the meeting. It was enough of a shock when they asked for my acceptance to do the job, before the final vote. Somehow I knew that Odd Hoftun must have spoken to lots of influential members of the UMN Board of Directors. Odd congratulated me and tried to comfort me by saying, "It is only a seven-year term, not eternity!"

Not everyone in EDB was happy about my having been selected to be Economic Development Secretary. Many of the seasoned, highly experienced men, who knew the UMN and Nepal much better than I, felt that they would have preferred a different choice. One shared with me the opinion that "Anyone who tries to follow Odd Hoftun's leadership will fail!" That was very helpful, because it gave me a clue of what I had to do. Admittedly, I could never rise to Odd's administrative level of competence. He was an <u>Administrator</u> of the highest order. "You see," confided one of my colleagues, "you have to run the work like a commander of an army – planning, recruiting, laying down the rules and regulations, and implementing the plans and strategies!" However, I could become a <u>Manager</u> soliciting the help of Project Directors, Project workers, and experienced Nepali personnel. Yes, there were many administrative tasks, but I would not have to "reinvent the wheel." The Projects were well organized and doing an excellent job. In reality, my work was to continue implementing and building on the foundations already in place. This is not to imply

Al is Yoked to a Heavy New Responsibility

that Odd was a Paternalist. Quite the contrary. He had started from scratch the industrial/technical projects for economic development. He had also trained and given responsibilities to the managers of the companies in Butwal as they achieved maturity and competence. The rules and regulations were the guidelines for progress and success. If there was ever a dwarf standing on the shoulders of a giant, this was it!

With so many Projects and Programs in operation, each with particular settings, demands, and problems, it was like a great balancing act to juggle them all without dropping a ball. To assist me, two EDS Associates were appointed, with Odd's and my blessing. They were Tor Mogadal, an engineer from Norway, and Lionel Mackay, an engineer from the UK. Together we reviewed the whole range of EDB's

Projects/Programs, Personnel Assignments, and the Goals/Objectives of each one. However, it was more than sitting in the office. Every six weeks we toured ongoing work onsite. This entailed much riding of buses, trekking ridges, wading through rivers, and praying for the stamina and strength of high-altitude Sherpa porters. I cannot go into detail about these visits and the heavy work in which we were engaged. Peggy was concerned about our riding in crowded buses and the time-consuming wait for them. She suggested we order a Suzuki jeep from Japan. Some insisted we import an Indian jeep, but Peggy had done her homework. She rightly convinced everyone that a closed two-door jeep from Japan was the way to go. With the use of the jeep, we could drive to the nearest point of road transport to the location of a Project, then walk the rest of the way. This saved many hours. While I was in KTM, I continued cycling to work which provided exercise and saved time. Visiting HMGN ministries and departments by cycle set an example for reducing transport cost. Their jeeps were larger than my cycle and more expensive to run.

The EDB staff prepared and sent to all Projects a survey to help document from their point of view what ought to be done in the future. This was in preparation for a Three to Five Year Plan to be submitted to the UMN Board in April 1981. Instead of EDB administration preparing this and circulating the Plan to Projects for their study, discussion, and debate, it was an attempt to start the process at the grass-roots level. Using previous plans as a base, we had broadly outlined a draft which the Projects could revise according to their own Plans, Budgets, and Personnel needs for 1981/82/83 in detail and note

Turbine Refurbishing, Butwal

the trends for 1984/85. To ensure People's Participation, the Project and Program Managing committees were to solicit what local farmers/villagers and their leaders considered their needs, problems, and possible solutions. With this information in hand all the Project members were to coordinate the needs and means to accomplish what would benefit the development of the whole community and achieve the goals/objectives of each Project. To share and discuss these reports, we arranged an EDB Seminar at Butwal for October 30-31, 1980. This was most successful. Prior to the meeting, I circulated a nine-page document on Development Definitions, Goals and Strategies, Problem Solving Methods, Proposed Impact Areas, Priorities, and Evaluation Guidelines. A brief description of our EDB Projects/Programs Activities was included for reference and acknowledgment, to illustrate their range and variety. This proved to personnel at all levels that their hard work was being recognized and highly appreciated.

Nevertheless, there was need for motivation as well. All of us were aware of "drudgery and narrow attention" caused by grinding, daily exertions. In the EDS office there were also piles of letters, complaints, problems, committee meeting reports, and inquiries from our donors wanting to know how we were using "their" money. Was I finished with my work after clearing those piles, or were there countless other matters to consider? One afternoon, I had a German Representative from Bread for the World visit my office. His main point was that his organization wanted to pay UMN Projects directly, not funnel funds through UMN. He said we were paternalistic in our actions! This I convinced him was not true. As he was leaving, he noted the stacks of files on my desk, saying, "When I leave my desk each day my desk is clear. A cluttered desk is the sign of a cluttered mind." To this I innocently answered, "Then what is the sign of an empty desk?" He left a bit more educated.

I had shared with my visitor my definition of paternalism, which I kept refining. "A paternalist is one who becomes the brains, conscience, initiative, and means of support for those in need who increasingly become dependent on others rather than learning to recognize, come to grips with, and seek to solve their own problems through involvement with others in the process of desired change. The other extreme is the passive observer who sits and waits for something to happen." It takes lots of patience to get rural people, who live close to the subsistence level, to make plans for development. Day to day they barely survive. They need a catalyst to help them get started. When newly appointed personnel got impatient and forwarded a Program Plan to "help" these people, I would thank him/her for the projected plan with budget and the like, and then advise keeping that Plan in his/her pocket. Instead, I suggested they start discussing with the villagers their situation, problems, and needs, dropping a hint now and then about that newly installed clean drinking water system in a nearby village, sharing that such a system reduced bacterial diseases by eighty percent. Leave it there! After awhile an elder would visit that new system and start discussing it with his neighbors. They in time inquired how UMN could help them if they made a plan to install such a system. That's when you say, "What a great idea! I'm sure they would agree to help if you send them a request!" Don't say, "I told you so!" Let it be their idea and help implement their plan for action as they proceed. That is one way to initiate a People's Participation Program. We had learned that plans from the top down rarely helped. It is better to be a facilitator than a dictator. Foreign Aid Agencies could identify the needs of people, for example, severe erosion on steep hills. Their approach was to offer to plant the trees, fence in the area, and to move on. Most of these Projects failed because the local

Al with His Piles of Papers

people were not involved in the planning or implementation. This was charity, not development; something was being done <u>for</u> them. In a few years, the trees would cease to grow because goats had bitten off the tops of the pine saplings and farmers had cut the trees for fodder and sold the fencing.

One day an AID official visited UMN Headquarters. The Executive Director was out, so he conversed with Frances Swenson, the Treasurer. He praised the work being done by the UMN and offered to help with funds and personnel. "What would you do if we gave you a million dollar grant in aid?" he asked. Without a blink of the eye, Frances firmly said, "We would refuse it! Your money would ruin how we do things." As the official made his chagrined exit he laughingly exclaimed, "Wait until I tell this story to those sophisticated wise guys in Washington!" One morning, I had a caller, one of our recently recruited German Agriculturalists. Having heard that I was an ordained pastor, he asked, "What are your qualifications for being Secretary of the Industrial, Economic Board?" I replied that there were three: 1) I had been an Iowa farmer who had planted and harvested, broken things and repaired them, bought and sold, planned and budgeted, 2) I had a Master's degree in Community Development from Cornell University, and 3) I had been smart enough to recruit him! Word got around – I was never challenged again.

For seven years, I worked as strenuously as I had ever worked. With the proficient assistance of my Associates, Project Directors, Managers of Factories and Services, those brave UMN people living in isolated villages where their assignment was, plus UMN Colleagues on every level, we attempted to assist all in need of some facet of development and to work with them to attain the fulfillment of their Basic Needs. We, in the modern age, are apt to take for granted these needs. In the raw and debilitating morass of Mass Poverty, basic needs include a clean and wholesome environment, an adequate supply of clean water, clothing, a balanced nutritious diet, shelter, basic health care, simple communication facilities, adequate power sources, total education, and cultural/spiritual needs fulfilled. It is realized that one must always go beyond basics, but a solid foundation of met needs serves to further more progress and growth. That seems to be the focal point of where we begin, not, we hope, where people will quit trying!

The UMN Economic Development Board Staff from Six Nations

Chapter 38

Family, Europe, Persecution, The Carters

It seems like there is constant change in a family, with comings and goings, settling in and starting new work. Hope worked at the Harvard Center for Urban Studies while Stephen completed his Ph.D. They settled in Austin, where he began teaching at the University of Texas. During Stephen's graduate studies at Harvard, Hope and he had toured India and Kashmir, with Stephen doing a year of Fulbright Studies, research in Sanskrit, and working with scholars in India. Hope studied Hindi at Banaras Hindu University, which came easily because she had a good grasp of Urdu, having lived in Pakistan. She also taught English to fellow students. Esther and Joe worked and did graduate study in Nashville, Tennessee for a time. After completing two master's degrees at Vanderbilt University, Joe worked as a reporter and classical music announcer for Nashville's public radio affiliate. He also hosted a daily business roundup program and conducted on-air interviews. They moved back to Cambridge, Massachusetts where Esther did her M.A. in Urban Planning in the Department of Urban and Environmental Policy at Tufts University. She then began work for the city of Boston and eventually oversaw the City's financing for affordable housing and community development. Joe was busily engaged in Public Relations at Boston University and Boston College. Stan and Jo Ann, with Tanya and Erik, moved to Florida. Stan worked at a Securities Bank and then opened his own brokerage firm. Jo Ann put her nursing skills to work at Dunedin Hospital. John visited us in KTM, coming from Japan where he was teaching English at high school level. His study of Japanese had paid off. With parental pride, Peggy and I listened to John as he shared his experiences. He was learning what it meant to become part of the regimen of Japanese educational bureaucratic administration. He toured many schools and helped with conversational English. As in Pakistan, the writing skills were acceptable, but students hesitated to converse in English. They were pleased to have an American teacher with whom they could discuss customs and idioms in the USA. John was impressed with the attentive study habits and diligence of the students. He mentioned this to a teacher and was amazed to hear the teacher apologize for the lack of discipline in these "modern" days. She lamented the fact that some of the pupils dared to raise their heads from their work! John admitted that he did not mention the study habits of many American students. He lived with a Japanese couple and enjoyed the food and getting acquainted with that culture. During one of his visits to Nepal, we introduced John to a new destination for tourism – Pulchoki Mountain, nine thousand feet above sea level. Fredi and Claudia Grob from Switzerland had introduced us to this marvel by driving to the top in their four-wheel drive Subaru station wagon. A few weeks later, Peggy and I maneuvered those hairpin turns in our four-wheel drive Suzuki jeep. Knowing that we could do it, we took John to the top, enjoying whole valleys filled with pink or white-blossomed rhododendrons, which bloom only above a six-thousand-foot elevation. The rhododendron is the national flower of Nepal. It was a sunny day with the distant Himalayan Range fully visible. What a treat to view that vista while enjoying the picnic lunch Peggy had prepared! All three of us had cameras and took full advantage of an elevated tripod. Another day, we made a trip to Nagarkot, for old time's sake, to again see those high peaks. Too soon it was time for John to travel back to his work, and we to ours.

Out of the blue, in May of 1981, came a startling request from a group of German churches: would Peggy act as bodyguard to Begum Bilquis Sheikh as she toured their circle of churches? Bilquis indicated she did not need a bodyguard as much as a traveling companion, but the German churches feared that Muslims would attack Bilquis because of her conversion to the Christian Faith and her forceful testimony. Peggy agreed to accompany her and took a plane to New Delhi, staying overnight at the YWCA, then traveling on to Amsterdam. What a hearty welcome she was given at the airport by Pete and Elsie Born and their daughter Rimka! They were friends with whom we had worked in Pakistan. Peggy was travel weary and rested most of the day in their beautiful home. Two days later Bilquis arrived. After a day's rest for her, they started on their tour of Amsterdam, Leiden, Rotterdam, and many other cities in Holland. Germany had cancelled her tour for security reasons. The translators were excellent. Most Europeans study four to five languages in school. The audiences were large and attentive, amazed to hear how God had worked in Bilquis's life. They were impressed by her strong faith, her courage, and her devotion to the Lord.

The next meetings were held in Belgium, then on to Sweden. There were impressive meetings in Stockholm. A pastor they met there was young and showy. Bilquis teased him about the pride of good looks. He took it well, but later must have wondered why she needed to say this. Taking a train to Orebru, they were met by Lilli Amman and Miriam Berg, nurses from UMN on home leave. What a joyous reunion! They had done a good job of promoting Bilquis's visit. The meetings were overflowing with many people asking searching questions. In Gothenberg, eight Muslims attended. They could not hide the hate on their faces. Two women had their prayer beads at their feet. They were convinced that Bilquis should recant and return to Islam. Another memorable evening meeting was drawing to a close when suddenly a young man got up and walked onto the stage. Peggy wondered what he was up to. He had one hand in his pocket, but there was no way that she could intercept him. Approaching Bilquis, he pulled from his pocket a small piece of paper and read his question: "Why do people hate us when we find life in Christ?" Bilquis embraced him and said, "Young man, they also hated Jesus in His time. He comforts us by warning about persecution and hardship for whoever truly follows Him. He has promised never to forsake us. We are in His care. Be brave and trust Him!" Greatly relieved, Peggy was grateful that there was a Bodyguard in heaven who did a better job than she. After more meetings and many farewells, Bilquis returned to the USA. Via London, Peggy returned to KTM where I was eagerly waiting to hear about her visit to Europe. She was exhausted and had a bad cold. It took some time for her to fully recover.

In Nepal, persecution of Christians was increasingly apparent. Since Nepal at that time was the only Hindu Kingdom in the world, there was much pressure from the Hindu population, and especially their priests, to preserve and foster their ancient faith. They did not return to the exiling of Christians but to legislation. His Majesty's Government had enacted the Nepal Act of 1963 which imposed stiff punishment for those changing from the faith of their father. It stated that for anyone charged and convicted in court there would be one year of imprisonment, three additional years for preaching or trying to persuade someone to be converted, three additional years for baptizing anyone – six or seven years in prison for being an active Christian witness. That was a stiff law, but not very often implemented until the number of those changing their faith was too apparent not to notice. In the 1970s and early 1980s, there was a steady increase in Christian conversions. They had risen from zero in 1952 to alarming numbers. That is why HMG started to vigorously apply the 1963 law. Many pastors and lay people were convicted and sentenced to long terms in prison.

Why this gradual increase? The missionaries were not proselytizing, which was forbidden in the UMN/HMG Five Year Agreements. But still the numbers grew. This was a people's movement. One astute Nepali leader explained to me what was happening. He thought that many in Asia felt their gods were failing them. They were questioning why they had to live in superstition and bondage, prisoners of rituals and traditions which contributed to their Mass Poverty. How could they overcome their fear of unknown powers, how could they be delivered from their guilt of sins? They sensed that they were lost in the unrelenting cycle of caste and soul purification, trying to win salvation by merit, and at the mercy of priests who took instead of giving. Nepali Christians were telling others about their newly found freedom. By grace through faith in Jesus Christ they found salvation, a new spiritual life, renewed minds, and changed habits, not because of religious strictures, but rather living a life of thanksgiving to God. Porters carrying heavy loads from India to Nepal would ask whether the person they met on the trail was a Christian. When a person said he was not, the porter would say, "Too bad, the future of Nepal is with Christ." Their enthusiastic witness was at just one level of society. Peggy asked a Nepali woman what was going on. She replied, "My whole neighborhood is going in the Jesus Way!" This movement was not the result of printed materials, evangelistic meetings, or organized groups. It was on a personal level of sharing the reality of a new relationship with the Lord.

Peggy and I were invited by a family for a Nepali meal. We had met in worship at the Patan congregation. Abraham shared his testimony with us. He related how, while driving a taxi in KTM, he had led a bad life, including cheating illiterate customers and drinking heavily. Providentially, he was converted by the testimony of his son-in-law. He was baptized and joined the fellowship of the church. After a few months he was arrested, convicted, and sentenced to a year in prison. During his last week of freedom, I shared with him my concern. He replied, "Don't feel sorry for me. Being in prison will give me an opportunity to witness to many I would not meet on the street." The Magistrate asked Abraham why he had changed his faith against the law in Nepal. Abraham replied, "Where were you Hindus when I needed help? Now that my life has been changed from bad to good, why must I go to prison?" There were few organized congregations. People met in house fellowship and prayer meetings. It was comparable to the early days of the church following Pentecost, as recorded in Acts 2:42-47. They prayed believing that God would answer their prayers. Laxmi, a widow with three children, had an illness that doctors and medicines could not cure. As a Hindu, she had spent much money at temples as well as at hospitals and pharmacies. One day, she shared this with a neighbor who had become a Christian. She told Laxmi about a prayer group in Patan who would pray with and for her. She went and shared her miseries and despair. They prayed and Laxmi was healed! Later, she and her three children were baptized. That family was another Light in the world, shining, singing, and sharing what God can do in His mysterious Ways. There were hundreds who gave similar testimonies. Yes, there was persecution, but faith was strong and vital. The movement is still vibrant today. At this writing, it is noted that there are over one million Nepali Christians in thousands of churches and house fellowships throughout Nepal. In recognition of this fact, HMGN declared Christmas as one of its National Holidays and welcomed decorated floats entered by Christians joining in public parades. Who could have imagined that in 1952?

In October 1981, Peggy drew my attention to an article in the "Kathmandu Times." It stated that President and Rosalind Carter were in Nepal for a month's trekking and relaxation. We were both thrilled to learn this. I went to the EDB office as usual and returned home having had a busy day. Peggy announced that she had a note ready to be delivered to the Oberoi Hotel where the Carters were staying. We drove to the hotel and deposited the note for President and Mrs. Carter, requesting an interview/visit at their convenience. We also alerted Drs. Tom and Cynthia Hale to what was happening, urging them to join us if the proposed visit materialized. They were close friends, both doctors and vital Christians. Dr. Tom had taken leave to make a new translation of the Nepali New Testament. We discussed how to deal with the requested visit. Peggy also made the suggestion that some Nepali pastors accompany us to give them a way to share with the Carters the persecution of Christians in Nepal.

Two evenings later, we received a telephone call from Carter's Security Chief that we could meet the President and Mrs. Carter the next afternoon at 2:00, with a twelve-person limit on our party. The three Nepali pastors, having been alerted, finalized their official letter to be read at our visit. Together with members of the Mennonite Mission, the Hales, the pastors, and Peggy and I met in the foyer of the hotel. As the time drew near, we inquired whether we were in the right place to take the elevator. It turned out that we were in the wrong wing! Scrambling to the correct elevator, we were whisked to the right floor. How graciously the Carters received us. Following introductions, a very nervous pastor read the letter. (Later he described to us how he wondered that he was reading those words before a President.) He did an excellent job. The President listened attentively and, putting them at ease, gently asked for more details about the persecution and where their churches were. He agreed that the Nepali Christians should press for religious freedom, but warned them that as they succeeded in their quest, the persecution would intensify. He shared with us his meeting in China with Deng Xiaoping about human rights. We shared what UMN was doing in Nepal. The Mennonites shared their concerns. Instead of the twenty minutes allowed, the Carters graciously gave us forty-five minutes. The pastors presented the Carters with a Nepali Bible and other appropriate gifts. As we were leaving, President Carter said, "Rosalynn and I are having supper with their Majesties the King and Queen of Nepal this evening. I will discuss this matter with them." A week later, we received a personal letter from the Carters about how they had brought up the persecution of Christians and what could be done to alleviate this concern. He stated that the King openly discussed the issue. His Majesty pointed out that it would be difficult to change the law because of the powerful pressure of the Brahmin priestly class. He would, however, give orders that the higher a case against a Christian in court went, the more he would favor leniency. In the next several months, one hundred thirty-two Christians were released and the number of arrests lessened. We were grateful to have a strong advocate in our corner, ready to courageously deal with human rights and religious freedom, not only in Nepal but around the world.

Jimmy and Rosalynn Carter Provide Real Help

Chapter 39

Hydroelectricity, Rural Development Center, Entrepreneur

The water power capability of Nepal is tremendous! From those towering Himalayan ranges, fast flowing rivers carry that precious commodity to the Hills and Terai. There is ample water for irrigation projects, safe drinking water schemes, and turbines providing electrical power wherever they are installed. The problem is to harness that potential and distribute inexpensive and reliable electric power. This was the issue Odd Hoftun faced while building the seven factories in Butwal to establish a vocational/industrial center. Being an electrical engineer, he planned some way to get the needed power. About a mile above Butwal, beside the road that winds its way south from Pokhara, Odd saw an ideal place to build a hydropower plant.

Hydropower Tunnel Project, Andikhola

The Tinau River was rather small, but the water rushed through a gorge cutting through the mountain's steep rock strewn sides. The engineers from Butwal carefully surveyed the gorge, studied the loose rocky formations, and devised a plan to construct the very first power plant in Nepal. This would necessitate the construction of a tunnel in the mountain running parallel to the river, a dam upstream, settling tank to remove sand and debris, and an intake to control the flow of water that emptied into the tunnel. The degree of descent was calculated to provide a forceful stream of water to the turbine and an electricity-producing generator to which the power lines were attached carrying power to Butwal and the Butwal industrial complex. Almost everything was in order for the first phase when a monsoon rain of twenty-seven inches in twenty-four hours flooded the whole project, severely damaging the work that had been done. They cleaned up the mess, made repairs, and put things back in order. It took two more phases to reach the goal of installing three generators producing a thousand kilowatts each, sufficient for the town of Butwal, its shops, domestic consumers, and the UMN Butwal center. There was also enough electricity to add to the electrical grid supplying power to the surrounding area. What an amazing feat and benefit to the whole community!

But the story does not end there. Prior to the construction of the paved road, Mission personnel had to walk the trails from Butwal to reach Pokhara, from which air flights were available to KTM and major cities. Odd and Tulis occasionally made that long trek of eighty kilometers. To the experienced eye of the Norwegian electrical engineer, there came into view the possibility for another Hydropower Project. Approaching the village of Galyang Bhanjyang, Odd noted the difference in elevation of two rivers, Andhikhola and Gandak, separated by a mountain. He wondered whether the drop in elevation could be used to construct a hydropower plant. With the Development and Consulting Service (DCS) Staff, he got permission from HMGN to survey the area and to develop a

A Sari Looks Good with a Hard Hat

plan. It took four years of preparation to make a feasible plan, submit it to HMGN, and await their permission to proceed. As EDS (Economic Development Secretary) in 1982, I had the privilege of signing the Agreement which was the Andikhola Hydel and Rural Electrification Project. Payment for the whole project was to be shared by HMGN and the Government of Norway, whose grants would be contracted to the

UMN Private Limited Companies in Butwal. Hoftun had wisely established the Butwal Power Company Pvt. Ltd. (BPC), the Himal Hydro and General Construction Pvt. Ltd. (HH), and five other Private Companies in Butwal. DCS would undertake the detail of planning the project and serve BPC as a consultant. This was Hoftun's method to develop viable companies and proficient Nepali Mangers on strictly a business basis. This also assured that there would be a trained and experienced work force at hand. To list the UMN personnel who worked on this Project would be a book in itself. I have that list and thank the Lord for their dedicated strenuous labors, each augmenting the UMN effort in research, development, and construction.

The basic Plan was to construct on the Andhikhola River a macro-dimensioned dam, settling tank, intake, tunnels, and other features similar to the project at the Tinau. Then they would dig a tunnel almost one-and-a-half kilometers long, lined with cement arches to prevent cave-ins, through the mountain to a collection area where the water inflow could be diverted to an Irrigation Canal, or to the two-hundred-fifty-foot Drop Shaft. This water would flow downward to the underground Powerhouse, the turbines, generators, and flow on through a one-kilometer tunnel to the Gandak River. The Power Plant would provide over five megawatts of electricity, enough to provide two hundred thousand people with electricity (three valleys full) for the first time in their lives. They would be able to have lights and use electrical water heaters, saving fifty percent of the rapidly diminishing forests. I wish there were space to describe the arduous task of building an access road around the mountain to the site, the infrastructure, the logistics of manufacture, transport, and construction. It was a gigantic undertaking, with many highly trained UMN engineers, Nepali managers, and newly trained workers operating as a finely honed team. The most dangerous job was for the HMGN Inspector who sat on the roof of the building filled with dynamite for blasting. Every stick had to be accounted for! A popular place was the onsite lunch/tea shop where we all enjoyed hot tea and delicious boiled rice and lentils. To encourage the Nepali workers to continue working, a savings plan was adopted. Workers were paid twenty-five percent above the local rates, which they invested in a reserve fund of Water Shares. This made it possible for them to eventually build new houses, start up in business, purchase farmland, irrigate their fields, or whatever.

There were many development spin-offs – more UMN and HMGN health clinics, schools, adult literacy classes taught by the wives of the UMN engineers living in simple Nepali village houses, clean drinking water systems, cooperatives, increased incomes for food, clothing, and houses. Many of the materials and large equipment were imported from Norway, all except the penstocks, zinc-coated power line towers, and machines needed in the Project which were manufactured in the Butwal factories. Did it make a difference? It certainly did! During a survey in the latter years of the eight-year Project, a village woman put it this way: "My parents barely survived the hardships they experienced. Now, with all these changes because of the Andhikhola Project, my husband and I have built a new house. I don't have to walk four kilometers each day to carry water on my head from the river. We have an irrigated farm and garden. I don't have to take a sick child fifteen kilometers to a government clinic which is sometimes not open. Our children are in the local school." Peggy would often join me in visiting that Project. We could drive our jeep right to Galyang town. Wearing those yellow hard hats, we observed and evaluated the work at hand – my job as EDS. It was reassuring to see in action the personnel we had recruited, the funds we had raised, the approved plans being implemented, and the steady progress made against great odds. Two years ago, that Project was chosen by the United Nations as the best example of Hydropower Projects in the world! With the able help of my new Associates, Anders Kammensjo from Sweden (Civil Engineer) and Tom Wong from Hong Kong (Industrial Engineer), I was able to carry on.

While all this was being done, UMN and the overseas donors made the Rural Development Center (RDC) in Pokhara a reality, fulfilling my earlier work of planning for such a rural resource center. We rented a large two-story building located at Mahendra Pol in Pokhara town to serve as the administration and teaching center. Our purpose was to improve the effectiveness of UMN's rural development projects by making available animal health care and improvement, agronomy and horticulture, tree-planting and forestry, industries in rural areas, research, and evaluations of the whole Program. RDC had its own Director, Administrative Staff, and specialists in the above mentioned activities. A five-acre farm was established to develop and demonstrate many improved farming techniques, supplies of improved crop seeds, and breeding services to raise the quality of farm animals. Especially beneficial was the reference library which proved to be most efficient in providing resource books, periodicals, and publications needed by personnel, visiting farmers, and UMN Projects related to rural development. In the seminar room of the library was a large notice board outlining the organization chart, the various services, and photos of successful rural development work. The RDC became the center for seminars, conferences, and consultations with government officials, farmers, and business people from rural villages. It was for me a delight to view the far-ranging efforts to improve the livelihood of so many rural people. The RDC had grown far beyond my early expectations. It reminded me again that change and development do not happen without the catalyst of exposure to new appropriate technology, expanded knowledge, and expert assistance, whether from a successful farmer or businessman, or from a caring resourceful person willing to share and to provide that extra insight or help. Our UMN personnel had something to share. Peggy also accompanied me in the round of Project visitation, especially Pokhara. From its small but most comfortable hotel on the shores of Fewa Lake, one could marvel at the beauty and vastness of the Annapurna Mountain range, view that pearl of a lake and the tree-covered hills, with delicious Nepali food served on the outdoor verandah! Across Fewa Lake there were numerous boat rentals, food stalls, handicraft shops, and travel agents to arrange a one to twenty-one day trek into the mountains. Best of all, our hotel provided hot showers and clean bedding. Our Nepali host and hostess cared for our every need.

One of the Purposes of UMN was "to train (enable) the people of Nepal in professional skills and in leadership." Odd Hoftun told me that one of the most gratifying aspects of his labors was to note the young Nepalis who had begun training in basic skills in the Butwal Companies become industrious students/workers in one of the Training cum Production lines. Some, having mastered learning a trade, became foremen and then managers of those companies. There they would further mature and do excellent work in the Butwal Technical Institute. Eventually, the day of opportunity came for one young man to strike out on his own. He apologized for leaving, but wanted to start his own business/shop, making plain that he heartily appreciated all he had gained at Butwal. He would never forget Butwal and how years before he had been a kid from the Hills, not knowing a spanner from a pliers. That was both a sad and proud moment! Sad because there would be difficulty in replacing that man, but also pride that another Nepali had become a professional and leader. He left with the blessing and reassurance that he was welcome to return to Butwal from time to time to keep in touch, or to get some help with a problem he was facing.

The Education Board had a new project in Pokhara. The Boarding High School (with three hundred boys) needed a large Assembly Hall. It was to be circular and well constructed. A search for a reputable contractor was made. The lowest bid, but most impressive promise for quality, was presented by (you guessed it) that young manager from Butwal who had started his own construction company and had finished a good number of building projects in the Pokhara area. He secured the contract, and his company, with their skilled workmen and quality workmanship, erected that Assembly Hall to the satisfaction of the Education Board/UMN. The next year, the UMN Annual Meeting was held in the Hall. Representative personnel came from every Project in Nepal for a weeklong business meeting. During one session, the story of the contractor was shared as a tribute to that young man and to the fulfillment of the UMN Purpose. A new entrepreneur had successfully appeared. This demonstrated and reinforced all the innovative work that Butwal did so well.

However, there were many more examples of entrepreneurial activity. Butwal Engineering Works perfected and installed mini turbines of ten to forty kilowatts in hundreds of villages and towns. What was needed was a flowing river nearby, which would be diverted to flow through a small channel and into the water intake, causing the turbine to rotate fast enough to spin the generator. This generator produced sufficient electricity to light up a small village, or power a flour grinding mill/oil press, or water pumps for irrigation. These mini turbines were manufactured in Butwal, transported to the site, installed, and made operational by working crews who taught the owners how to use and maintain the equipment. Rural people became the entrepreneurs in their rural setting. They could now process their crops, light their houses, and become independent. This made life easier for them and convenient. They no longer needed to carry their grain for many kilometers to a distant mill. They could run their own enterprise and help the neighbors from other villages. That is the way news of work-saving devices spreads. Other farmers and villagers visited Butwal to start the process of obtaining water power. Maintenance crews from Butwal were kept busy in the early stages of installation and use, because the new owners were not able as yet to cope. This was part of the learning process and growing awareness of innovation and development. Increasingly rural villagers, independent farmers, and businessmen saw a ray of hope to escape poverty by latching on to the changing situation.

Chapter 40

Namche Bazaar, Peggy's Hospital Work, of Love, Faith, and Hope

Peggy surprised me one morning by announcing we were going to trek to Namche Bazaar which is on the way to Mount Everest base camp. That shocked me! She said she had bought the tickets to fly from KTM to Luklah. I consulted my work list for that week and noted there were four very important committee meetings at UMN Headquarters for which I had done a lot of preparation as EDS. This was a disappointment for her, but she was determined to go. She asked Opal Miller, an Iowan from Rockwell City, to accompany her. Opal agreed to go, saying that her work as typist at the Hospital was up to date, and she had always wanted to do that climb. Peggy said that she did not want a younger companion, because it would be embarrassing not to keep up. Opal was sixty-seven and Peggy fifty-seven. Peggy had heard that many UMN young couples had made that trip, and many more tourists enjoyed the struggle to reach Namche Bazaar and on to Mt. Everest base camp.

Peggy and Opal packed their backpacks with all the warm clothes they had. I drove them to the airport, helped them through ticket lines, and prayed they would make it safely. They boarded a Swiss plane (Porter Platus) adapted for flying to high elevations. Most mountain climbers trekked the one hundred fifty miles from KTM to Namche carrying a heavy load to get in shape for that treacherous ascent of Mt. Everest. They hired many porters to carry the rest of the equipment and supplies, which made quite an impressive entourage. Flying was not as strenuous, but it was risky. Even though the morning was clear in KTM, would it be clear at the eight-thousand-foot elevation where they wanted to land? Many times fog or snowstorms obscured the landing site among those lofty giants. The landing strip started at the edge of the mountain cliff and ended in just a hundred yards at the stopping point. It

234

took great skill and courage to fly those planes – the pilots loved the challenge. Peggy and Opal safely landed, disembarked, and were met by a crowd of porters who for hire would carry their backpacks. This was their livelihood. The load for a tourist was a water canteen and a camera! They hired two porters and started up. The path was level for a little way, with rushing rivers, short pines, and glorious views of mountains. Soon the path became steep and rocky. It took one's breath away! About midpoint they entered the Everest National Park where they paid the fee and looked for a teahouse to spend the night.

The next morning early, they continued climbing, with nary a level place. It was always upward. Often they stopped to rest, taking many rare photos. They climbed all day, until Peggy suffered stomach cramps. Opal was for going back, but Peggy was determined to make it. However, the pain persisted and they had to rest. The porters cut ferns and branches to make a "mattress." Peggy and Opal spent a fitful night at that high elevation in their sleeping bags wearing all the clothes they had to keep warm. The porters made a campfire and guarded them from wild animals while stoking the fire all night. Peggy had somewhat recovered, so they climbed the next morning until they reached Namche Bazaar at ten thousand three hundred feet above sea level. How relieved they were. Checking into a large lodge, they enjoyed two days exploring the sights. The paths were strewn with shops that sold yak meat, flour, sugar, fresh breads, souvenirs, Tibetan dress. Many of the shopkeepers were women in their colorful long skirts, with aprons for those married, and strings of semiprecious stones. These were hardy people used to carrying heavy loads and braving the hostile elements. Surrounding them were those magnificent snow peaks. They had a front row view! Sorry to leave, Peggy and Opal now had to face the descent to Luklah, although it was easier to descend than climb upward. They had to make way for a Canadian Everest Team making their way up that steep incline. After spending a night at a tea house, they reached the point from which they flew back to KTM. Opal had a bad cold which turned into pneumonia. We visited her at a guest house where she was recuperating. A Nepali woman, hearing their stories of Namche Bazaar and noting Opal's illness, blurted out, "Well, two old women like you had no business climbing our mountains!" Perhaps true, but Peggy and Opal, admitting they wouldn't try it again, always said it had been an adventure of a lifetime. Perhaps, also, committee meetings were a boon to save an "old" man from that treacherous trek!

As anticipated, Peggy found the appropriate assignment that Gordon Ruff had said she would. It was in the Patan Hospital, recently completed under the supervision of Tom Wilson from Scotland, whom we had met with his wife, Moira, in Pakistan. The new edifice was a replacement for Shanta Bhawan. It was the District Hospital for Lalitpur – a caring/teaching institution of the highest quality, a model which the HMGN officials praised. King Birendra and the Queen cut the ribbon at the inauguration. On touring the facility, the King was duly impressed and requested to see a restroom. He pulled the chain of the stool to see if the mechanism worked. It did, and he wondered if such an operational thing could be installed in the palace! The Patan Hospital was a one hundred thirty-eight bed institution which offered general medicine, surgery, pediatrics, gynecology, obstetrics/maternal/child health, physiotherapy, and dentistry. Peggy joined Rut Petersen from Sweden in the Social Services Department as Hospital Visitors. In Peggy's words, "I happen to be one of those who loves my particular assignment...The Doctors are so busy they have little time for talking with patients. Often we find that Nepali patients are too shy to ask questions of doctors. My duty is to personally visit from sixty to eighty patients a day and help answer their questions, concerns, worries, and fears. 'Will I ever be able to use my arm again?' 'Will they have to cut off my two toes with gangrene?' 'Will the lumps on my child's head mean permanent damage?' 'Who will take care of me and my four small girls, because my husband has just married again to get a son?' (Very common. Poverty is everywhere. Forty percent of our patients cannot pay their comparatively low hospital bills.) 'What am I to do now – my husband brought me here, but because I am ill and unable to work, he has not come back for me?' All of these questions and many more were asked me just today!"

It takes a loving heart to hear such woes and needs, to help patients get some personal care, praying for all but especially for those who need extra special grace and healing, encouraging those in despair, sharing that many love them, that Christian compassion reaches out in Christ's love and through the sacrificial giving of Christians thousands of miles away. Peggy carried a bag of reading material for the patients. Included were "Time" magazine, the Gospel of John, histories of Nepal, stories about Christ's life, devotional books. It was against the law to hand out such material to a patient. Peggy displayed them and let the patients make a choice. Many chose the God Books, as they called them. One woman had been brought to the Hospital from a distance of four days – walking, carried, riding a bus. She was paralyzed from below the waist. For six weeks she lay there, but always asked Peggy for a book, which she read

236

thoroughly. The day came for her discharge; she had fully recovered. Her husband angrily complained to Peggy that his wife could not take those God Books home with her. Peggy explained to him how close to death his wife had been. The doctors had done all they could and requested prayers and loving care as a last resort. That very week, Rut and Peggy had prayed for five in such a life-threatening condition – four of them had survived, one of whom was his wife! She asked, "Should you not at least honor the God who has so miraculously healed your wife?" He thought for awhile, then said, "Oh, let her take the books." Note that it takes great faith in the Living God to pray for the "impossible" to happen.

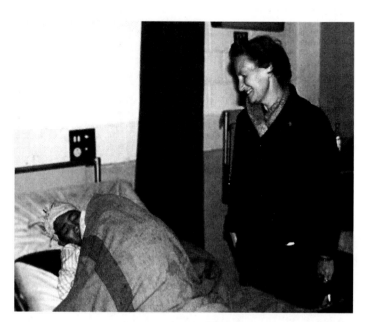

It Takes a Loving Heart

Can you imagine and appreciate how day after day Peggy and Rut ministered to so many in need? Peggy would come home utterly exhausted. In the evenings, we shared what God had wrought that day at Patan Hospital and in my work (which was not as emotionally demanding as Peggy's). Peggy and Rut made an excellent team. Each morning they prayed for patients they had seen and for those they would meet that day. Then, they went their separate ways to visit every ward. One morning, all went well until Peggy reached the obstetric ward, where she heard loud words of accusation and wailing. There in a bed lay a young mother who had given birth during the night. Standing at opposite sides of her bed stood a husband and wife forcefully arguing. Peggy cautiously entered the ward and stood quietly until the agitated couple took notice of her. She inquired whether she could be of help. Both husband and wife began to shout out their points of view. She learned that the wife had had four daughters and no sons, which in Asia is an unfortunate situation, because men demand that the wife have sons who will care for them in old age and carry on the family name. Besides, having to arrange the weddings for four girls is an expense that often breaks the bank. The wife explained that she had tried to have sons, but this was

237

denied her. To placate her husband and to bring sons into the family, she had suggested that he take her younger sister in marriage so that she could have the sons he wanted. This he did. It is customary to take another wife to solve such problems. At this point Peggy interjected, "Well, what is the problem?" The wife replied, "Last night my beautiful younger sister gave birth to TWIN GIRLS!"

Many women in developing countries suffer untold hardships – poverty, lack of education, unequal status as a woman in her marriage, disgraceful humiliation of being treated like chattel/mere property. The odds are against them no matter how they strive to cope. One such twenty-four-year-old woman with two small children was ordered by her landlord to leave the house as he did not want any Christian people coming to their house as visitors. She was not a Christian but had Nepali friends who were. Her husband had taken another wife two years previously. Peggy tried to find work for her so that after this patient left the Hospital she could launch out on her own. The Hospital remitted all the fees; she had been a patient, nearly dying from a self-induced abortion. Peggy wrote, "Rotten husband, he still wants to come at night!" Out of our own funds Peggy bought her a sewing machine, paid for sewing lessons, and visited her from time to time to see how she was doing. This was gratifying for Peggy. However, her regret was that while she was able to help this one, there were so many more.

At the Wednesday Fellowship meeting where about thirty Nepali women, members of the Patan Congregation, would meet to pray and share how the Lord had blessed them during the week, Peggy was refreshed and blessed. Those newly converted Christian women were fervent in their prayers and openly shared their life in Christ. One of the women was a leper whose name was Somita. She had been healed but carried the scars. She shared a problem that arose that morning. A young man had been left on the rock pile in front of her hut. She wondered what could be done. Peggy responded by saying that she had her jeep at the Hospital. With Somita's help they could get him some care. And that is what they did. He was in bad shape – all his clothing had to be burned, and he was completely shaved and bathed to get rid of lice. One of the other patients in the ward was heard to ask, "Who brought this poor, sick, dirty fellow to the Hospital?" Another patient answered, "It was the Christians, of course, who else would do it?" Later it was discovered that the sixteen-year-old boy was extremely ill with tuberculosis. He would have to have treatment before leaving for home, which he received. He related how he had come from a village where food and work were practically unavailable and, finding no work in Patan, had become very ill. A brother and two friends had searched for and found him, but with no money or work themselves, they did not know what to do. Having heard that Somita was a Christian, they left him on the rock pile in front of her hut, hoping that she would help him. Eventually he did return to his village, thankful for that loving care by such faithful Christians. There was a little ray of hope.

Peggy is Offered a Baby

Imagine a mother offering her newly born girl to Peggy for adoption! Peggy was shocked that a mother would give away her child. She told the mother that at her age, how could she raise a child, already having our four. The woman replied, "This is my eighth child. At home I have three sons and four daughters. My husband is a night watchman in Kathmandu, not earning much. How can we ever survive? We are so poor!" In order to do something, Peggy talked with the Accounts Officer in Social Services, a gentle caring Nepali man. It was his job to decide which of the forty percent of patients who could not pay their fees would have them forgiven. Day after day, he had heard the same plea to remit the costs. He patiently shared with Peggy that this woman may be poor, but one had to be careful not to be hoodwinked. She had a husband who was working; surely he could pay up. Peggy insisted she was convinced from what she had heard that the woman was poor and in need of help. To prove it, she would drive her home in the jeep, see for herself what the situation was, and report back. I drove the jeep that Sunday afternoon with Peggy, the mother, and child to the village about twelve kilometers from Patan. We were greeted by the seven children who were mud-plastering the roof of their mud house. They served us some uncooked soybeans from their small garden behind the house. They all shared some well-used rags at night to keep from freezing. They were poor! Once a month we drove out to see them, taking rice, wheat, fresh vegetables, and some powdered milk. Peggy had proved her point. That is what love, faith, and hope look like in action.

Chapter 41

Visiting Integrated Projects: Bojha, Nawal Parasi

One of the distinguishing features of UMN Project programs was the integration of services, personnel, and local development in the three Boards: Medical, Education, and Economic Development. This was a coordinated effort to meet the needs of communities holistically. For example, agriculturalists and foresters under EDB were seconded to the Projects under the administration of the two other Boards. This enabled these specialists to concentrate on the problems and needs of the community as a whole, not having to travel from Project to Project, but rather concentrating on a given area. They joined a team of support personnel already busily engaged in the Project's major thrust of work. In another instance, civil and mechanical engineers, along with maintenance consultants, worked in one of the four Medical Board's UMN Hospitals (Patan, Tansen, Amp Pipal, or Okhaldhunga), or at a construction site of an Education Board's Project. This functional sharing of personnel made possible wide ranging service/development efforts, which proved highly successful. According to the requests of a Project and their appropriate Board, personnel, funds, and shared Plans were made available. As Economic Development Secretary, I worked with the newly formed Coordinating Committee to fill personnel needs ranging from agriculturalists, workers/community motivators, foresters, horticulturists, food technologists, water and animal health fieldworkers, the full range of engineers/business consultants, and whoever else was needed in a Project. Our purpose here is not to confuse the reader, but place our visits to Integrated Projects into the proper context.

Gwen Coventry, a nurse who was assigned to the Tansen Hospital Staff, encouraged Peggy and me to visit the Bojha Program. This Health Clinic was an extension of the Health Services Board, working in close cooperation with the Tansen Hospital.

Having seen the plight of the villagers of Bojha on occasional visits, she helped them to apply for aid in establishing a Community Health Program, which in due course was approved. Instead of trekking almost two days east of Tansen, she rented a house in the village and aided the local citizens in building a Health Clinic for human and animal care. Peggy and I met Gwen at the bus station where we boarded and were on our way down the steep descent from KTM toward Pokhara. All went well for the first fifty kilometers. Then, hearing a noise from under the bus, the driver stopped to investigate. The long exhaust pipe had come unattached. The pipe was stored in the aisle of the bus, and we continued a bit farther.

Again we stopped and, this time, were advised to disembark to board another bus, which surely would appear in due time. We waited and waited. Finally, there was

The Second Bus; Frying Pan to the Fire?

another bus which stopped, prepared to take on passengers. Gwen told us to not say a word. She bought our tickets. Then she informed the driver that there were fourteen pieces of luggage (supplies, etc. for the Project) to be transferred. He wasn't too happy about this, but the bus crew did it. We made our way in that overcrowded bus

242

to the town, where we were to meet porters from Bojha who would carry everything. Gwen supervised the whole operation, weighing every sixty-pound load to determine the wages. Some men carried two loads to earn extra money. It took a long time and, added to the bus incident, we got a late start for Bojha. After walking about an hour, having crossed the river on a swaying suspension bridge, we noticed the approach of dark threatening clouds. We hurried toward a teahouse where Gwen checked us in for the night. Our Nepali hostess provided ample boiled rice, lentils, and hot tea. After awhile, all sixteen of us crowded into two fairly large rooms, spread our sleeping bags, and settled in for a bit of rest. Exhausted, we were almost asleep when the rats on the rafters started a game of soccer. We heard them scrambling for position. Suddenly, something thudded on us. Thinking that a rat had fallen, I switched on my flashlight. A small piece of a plastic doll had scared us stiff! We slept fitfully. All night, I kept hearing a scratching sound near my thin pillow. Pulling my sheet around my ears, I finally fell asleep. In the morning, we were wakened by the crow of a rooster in the basket near my head!

After a light breakfast, we started for Bojha, about an eight-hour trek. We followed the trail adjacent to the river, climbing up hills, then down to the river again. It was hard going. Peggy and I carried our water canteens and cameras. The porters stayed ahead of us with their heavy loads. Gwen pointed out a village where we were advised never to stay – too many bedbugs there! On and on we went. We came to a river which we crossed in a dugout. There was the full panorama of the Annapurna Range forty miles in the distance and many terraced hillsides. Since it was quite warm, we often drank from our canteens until they went dry. Have you ever been thirsty? I mean really thirsty! Peggy and I were nearing dehydration when Gwen stopped in a village to provide us with curds and whey, which helped. It began to get dark as we neared her little house on the hill. I used the flashlight to keep us on the trail. We made it! There were no rats, no roosters, no noise. We slept soundly. The next day we toured the Dispensary and surroundings. The personnel were busy with their work. At the clinic, we met Probu Dhan and his wife, Jyoti, who had worked for many years in UMN Projects. Many patients had trekked many miles to seek care; some brought their animals also. We were duly impressed! Here was an opportunity to talk with and see EDB-seconded persons in action. They were doing an excellent job in a difficult situation.

The clinic had been constructed on a level stretch of land, surrounded by the village and very high hills. The nearest Government clinic was twenty-five kilometers away. During the night we witnessed the slash and burn method to clear hillsides for planting corn. Ashes increased the fertility of the soil. The village houses had thatched roofs. Ears of corn were drying up on poles to keep them safe from rats. Life was simple and very harsh. After two days, Peggy and I bid our farewells and engaged a young porter to help us retrace our steps to the Pokhara road. The journey was tiring but without incident until we reached that suspension bridge. It had been damaged in a wind storm and was teetering dangerously. Hesitating, we asked where the next bridge was. Informed it was about three kilometers downstream, we crossed that damaged bridge and lived to tell about it. Peggy and I paid the porter and prepared to bid farewell, but he wanted to visit KTM for the first time in his life. The three of us rode the bus and arrived home. We entertained our young porter by showing him the sights of KTM. He insisted that he sleep on the carpeted floor of our living room, and seemed to be comfortable. Then, he was on his way back to Bojha. We slowly and fully recuperated.

Peggy did not accompany me on the visit to the Nawal Parasi Hills Development Project (NPHDP). Traveling to this Project meant driving on the East-West highway in the Terai. I drove the jeep, along with two nurses who would inoculate a whole village, to the place where you turn off the highway and drive two miles to the end of the track. There a Nepali household agreed to watch and protect the vehicle. It was a grueling nine-hour trek up steep and winding trails, through pine forests, and occasional rock slides where one cautiously crossed over those sharp edges. Reaching Buling-Arkhla before nightfall, we were welcomed by staff and entertained with a good hot meal. NPHDP had a number of programs: drinking water and sanitation, agriculture, reforestation and erosion control, animal health, rural industries, health, irrigation and public works, and education. This village was larger than Bojha, but had similar thatched roofs and farmyards. In talking with personnel, I inquired how the production in agriculture had increased with the introduction of new strains of corn and millet. Others were helping the villagers generate cash income through meaningful employment, encouraging local people to participate in all aspects of the development programs, measuring whether basic human needs were being met, promoting self-reliance and training, assisting with planting trees and protecting what was still left, facilitating the integration of development efforts into local institutions, and making contact with government services.

It was gratifying to observe the progress being made and the awareness of the local villagers in continuing to solve their own problems, with limited UMN resources. That was the main indicator I hoped was improving. It is one thing to have development goals. It is another to see what progress is in evidence. On the third day of the visit, they guided me to something they were excited about. At a higher level than the village was the newly installed water turbine. They proudly showed me the intake channels, the source of the water (a rather small stream I thought), the water turbine from Butwal, the attached machines for milling grain and sawing logs into lumber, and the generator which when operational would produce electricity for the adjoining villages. The Project Director had the men form a large circle according to their custom of discussing any problem or issue. One after another, they related how the whole program had been initiated, planned, and implemented. It all began when the UMN workers had talked with them about the problem of having to carry their grain to a distant mill for grinding. They related how far they had to go, the time and effort it took, and wondered whether anything could be done. Gradually, it had dawned on them that they wanted their own mill. But how to get one? Of course, I had seen the turbine plan in reports from the Project, but I was surprised to find how much progress they had made. To make the story short, village leaders had made a request to UMN for funds to construct the mill. It had been a good investment. This was rural development.

That night they held a full moon festival. They were Maggars by ethnic group. It was quite an affair of music, dancing, drinking the local brew, and enjoying a pig which had been roasted over a pit of fire. A few UMN people did put in an appearance as a sign of friendship, but this was mainly a private affair. However, we did "enjoy" the loud beating of drums, the chants, the joyous shouts which went on all night! Early the next morning, it was time to make that long trek back to the jeep and to return to KTM. I was disappointed that the household children had smeared mud on the side view mirror and license plate. (Or had the "neighbor children" done it as they explained?) There were similar integrated Projects at Surket which I did not visit, but Peggy and I flew to Jumla to visit the Technical/Vocational School there, an Education Board Project engaging Economic Development Board personnel. As those Projects and others followed the same pattern, it would be repetitive to give more details of visits to integrated Projects.

Chapter 42

A Rana Wedding, New Friends, UMN Annual Meetings

Living in another continent and in different cultures than your own is exciting and broadening of perspective and attitudes. Though there is a common web of home, family, neighbors, friends, and places in each, there is also an expanding wealth of relationships and experiences. Peggy and I were privileged to be invited to the marriage of the only son of our landlords, Colonel and Mrs. Rana. They had two daughters, one of whom had already married. We had a really good relationship with the Colonel's family. We lived in the ground level rooms, and they upstairs. They asked to use our large living room for the wedding teas and dinners. We were pleased to oblige.

On the appointed days, strictly set by the Hindu priests according to astrological calculations, the front yard became a rainbow of colorful buntings, streamers, Nepali flags, shamiana tents, arches, and centrally located geometrical triangles that were works of art. A small fire pit was surrounded by quite an array of flower pots, clay animals, ferns, and the like. We thought they were floral displays, but learned that they were their family gods! There were bowls filled with colorful powders, sticks of wood, and brass water pots meticulously arranged by the priests, as was the timetable of events. On the appointed day for beginning the ceremonies, through our decorated tin front gate came an army marching band playing tunes unfamiliar to us. They had bright uniforms and moved with precision. While they rested, another group arrived with the traditional long looped horns and drums. We were entranced! Streams of guests arrived to be greeted by the host and hostess. High ranking military officers with their wives arrived – the men in full colorful dress and the women in fabulous red/gold saris. Behind the scenes the groom and bride were being dressed for the occasion. Gold necklaces, rings, and bracelets adorned the bride, family, attendants, and guests. (It would take a separate book to describe the rituals and ceremonies which continued for three days and nights.) We missed one ritual. No one had told us. It took place at 2:00 am.

The army served banquets, which were sumptuous and delicious. Our living room was the main dining room, with tables filled with huge serving platters and bowls. Nepali sweets and rice puddings were the desserts. Toward evening of the last day, two horse-drawn carriages complete with large red umbrellas appeared to give the groom and family children a ride around the square. We never discovered what the bride was doing at that time. Gifts were exchanged, farewells made, and three glorious days and nights came to an end.

During chats with the wedding guests, Peggy in a white sari had been introduced to a Nepali couple who spoke perfect English, were openly friendly, and showed a zest for life. They were Colonel Narendra and Sheilah Singh. Peggy introduced them to me,

Peggy with Narendra and Sheilah Singh

and that was the beginning of a friendship that has endured to the present time! These new friends invited us to visit them sometime, which we did, surprising them a bit, I think. You know Peggy never let an invitation go unanswered! We had an inspiring evening: a full course of Nepali/Indian food, comfortable cushions on which to relax, and a mutual sharing of our heritage, families, children, our work, and humorous experiences. We bonded right from the start. Narendra was a Nepali from Nepalgunj, but had served in the Indian Army. Sheilah was from the renowned Hoti family in India. They admitted that what struck them at the marriage ceremony was how well Peggy wore her sari – few foreigners did. We also reviewed the histories of India, the USA, Nepal, and Pakistan. We had a grand time! Of course, Peggy invited them to our house for dinner, which they graciously accepted, saying, "But don't go to a lot of work." Peggy replied, "Of course not!" Then we all had a good laugh. They did not as yet know her art of hospitality and food preparation.

About once a month, we would exchange alternating visits in their home or ours. Narendra told us how he had joined the Maharajah of Jaipur's bodyguard. They performed their duties as ordered, but when there were lady guests in attendance, those military men in full dress uniform were assigned a whole night of dancing. This was to provide "appropriate" entertainment, as Narendra explained. Sheilah had been schooled in a convent and strictly brought up. She was able to talk freely about religion, comparing her Sikh faith with ours. We have rarely ever met such a knowledgeable, tolerant, loving couple in all our lives. Often we would discuss our philosophies, theologies, values, issues, politics, and world views. It was invigorating! Every two to three months their daughter, Jyoti, would visit her parents. Jyoti, her husband, Rajesh, and their two children lived in Agra where they operated

the Lauries Hotel. She was as vivacious as her mother and as witty as her father. What fun we had!

One evening, we were introduced by the Singhs to a new couple, Captain Anandan and Dr. Kanti Nayyar. They were from New Delhi. He was a retired Naval Officer and she the Doctor in attendance at the Indian Embassy in KTM. They

Sheilah Singh and Dr. Kanti Nayyar at Nagarkot

were Hindus. Again we experienced the bonding with new friends. The circle and range of our discussions and shared experiences multiplied. In the ensuing months and years, we shared picnics and tours to Nagarkot, Pulchoki, Nagarjun, and other sights in Kathmandu Valley. We now had three loci for dinners, teas, and special occasions. Being entertained at the Indian Embassy was a rare treat. Dr. Kanti was extraordinarily gifted professionally and culturally. Soft spoken and gracious, always thoughtful of others, she continues to be a role model of decorum and wisdom.

One afternoon, a tourist appeared at our door seeking help from Peggy. She had been advised by George Sadiq, our Urdu teacher in Pakistan, who was now a US citizen living in Dover, Delaware, to contact Peggy if she ran into trouble in Nepal. This woman was planning to run from Darjeeling, India, across the length of Nepal, to the upper regions of India. Her problem was getting permission to do this. Peggy took her to the American Embassy and sought their assistance with the Nepali government to help her obtain permission for her long distance run. Narendra made a few contacts. The Embassy followed through, and Ms. Douglas was on her way. We heard nothing for a month, then there she was at our door again with huge blisters on her feet from running on those hard surfaces. She looked exhausted but determined. Peggy and Sheilah took her to Dr. Kanti who treated those sore feet. In two days off the runner went. We hoped that she had completed her ambitious plan, but we never heard from her again. She turned out not to be a new friend!

A Nepali woman named Mitthu Sanjeel *was* a new friend. Peggy met her at Patan church and hospital. Her story needs to be recorded because it is so unique. Mitthu was born in a small village near KTM in a farmer's mud house. As was too often the custom in those traditional societies, she had an arranged marriage at the age of eleven. At fifteen, she got leprosy. Disgusted, the husband, her in-laws, and parents all put her out on the road to die. She wandered off to find help. Eventually, she learned of a leprosy mission hospital, to which she made her way. They admitted her, treated her, and cared for her until the disease was controlled. Mitthu decided to learn to read and write. Bright and capable, she learned to read the Bible. Then came a wonderful revelation: "Someone loved her!" Up to this point she felt no one loved or cared for her. Now, she learned that Jesus loved her. Encouraged, she learned weaving and handicraft skills and began to support herself. She heard of Patan church and was baptized. Mitthu became one of the most effective witnesses in Nepal, sharing with everyone everywhere about how Jesus had found and helped her to health, faith, and a renewed life. Still today, in Nepal, she is a glowing witness. She became the first woman graduate of the KTM Bible School (now a seminary), where Peggy taught Old Testament and the Prophets.

At the Patan congregation we met another Nepali family. Radayshyam and his wife, who lived near us, were members. He was an elected deacon (steward of care and outreach). Radayshyam had his auto repair shop attached to their house, which was constructed with galvanized sheets for protection from the elements. He did an excellent job of servicing our jeep. It was inspiring to hear him lead in prayer and bless the offering. The vitality of his faith and spirit was contagious and uplifting. If anyone was ill he would see that they got treatment – and much prayer. If someone was in trouble and being persecuted, he would fearlessly turn up to help and encourage. He reminded us of Stephen and his faith and ministry as recorded in the New Testament, Acts chapters 6 and 7. From time to time, he would join a team visiting a remote area in the mountains and hills to preach, testifying to the reality of Jesus and His saving Power. In one village, an anxious father urged Radayshyam and his companions to come to his house to see his very ill son. They made their way to the house where they found a twelve-year-old boy who could not speak, walk, or eat and could not bear the pain of being touched too firmly. This was a time for prayer and action. Together with the father, they hired porters to carry the boy, suspended in a canvas sling, to the nearest bus leaving for KTM. They made a painful journey. Arriving in KTM, Radayshyam and his companions got the father and his son settled as comfortably as possible with quilts in the church, where they were fed and cared for. Many of the church members brought food, clean clothing, and prayed for healing. Hearing of this, Peggy arranged for the boy to be taken to Patan Hospital. Unfortunately, an inexperienced doctor gave the verdict that the boy should be taken to a nearby mental hospital. Peggy and Radayshyam would not hear of this and found a senior Doctor who began treatment. After a few weeks, the boy had recovered to the point of being able to travel home. His Hindu father could not stop thanking those who had cared so lovingly for his son. Peggy, of course, made sure that there was no charge by the Hospital. We all thanked that faithful steward, Radayshyam, for being a true deacon and for demonstrating Christian love in most remarkable ways. We prized our friendship with him and his family. Many similar ministries of grace and love could be recorded here.

Every year, usually in October after the monsoon rains had ended and the weather was pleasant, the representative members of UMN Projects and Programs met for the Annual Meeting. This was a time for reviving long-standing friendships and making new ones. Since the Projects were located in many places throughout Nepal, some of the recruits were new to some of us who had come earlier. About three hundred were in attendance, though the number fluctuated because of home and sick leaves and retirements. It was a big affair which lasted about four to five days. In the early years, ten days were needed for all annual reports, financial audits, committee meetings, and future plans to be completed. With few roads in Nepal then, it took much time and effort to trek so far, so often. We eagerly looked forward to hearing the invited speaker, usually from abroad, the Bible Studies, devotions, hymn/chorus singing, well-planned meals, and fellowship. One felt that this was a family reunion.

The UMN Director presented an overview of what had happened the previous year with material from the Project and Program annual reports. In 1987, we heard that in addition to the expatriates, twenty-two hundred Nepali colleagues were engaged in the various Projects. After the Treasurer had shared what all the work cost, the Education Board Secretary reported the achievements, problems, and plans under his supervision. The Health Services Secretary did the same. Next it was my turn to report on the progress of the Economic and Rural Development work. I will spare you that long involved paper which had taken much work in the office and the field to prepare.

The floor was open for the whole assembly to question each Secretary concerning facts and figures, possible misinformation, and nitpicking. Some members thought that EDB's budget and work were too large. "Small is beautiful," they said. "Why spend so much on the Andhikhola Project? It would be preferable to conduct a series of small programs rather than spend millions on such a huge one." My answer was, "That Hydropower Project will provide electricity to two hundred fifty thousand people in the District. There are about ten small programs possible as spin-offs – think big!" An intriguing question was, "Why do you in Butwal engage in lawbreaking activities? You folks are dishonest!" Even Odd Hoftun held his breath on that one. I explained that there was a rumor floating around, but it was a false accusation. Then I related how the Butwal Mechanical Workshop had sent their purchasing agent to India to procure some roller bearings for use in the turbines. He had completed his purchase, but had been stopped at the Indian border customs. It was against the law, they insisted, to export anything that had been imported into India from abroad. There it was plainly stamped on the boxes "Made in Russia." The agent had to return the bearings to the factory, which he did. The business officer accepted them and requested that he return the next morning. The agent again transported the purchase to the border. This time the boxes, now stamped "Roller Bearings," sailed right through. When asked if that was immoral, I replied, "Our agent did no wrong; the Indian factory changed the boxes." In Nepal, that is called doing business! To apply this to daily life in Nepal, I related how Peggy had seen a bright new tin of cooking oil stamped "Made in the USA, Not to be sold" in a shop. When she asked the shopkeeper about this, he replied, "Madam, you can buy that tin, or some of these bottles which we fill from that tin." I saw a lot of sheepish faces. No more questions!

Chapter 43

Problems/Opportunities, Peggy's Contacts and Joy

One can either ignore problems or seek to solve them. Sometimes problems are a catalyst to a greater good or benefit. Nothing ventured, nothing gained! (Recorded here are excerpts from Peggy's notes and letters. They are not chronologically presented.)

I can never forget a small, poorly dressed woman who entered the Patan Church, looking for a place to sit. I moved over to make room for her. With a faint smile she sat down. This was the first time she was visiting a church, and she wondered whether she would be welcomed. For the occasion, she wore a clean bright red outfit. It was Christmas. With absolute attention she knelt looking upward for each part of the worship service, not wanting to miss anything, as if committing everything to memory and spirit. One could feel the depth of her devotion to the God of her newly found faith. This made such an impression on me that I will never forget that precious soul, freed to become able to worship in spirit and in truth.

A young Brahmin became a believer, but then had no possibilities for a marriage arrangement. He noticed an attractive young Hindu lady where both were studying. They met in classes and assemblies and struck up a friendship. One day, he asked her if she would consider marrying him. She said she would think about it. He then said to her that there was one condition; she would also have to become a Christian. This gave her pause for deep thought, but after due consideration she decided to marry him. (A marriage that is not arranged by the family is called a "love marriage." Peggy did not record what turmoil this must have caused her family.) He arranged for her to study the Bible with a Nepali woman from his church. As she read and studied, she became convinced that Jesus was the Way. What a surprise that young man got when she remarked to him that she no longer cared if he married her or not, because now she belonged to Jesus!

Another such problem arose when a Hindu man and Buddhist woman fell in love. They lived near the border with China. Both were skilled carpet weavers. In that remote area neither had close family ties. Who would marry them? While they were considering this problem, a young Christian woman witnessed to them, and both decided to change their faith. A local Nepali pastor baptized them. They married and moved to Patan, because in a city they could make a new start together. They became members of the Patan congregation, started a carpet weaving factory, and were most successful. Al and I often visited that factory and bought some carpets, which were first quality! Years later, they gave us a small throw rug as a gift of friendship. They never tired of telling their story of providential care and blessing.

During a flare-up of intolerance and persecution of Christians, KTM police at random raided their homes and churches to arrest them. Among these was a woman named Sharada. She was leading a Saturday morning house fellowship in her home. The police arrived and were about to arrest all of them, accusing them of speaking against the King and the Government. Sharada served the police officers tea while she insisted that such accusations were untrue and unjust. Forcefully, she made her case. Then she told them that in a little while there would be a time of worship at a nearby church. She challenged them to accompany her to that worship where they would see for themselves that Christians worship God only and pray for the King, his family, as well as the government. She was so adamant and courageous that the police departed, after giving her threatening warnings!

It was the custom at the Patan congregation for awhile to invite newcomers to stand and identify themselves, giving their name and village/town. This was a gesture of acceptance and recognition, making visitors feel welcome. However, after a few weeks we noticed that this was no longer being done. We inquired and were told that people who stood and identified themselves were visited by the police and interrogated. Present at those services were plainclothesmen noting names and addresses! That serious problem was solved by having the elders and deacons recognize and greet visitors privately.

Raja and Dainty (not their real names) were both the first and only Christians in their families. The marriage day was set, but such fierce opposition from his family arose that they decided to get married in an hour. The bride-to-be was stressed, wondering what she would wear. A friend called me (Peggy) and blurted out the problem. I quickly selected a fine sari and took off in the jeep to where she was trying to get dressed. Hurriedly, we helped her, piled into the jeep, and rushed to the church. The wedding was beautiful in its simplicity, but the young bride found it so disappointing to hurry through the ceremony in such a fashion that she had very real emotional problems the first few days. My friend and I were called to the home where she was staying. We talked with her, tried to console her, and prayed with her. Members of the church brought food and gifts, giving empathetic support and fellowship. Within a few days the new couple made the necessary adjustments and were able to cope. They were determined to make every effort to love all the members of his family and to show how much they cared for them. As a result, the entire family on both sides, faced with the reality that those two young people really loved each other, gave their blessing. Love conquers all!

R and S stayed with us in our home at our invitation when they needed medical care. She was in her thirties, as was her husband. She had been suffering ill health for nearly five years and had tried all kinds of home cures, magic, and witch doctors. I suggested to her that she see our doctor in Patan Hospital. He discovered that she had a diseased gall bladder, which had to be removed. They found fifty-six small stones! After a few days of recuperation, she joined her husband at our home while convalescing. We wondered why she had delayed so long to have an operation. It was later that we learned her father was a practicing medicine man, a shaman. But, the story does not end there. About six months later, R had the same problem, so again they traveled to KTM and stayed with us. He had only three or four stones, but they were large ones. His convalescence was longer and more difficult as the incision was slow in healing. I was told that this happens in tall men sometimes. In any case, S was quite worried about him. Then, one morning, they stood in the kitchen talking to me while I was getting breakfast ready. She related that during the very early hours Jesus had come and stood by her bed telling her, "You don't need to worry. He will be all right." At the same time He had placed his hand on her head. She had jumped out of bed to see if she had left a door or window unlocked and someone had gotten in. Going back to bed, after about two hours, she had the very same experience. We were all amazed by what had happened. This changed their lives considerably. Back in their village they kept a Bible on a table in the living room and put posters of Bible verses on the walls of their home and office despite opposition from their families who were strict Hindus. We visited them in their home some months later and saw that their neighbors who shared the duplex had recently built a small, temple-like structure representing a god to be worshiped right in the front courtyard. With subtle and not so subtle pressure from family and friends, we wondered what would happen in the future.

Nirmit was a highly regarded and influential teacher in KTM. After getting a very high promotion, she made every effort to avoid any indication that she was a Christian. Even though she had been born into a Christian home in Darjeeling, she rejected the church and her family ties. Her former friends were disappointed in her. After some time, she became ill and was diagnosed with third-stage cancer. She went to the Vellore Hospital in India, a Mission medical center, where she received first-class treatment. She also met a group of vital Christians with whom she found faith, comfort, and renewed fellowship in the church. Back in KTM, accepting retirement from teaching and making many adjustments, she joined our small Bible study group for seekers, sharing what had happened to her in India. She became a vibrant Christian, full of joy and praise! It was a blessing to visit her. Joining her in prayer was like opening a window into heaven. Her prayer was that she be given at least a couple of years in order to be a witness for the Lord, because as she put it, "For fifty-five years I have not done anything to honor my Lord!" She lived another three years.

S was married off at fifteen and spent a miserable life in her husband's household. His mother demanded that she do the most menial tasks in that extended family. She suffered many insults and hardships. Becoming seriously ill, she returned to her own family, who helped restore her to health over the next two years. She did not see her husband all that time. However, one day they could hear a wedding party going by the house with horns blowing and drums beating. It was her husband coming to take a new wife from one of her close relatives! For some years, she lived with her parents and during that time, with great determination, got an education. She became an excellent teacher, ultimately serving as headmistress of a large boarding school for girls. Sadly, she became ill again and this time was advised to get an operation in Delhi. She lay awake the night before the surgery, quite anxious about what would happen. Drifting off to a light sleep, she became aware that she was seeing as in a vision or dream first the image of the Buddha, then Lord Krishna, and then a blinding, brilliant light. To her amazement, she sensed a comforting peace and inner strength. The next thing she knew it was morning. Her operation was successful, and she spent time recuperating. Her strange dream lingering in her mind, she wondered what

Peggy's Bible Study Group

meaning it could have. One day, as her young Christian nurse was attending her, she felt led to share the dream with her. The Nurse listened attentively to the description of the intense light. S asked her what that could be. She replied, "Have you ever known that Jesus is the Light of the World?" She picked up a Bible and read scripture to S. Suddenly, the significance of her dream dawned upon her. Jesus had contacted her and given her His Presence and Peace. One early morning at a pool in a river, I witnessed her baptism. Al could not attend because it was policy that UMN-ers should not join in such ceremonies. I couldn't miss out on that! S became a secret believer, not openly attending public worship, although she did attend one of my Bible studies for several years. The reality of her faith and actions was apparent. One evening at our home after dinner, she sang a hymn she had composed. It was deeply inspiring. Another guest asked whether she had ever partaken of the Holy Communion. She shook her head and said she had read about that in the gospels. I asked Al to bring in some bread and grape juice. She had her first communion in our home. There surely had to be rejoicing in the heavens!

A young village woman was deserted by her husband. She was devastated, made to be an outcast, and poverty-stricken. At a loss for what to do, she begged help from a pastor and his wife, because she had heard that they took care of needy people. They made her one of the family until she could recover somehow. This meant she joined them for family devotions, the reading of the Scriptures, and prayer. She became a believer. After some time, she left with a man from a mountain village in the far north. Two years later, the UMN Director and a visiting Bishop from Australia were trekking in the mountains. To their amazement, they heard that in one isolated area there were many Christians. A local leader asked the visitors if they would worship with them. He sent out word to the surrounding villages, and two hundred Nepali Christians appeared! During their worship, the Bishop asked whether they celebrated the Holy Communion. They had not even heard about it. The visitors prepared the elements, and all partook. What a demonstration of faith and unity of believers! All two hundred believers attributed their conversion to that very same woman who had been deserted by her first husband. She was an extraordinary effective witness of the power of the living Lord Jesus.

This is a small compilation of the contacts Peggy had with the thousands of people she had met, helped, encouraged, prayed for, and empathetically listened to. She always insisted that she did not have to go looking for someone to help or witness to. In the midst of her daily schedule of work and contacts, they had come to her. Peggy said that happiness in life could not be found by doing things for oneself, but rather by doing things for others. This she did tirelessly; this was her Joy! And this also was a reaffirmation that in Christ she had Something to Share. Joy is the summation of all things that are eternal and true which endure because "God is at work in everything to bring forth good." (Romans 5:28)

Chapter 44

Family, Elections, Earthquake, Hong Kong, China

Returning from a short furlough, I flew directly to KTM, while Peggy accompanied our Granddaughter Tanya. They traveled via Singapore and Thailand where they visited Carol Mumby who had a carpet exporting business in Bangkok. She gave them a royal tour. This was Tanya's first time abroad. Peggy enjoyed describing the fascinating sights and sounds of that Buddhist culture. Tanya was a bit overwhelmed during her two months' stay with us: traffic on the left, cows settled in intersection safety zones, and our "primitive" bathroom accommodations! We had a great time celebrating her sixteenth birthday. Peggy used her last cake mix for this special occasion. However, as she prepared to put on the frosting, it broke into four sections. A heavy application of frosting solved the problem. Tanya studied the box and exclaimed, "Grandma, this mix is outdated by over six months!" So much for saving treasures for special occasions.

Peggy's brother, Dick, and his wife, Merna, visited us. As an electrical engineer, he was giving twelve lectures at the Paloni Institute in India. Peggy drove them on the circle of UMN Projects: Pokhara, Andhikhola, Tansen, Butwal and KTM. Koruna Biswas joined them on that tour. She was the oldest daughter of Joy and Benoy whom we had known from Pakistan. Dick never did enjoy driving our jeep on the "wrong" or left side of the road. They were especially glad to see the industrial development at Butwal. Odd Hoftun gave them the tour, including the water-powered turbines manufactured there. Too soon, it was time for Tanya to return home. We flew to New Delhi, where we met Dick and Merna. The five of us hired an "air conditioned" taxi to visit Agra, because it was so hot. Crowding in, we discovered a single hose jutting from the dash board, which helped the one person directly in front of it. We toured the Taj Mahal in that one-hundred-ten-degree heat. Four of our party were very uncomfortable. Taking refuge with Jyoti Lal in her hotel, we were served cold water and delicious sandwiches. She saved our lives! The next day, Dick, Merna, and Tanya left for JFK in New York. We had had a wonderful time together – a rare treat for us.

We were invited to the wedding of Aphuno Chase and Parimal Roy, who had met at the Union Seminary in Pune, India. Because of the distance, Peggy and I traveled by plane to Parimal's town. I don't remember the name. It was north of Bombay (Mumbai) in the Rajastan area. What a grand affair! Aphuno's family came from Nagaland to join in the festivities. Since Aphuno had no living father, I walked the aisle with her. We were blessed to be part of the ceremony, the feasting, the joy of family being together. Peggy and I considered it a great privilege.

Sometimes, a work assignment can have multiple effects. We were planning a short stay in Hong Kong, to rest a bit. The UMN Director requested that we also travel to South Korea to interview two couples who had applied to UMN – the Ritzes and the Sibleys. We did this and had the opportunity to worship with five thousand Koreans at one of their five Sunday services at Young Nak Presbyterian Church in Soeul. The congregation, which was started by Presbyterian Christian refugees from North Korea, is still growing. Doctor Kyung Chick Han is the senior pastor. Being in that area, we recalled visiting John who had taught in Utsunomiya, Japan. It had been delightful to be with him. He was boarding with a Japanese couple who grew and sold bonsai trees. He took us to all his favorite restaurants, where we learned how to grill our veggies and meat right at our table. His fellow teachers arranged a buffet dinner at a local hotel to honor us. One teacher confided to John that he wanted to personally meet the mother who had reared a son who didn't drink sake! Introduced to edibles we had never even heard of, we tried them all. John, of course, gave us tours of many places, including Nikko, Tokyo, Kamakura, and the pottery town of Mashiko. He had thoroughly enjoyed his teaching stint in Japan, also seeking to master yoga-related exercises while there. He now teaches yoga at the Harvard University Wellness Center and in other classes in the Boston area.

At the Annual Meeting of the UMN Board, our Presbyterian members and others pressed me to become a candidate for Director of UMN. I had given a thorough summary of the previous year and challenged them to initiate new opportunities. I closed by quoting Pastor Robert who noted at worship, "Fellow missionaries, many of you appear to be weary and exhausted. Do what is possible and let God do the impossible!" That seemed to strike a chord! When it came time for my seven years as EDS to end in six months, there was strong pressure that I serve another term, because UMN was encountering difficulties in finding my successor. At sixty-four, I did not think this a good idea. I suggested instead that we divide my EDS duties into two Functional Services and elect secretaries for each. This was accepted. They found those secretaries in-house, already serving as EDB staff workers. After rounds of discussions, it became apparent that the following should be appointed: Lionel Mackay would become EIDS (Engineering/Industrial Development Secretary), Wynn Flaten would serve as Assistant Engineering/Industrial Development Secretary (AEIDS) and also the KTM-EID Associate, Jim Alexander would serve as RDS (Rural Development Secretary), with Stan Freyenberger becoming ARDS (Jim's Associate). This list may be confusing, but it is hoped you now appreciate the enormity of my responsibilities and duties for seven years! My new assignment was to be Development Consultant, assisting those newly installed men in getting acquainted with everything involved in their work, explaining again and again what we had been doing, why we had done as we did, and encouraging them by saying, "If I could do it, you can too!" They learned quickly and soon made changes to fit their way of doing things. I had to get used to being on the periphery, not at the heart of matters. But, it was a relief for awhile.

The UMN Director, Howard Barclay, was to have a three months' home leave (July, August, and September). You guessed it, they appointed me to become Acting UMN Director! This came as a complete surprise. I agreed but insisted that I would not have time to visit Projects – this was to be a desk job. My, what was loaded onto that desk! With the able help of Anders Kammensjo as Assistant, an experienced Treasurer, Betty Young as UMN Secretary, and others at Headquarters, we carried on. You can imagine the work involved in handling the business of all the UMN Projects and Programs. I leaned heavily on the Directors of those Projects. Out of the blue, there was an added dimension of responsibility – a severe earthquake. To describe what happened, allow me to quote what Peggy wrote on August 27, 1988 to those concerned. "Late News Bulletin! One week ago, Sunday morning at 4:46, Al was only half asleep. I was sound asleep. Then struck the most severe earthquake of fifty-five years. I was dreaming that I was at last having a chance to ride a bucking bronco. The floor was shifting, the bed was rocking. By then I realized what it was and reached out for Al. He was already out of bed. Neighbors everywhere were making a great clamor as they ran out of their houses, including Colonel Rana's family upstairs. The damage was extensive. At least six hundred died in Nepal. Many more were injured. Twenty-seven died in our nearest sizable village where a great many houses collapsed. In Okhaldunga, which was at the epicenter, our small village hospital was so badly damaged that it will have to be rebuilt. Four of the houses our staff live in will also have to be rebuilt. The mother of one of our Canadian doctors was visiting. She was buried under rubble, and it took fifteen minutes to get her out. Another house with our Finnish people suffered much damage – two walls collapsed but no one was hurt. Half an hour later as the young mother walked through the rubble she fell and broke her arm!"

As Acting UMN Director, I appointed a Disaster Relief Committee, inquired whether any other Project people had suffered any damaging effects, and organized the HQ Staff to deal with differing aspects of what we had to do. Instead of attending all the HMGN meetings to deal with the crisis, I appointed members of my staff to represent UMN, to prepare daily reports, and give them to Betty Young who collated the Minutes in the Report. We met each morning at 9:00 to scrutinize the report and to discuss the situation. In the meantime, I had sent two chartered U.N. planes to pick up the worst injured, both expatriates and Nepalis. We sent in supplies: food, water, medicines, blankets, and large tents for shelter. I also called a meeting of every UMN-er in KTM to share what was happening, what was being done, and to study what more could be done. There were many helpful suggestions. Calling an extraordinary Executive Committee meeting to review the situation and make a decision of how much UMN could contribute to HMGN for relief operations and rehabilitation, we made the decision to give one hundred thousand rupees. It was my privilege to present that check at Singha Debar. We were televised! Narendra and Sheilah said, "You should go into films." The UMN Director returned, and I left on his desk the full report of what we had done with a few suggestions regarding pending work. To my utter amazement, he never called me to discuss anything. I felt marginalized with a bang.

Thankfully, we were due for home leave. Peggy had planned and made reservations for us to fly to Hong Kong for a few days of relaxation and shopping. It was good to be back. We made the rounds of restaurants and shops we knew well by now. Peggy had in mind the gifts for family, relatives, and friends in the USA. I purchased our first video camera to record Project work and favorite scenes of Nepal. We spent an enjoyable evening with Tom and Mamie Wong and their son, Justin, who were also on home leave. The rides on the Star Ferry in the harbor were as exciting as ever. Continuing on our way, we flew to Beijing by Northwest Airlines. Peggy had chosen a Chinese hotel near Tiananmen Square. It was a new experience for us, eating only Chinese foods, served with all the trimmings. The service was superb!

On October 1, 1988, we made our way through congested streets to Tiananmen Square to join the crowds of thousands celebrating the fortieth anniversary of the Communist victory over General Chiang Kai-shek and his armies. Too apparent was the pollution, which almost blotted out the tall buildings under construction. The Square was overflowing with about a million people. There were a profusion of colorful flower displays, animated dragons and bears, and huge portraits of Marx, Engels, and Mao Zedong. National red flags with that one large star and other small ones were everywhere. A sculpture depicting the Workers' Revolution with men and women in stone was most prominent. Surrounding the Square on three sides were the mammoth State Buildings, festooned and decorated to fit the occasion. In front of the Square, a wide boulevard of five to six lanes in each direction, complete with Russian street lamps, was used by thousands of cyclists. Across from the Square is the famous Forbidden City with a large photo of Mao Zedong above its entrance. Peggy and I were busy taking pictures and enjoying the festive affair, even though in the back of our minds we recalled the suffering during the consolidation following the Cultural Revolution when every part of society was forcibly molded to Maoist ideals.

The next day, we spent touring the Forbidden City, which is the world's largest Museum with its vast arrays of palaces, halls, towers, marble bridges engraved with dragon and phoenix designs, broad streets, all surrounded by walls of the Outer and Inner Courts. There are almost a thousand structures, each one a work of art. By taxi, we traveled to the Ming Tombs the next day. Fifty kilometers north of Beijing in the valley near Tianshou Mountain lie the mausoleums of thirteen emperors of the Ming dynasty, ranking in popularity with the Forbidden City and the Great Wall. The approach is impressive with its archways and pillars and the Road of Gods lined with stone sculptures of lions, camels, elephants, unicorns, horses, court officials, and warriors. We descended ninety-six feet step by step into the tombs. After viewing this phenomenon, we drove to a section of the Great Wall at Badaling. Here is another wonder of the world. Begun in the third century BC, the six-thousand-kilometer wall extending along the northern border of China was a means to "keep the barbarians out." Many millions of slave laborers were forced to work there and many were buried in the stonework. Viewing the mountainous landscape from that Wall, we walked for some distance as it snakes its way through treacherous terrain. Then we returned to Beijing and on to Hong Kong to embark for the USA, via Honolulu.

Arriving in Los Angeles, we met daughter Hope from Texas (by prearrangement). The three of us took a bus to Thousand Oaks to visit Begum Sheikh, who was impatiently convalescing from a successful triple bypass operation. Her daughter, Tooni, from Pakistan was there. Tooni's husband, Sher Khan, also joined us. It was a joyous reunion! The next day, Peggy, Hope, and I flew to Dallas and on to Austin, where Stephen was still teaching at the University of Texas. They had bought a five-acre plot in the Hill Country and lived in a cozy stone house. It was an exciting exercise to throw frisbees, trying to keep them from their two dogs. They treated us royally, but we had to travel on to Des Moines and Carroll to make that our base with my sister Carrie, for a tour of our seventeen churches in Iowa, and to visit friends and relatives, discovering again the joy of family.

Chapter 45

Packing, Moving to Patan, Closing Down,
In Retrospect

As we prepared to return to Nepal, an invitation from the Presbyterian Hawaiian Council of Churches requested us to visit and share with their congregations the thrust of mission and development. This communication was processed by our USA Mission Office. Evidently, someone heard we were heading toward Nepal and happened to be available. We spent a most inspiring month in Hawaii. On our arrival in Honolulu, we were welcomed with leis and taken to spend the first five days on the seventeenth floor of the Outrigger Hotel. A most comfortable suite of rooms gave us a full view of Waikiki beach all the way to Diamond Head. The cuisine was superb! Each day a member of First Church drove us to the famous sites of Oahu Island. We were embarrassed by all the attention. Especially intriguing were the flowering trees and shrubs. After those five days, we averaged two to three meetings a week. They flew us to Kauai Island to continue meeting with many congregations. We had rarely met such enthusiastic Christians wanting to hear what was happening in Nepal, Pakistan, and the Lord's Kingdom. Touring Waimea Valley, the "Grand Canyon" of that island with its many colored layers of lava formations, was a highlight for us. We were in Paradise and had never experienced such "working" conditions.

I record this to contrast with what lay ahead of us in KTM. We had less than a year to finish our work and plan our retirement. Packing is a strenuous task. It was heartrending to sort through possessions which had accumulated over almost thirty-five years in Asia, mutually deciding what to keep or dispose of. Since we were still working, it was mostly evenings and holidays when we found time to sort. We decided to sell, or give away, the furniture as it was too expensive to ship. My library had to go as well. The Islamic materials I arranged in the UMN Headquarters library, plus many reference books on development, economics/business, and the like.

Theological books were distributed to local pastors and Nepali elders and deacons. I was parting with "dear friends." Good books become an integral part of one's psyche. I was glad to have something to share with Nepali leaders that they could use in their calling to minister to the needs of the Nepal Christian Fellowship. Official UMN reports and documents were sent to the UMN archives, which Betty Young so ably managed. Peggy gifted most of her saris, home furnishings, and devotional/biographic books among her dear friends. She, too, suffered during this process. We bought fifteen tin trunks and began to carefully fill them. We had to buy another five to complete our task. Having painted on each trunk a number and Stan's Florida address, we locked each one with brass padlocks made in Nepal. These were stored in the Rana's kitchen on our floor. They assured us that no one would even touch them.

With our suitcases packed and the bare essentials to cope for the next six months, we moved to a small apartment in Patan, adjacent to Patan Hospital. This made it easier for Peggy to continue her work, but it added a mile to my cycling to work at Headquarters. Continuing as Development Consultant, I did visit some Projects to orient new recruits and aid in future plans; however, I didn't meddle with the Project Directors. Another task was to share with donor visitors in the Board Room what UMN was attempting to do to meet the needs of Nepalis. One group of twenty-four from Minnesota listened attentively, asked many pertinent questions, and at the end inquired whether the sun would shine the next day. During their visit, cloud cover had hidden the mountains from view. I was in a bit of quandary for a moment, but assured them the sun would surely shine. They applauded, until I revealed that there also might be clouds, though surely above them the sun would shine in all its glory! They moaned in perfect harmony.

Peggy was as busy as ever. With her wealth of knowledge about the hospital and patient care, she often gave guided tours for visiting groups. One such donor group was from Japan. She took them from ward to ward, explaining the system of care and giving numerous instances she had experienced. As they entered the pediatric ward with all those beds of infants and young children, suddenly one of the men said, "I can't go farther. I'm having a heart attack!" Quickly responding, Peggy started to call the heart doctor, when he said, " No, I can't bear to visit this ward or any more!" Other visiting donors were amazed at how much was being done, by so few, with so little funds. Inspired by what they saw and learning that the cost for one patient per day was seventy-nine rupees (then two dollars), on reaching home they began to raise the funds to care for one hundred patients each month. What a blessing!

We also invited the Project Directors, when they were in KTM for meetings, and their families to our home for special recognition and thanks for our years of being on the same team. Peggy and Sanu, our helper, served a sumptuous lunch for all twenty-seven! I had prepared a short devotion based on the Book of Habakkuk and a long review of their accomplishments. When I spoke of how proud and grateful the Economic Development Board (EDB) was of their unstinting contribution, I made quite a few references to EDB; that is, until either little Ruth or Fiona Mackay said loudly enough for all to hear, "Daddy, tell Uncle Al that it is not EDB, but ABC!" The whole crowd roared. That shortened my speech a bit. A great surprise was the visit by Benita Biswas from Toronto, the youngest daughter of Benoy and Joy. Benita solved the taxi and bus costs by borrowing my cycle. To find out where the sights of KTM and Patan were, she asked Sanu to hop on the back and direct her. They struck up a close friendship, and even Sanu visited places she had not seen! Not to be outdone, Benita's sister Onila enjoyed a week's visit, insisting on going whitewater rafting, among many other excursions in the KTM Valley.

Peggy and I were invited to lead a retreat for the staff families in Butwal. We sent them a questionnaire about their self-image, attitudes, motivations, problems, and projections for the future. Their answers were confidential; we never saw them. That weekend, they shared examples of their responses to the questions. Peggy and I led biblical studies on each category, including the sharing of what our answers were. It was a rewarding time of fellowship. That would be our last time in Butwal. On our way back to KTM, we stopped at the Andhikhola Project to visit the families and marvel at the progress being made at that Hydropower and Irrigation site. They took us to a neighboring village to show us the safe drinking water system that had been installed and the enthusiastic women and girls who didn't have to carry water from the distant river anymore. Most impressive was the worship in Nepali, with a big group of Nepali Christians who sang, prayed, and shared the joy of their faith and devotion to God. The staff families were all there. It was especially enriching to hear those UMN children loudly singing choruses in Nepali! Continuing on our way home in KTM, we made another stopover at Pokhara to bid farewell to the Rural Development staff and families. We spent time at our favorite hotel, soaking in the beauty and tranquility of the lake and mountains.

Narendra and Sheilah Singh invited us to many dinners, but the occasion of his mother's seventy-ninth birthday was a highlight. Captain and Shanti Nayyar were present. Narendra's brother, who was a member of the High Court of Nepal, and his wife and son joined us. The second oldest Rana was also present. A pilot from the Royal Airlines of Nepal and his wife feted that joyful occasion, as well as daughter Jyoti and her husband who had arrived from Agra for the celebration. What a hilarious time we had! I videotaped the affair and prize that CD to this day. Peggy baked a birthday cake with seven candles, explaining that seven is a perfect number. What a feast we enjoyed! Narendra and I also entertained the celebrants with stories, jokes, and memories of times shared. Sheilah asked me to sing The Lord's Prayer, which I did. We were good family members present on an auspicious occasion, never to be forgotten. Peggy joined in a bit of folk dancing, but I refrained warning them that I was a "toe smasher."

Nima and Angdoma invited us for a daylong visit to their new home in Lazimpat, near the American Embassy. Their whole clan was there to join in the festivities. At folding tables, delicious hot Tibetan tea was served in ornate silver mugs. Two Buddhist monks were there to read, in rich sonorous voices, their scriptures. Angdoma admitted that she could not understand what they read, but it was supposed to bring good luck to have them. At noon, the finest dinner one could ever imagine was served out on the lawn where we gathered at tables of steaming hot rice, meats, fruit, nuts, and chang (rice beer). It was a most delightful day. We would miss our dear friends who were such close ones. How gratefully we recalled all the Buddhist celebrations and special occasions at Boudhanath.

During the last month, Peggy's sister, Hope Abigail, came from Brazil to see for herself what we had been doing. She and her husband were Presbyterian missionaries there for thirty-three years. It was a time of sightseeing in KTM, and spending time atop Pulchoki and Nagarkot to wonder at those mountains. Sanu invited us to her village to meet her mother and sister. The brilliant yellow mustard plants were in full bloom. Hope was struck by how simple the Nepali mud-brick houses were, but overwhelmed by the gracious and generous hostess, Sanu. As a nurse, she was eager to visit Patan Hospital and view firsthand what Peggy had communicated in her letters. We attended the Patan congregation worship. Hope said that though she would have understood more if people spoke and sang in the Portuguese language of Brazil, she could sense the vitality of faith and devotion of those Nepali believers.

She felt an affinity with newly found brothers and sisters in Christ. Peggy introduced Hope to our UMN people and to many of the Nepali people with whom she had worked and helped in special ways. That time ended too soon, and we had to let Hope return to Frank and her family: David, Deborah, Johnny, Daniel, and Stephen.

There were also the rounds of dinners at the Indian Embassy, the Chinese Council, with the HMGN (His Majesty's Government of Nepal) Secretaries with whom I had "impatiently" worked getting permission for Projects/Programs, and with UMN families, one of which was Anders and Birgit Kammensjo. They again apologized for calling us Eggy and Pal in the early days of our acquaintance. We would miss them, and many many others. Farewells at Patan congregation were the most difficult. We had sat in worship in the midst of healthy Nepalis, but also the crippled, the lepers, the blind, men who had served time in prisons for their faith – saints in the Kingdom of God. We had shared with them the common cup of Holy Communion and the broken bread. In prayer and praise, we had deeply experienced the vitality of our mutual faith, hope, and love. Enriched in Spirit, we commended those dear brothers and sisters in Christ to persevere and carry on.

During those final weeks, Peggy and I reflected on our eleven years in Nepal, that had so rapidly passed. Our love and devotion to each other had deepened and matured as we shared in a ministry the Lord so graciously opened up for us to follow. Our work had not been easy, but it was a never-to-be-forgotten experience. What strategic changes had occurred, what transforming progress in education, health, and rural industry and appropriate development!

While all the problems related to Mass Poverty had not been solved, an innovative beginning was in place, not in theory but in reality. The Goals set by HMGN and their efforts for economic and basic needs Development, together with the implementation of UMN Goals and Purposes in its Projects and Programs, were being realized. During those eleven years the death rate of children caused by malnutrition and diarrhea, which in the first five years had been fifty percent, had gradually been reduced. The life expectancy had been raised from twenty-seven to forty-seven years. Schools, hospitals, clinics, and vocational/technical institutes were increasingly opened and maintained. Having noted the prototypes in the UMN's institutions, HMGN adapted much for their outreach. Increasingly, Nepalis were the Managers/Directors of services and commerce. Some UMN Projects were handed over to the Government, for instance, the Butwal Power Company and Grid. The Government was requesting UMN specialists to join in Teaching Institutes and Hospitals.

Overt persecution of Christians was almost nonexistent, except for six arrested and convicted men from East Nepal. From the local to the District to the Supreme Court, their appeals were dealt with. The Judges asked them why they had converted, to which those humble, almost illiterate men replied, "We did not convert – only God can convert the human soul." Case dismissed! The Nepal Body of Believers had grown from fifteen hundred in the year we arrived (1978) to forty thousand in 1989. Spread out into all Nepal were Christian groups who actively witnessed and lived worthy of the gospel. They were building worship centers, legally able to register the land plots and assemble at will. They were establishing primary schools for villagers denied education by isolated distances. Orphanages were springing up, social services to the community were extending a helping hand to the needy. In Galatians 5:6 we read, "The only thing that counts is faith expressing itself through love." Yes, Peggy and I were to retire, but we could return to the USA with the satisfaction that our participation was continuing to flower and grow.

Part IV: Retirement and Florida

Chapter 46

From Nepal to Florida Via Hong Kong and China

As hired and agreed upon, the Mendies sent their rattly old bus with crew to transport our cargo freight to the airport. They made quick work of emptying the Rana kitchen, putting all twenty-seven items on the seats and aisles. Bidding farewell to the Rana family, Peggy and I took seats in the bus and headed for the KTM airport. Two weeks prior to our departure, Peggy had sold the jeep to a Nepali car dealer. She and her sister, Hope Abigail, were driving to the Blue Star Hotel for some shopping. In the rear window was a For Sale sign and the amount. A car followed them to the parking area and the deal was done. The buyer let us drive the jeep for the last two weeks. As the reader may remember, I dread customs inspections. With the help of a small army of porters, the twenty-seven items were neatly arranged on the platform. The Inspector was summoned. We showed him the fat list with every last thing itemized. He ordered that all, everyone of those trunks and suitcases, be opened! I had the keys and did what was necessary. He made a cursory survey and signed the manifest. (We did not complain.) After thanking those young helpers and tipping them, Peggy and I went to the passenger terminal and checked in for our flight to Hong Kong. As the plane circled KTM, we viewed for the last time a place very dear to us. The patchwork of farms and red brick houses, the Valley, and many villages and towns we had visited came into sight and vanished. Our mission to Nepal for eleven years was ending, but we hoped and prayed that the ministry we had been privileged to experience would continue to grow and mature. We knew that the UMN Projects and Programs and the Nepali Church would carry on. We had shared what we could.

Peggy and I proceeded to Hong Kong with a good bit of trepidation. It had been about two weeks since the Tiananmen Square June Fourth Incident (Six Four). Nonetheless, since Peggy had made reservations through China Travels well in advance, we hoped that our itinerary was still possible. It was great to visit again the arcades and restaurants in Tsim Sha Tsui, take the Tramway to Victoria Peak, ride the Star Ferry, and feast at Jumbo Floating Restaurant. As part of our shopping tour, we visited the travel agency to inquire if all was "go." The young Chinese woman smiled and informed us that the previous day the letter of permission had arrived saying that it was safe for tourists to visit China. She gave us the little red carry-on bags, badges to wear, and assurance that we would be met at the airports by their personal representatives, who would arrange taxis to take us to the hotel at every stop. What a relief!

Two days later, we boarded a train for Guangzhou (Canton), now a most impressive Finance/Industrial Center. We did a bit of sightseeing waiting for our plane to Xi'an (pronounced She-on). As promised, there was a China Tour Representative to see we boarded the right plane safely. On our arrival, another one met us and by taxi deposited us at the Hotel Xi'an, a four star hotel much grander than what we had reserved. For three days, we toured that famous city where the Silk Road from the Middle East terminated. One could easily imagine the camel trains being unloaded with fineries of silk, gold, and precious stones. What spectacular sights: the City Wall near the hotel, a fifty-foot-high military defense system surrounding the inner city; the Bell Tower, over a hundred feet tall, which marks the exact center of Xi'an, where rare pottery adorned the walkways; the Drum Tower, almost identical to the Bell Tower, with its huge drum used to signal the time of day or night and to alarm citizens of fires or attacks; and the Big Wild Goose Pagoda, a two-hundred-foot-tall series of walled-in floors and steps, now a Museum of Buddhist art.

On the second evening, we took a short stroll near our hotel. To our surprise, long tables of curios, art pieces, and handicrafts had been set up. This pleased Peggy, and the vendors were most pleased to have their first customers in two weeks. Peggy bought a jade piece commemorating the story of a worker on the Great Wall. A girl, whose family was forced to send one male worker to help build the Wall, disguised herself as a man and worked in place of her father until she died and was buried in the Wall's roadway, as so many others had been. The shopkeeper related this story with feeling. Peggy did not bargain much! On our way to the hotel, we came across a group of young men playing table tennis with lots of enthusiasm. We paused to watch. Suddenly, the games stopped, and the high school students greeted us, inquiring from where we had come. We said the USA was our homeland, but we had worked in Pakistan and Nepal for thirty-five years and were on our way home to retirement. Cautiously, they asked if we felt safe, whether we had heard of the disturbances, and was word getting out? This was said almost in a whisper by those near us. We nodded and assured them that the whole world had heard and was deeply disturbed, but helpless to do anything. They nodded. Then one asked, "What is freedom?" This initiated a twenty-minute discussion of that question. We did our best. Taking our turn, we asked, "What does freedom mean to

Tiananmen Square

you?" The best answer was from a young lad who quietly said, "In a controlled situation, we aspire for a changed future at our peril! Is it really true that in your country you are free to do and say what you want?" "Yes," we replied, "as responsible family members and citizens, we are free to be, become, say, and do within the boundaries of law and order and respect for others. We have the right to our own opinions and views, but others have the right to agree or disagree. What makes the difference is the system in place." How we would have liked to adopt them all and enroll them in a high school in the USA!

On our last day in Xi'an, we took a bus tour into the countryside. We got a glimpse at last of village, town, and rural life. There were many laborers in the fields and hundreds of cyclists on the roads. We visited an agricultural commune, so neat and clean that it must have been on the tour's route for some time. Some men were drying rice, raking the grain to help it dry. There were stacks of hay and fodder. Animals were herded to water. The bus stopped for our refreshment at an immense array of shops and vendors. They were actually selling produce, handicrafts, and Coca Cola! We hoped that this was indeed free enterprise. Proceeding on, we arrived at the world-famous museum of the Terra Cotta Warriors. Outside the entrance were a few statues of soldiers, horses, and a chariot on display. However, after buying our admission tickets and being sternly warned not to use a camera, we entered the museum proper, the size of three football fields! There in battle array were over seven thousand life-sized warriors, with horses, chariots, and weapons lined up facing the King's burial throne. No two were alike. Clay replicas, they had been molded and baked in pottery furnaces and buried for over two thousand years. That was an astounding sight! We were riveted there until the bus driver announced that the bus was about to leave for Xi'an. Peggy and I had much to discuss regarding our three days of being enriched by people and sights in a culture so different from our own.

We landed the next day in Beijing. Again, we were met by a China Tours representative, taxied to a five star hotel two blocks from Tiananmen Square, and settled into a room on the seventeenth floor. They were certainly keeping us safe and well cared for. We had reserved the same Chinese hotel we had the previous year – this was pure luxury. My, what a panorama that room made possible! No pollution this year; the skies were clear, the air fresh and clean. Recent rains had done the trick. The next day, we went shopping and sightseeing on foot. However, Tiananmen Square was completely off limits, guarded by Police and Army units. We were cautious. The forces that had crushed those students and workers in their demand for political reforms were scattered at intersections and at strategic positions.

We again visited the Forbidden City, the Zoo, several Parks, and the Temple Palace. We had time to see things we had missed before. China Tours hired a taxi for us to visit again the Ming Tombs and the Great Wall of China. Two young men, one the driver, picked us up at the hotel, drove past Tiananmen Square and the Forbidden City, and on to the highway. Peggy and I kept looking for signs of damage and wreckage, but there were none we could see. The cleanup had been thorough. As we traveled and introduced ourselves, we assured them that, judging from the news accounts we had read, we were sorry for the loss of life. Gradually, they began to share what they had seen and heard during the confrontation. It was a frightening account, too gruesome to record here. We remained silent and nodded from time to time. Later, Peggy and I were struck by an amazing insight – neither these taxi men nor the high school students had ever said anything against their country. This could have been an instinctual safeguard against being exposed and punished, or was it that these loyal survivors, in spite of all the regimentation and curtailment of freedom, had pride in their nation?

Since it was such a clear, bright day, we could more plainly marvel on seeing the Ming Tombs and the Great Wall. (Descriptions have been previously given and are not repeated here.) The difference was this time there were not as many visitors, which made it easier to explore the sights. We could look into the Guard Houses on the Great Wall, and exhaust ourselves on those countless steeps and steps. Through our binoculars and camera lenses, we could see the horizons and distant walled peaks. We thought of the suffering of those laborers as they had been forced to construct that edifice, which ultimately failed to keep out invaders. Then, it was back to Beijing

At the Great Wall

and our hotel. That evening we celebrated our wedding anniversary in the lofty top-floor restaurant. We were served an elegant dinner with a generous slice of Black

Bullet Hole (Upper Right) in Hotel Window

Forest cake for dessert. However, we missed our family and friends even more, because we were the only ones in that dining room, except for the waiters. That was a lonely moment! On returning to our room using a different elevator, we saw a large window which had been "frosted" by a stray bullet, a memorial to unsung heroes. We thanked the Lord for family, freedom, and new friends.

Early in the morning, we caught our flight to Hong Kong for our two-day layover. We stayed at a hotel near the main shopping center. Joining us for dinner at the Jumbo Floating Restaurant were Tom, Mamie, and Justin Wong. The four-course dinner was superb. From a tank at the entrance, we had selected the fish, which was served with all the trimmings. The next afternoon, Tom showed us where he was working, conducting computer survey studies of the industrial finances of Hong Kong – really complicated and impressive. We thanked him for all the work at UMN he and Mamie had done. It was good we did, because several years later Tom died of stomach cancer. On Sunday, we joined the Wongs and about a million others on a Sympathy March from downtown on to Victoria Park to register their reaction to the massacre in Beijing. A replica of the Goddess of Democracy, which the workers and students had erected in Tiananmen Square, towered over the park. They were singing, shouting, and giving forceful speeches, as the citizens of Hong Kong demonstrated their solidarity with those courageous people of Beijing. That experience was the pinnacle of our visit to China. We flew to Los Angeles via Hawaii and customs, declaring our unaccompanied luggage hopefully on its way to Tampa, Florida. After a night's rest stop in L.A., we continued on. We were near exhaustion, but it had been an exciting time and a fitting departure from Asia. Our minds and hearts were in a whirl as we recalled where we had been and what we had done. Was it really true that this flight would be the end of thirty-five challenging years? We were going home to family and so much more. And we laughed – we had never owned a home in the USA. We were homeless! After that long, tiring flight, we landed safely at the Tampa International Airport.

Jo Ann, Tanya, Erik, and Stan

Standing at the Gate were Stan and Jo Ann, waving their greetings. They called, "Welcome to Florida!" Having stuffed our bags into the trunk, we settled back as we whizzed along on the Causeway. There were many questions and replies by all. Soon we were in Palm Harbor and at Sandy Hook Road. Tanya and Erik were there to greet us. My, how they had grown! It was good to be back in that land of "unboiled water," though we often hesitated before filling a glass from the water tap. There is something amazing about being with family.

Relaxation is one dimension, but there are others – the diminishing of distance and isolation from loved ones, the comfort of knowing all is well, the filling of the gaps in relationships, and heartfelt thanks for all God's blessings. There are many more, but I hope you sense what Peggy and I felt as we accepted Stan's and Jo Ann's loving hospitality. Unfortunately, this also meant that Tanya had to move from her room and bed to make way for Grandma and Grandpa. But we never heard a word of complaint from her. Erik, too, shared his home and space.

Four days later, customs called to say our luggage had arrived. Stan and a friend rented a U-Haul to help me retrieve our belongings of thirty-five years in the Subcontinent. Clearing of customs was quite easy, especially when they asked what was in a randomly selected trunk/suitcase and I read out the contents from that fat list without fail. There was one exception: number seventeen, filled with the eight by ten carpet from Pakistan, had not arrived. We loaded the rest and deposited them in the Econo Mini Storage. Two days later we collected number seventeen. Mission accomplished!

Chapter 47

House Hunting, Orientation, Quite Settled, A Home, Texas

For the record, we arrived in Florida June 1989. You should know that it had been quite a conflict to decide where to retire. All four children wanted us near them. The problem was we had heard of and experienced the snowy bitter cold of Boston and the Midwest. Texas was too gun-toting for us – we had watched Westerns. Stan convinced us that being in Florida would remind us of Pakistan with its sun, fruit, heat, mosquitoes, and that in the winter everyone would want to come and visit! We decided to give it a try. Stan and Jo Ann had a large two-story house with a large patio and screened-in swimming pool. Stan and Erik entertained us with their abilities. We named Erik "Fish" because he dived, swam, did handstands, somersaults, and learned how to duck the beach ball Stan threw at him. He seemed to enjoy the attention. Tanya's birthday was duly celebrated. Fondly we recalled the expired cake mix in Nepal. Jo Ann's angel food cake was fresh and delicious.

After several days of rest, adjusting to time change and travel weariness, we began to seriously search for a house. Researching the Yellow Pages, consulting with Stan and Jo Ann, and scanning the newspapers, we began to make a list of reputable realtors. It was quite overwhelming because we wanted to live in a friendly neighborhood, near good shopping, and not to spend a fortune, which we did not have. Stan found a bargain price for an excellent used Mercury car and helped us through the negotiations. That car helped us to become mobile and lost a few times. We were attracted to Highland Lakes, a vast settlement of seven hundred fifty new and used condominiums just off US 19, a busy four-lane highway. Forty years before, that whole area had been a mass of orange orchards. It had become a honeycomb of furnished and unfurnished condos built around one large Club House, a Golf Course, and two smaller Club Houses. The sign said "Private Retirement for Fifty-Five and Older." We qualified! Stan and Jo Ann suggested that in the first instance we not buy, but rent a place, so that if we found we didn't like it we could move. Otherwise we would be stuck. This proved to be sound advice. Unexpectedly, one happy day, a lady realtor called and showed us a five-room condo which was for rent. We decided to take it. This meant moving again, retrieving our stored luggage. We furnished the condo and stored the excess in the attached garage. At last, we had a place to call our own. This had taken three weeks, which meant that Stan's family must have been weary by that time, though there never was a complaint. How grateful we were for their love, patience, and help.

In the thick of that search we were becoming oriented to life in the USA. I had to enroll in Social Security and in the Presbyterian Pension Plan. Talk about paperwork and visits to offices. There were bank accounts to open, medical and dental help to arrange, and aisle upon aisle of products at Publix supermarket to marvel at. Most shocking were those long aisles of cat and dog foods, toys, and accessories. We thought of the villagers of Pakistan and Nepal who had barely enough to keep alive. What a contrast! Driving the crowded roads was another challenge. There were times I was tempted to take the left-hand side. Speaking at a local church one evening, a question was asked how we liked the busy roads in Florida. I answered that it was confusing because Americans drove on the "wrong side" of the road, but it was less crowded than in Pakistan, where roads were filled with goats, oxen, bicycles, rickshaws, buses, pedestrians, cars, and horse-drawn carts. As an example, I shared what it was like to ride in a motor rickshaw. Once one got used to the constant weaving in and out of traffic, one noticed the speed and dexterity of the driver taking turns at full speed, honking the horn every ten seconds, and the like. I related an experience of Dr. Winnifred Thomas who traveled daily from FC College to the Anna C. Weir Clinic in old Lahore. She was a brave soul. All went quite well until one morning the rickshaw driver went faster than usual, more erratically, and at a sharp turn landed the machine on its side. A Constable was called to inspect the accident. He asked for the driver's license. The driver said, "My brother has it – he loaned me the rickshaw today so I could practice!" Fortunately, Dr. Thomas only suffered minor scrapes and bruises.

Peggy and I enjoyed our condo. We even bought a TV and microwave. McDonald's was only a five-minute walk away. We took refreshing walks around the pond, joined in on activities at the Club House, and got acquainted with our neighbors. We worshiped at a nearby Presbyterian Church. Occasionally we invited Stan and family for a Pakistani dinner of rice pilau, chicken curry, flat bread, spiced veggies, and cake and ice cream. Peggy had not lost her touch! Selma Miller, who lived adjacent to us, was a champion neighbor. In her nineties, she was mentally sharp as a teenager. Selma, a widow living alone, was from Michigan, but had done her Nurse's training in the Cook County Hospital in Chicago. She entertained us with many fascinating experiences. Of course, she wanted to know where we had been and what we had done – everyone has a story! Selma admitted that judging from our over-stuffed garage, she had surmised we were army people. To her surprise, we told her she was living next to missionaries! She did not blink – she was Lutheran. Once every month,

Enjoying Life at 1313A Whitebridge Drive

Selma would invite us to lunch at her condo. These were precisely planned and served complete with linen napkins and goblets. There was always a bouquet of flowers and lots of lively chat. Of course, Peggy invited her to our condo for lunch and the same type of hospitality! Then, one day Selma remarked that since we were close friends we could use paper napkins and Peggy was not to serve such grand dinners, as they took too much

effort. We were family, not neighbors! Her daughter, Katherine, visited her mother quite often. She, too, was impressed with her mother's weekly shopping list, with every item for meals outlined in minute detail. We felt settled in and were thankful for being part of a retirement community.

One morning, as we were taking our daily walk around the pond, Peggy suggested we consult the Club House notice board to see whether there was a condo for sale. There it was on a three by five card: Condo for Sale. Call John – at this number. We hurried home and called immediately. John gave the directions, and we fairly ran to his condo. It was just around the corner from us, not fifty yards away. He took us next door and introduced us to Emma Meir, the owner of 1313A, Whitebridge Drive. She gave us a tour of that clean and I mean meticulously tidy condo. It had a large living/dining room combination, with a fully equipped kitchen opening off the dining room. The master bedroom had an attached bathroom with tub and shower and a walk-in closet. At the end of the hallway was another bedroom. A separate bathroom was halfway down the hall. It had nine hundred thirty square feet of floor area. The patio had a flagstone base, and the outer wall had tendrils of creeping vines. We told her we liked what we saw, inquiring the cost. She said, "It is worth fifty thousand dollars. You will be the second residents of this condo. My husband, Charlie, bought it after selling our restaurant in Long Island. He died six months ago." Peggy remarked that was a little more than we had expected. Emma reduced it two thousand dollars, because she said she was pleased to know that a couple with a German name was buying her condo. We shook hands. I ran back for the checkbook, paid the down payment, and discussed what furnishings she might be selling. She had her list and prices. We needed most of them so made another deal. As we left, Emma reminded us that the front walk and open verandah had to be swept daily to keep things in shape. We liked her very much! We also set the closure date and terms of sale. She thought we should not have any trouble getting the approval of the Highland Lakes Executive Committee. Emma thanked us for answering her card so quickly – fifteen minutes after posting! She had dreaded having to show critical strangers her home. John drove us to the Title Company where we made the arrangements to close, apply for a mortgage, and occupy our home.

On December 1, 1989, we began to shift things to our new home. I carried over the light and fragile items, but wondered how to empty our garage. We had ordered a new sofa from Haverty's, which was delivered by truck. I asked the men if they could transport our heavy items. They said they had to get permission from their boss. At noon, they arrived and made short work of moving our things, depositing them in our attached garage, line by line, pile by pile. It took two weeks to position everything, that is, except the many boxes of documents and knickknacks from overseas, which continued to adorn the garage. We were pleased to learn that our maintenance fee included the lawn being cut, cable TV, hedges trimmed, and water. Electricity and telephone were our obligation. Across the street was a swimming pool reserved for residents. We enjoyed exercising there and getting some suntan. Peggy could swim, I could not. Wading was my favorite. We met many new neighbors at the pool and Club functions, but noted that they were "older." People were impressed that Peggy still wore saris. They were comfortable and always in fashion. She was asked to demonstrate how to arrange six yards of silk so skillfully. Gradually, we had settled into a friendly community and felt quite at home.

Hope and Stephen invited us and Stan's family to celebrate Christmas with them in Texas. John, Esther (pregnant with Arin), and Joe joined us from Boston. Stephen was a Professor at the University of Texas at Austin in the Philosophy Department. He also taught South Asian Studies. His long years of Sanskrit study and research were paying off. Hope was working for an air charter outfit called The Golden Goose Company. The "Head Goose," an eccentric Texan retired from the oil business, decided to charter out his planes for the write-off. To his surprise, the Gulfstream IV (G-IV), which was the first available for charter, was in great demand all over the world. He hired Hope ("Little Goose") for her international experience. Having consulted and gotten the approval of Stan and Jo Ann, we accepted. To accommodate everyone, Hope was renting a ranch for us to stay in. That sounded just large enough! You can imagine the hurried shopping and packing the car – we were eager to launch out on this grand adventure. It was only eleven hundred miles away! Tanya and Erik wanted to ride with us. Stan and Jo Ann were to follow a day later. The first day, we made it to Mobile, Alabama, where we found a good motel. We got an early morning start, because Grandpa had set his watch an hour the wrong way in anticipation of the time zone change. It was dark and raining hard as we drove on Interstate 10, barely able to navigate. Fortunately we spotted a place to have breakfast. That helped to ease the situation. As it cleared, we made good time and arrived at Hope's house in the Hill Country southwest of Austin by late afternoon. The temperature was cold. After supper, they directed us to the ranch where we settled in. The next day, Stan and Jo Ann joined us. We gathered logs and mesquite tree stumps to stoke the fireplace in the living room. That night it snowed. The next day a frigid cold wave invaded Texas – down to zero! We had insulated the outside water taps, but the tank froze. Peggy and I kept a fire roaring through the night. The others slept under heavy quilts fully clothed. We tried to emulate Texas ranchers who took such things in their stride. Next morning, the sun made a glorious appearance. It began to warm up – there was now some hope of surviving.

We had a memorable Christmas celebration at Hope's house complete with wreaths and tree. She and Stephen prepared a sumptuous dinner with all the trimmings and desserts. It was good to be together as family. We had agreed to give one gift to each person. There were a few extra ones, but we knew Peggy would do that anyway! A special gift was given by Hope to Erik – electronic drumsticks. I know Stan wondered if this was revenge for some of the hard times he had given her in earlier years. However, the gift backfired. Erik zestfully drummed on every surface including Hope's dog's head. The "hypersensitive" (as Hope called him) hound and "wimp" (as the vet called him) rose up with a howl, then snuggled back into his blanket with a reproachful stare. Apologizing to Malone, Erik put the drumsticks away. We sang carols and shared Christmas experiences. Peggy and I sang an Urdu carol and told about some of the customs and traditions of Pakistani Christians. It was cozy in front of the fire. We were having a great time. We went back to the ranch for another night. Thankfully, the weather had improved.

With Hope and Stephen

The next morning, Hope arrived to lead us on an exploration of the ranch. We trudged through two inches of snow. Tanya and Erik had a wonderful time. They hadn't experienced snow since they left Nebraska years before. There were snowballs and a small fort. Tanya and Erik enjoyed the crackle of ice breaking under their boots and trampled many ice-covered puddles and brooks. On our return to the ranch house, we dried our wet coats and gloves, while drinking mugs of hot chocolate with marshmallows.

It was time to depart the next day. Tanya and Erik joined Stan and Jo Ann. They made it back in one long day and part of the night. Peggy and I traveled west to visit dear friends in Arizona. Having retired, we were in no hurry to return to our condo, which we had left securely locked. It was a relief not to have to hurry, to put in a day's work, and to somehow cope with the pressures we had known. We decided that retirement was not so bad after all.

Chapter 48

Texas is Big, Tucson, Phoenix, El Paso/Juarez, and Home

Texans "modestly" brag about their expanse of territory, with ample proof of its enormous two hundred sixty-two thousand seventeen square miles of land. Passing through the Big Country we were amazed by the hills and dry lands, rushing rivers, ranch upon ranch, large herds of cattle, thick groves of trees and water holes, sagebrush, wildflowers, but no gun-toting cowboys, which caused us to revise our Western image. However, we learned that it was in vogue to have a gun rack in the back window of your pickup truck, complete with an impressive gun. At food, gassing up, and exercise stops, we met charming, friendly people speaking with a definite accent. I thought I could have corrected that with some intense phonetic drills as I had done in Pakistan. Peggy wisely reminded me that a better way would be to pick up their drawls and y'alls. At times we got somewhat bored by the repetitive views in that big state. I recalled the story of a Texan college student who invited an Asian Indian to visit his home in Texas. Informing his guest how big this State was, he exclaimed, " Texas is so big you can board a train at Lake Charles, ride two days and a night – and still be in Texas." His Indian friend remarked, "I know. We, too, have trains in India like that!" After a night's motel stop, we continued on toward Tucson, Arizona.

We were to visit two friends of long standing: Lydia Thomas and her sister, Leona Behneman, who had moved from Carroll and Arcadia, Iowa to Tucson in retirement. We were royally welcomed and made to feel right at home. Peggy again thanked Lydia for all the dresses and blouses she had selected which were on sale and put in layaway. Lydia recalled Peggy's mom coming to collect and send them to Ames. She also recalled Beulah's love and devotion for Peggy. She had always proudly brought Lydia up to date on all that Peggy was doing. Lydia also shared that she knew the "cost" of Beulah's efforts to provide the loving support of her daughter – it took lots of egg money! We reviewed many endearing memories. They brought us up to date on how Lydia, Leona, and her husband Elmer had migrated West after selling their farm near Arcadia. Elmer had passed away several years before. Lydia showed us the file of letters Peggy had sent from Pakistan and Nepal. Remarkably, they could share in what we had done in those two countries as if they had been there. We filled in the spaces and behind the scenes of what we had experienced. We hosted them to dinner each evening in their favorite restaurants and explored the parks where we were duly impressed by giant cactus plants standing as guards to strata of balancing rocks. One day, we drove with them to a Native American reservation. Every two weeks they and others from their church made quilts, lap robes, and sweaters to distribute and taught basic skills in handicrafts. How lovingly we all were received. On Sunday, we attended the Presbyterian Church, where to my surprise and joy I met a fellow classmate from Princeton Seminary who was the Pastor. We had a short but rapid-fire visit following the worship. What a small world! Too soon we had to leave those dear friends and be on our way. Life is a series of Hellos and Goodbyes.

Heading north we reached Phoenix where we were to meet Hans and Trudy Hebert. We had met in Lahore while they were on holiday in Pakistan from their work with USAID in Bangladesh. Mutual friends had invited Peggy and me to dinner at an outdoor restaurant on Fountain Road, Gulberg. We struck up a friendship and have corresponded to the present. Hans and Trudy lived in a house fully decorated in Southwestern style. There were hunting trophies of deer, salmon caught in Alaska, and artful handicrafts they had created. Their hospitality cannot be matched by anyone! All four of us have a sense of humor, a full resume of jokes, anecdotes, and stories from many lands. Each summer they made trips to Alaska to visit their two sons and their wives and children. That's when the fish stories started. Hans told us of the huge size of the salmon they caught and how they ate their fill, canned some, and shared the rest. Those fish, according to Hans, were almost as large as whales! They loaded their caravan with the tinned delicacies and drove along the Alaskan Highway. One year, they were driving along when a man opened his car window yelling, "Your van is on fire!" Hans jammed on the brakes and grabbed the fire extinguisher. He made some headway putting out the fire, but his cylinder was too small. A large semitrailer stopped behind them. The driver leaped out, grabbed his large extinguisher, and put out the flames. That's the good American way! On examination, they learned that the air conditioner had overheated. They stopped at the next large town to have it repaired. That was a close one. Once a year, they visited their five children widely separated throughout the USA.

They had invited us to show our slides and share our experiences in Pakistan and Nepal at their church. Peggy wowed them with those personal touches of helping people in many ways. I shared the work of the Projects and Programs in both Pakistan and Nepal. The question period was intense with searching, penetrating inquiries. They knew what mission was all about, having heard the experiences of Hans and Trudy. That evening, we discussed how informed the group had been, interested in what was happening in distant lands. They were not, like so many others, parochial and insulated from the world's problems, the needy in many lands. Hans and Trudy took us on many trips to see the grandeur of Arizona, including the elite retirement communities of Scottsdale, with mansions built on the rocky edges of the mountain and overflowing to the adjacent hills. We were not envious or resentful, but we did wonder whether the residents were happy and content. It was their world and they could afford to use their resources as they wished. I guess we were awed by the contrast with what we had experienced in trying to help those in Mass Poverty.

That inevitable last evening, we four sat in front of the roaring fireplace and talked of many things, but the highlight of our conversation centered around friendship. We had enjoyed the dinner at their choice of restaurants which is the custom of visitors thanking hosts. We were good friends. A friend has been described as someone who knows all about you – good or bad – and still loves you. I like that! Peggy and I had friends in the USA, in Pakistan, in China, in Nepal, in India, in Scandinavia, in Europe, in the UK, in Canada, and elsewhere. Those dear friends were the living blocks of many shared "good times" and "troubled times" – all part of that meshwork of the most significant relationships one has the privilege to experience. We celebrated being friends, knowing that even after a long separation of time and distance we could meet and begin to take up the thread of where we had left off, as if we had never parted. We four had learned that in a cold, cruel world where there is so much anger, violence, and exploitation, the more excellent way is one of love, trust, integrity, and the building up of people, not tearing them down or using them for selfish ends. In our moments of sharing we began to name and recall many of those distant friends and the fond memories of how we had become friends. That's better than discussing politics!

We traveled in the direction of El Paso, Texas, where we planned a shopping visit/tour of Juarez in Mexico. Peggy and I had never been in Mexico before. Crossing the border we entered a festive city, with loud blaring music and colorful costumes. Peggy wanted a new handbag. We found several leather shops with counters filled with bags and other leather goods, finely tooled. She bought two deerskin bags, a chess set for Erik, and lots of handicrafts. I looked at the impressive sombreros, but decided they would make me look too tall and handsome. We treated ourselves to a genuine Mexican lunch, with all the trimmings. Those spices reminded us of Pakistan and India. For entertainment, we were privileged to watch a young boy and girl dance with grace and gusto to the tunes of the Mexican band. It was a rare treat for us to see them in their colorful costumes. Peggy discovered the Guayabera shirts, so richly embroidered. She insisted we buy four in a variety of colors. They were almost identical to the ones I always wore in Pakistan. One doesn't have to tuck in the shirt tail – they are most comfortable. We had no trouble with customs. They casually asked, "What did you buy?" We showed them, and they waved us through.

The next morning, we joined a tour of the border organized by a Special Interest group. Their van picked us up at the motel to transport the group to the Border Fence on the outskirts of El Paso. We walked along the border on the USA side. The guide explained how the illegal Mexican and Central American workers entered into the USA through holes in the Fence. To reinforce his description, he showed us many holes dug through its base. First, they had to cross the Rio Grande, then search for a hole and make a dash for safety in the USA. We asked many questions: Where are the guards? Why leave the holes open? Why do they cross over the border? He answered that the guards had a lot of territory to cover. They could not be everywhere at once. People cross the border to escape poverty by trying to find a place to work to support their families. He shared something we had not known. "At first," he stated, "we closed every hole as rapidly as we could. Who do you think were the first to complain? Not the 'wet backs,' but the owners of those large factories strung along the highway adjacent to the Fence!" He pointed to the long string of factories and, shaking his head, asked, "Why are those factories so close to the border?" With a glint in his eye, he explained that many famous brand items are produced in those factories. Using illegal immigrants to work at a low wage, they can put on the tag "Made in the USA." Profit was the goal, not rescuing those in Mass Poverty.

As we headed back to Florida and home, Peggy and I could barely endure the pain of seeing the plight of those desperate workers. Our view of the immigration problem had a new focus. We recalled our visit to the Statue of Liberty and reading "Give me your tired, your poor, your huddled masses yearning to breathe free." Not only in the USA but also in many nations of our world, cheap labor is encouraged to enter and slave, until they become a recognizable minority, a threat to the citizen work force, and considered a liability. How thankful we were to have worked in Pakistan and Nepal, assisting many to attain quality of life in their attempts to reach out for development, not exploitation.

Chapter 49

Settling In, Brazil, Iowa, Family Reunion, Boston

During the Spring of 1990, we were fully occupied settling in and enjoying our first home, which gave us a sense of responsibility and challenge. Furnishing those bare rooms was a means of getting acquainted with local shops and stores. The living room soon became a comfortable lounging repose with an expensive sofa from Haverty's, a Lazy Boy recliner, a china closet from Reliable Furniture (filled with second/third hand bargains), another smaller sofa for the second bedroom, which became the TV/Computer room, a new fridge, and so on. Quite a few discussions arose over the problem of positioning Beulah's paintings, family photos, and artifacts from Pakistan and Nepal. After a few days, my left thumb recovered from the hammer blows that were not accurately aimed at the nail. The carpets from abroad were strategically placed. How pleased we were to add those colorful art pieces. They partially covered the greenish yellow wall-to-wall carpeting. I knew that in the near future Peggy would purchase new drapes, which would be the first step to installing new carpeting to match the color scheme. She had the knack of planning ahead and subtly convincing me that I was right in selecting the color schemes she had chosen. There came a day when we could just sit and enjoy our tea/coffee and homemade cookies/cake breaks. How satisfying!

Of course, there was a front lawn and empty flower beds. The mowing and trimming of hedges were done by the maintenance crew, but we wanted to add colorful beds of roses, perennials, and border flowers. We were soon warned, however, that we had to personally care for what we planted. This convinced us to plant a bougainvillea vine on the south side of the house where it would get lots of sunshine. So there! However, when pruning the roses and that vine, I discovered spiny thorns which kept me alert. Daily walks around the pond, wading and sunbathing at the pool, visiting neighbors, and shopping kept us fully engaged, but we loved it. Stan brought a computer and taught us how to use it. This was a great gift. After some frustrating attempts, we got the hang of it. No more carbon papers and duplicating machines!

In early July, we visited Hope and Frank Arnold in Brazil. We took flights from Tampa, Miami, and Belem to Fortaleza. The mighty Amazon River and wide expanses of forests were an impressive sight. It was hot. Even though the hotel in Belem boasted about their air-conditioned rooms, that noisy fan and wind tunnel were a disappointment. It was good to be with Peggy's only sister, Hope Abigail, Frank, and their son, Stephen. They gave us a rousing welcome at the air terminal and pampered us with matchless hospitality. Hope and the helper served us typical Brazilian meals – flavorful, delicious food. Peggy and I marveled at what a rich culture we were in. We especially liked the dominant colors of orange and blue, the festive air of open friendly people warmly greeting us and proudly welcoming us to their nation. They inquired from where we had come. We answered, "Florida." "Oh, tourists!" they replied. They spoke in Portuguese and simple English phrases. Adding some gestures, we communicated quite well.

What a blessing that we could reminisce and share family and work experiences with Hope and Frank. They had been assigned to establish a Presbyterian Seminary in Fortaleza. Frank was Dean of Faculty, teaching Church History, Theology, and Biblical Studies, plus counseling. It seemed that he was also the head of construction, renovation, and author of the curriculum. Hope had her office keeping records of students, grades, and I think doing some matchmaking! Since she is an accomplished pianist, she directed the choir and gave piano lessons. We met many of the students and were impressed with their faith, convictions, and serious pursuit of ministering in a congregation somewhere in Brazil. On Sunday, we worshiped in the church Frank was pastoring. He was brave to request that I preach. Not having mastered the language in a week, I certainly appreciated the young man who translated for me. They sang the hymns with emotion and deep devotion. We almost felt we were back in Asia.

Brazil has hundreds of sandy beaches. Fortaleza's beach is superb. One afternoon, Frank drove us to the beach filled with fishing boats complete with nets and sails, food stalls, and shady shelters. Everyone except me went swimming in the slightly rough Atlantic. They had a great time until Peggy called to Stephen for help. She was caught in a riptide. At first he thought she was joking, but she wasn't. He helped her swim parallel with the beach until she was free. Peggy also got a painful Man of War sting on her leg. Sipping juice through a straw stuck into a fresh coconut helped us all recover. Generous servings of grilled fish and chips also helped. Another day, they gave us a tour of the hills and rocky mounts, with villages clustered near rushing streams. Brazil has a plethora of spectacular natural wonders. It is larger than the USA and soon will become a superpower nation. After church the second Sunday, Hope and Frank treated us with the most fabulous buffet at a large hotel. Then it was time to depart. Several new friends went all the way to the terminal to bid us farewell, insisting on giving us gifts. How grateful we were to have had that special time with dear family.

A telephone call from Judy Churchsmith alerted us that her mother, my sister Carrie, had cancer and was undergoing chemotherapy. We quickly made plans to drive to Iowa. Never having driven to Iowa from Florida, we contacted Triple A for maps and information as to which was the best route. They were most helpful. Early one morning we left Palm Harbor, headed for I-75, and continued toward Atlanta. Planning to go beyond that busy city before our first night's stop, we had a surprise as we entered the outskirts – cars were six abreast and rocketing at seventy-five to eighty miles per hour. We went with the flow of traffic, hurriedly read the signs, and swooshed through in record time. Ben Hur would have been proud of us! The motel was most welcome. The next day, we drove through Chattanooga and Nashville. We spent the night in Indiana. Braving St. Louis, we continued on to Carroll, Iowa. It was a treat to see the waist-high corn and leafy soybeans simmering in that hot July weather. But, it was not good to see Carrie, much thinner and drawn. However, she was brave and determined to recover. She was strong in faith and had told her pastor she would again sing in the choir and do her work as an Elder in the church. Many in that congregation were praying for Carrie and her family, bringing prepared hot meals and salads. We all did what we could. She was pleased that we had come.

Such situations draw families together. Soon we were joined by brother Floyd and Lou from Rockwell, Iowa; Wayne and Mary from Stroudsburg, Pennsylvania; Hope from Austin, Texas; Jimmy and Joy, Larry and Cheryl Cruchelow and their children, and Judy and Fred. (Stan and Jo Ann were both working, Esther was expecting.) We all helped with meals and caring for Carrie. One evening, when she felt strong enough, we had a picnic at Swan Lake near Carroll, where she and her husband, James, had often fished. Carrie told us how James, who was part Iroquois, had taught her to put a worm on the hook, spit on it, and cast. We all shared some fish stories of our own, happy memories of family experiences, and enjoyed being together again. Peggy and I visited the cemeteries at Wheatland, Wall Lake town, and the one south of Wall Lake. Positioning the cut flowers on many of the graves, we fondly recalled how beloved all were to us.

Floyd told us about his heating and air-conditioning business, sharing amusing incidents of how customers made life difficult for him at times. Wayne related the woes and dangers of his bowling ball refinishing factory. He said it was a matter of time until the lacquer fumes would ruin his health. Jimmy and Joy were working at the State Capitol in Des Moines in the Revenue Department, mastering the art of computerized systems. Larry was putting his skills of rescuing the wounded in Vietnam to work as the first Director of Carroll County's Emergency Ambulance Service. Cheryl had her job, too. Fred and Judy kept busily engaged in their Real Estate enterprise. Hope was still working for her Texas tycoon, arranging charters for his fleet of planes. Someone had called asking for a discount on a plane for President George H.W. Bush to campaign. Hope had consulted with the Head Goose who replied in his best John Wayne fashion, "Tell the cheapskate to drop dead." Peggy and I brought everyone up to date on Pakistan, Nepal, and the joys of retirement. We made it sound so easy and fulfilling that all wanted to retire. We also told them about the hard work of moving, settling in, and getting adjusted to this land of "unboiled water." Carrie seemed to be stronger and confident of recovery, so we bid our farewells and went our separate ways.

Peggy and I headed east for Boston. On August 3, Arin had arrived after a difficult pregnancy. It is a long way from Carroll to Boston. We thought I-80 would never end. Finally, it did when we switched to the Massachusetts Turnpike. Navigating to find Oak Square, where Joe and Esther lived, was a big challenge of starts and finally finishing. You can imagine the excitement and exuberance of seeing our second grandson. Esther and Joe never tired of showing us that new bundle of joy. Joe had already photographed the full range of Arin's arrival from the delivery room, the mother in the bed with child, his holding of Arin for the first time, to numerous posed and non-posed views of a happy family. Grandma Peggy held that boy with great pride and decided he was a composite of the Hunter and Schlorholtz families. However, Arin had a serious colic disorder. It was difficult to get him comfortable and asleep. This necessitated a brigade of comforters: Esther, Joe, Peggy, Uncle John, and Al. Each of us used artful methods to demonstrate our skills. Arin appeared to be loudly expressing his individuality. Especially after his feeding, we had to try to burp and comfort him. Joe developed quite a bit of expertise by applying pressure to Arin's tummy. Arin, like Stan, suffered from a colic disorder. We hoped that he would soon outgrow the painful pressure as Stan had, which he did.

We joined in the cooking, ordered savory fish and chips from Captain D's, and helped with household duties as best we could. Observing Arin's daily bath delighted us. Nothing compares with the fragrance of a newly bathed baby wrapped in soft woolen blankets. Noting that Esther and Joe were lovingly and ably coping with their bundle of joy, we took our leave for home, relieved that babies are born to younger parents!

Chapter 50

Fiftieth Reunion, Carrie, Trip West, Mission Conference, Boston

In the Spring of 1991, an invitation to the Wall Lake High School annual reunion arrived. This was not a mundane invitation. It reminded me that in 1941 I had graduated from that school. I thought it was a long way to drive for a one-night stand, but Peggy insisted we go. Flora (Armstrong) Bazzone wrote Peggy saying that their Class of 1942 was having a special gathering in preparation for Peggy's fiftieth the next year. That clinched the decision. We made plans to attend the mid July auspicious celebration. Recalling how hot it is in Iowa during July, we were grateful for the car's working air conditioner. You know the route we took, so I'll not repeat it here. Arriving in Carroll and having been alerted by Judy that Carrie's remission had ended, we were apprehensive for her health. However, she was adamant we stay with her and bravely joined us to attend the Annual Banquet. Carrie graduated in 1932. She told us that her favorite teacher had been Marie Doxi who taught Math – the best teacher she had ever had. (That was prior to Marie's marriage to Uncle Steve Hoft.) The banquet was held in the Gym to accommodate the two hundred plus graduates. We registered and joined our respective classmates in separate classrooms, the better to renew our memories of younger days. One fellow grad stated he never missed the reunion, because he could note how others had grown older and rounder! I was tempted to hand him a full-length mirror, but one has to be on one's best behavior at such events.

Thoroughly enjoying the ham dinner with all the trimmings, plus pumpkin pie, we sat in Class Groups. Since Peggy's class was next to ours, we sat together at the extreme edges of both groups. Of course, there was a program welcoming us, an address by Dr. Underwood who had been our teacher and Principal, jokes by the master of ceremonies, then each class was introduced and invited to stand to be recognized. Since we were celebrating our fiftieth, we were introduced last and requested to give a short resume of our life's work. Somehow, I was the last one in our class to speak. (I have often wondered how they knew my talk would be longer than the rest!) Actually, I only highlighted how Peggy and I had ministered to the poorest and most disadvantaged people of Pakistan and Nepal, giving a few examples. I closed by thanking everyone who had helped prepare Peggy and me for such a task and affirming that I was proud of my Iowan heritage. It was well received. The Mayor's son, now the Head of the Popcorn Factory, said he could have listened all night! We had a great time and regretted that we had not attended more often.

However, we were saddened to hear the diagnosis that Carrie's cancer had again reasserted itself. She had gone into remission late in the fall of 1990, kept her promise to sing in the choir, and resumed her leadership role in the church. But now we noted her loss of weight, her weariness, and discomfort of the chemotherapy pump. Peggy and I did what we could, preparing meals, cleaning, doing laundry, and praying for our dear sister. Those were troubling times. Judy came to take over for awhile. She was very concerned. It was her suggestion we accept the invitation from our Denver friends, the Barths, whom we had met in Nepal. This would give us a break and also a change for Carrie. We knew how loving and efficient Judy is. Still, we were reluctant to leave, even for a short time. Dr. Barth and his dear wife showed us some of the wonders of Colorado, including Loveland Pass and the Eisenhower Tunnel. What a surprise to throw snowballs in July! On our return to Iowa, we visited niece Patricia (the daughter of Uncle Cliff and Aunt Elma Hoft) and Don Vogel at Grand Island, Nebraska. We enjoyed dinner at the country club, as we enjoyed catching up on news of their two girls now married with children. Family ties are precious – one has to work at maintaining those threads that bind us together. Back in Carroll, we noted things had not changed for the better; there was that persistent cancerous growth and Carrie's deterioration. We did not know how much longer she would live. How thankful we were that Jimmy, Larry, and Judy would carry on with their mother's care. Stan, Jo Ann, Tanya, and Erik visited Jo Ann's family in Lake City and Aunt Carrie. Soon we had to bid farewell to all, because we were invited to participate in the Missionary Conference in New Wilmington, Pennsylvania.

To our surprise, Erik, now eleven, wanted to accompany us. Occupying the back seat, he kept us amused. We discussed his schoolwork and were told that Math and Science were his favorite subjects. He liked to use his dad's computer and missed playing computer games. He had some trouble with his multiplication tables, from the sevens, eights, and nines. We played a game of reciting those troublesome numbers, discovering that Erik really didn't see the need for mastering them. We talked about that. He gave it a few more tries, but quickly got bored. We shifted to who could first identify a Volkswagen. That was fun. Eventually we arrived at the Conference Center. It was easy to find, because we had instructions to enter by a certain route, note the one traffic light in the town, and make a few turns after that. About two hundred fifty were present for the weeklong retreat. It was exciting to meet friends we knew from Pakistan and others who had served in Egypt, the Sudan, India, Japan, and Korea. We were the only ones who had worked in Nepal. There were busy days of breakfast, devotions and Bible studies, prayer sessions, lunch, and afternoon group discussions. Following the evening meal was the main meeting of the day, with readings, loudly sung choruses and hymns, and the main speaker giving mostly inspirational and challenging messages. Each participant had been requested to bring artifacts from abroad to be displayed. We had brought with us quite an array. Also on the program were a series of slide presentations depicting the wide variety of missionary outreach in the world. Peggy and I had brought along our slide projector and more than ample slides. We made a joint presentation of our mission in Pakistan, which highlighted working in a Muslim land; our teaching at Kinnaird and Forman Christian College; the medical, social, and educational programs; and the development of the Pakistani Christian Church. We then shifted the presentation to Nepal and our work with the United Mission to Nepal. This drew everyone's attention, because they had only seen slides of Pakistan from our colleagues who had also served there. Especially the young people were impressed with Nepali culture, Hindu and Buddhist religions, the UMN "appropriate technology" Projects and Programs, and the rapid growth of the Nepali Christan Fellowship. Many questions were asked. For some this had been an introduction to a strange new world, with its problems and potential. This was also the intent of the Conference. It would be interesting to learn whether some of those young people actually made it to the mission field.

Peggy and I relished the fellowship and interchange of experiences and blessings the Lord had showered upon so many, representing many different States. It reassured us that Someone greater than all had called, prepared, inspired, and sustained such a large group of Presbyterians to "Go into all the world..." One speaker I recall spoke on "The Extra Dimension." His main point was that each person and mission had made plans and set goals to be achieved in the next year, including the financial and personnel needs. Time after time at the end of the year, when the reports had been prepared, it was noted that more than anticipated results had occurred! This, he said, was the Extra Dimension of God's Presence and Power in the midst of mission. He also commented that some fervent people had thought it was due to their prayers and efforts. That is true in part but not the full account. He reminded us that mission was not merely a human effort, but rather the divine Plan and Purpose being implemented through the loving witness and service of ordinary humble persons doing God's Will in God's Way. It is a privilege to be a part of such a cause and movement.

We finally arrived at the Hunter Schlorholtz residence. They were pleased to see Erik with us. Arriving in time to help celebrate Esther's birthday on July 30, we joined the festivities, which were fully photographed by Peggy, Joe, and Al. John also was present, but he was not well. Suffering from a severe bout of Chronic Fatigue Syndrome, he was thin and tired easily. His program of a vegetarian diet, yoga, and more rest was showing some success. We were anxious about this and wondered how he could continue his work in his bookstore in Harvard Square. But John was determined to get well and to attend library sales in search of first editions for his store. Arin was in full swing, walking with quite a bit of confidence. He won our hearts with his perpetual motion. However, he also kept us alert making his sudden moves. Surrounding him were many toys, including a white teddy bear which he loved to wrestle with and hug.

August 3rd was the big day: Arin's first birthday anniversary! Esther and Joe invited a good number of neighborhood children and especially Shelley and Larry Rubin-Wills' daughter, Jessica, and their son, Daniel. Shelley and Esther had been classmates at Radcliffe/Harvard. Their friendship has endured even to today. In the midst of that circle of excited invitees, including Erik, Esther and Arin were kept busy opening the gifts and recording who had brought what. My, what fascinating gifts! Arin had a ripping good time opening them, so artfully wrapped. Some of the children tried to explain how to wind the toys and make them perform, but Arin's attention moved ever forward – there were so many enticing gifts! Joe was kept busy gathering the wrappings and recording the whole affair. Arin needed assistance blowing out that big number one candle. There were many volunteer blowers. The fitting menu of birthday cake, cookies, sweets, and Kool-Aid was served. Balloons and streamers began to pop and tear, but by then it didn't matter. How glad we were to be there.

Search as you will, I doubt you could ever find prouder parents and grandparents. We had every reason to count our blessings.

The drive to Florida seemed long and tiring. We were still savoring that happy time in Boston. I-95 threads its way through many difficult cities and towns. Erik liked the George Washington Bridge, the panorama of New York City, and the McDonald's we frequently visited. He was happy to be home – his homesickness had been apparent. He loves his mom and dad, even Tanya, his big sister. It had been a long trip. Peggy and I had also managed to survive. Be it ever so condo, there's no place like home!

Chapter 51

A New Venture, Interim Pastor, Chesterfield, The Deep South

During the Fall of 1991, we were kept fully busy caring for our condo and yard. Almost daily we walked around the pond and sat on the bench near the Club House to admire the beauty of the lawns, the flowering shrubs, the live oak trees, the young alligator, and the array of white condos. We greeted friends who joined us as they circled the pond. Three rounds of the pond equaled a mile. We did a mile per day to counter the ample meals Peggy prepared. The Publix store nearby had too many enticements. Of course, frequent trips to McDonald's didn't reduce the calorie intake. We were compensating for all those dal bhat meals in Nepal. Let's face it, there is too much good food in the USA. We also purchased a set of dumbbells and did calisthenics. Then it happened – Peggy discovered in the "Presbyterian Life" magazine a plea for help from the New Harmony Presbytery in South Carolina. There was a shortage of pastors. Peggy and I wrote to the Stated Clerk, Rev. John B. Evans, to inform him who we were, what we had done, that we were retired, that our four children had left the nest, and that it might be possible for us to help in some needy congregation. By return post, we received a reply: "How soon can you move to South Carolina?" An exchange of correspondence followed, and we accepted the Call to the Chesterfield Presbyterian Church. However, we first celebrated Christmas with Stan and Jo Ann, sent boxes of gifts to the others, and circulated three hundred Christmas letters to our friends around the world.

Another move! We packed, gathered what we could haul in the car, and locked the door of our condo, having informed the Executive Committee what was afoot. They promised security and regular yard work. Making our way, we arrived in early February 1992 at Chesterfield. Deacon Sam Davis showed us the town, the church, Main Street, and the manse on Ivy Street. The manse was a single-floor ranch style four-bedroom house. We were told it had been completely refurbished in May 1979 with a new heating and air-conditioning system, painted inside and out, old ceilings replaced, curtains made for all the windows, and wall-to-wall carpeting installed. We loved it from the start. Settling in, we found the local IGA/Piggly Wiggly grocery stores, the Post Office, two department stores, and Gene Stephenson's hardware. All these were on Main Street, making it a simple matter to shop and converse with many friendly people. Quickly noted was their distinctive Southern accent, so smooth and lyrical. Peggy and I were determined to learn an approximation as soon as possible. In Chesterfield, one doesn't give a ride to someone, one "carries" them. You also "give a holler," not a call. We were readily endeared to the customs and traditions of the South. How grateful we were to have the privilege to be part of such a rich culture. We were "fixin" to do our best.

It was also time to be the Interim Pastor. The present church building had been erected in 1925. But the history of that congregation had begun in 1812! It was of brick construction, complete with steeple and bell tower. We were given a thorough tour of the sanctuary, the attached church school, and the large fellowship hall by Frances McRae, Clerk of Session. She was the role model of all Southern women: a quiet disposition, glorious white hair, soft spoken, humorous, diplomatic, charming, gracious, firm in her opinions, a dedicated Christian, a staunch Presbyterian – you name it! She had taught English at the local school for thirty years and retired to her lovely home on East Main Street. Whenever we wanted help with any troubling issue or situation, we first consulted her because she knew the history, personality quirks, and pedigree of every member.

My sermons were Scripture-centered, good firm Reformed doctrine, with faith lessons. (I am tempted to record ten or so sermons here, but space denies you that blessing.) The active congregation numbered about fifty-five, because ten years previously a young pastor had split the congregation and started a new church. This soon failed. Many did not return; they joined the local Baptist Church which was predominant in the town. To comfort the flock, I shared that quality, not quantity was better. From my own experience, I related instances of being part of a minority of Christians in Pakistan and Nepal, trying not to use too many references to our ministry abroad. Congregants reassured me they were most apt and enlightening. Par for the course, Peggy soon knew the names and addresses of every member. Her open, friendly manner endeared her to many.

Prior to the worship, the Bible Class met. They requested me to teach and Peggy to put things into perspective with illustrations of faith and love in action at the local level. Faye and Carolyn Bell, our neighbors, insisted we were prophets! He was the town's leading lawyer and an Elder – who could argue with him? Don and Carolyn Rivers, our neighbors up the hill, faithfully attended. He was a retired Funeral Director. Dorine Douglas, who managed her handicraft and flower shop, attended as often as her health allowed. Frances McRae never missed. Gene and Libby Stephenson were faithful in attendance and participation. Buck and Agnes Lawrence were the question masters. He had flown torpedo planes in the Pacific campaigns. His base of operation, the Yorktown, had been sunk. They had the largest collection of Indian arrowheads in South Carolina, most of them mounted and identified. This was the class that really studied the Bible and was eager to learn and apply it to daily life. Questions of interpretation and application kept me on my toes.

Visitation of the members was never a duty but rather an enriching experience. Everyone had a history to share. A few were bedridden caused by age or illness. They especially were grateful that we were living in Chesterfield, not just a pulpit filler on Sundays. They were much appreciative of the reading of appropriate Scripture, a bit of counseling and comforting, and prayers. Without exception, we were served tea with cookies. One can rarely surpass Southern hospitality. There were hospital visits at Cheraw, thirteen miles to the east. Sorrowfully, we conducted funerals also. Sadie Clark's daughter, forty-two years of age, died of cancer. Sadie's son was the town's dentist, but he attended the Methodist church. There were no marriage ceremonies, the congregation was aging. Confirmation of personal faith in Christ was a joyful way to welcome the youth into the fellowship of the church. Finding an organist was always difficult, though always successful. The monthly meetings of the Session, with long agendas, afforded an opportunity to become acquainted with the strong views held by both the traditionalists and the progressives. I spare you the details, but meetings were lively and most informative. Faye Bell kept us within the law; Frances McRae poured oil on the troubled waters. During the summer attendance dropped. The remnant informed me that church attendance was similar to Route 9, which runs through Chesterfield. In summer, it was "up" to the mountains and "down" to Myrtle Beach.

Chesterfield was up-country from the lowlands to the southeast of the State. The sandy clay was well suited for growing cotton, but when demand sharply declined

King Cotton was dead. That slump brought poverty to the region. Pine forests and vegetable farms became more prevalent. Stately old plantation mansions badly deteriorated. The slaves had won their freedom but not employment opportunities. The Slave Market in Cheraw is now a museum. Peggy and I often visited Tom Jones in his little grocery store on the outskirts of town near the African-American population. His rich encyclopedic knowledge of the history and happenings of Chesterfield was phenomenal. We learned that the very first declaration of secession from the Union was signed at the Chesterfield Courthouse. The citizens of Chesterfield were staunch loyalists to the South in the Civil War of the 1860s. Hearing their strong opinions, we gathered the war had recently happened.

Spring is the season of flowering trees and shrubs in Chesterfield. First are the Dogwoods and Azaleas, followed by Plum, Apple, Peach, and every bloom you can name. The whole town was a showcase of color and scent. Tom Jones invited us to view his backyard bed of the most beautiful Daffodils, a hundred of them, rich golden blossoms nodding and dancing in the breeze. Everyone took special care of their yards and flowering exhibitions. Maude Garland was proud of her Azaleas, inviting us for lunch so we had sufficient time to drink in the beauty of her fifteen-foot hedge. She drove a long Cadillac around town, sometimes parking in the wrong zone and missing stop signs. The police never gave her any trouble. After all at ninety-one, she was queen of the town! I recall that we invited Drs. Tom and Cynthia Hale to present their work of raising funds for medical students, enabling them to serve overseas without a load of debt. They, too, were impressed with the showy spring. Hope and Stephen drove all the way from Texas to join in the "Chesterfield Adventure." Stan, Jo Ann, Tanya, and Erik drove up from Florida to spend a few days. We joined Esther, Joe, Arin, and Joe's mother in West Virginia, where they had rented cabins in the woods. We had a good time with all of them and marveled how big Arin had become. He still was as lively as ever. Touring the area, we stopped one afternoon at the Green Brier Hotel. Seven Presidents had slept there. It was so very expensive, we commoners ordered only ice cream, pastries, and tea. The fountains in the shade of those mighty oaks had water with a heavy concentration of sulfur. Curious onlookers watched me pretend to take a sip. I declared the water was better than Florida's. As they gasped with surprise, I admitted not having drunk one drop. The odor was enough.

After worship on Sundays, almost everyone patronized the restaurant near Mellon's Veggie and Fruit stand. They served authentic Southern dinners: mashed potatoes, southern fried chicken, mustard greens, hot biscuits, the works! Sharing tables to help accommodate everyone, friends and neighbors celebrated together. Our other favorite eating place was the Fish Diner at Rockingham. When Peggy's brother, Dick, and his wife, Merna, visited us, we took them there for the best seafood dishes in South Carolina. We had a grand time, until late that afternoon Peggy complained about pains in her lower abdomen. I drove her to the Cheraw Hospital for examination by Dr. John McLeod, our member Eva McLeod's grandson. X-rays and examination showed that she was suffering from an acute attack of diverticulitis. Dr. McLeod said I was right to bring Peggy to the hospital. To play it safe, he consulted with the surgeon how they would operate if necessary. Peggy spent eight days there – daily I visited her. From the church members and friends, many cards and bouquets were sent to cheer her and "Get Well Soon." She was cautioned to carefully watch her diet, abstaining from nuts, strawberries, hard rinds, and the like. That had been a close call.

For the speaker at the World Day of Prayer, Peggy invited her close friend, Joy Biswas, from Toronto, Canada. Joy did an excellent job. For the first time in Chesterfield history, Peggy arranged that African-Americans members from nearby churches join in. This raised many an eyebrow, but she had convinced the Session and Women's Group to reach out and broaden the horizons of sisterhood. She related that in Pakistan women of every station in life attended the World Day of Prayer. The whole group ate lunch in our Fellowship Hall. That's my Peggy! Racial feelings at that time were still present in Chesterfield. The neighbor across the street from us made it plain that she did not think heaven was integrated. Yet she had taught in the town's integrated school for many years. Peggy tried but could not convince her to change. That is when we learned why slaves had sung "Dem Golden Slippers" and "Walking All 'Round God's Heaven." Slaves and children of slaves were forbidden to wear shoes to school, even in high school, if they were allowed to attend. Thankfully, that situation has changed, although not completely.

In April 1994 after Easter, we took our leave. Parishoners offered that we could use the manse and serve in Chesterfield for as long as we lived. And they meant it! At our farewell dinner in the Fellowship Hall, Peggy and I thanked them for the privilege we had had to be a part of their community. We shared how sad we were in leaving. For personal and family reasons we needed to return to our condo in Florida. Betsy

Vaughn, whose husband John was a Patrolman, presented a crystal pitcher, the parting gift from the congregation. Her sister, Suzanne, and Dan and Lynne Beaver were also present. It was an emotional affair. In those two years we had become a family of faith and love.

Arriving home and settling in again, we truly missed those dear ones in Chesterfield. What a blessing they were. Peggy and I discovered that the Deep South is north of Florida, which has been diluted by snowbirds and Yankees like us. We missed those Carolina pines, the gracious new friends we had made, the aura of distinctive Southern culture, the fish fries and hush puppies that Faye Bell excelled in cooking, the burst of spring blooms, the camaraderie of kindred hearts and minds, the firm resolve of character and loyalties of those Great People. We are indebted to them and continue to send our Christmas letters to those beloved souls.

Chapter 52

Family, Parish Associate, Programs, Visitations, Concern

Soon after we got comfortable in our condo, we celebrated Jo Ann's and Erik's birthdays. We all met for dinner at Outbacks. Erik invited seven of his close friends and us to a pool celebration. Peggy and I had never seen such energy and enthusiasm as those boys did every aquatic trick and maneuver possible. All were expert swimmers and dove into the pool with great dexterity. There was a game of pushing one another into the pool and another where they had a beach ball tournament. Jo Ann had baked a mouthwatering cake, a big chocolate delicacy. All helped Erik in blowing out the candles. After the gift opening, he and his friends continued to enjoy the water sports. In June, we helped Tanya celebrate her birthday. It was a family

affair at the pool. Stan kept bouncing a beach ball on the unsuspecting heads of Tanya and Erik. We recalled Tanya's sixteenth in Nepal. Jo Ann's cake didn't collapse! We felt at home.

Esther, Joe, and Arin Visit for a Birthday

Esther, Joe, and Arin visited us for a whole week every year during the school break in April. Welcoming Florida's sun, heat, and warm water, they escaped the chill of Boston. Much time was spent in the pool and sunbathing. Arin liked to dive off the rim of the pool making a big splash. However, one of the older residents got annoyed and exclaimed, "We have rules about No Diving – this is not a hotel pool!" Arin was crushed. Peggy set that critic straight. There were rounds of mini golf at the Congo River Course, feeding the alligators in the pond, and enjoying the pirate motif. Water World was another adventure. To save time and effort, we often enjoyed takeout suppers from Boston Market where rotisserie chickens, hot potatoes, veggies, and rolls were served. In the evenings, we showed slides of Pakistan and Nepal and talked about many things. Esther had shifted from working for the City of Boston and told us about her work in a Boston bank, where she was director of community development. Joe related the challenges of public relations work in Boston colleges. We got the idea that they were permanent Bostonians. John, Hope, and Stephen joined us when they could. To help make ample room for family, we added a room in front where the flagstone patio had been. This enlarged the living room area and gave us more sunshine and space. Sitting on the sofa or Lazy Boy recliner gave the impression that we were sitting in the flower beds. We spent many pleasant hours there reading and relaxing. It was worth overcoming the resistance by the Executive Committee to grant permission to build that extra room. Pointing out that two of the five members had enclosed porches shifted the odds in our favor. Peggy was an able negotiator. Her bargaining experience while buying carpets, brass, and jewelry in Pakistan and Nepal gave us the cutting edge.

In September, we received a call from Dr. Raymond Guterman, the senior pastor at the Northwood Presbyterian Church in Clearwater. He had heard my talk at a Presbytery meeting and was in need of help in his congregation of over twelve hundred members. Dr. Mask had to resign because of ill health; they needed a replacement. Elder Paul Wagner and Raymond invited me to meet them for lunch where they offered me a job. Having agreed upon the terms and job description, I was hired as the Parish Associate to begin October 1, 1994. It was to be a ministry of nineteen hours per week. I was serving a three-year term on the Presbyterian Church's Self-Development Committee which studied about twenty-five applications for funding grass-roots social/economic projects from around the world. Northwood accepted my request that I take time off to attend the General Assembly quarterly meetings held in widely scattered cities like Washington, DC, Seattle, El Paso, Atlanta, Mexico City, Puerto Rica, and Tulsa.

We were acquainted with the church, having attended the worship there occasionally. It was a mile east of the Countryside Mall on State Road 580. Peggy was pleased that we could be active members. She joined the choir, served on the Worship and Mission committee, and made lots of new friends. My ministry included many aspects, such as assisting in Sunday worship, home and hospital visitation, teaching in the church school, and conducting biblical studies and lectures. At times, a Parish Associate is the overworked gofer. The staff were friendly and helpful in getting me acquainted with the roll of members and those with special needs. I bought a Pinellas County map and soon found where members lived (getting lost a few times). In those days there were no GPS gadgets.

At the close of worship one Sunday, Peggy noticed a "foreign" woman sitting alone. She introduced herself to Cicile Sawaris. Cicile was a bit cautious, but noting the two twenty-two karat gold bangles on Peggy's wrist, she surmised that this woman had traveled and appreciated good things. Cicile said she had attended Northwood for some time and was disappointed that no one really had made any overtures of friendship. She had decided this was the last time she would attend. A U.S. citizen, she had immigrated with her two daughters from Egypt twenty years previously. Cicile and Peggy struck up an immediate friendship and often sat together. Peggy kept introducing her to everyone. Soon she had lots of contacts and well-wishers. Peggy was pleased to have found a new friend. She always greeted people who looked lonely and a bit uneasy. The Lord blessed her ministry of including one and all. She had had a lot of opportunity to greet and reach out to people throughout her life. That is a gift which some have, but not many put to use in a constructive way as Peggy did.

Eventually, my participation during worship was the pastoral prayer and blessing the offering. Some adoring fans remarked that my booming

How to Wear a Sari

tenor during the hymn singing inspired them to put a little more gusto into their pipes. At Pentecost, I was requested to share verses of scripture in different languages. I recited or read these in Latin, German, Greek, Hebrew, Urdu, Nepali, and English. I realize that list is short, but they were the only ones I knew. At the close of worship, the senior pastor greeted members at the main door of the vestry. I was assigned the side door which had a shorter line. One critical woman chided me for not wearing a black robe. She thought I was being obstinate, until I told her I had given my robe to Pastor Arthur in Lahore, Pakistan on leaving that country. She did not realize a robe cost at that time four hundred dollars. Cicile, hearing about this from Peggy, insisted on buying the material and making me one. She is an accomplished seamstress. So there!

Northwood had many active programs. Peggy attended the Women's meeting, I the Men's, which met each month. There were Sunday school classes for all ages. Peggy and I joined the Serendipity Class taught by Jane Sutton, Ron Roberson, Rick McNeill and others. Ron was famous for his timeline presentations of the gospels and epistles. It was actual Bible Study, relevant to our faith and actions. Peggy often shared the parallel application from Pakistan and Nepal. This was most helpful and illustrated the topic at hand. Eventually, my portion was to answer questions which the teacher referred to me and to interpret difficult theological/philosophical passages. They used me rather than a Bible Encyclopedia. It was good that I had about thirty-five years of experience dealing with such matters. During the fall and spring, the midweek potluck suppers were scheduled. They were well attended. This was a time for getting acquainted with many in a social setting. Usually, an invited speaker, films, discussions, and the like highlighted the evening. Peggy made a great hit by contributing her magic of cooking: chicken curry, kabobs, rice pilau, and spicy foods, served with pita bread. She was also requested by the Women's meeting chairperson to demonstrate the wearing of a sari. All were envious that they did not own such colorful material or know the secret of how to drape six yards of cloth so elegantly. Other lectures Peggy and I gave, complete with appropriate slides, were on World Religions: Hinduism, Buddhism, Islam, Judaism, and Christianity and How Great is Our Faith, a review of the major doctrines of the Reformed Faith, with examples of application.

Each spring, there was a fundraising program called Night on the Town. Many talented members volunteered to put on an act, play an instrument, sing, or tell jokes. The first year Peggy and I enjoyed the program as spectators. The next year Peggy suggested I sing for that rapt audience. What to sing? We finally decided that I should impersonate Pavarotti singing "O Sole Mio" in Italian and then substitute in English humorous lines about Raymond, the choir, and notable members of the congregation. Billed as "The Poor Man's Pavarotti," I dressed in his style, bought a false beard, and held a large handkerchief in my hand. The church pianist accompanied me. Warming up the crowd, I imitated Pavarotti's voice to share a recipe of Snow Pie. Then I sang "O Sole Mio" in Italian. Peggy took the mike and said to me, " Mr. Pavarotti, you are using Italian – sing in English!" That's when I substituted those comic lyrics. It made an amazing hit. No one had ever imagined that I could belt out with tremendous volume such an operatic jewel. Of course, they suggested I join the choir. I replied that I was not the volunteer type of singer – they couldn't afford me! Actually I had more than enough to do.

Most exacting and challenging was to do pastoral calling. This is not to entertain members, but rather to visit people in their homes or wherever they are. Each week, I laid out a plan to see at least ten family/single members. I contacted them and arranged a suitable time to meet at their convenience. Visiting new members was the easiest. It involved personally welcoming them, hearing their life's story, and explaining the Church Program and Activities they might like to join. We had learned from experience that members remained in the congregation if they actively participated in something that interested them. They felt they were part of a warm fellowship rather than mere spectators. One of the joys was to visit people in Nursing Homes and Retirement Communities. These members were expecting a visit. Lonely, unable to attend worship or church activities, far from immediate family, and trying to deal with some disability or illness, they needed cheering up, encouragement, and prayer. I visited them once a month. They did not have busy work schedules as most members had. There were a number of retirement communities, such as Brier Creek, Top of the World, Regency Oaks, Mease Manor, and others. Slim and Betty Roberts were residents of Regency Oaks. They were nearing their nineties. Slim always greeted me with, "Pastor Al, are you behaving yourself?" "Yes," I replied. Then he asked, "When did you start?" Both had endured cancer, chemotherapy, and radiation. During a checkup, their Doctor told them there probably would be another attack. They asked me whether they were doing the right thing by telling their nephews and nieces they would not take another round of treatment just to add a few months to their lives. We prayed about it. I advised it was their decision. They affirmed that their faith was strong enough to face whatever came. A few months later, the cancer was back. They persisted in their decision. Slim died two months later. At his funeral, I related their decision, highlighting their faith, love, and hope. People openly wept. Three months later Betty passed away. Those were difficult times for the relatives and for the pastor.

Visiting members in Hospitals and Nursing Homes was also challenging. I have made hundreds of visits. It pays to listen, find rapport and encourage the patient, read appropriate Bible verses, pray, and reassure each one that God loves them and is in their corner. For example, Andy Andrews assured me that his Lord would care for him all the way. Then he added, "Pastor Al, I want to teach you pastors something. At my funeral don't say "The Lord gives and takes away." Say instead "The Lord gives and receives!" A year later, I shared his request with the mourners. After the service, his three little grandchildren were lingering with their mother. I told them that their Grandpa had it right: God is Love, Light, and Grace. The Lord had "received him with the blinding Light of His Presence." They threw their arms around me and said, "Will you be our Grandpa?"

There were also visitations to help celebrate birthdays and anniversaries, bless a new home, thank the Lord for a newly born child, counsel the youth to try another way (and they did), rejoice with a couple reconciled after a separation or divorce. Especially enjoyed were the evening dinners served by Cicile, who introduced us to Egyptian and Sudanese foods. Another highlight was having lunch with Carmele Andrews with her charming North Carolinian accent and sumptuous Old South delicacies. Jessse Loy, Ruth Teal, and Mildred Wilson were also special friends. A Parish Associate has to be all things to all and full of grace and truth.

However, there was a gnawing concern. At times, there were indications that Peggy had problems with her memory. Our Dr. Susan Baldi referred her to a neurologist for examination and therapy. A course of treatment was prescribed and followed. I wondered how we were to deal with this perplexing turn of events.

Chapter 53

Trip to Europe Planned, Change of Plans, Difficult Times

Peggy began to successfully cope with medicines (Aricept and another strong medication) for Dementia and Alzheimer's Disease prescribed by Dr. Barnhill, the neurologist. She was able to answer twenty-nine out of thirty questions in memory tests. Each month, we visited that office in Dunedin Medical Arts building for a checkup. This was heartening. I wondered how long Peggy would respond favorably. Her health improved, and she was able to return to what would be called a "normal" life. A month later, an email came from Hope Abigail and Frank Arnold inviting us to accompany them to Europe, where Frank had relatives in Stuttgart. We happily accepted that invitation and planned an itinerary, not just to include Stuttgart, but also to visit UMN colleagues in Germany, Holland, Norway, Sweden, and Finland. It was a combination of Air/Eurorail connections. Barbara, at Triple A, made the reservations, gave us maps, and thanked us. Our trip had inspired her to take the Scandinavian tour sometime. We were excited in anticipation of visiting so many of our close friends and exploring countries of Europe we had not seen. It was fun to shop for suitable travel wear and new roller bags. I had some leave time earned, so Northwood would have to carry on without my services for three weeks, two of which were vacation merits. As the departure date neared, Peggy went in for a medical checkup. Dr. Walter gave her an examination and was pleased to okay her trip to Europe. Then, performing a routine breast exam, he reported he had found a lump! Peggy said that it could not be true, because she felt fine. However, he made an appointment for an x-ray and other tests. To our great shock it was confirmed – there was definitely a lump. The doctors urged immediate surgery. A few days later, Peggy underwent a partial mastectomy and spent a night at Countryside Hospital.

We were both devastated! Who could have predicted this? Our family doctor approved the surgery and then advised Peggy to undergo chemotherapy even though the cancer had been discovered before it had reached the lymph nodes. This would reduce the chance of a recurrence by eighty percent. A Health Worker was assigned to visit every other day, and Peggy had chemotherapy for the next six months. Of course, we had to cancel our proposed trip to Europe, but we were grateful that the cancer had been diagnosed early. What would have happened if during the trip the cancer had spread more widely because we were unaware of it? Even though this gave us some comfort, it didn't ease the brunt of Peggy lying in a hospital bed in our new room, with nausea, a catheter, and lots of discomfort. That was a difficult time. Reluctantly, I requested Triple A to cancel our trip and to retrieve our down payments. I apologized for wasting so much of their time and effort. The surgeon, Dr. Hume, wrote a letter of explanation, which helped us to be fully reimbursed.

Another change was my having to prepare meals, attend to Peggy's every need, keep the condo clean and bright, and be prepared anytime night or day to respond to her call for help. I slept on the living room couch to be near her. In order to continue my work as Parish Associate, it was agreed that I do all my visits two mornings a week to coincide with visits by the Home Health Nurse and helpful neighbors who looked in on Peggy. How thankful I was that she also took naps in the mornings. I drank more coffee and buried myself in the work at hand. Stan and Jo Ann visited often and did everything possible. Hope, Esther, and John flew in on occasional weekends.

Even the partial loss of a breast is a blow to one's self-esteem. This caused Peggy much concern. I assured her that we could cope. She could count on my love and devotion. I did hear at church of a husband who never embraced his wife after she had a mastectomy. Pity that poor wife! I convinced Peggy that I had taken seriously the marriage vow "in sickness and in health." Eventually, we purchased a padded bra which restored her self-esteem. The aftereffects were difficult to cope with, but she made good progress and later was able to be up and around. Then came that joyful morning when she announced herself well enough to attend worship. Everyone was pleased to see her. When some desired a blow by blow account of what had happened, I came to her rescue by saying it had been a most difficult ordeal. You will note, dear readers, that I have omitted many details and trials. It is hoped you will read between the lines and imagine what that time was like.

It pleased me to discover that Peggy was using the computer more and more. She had to be somewhat inactive, yet occupy her time constructively. She had enough energy to record some important things. To my amazement she made a list of Workable Verses from Scripture. These included passages referring to God's faithfulness, prayers for healing, Jesus' teachings on the abundant life, death, resurrection, and eternal life in heaven. In the watches of the night, evidently she had been searching for help from the Lord. Other printouts were short true stories about many people she had known in Pakistan and Nepal. (Several of these I have recorded in this book.) There were also pages on the challenges of mission overseas, the nature of valid mission, rare experiences, and notes regarding the Ten Commandments applied to modern life and action. She made the point that one is not saved by keeping the Law, because that is humanly impossible to fulfill perfectly. Neither were the merits of good works to be considered adequate, nor were human wish and resolution enough. Only by God's Grace through faith in Christ's atonement, giving His life on the cross, could the penalty of sin be paid for. God freely granted one the forgiveness of sins and the assurance of salvation. Peggy, in the throes of illness and the threat of death from cancer, had done some serious thinking about the really important questions in life.

There is one more and most overwhelming account to record. No one except me, not even our children, has ever seen or read what I am about to transcribe. Peggy entitled it "A Difficult Letter to Write But Essential."

To Our Dear and Much Loved Ones,

It is my hope that you will accept this letter in the spirit of sincerity with which it is being written. Since none of us knows how much time God has allotted us, I feel I must share these heartfelt thoughts with you now. However long that may be, I would like to have one last chat with you. I regret so much that it was always very very difficult for me to speak of some of those things that are most important. Perhaps it was because we did not know just how to approach you. Perhaps it was typical of the time in your lives and mine, and perhaps it was because we did not live lives that generally fit into a once-for-all pattern. Should it be God's Will that your father and I enter into eternity together, I am certain that he will agree with me, since most of what is contained herein, we have talked about many times.

To all of you, I ask your forgiveness. Though your father and I tried to do what we felt was best, it is I who so often failed, often miserably. And as hard as I tried (admittedly, perhaps not hard enough at times), with all my heart I can say that I tried and many of my faults have stayed with me I know. Now in my later years, I hope that my lack of patience wasn't as glaring as in earlier times. Perhaps my discipline was too sharp. Most sincerely I say that my intention was only for your welfare. For my other shortcomings, some of which only you are aware, please forgive me.

Each of you children brought your father and me many joys, moments of pride, and happiness. This was especially true in your younger years. Your father and I tried our best to guide and encourage you along each step of the way. We are pleased that at least you took our words to heart and continued your schooling. We can only regret that we did not have the finances to encourage you in more study, though we know that higher education does not always guarantee anything, except perhaps a smoother road in life. In any case, I urge you each to add up your many blessings and thank the Lord.

Finding ourselves in a totally foreign culture, with multitudes of pitfalls for young people, there was no pattern set by which I could establish what a good parent ought to be. My goal, as I am certain was your father's also, was that you would be able to integrate yourselves into and appreciate that culture at its best, and above all to be loving and appreciative of all people, who though different from us, were also God's wondrous creation. This still meant that sometimes there were clashes of our Western background with that of the Eastern culture in which you were raised.

In closing, again I ask all of you for your forgiveness for my shortcomings. And while no doubt failing in so many ways, it was always my intention to guard you and to guide you in areas with fewer difficulties along life's path. In passing from this life into eternity, there is little of real value to leave behind, except kind words and deeds. This phrase sums it all up: "One kind word said to the living is worth more than a million tears shed over the grave." I know your father would join me in encouraging and challenging you to strengthen your faith. Rest assured that we shall all come together again in eternity.

I have nothing to add or to subtract, except to affirm that Peggy dearly loves her children. She never showed me this letter. While searching through some old files, I recently found it. Peggy is a most remarkable person. She met the considerable challenge of raising children in a culture different than her own, gave herself unstintingly to their care and nurture, and though they did not necessarily conform to the path she thought best for them, she has always been proud of "her four."

Chapter 54

Norman's Birthday, Levey No. 7 Reunion, Willard's Surprise

In April 1996, there were two coinciding events: one was the celebration of Peggy's older brother's birthday, the other was the School Reunion. Because driving from Florida to Iowa was too great a distance for us, we boarded a plane in Tampa and flew to Des Moines, via Chicago. After renting a car, we settled into a motel near the airport. For the previous three weeks there had been a flood of emails to make firm reservations, motel choice, and flight schedules, ensuring everyone arrived on the same day early enough to assemble at the same motel. Dick and Merna, Frank and Hope Abigail, Harry and Helyn joined us as arranged. That first evening, we had a joint dinner at a posh restaurant near the airport. It was good to be together as a family again. We each shared updates of activities since our last gathering and made sure we were on track for the next few days.

Hoft Family Women

At noon, we met at Perkin's restaurant, having reserved their small banquet room. Dorothy arrived with Norman, whose birthday we were celebrating. Norman was living in a Nursing Home because of advanced Alzheimer's Disease. Dorothy still worked as Manager of a local community retirement unit to keep solvent. We were pleased that Norm recognized and warmly greeted his brothers and sisters. During that more than ample luncheon, which was thoroughly enjoyed by all of us, especially Norm, the banter and reminiscing began. As Peggy's chauffeur and husband, I tried to allow those slightly exaggerated long-standing family experiences to stand unchallenged. However, it warmed my heart to see Peggy actively engaged and communicating. The impetus of familiar and endearing memories seemed to spark her recall and participation. I was amazed how she remembered and shared incidents from childhood so enthusiastically and well. Such is the magic of family familiarity and heartstrings! Norm joked and played tricks on those nearby. Dorothy told us that in the nursing home he sang a lot and interacted warmly with other patients and attendants. She said that unlike many other patients, Alzheimer's had made Norman more congenial. He was thrilled with the cake, blew out the candles, and requested extra ice cream. We all sang the birthday song and a few others. How good it is for families to get together and enjoy celebrations and remember and relish the love and nostalgia of one's childhood and youth. Our parents had passed on. Here we were, aging parents of the next generation. We hoped that our children would carry on the line and reminisce together as we were doing. We had certainly given them enough raw material to work with. Our concern was that they would remember the good things, not the unpleasant. It was time for us to bid our farewells.

The following morning, we drove to Lake View where we had reserved two nights at the Tjaden's Motel/Cafe. We were three miles from Wall Lake and the Levey #7 Reunion. At 11:30 sharp the next day, we arrived at the Lutheran church basement, registered, attached our name tags, and began trying to put names with faces. Many years had passed since these graduates of that small one-room school with all eight classes had met. Prominently displayed were two large maps of the North American Continent and Levey #7 Township. Graduates were requested to place their names on the former map where they now lived and on the other where they had lived while attending Levey #7. The organizing committee of seven graduates had done a lot of work in preparing for this event. Tables were decorated in red and white and country school memorabilia. Exhibit tables were loaded with articles which former pupils had created, such as artwork, embroidery, and wood projects. A few old copies of the textbook readers printed in 1911 were on display. The exuberant exchange of greetings was deafening.

On cue, Ken Bundt, as master of ceremonies, rang the old school hand bell, all said the Pledge of Allegiance and sang a few songs. A booklet of familiar songs had been printed to save us from the embarrassment of not knowing the words. Roll call was held, requesting both name and address. More than forty former pupils and twenty-

317

nine spouses and guests responded. Pupils had come from Missouri, Florida, Wisconsin, Alabama, Alaska, Colorado, Nebraska, Washington, and Iowa. Corsages and a large apple were given to three former teachers: Josephine Lawler Clifford of Carroll, Leona Batz Belt from Wall Lake, and Lois Crowe Ernie also from Wall Lake. Each of them was in their nineties! (If you care to refresh your memory of the Levey #7 School, see Chapter 5.) The ham steak dinner, with all the trimmings, was catered by Faye Kruse of Tjaden's Cafe. You can imagine the hubbub during the meal – it was a happy reunion to be sure.

The school bell rang again. "School is now in session!" exclaimed the master of ceremonies. "Today, we will reminisce about our school day experiences, whether they are remembered as the worst of times or the best of times. Please limit your response to five minutes; we have lots of pupils." May the following selections be shared:

Hope (Hoft) Arnold:

> I recall going through the snow, mud, and rain to get to school, warming up around the pot bellied stove, how special our Christmas programs were, and the time three of us girls were playing school in the coal shed during noon recess when a skunk surprised us, sending us on the run. The smell, thankfully, didn't linger long on us. It stayed in the coal shed.

Virgil Auen:

> I rode a buckskin horse to school, threw the reins over her neck, and she'd go home. At night I walked home. We lived one mile south of the school. I got a new bicycle for my tenth birthday. I rode it to school and had to give all the kids a ride.

Teacher Leona Belt:

> World War II was in progress at that time, and the school children were asked to help by collecting, at seventy-five cents a sack, silk from milkweed pods to be used in parachutes. We had a lot of sacks hanging on the fence to dry. Ration Books were issued for tires, sugar, gasoline, and other things. It was the rural teacher's duty to issue these – one to each family. People were already

lined up as I arrived at 7:00 am. I had forgotten my lunch and toward lunch time I was getting hungry. I called Rose Finger and asked her to bring me a sandwich when she came. I had little time to eat it. By supper time, I was exhausted and hungry. Then I heard a car and footsteps running up the stairs. There was Peggy (Hoft) Schlorholtz with a tray of hot food. I don't remember everything, but I do remember the pork chop and hot tea. No food ever tasted so good.

Kenneth Bundt:

I remember the good times sledding and skiing on the roads and on Bieret's pasture. Also special were the ball games and outdoor activities.

Larry Bundt:

I remember the Arnolds moving here from Germany. Klaus and Deter started school and were unable to speak English. Communication was a bad situation or problem for a long time.

Klaus Arnold:

Families took turns at times preparing lunches for the pupils. They fed me an ear of sweet corn. Of course, I was offended and threw it over the fence to the cows. In Germany, corn on the cob was not for humans to eat. The teacher paddled me for that. [Klaus, who spoke fluent English, came all the way from the State of Washington to attend the Reunion. He sold insurance and made us split with laughter.]

Lucille (Bieret) Geake:

Our parents brought treats for our birthdays. One Sunday afternoon, a few of us went to Hope Hoft's house and made a birthday cake for Miss Leona. We surprised her the next day. Mrs. Hoft made the best chocolate cake with chocolate and white frosting.

Shirley (Drost) Heim:

> I remember Harry Hoft smashing his piece of angel food cake with his lunch pail. I played Gretel and Jim Roth was Hansel in the Hansel and Gretel play. He was the "love of my life" at that time.

Dick Hoft:

> I remember Miss Crowe as the strictest teacher ever. She ruled the school in a firm manner, but she taught me everything I needed to know, even to do a graduate degree. My brother Norm, my sister Peggy, and I had a lot of fun riding a horse-drawn buggy to school.

Harrison Hoft:

> A favorite memory is just the location of the school – a very rural setting with dirt and gravel roads leading to it. I remember walking on those roads to school, the hills, fields, a creek, and just how pretty the way was. I'm so glad to see my schoolmates today and to reminisce.

Peggy (Hoft) Schlorholtz:

> I dearly prize the days I spent with many of you in Levey #7. Iowa has the best school system in the USA. We learned the basics in that rural school and had our characters formed by excellent teachers, parents, and you dear classmates. There is nothing like it.

More quotes may be found in the Memories of Levey #7 Reunion folder, but we must carry on. It is noted though "that be it ever so humble, there is no substitute for a school where a basic foundation is made, with all the help and blessing of loving parents, neighbors who care and share, and teachers who make a lasting impression. We are dearly and truly indebted to all, even those fellow pupils who vexed us at times!"

Later that year, a plan was made to surprise brother Willard in Huntsville, Alabama. His wife, Betty, made sure he was in town the day we all arrived from many directions. Dick and Merna had brought Dorothy with them. Norm was not able to make it. Peggy and I drove to Atlanta, and Frank and Hope Abigail gave us a ride to the party. Harrison and Helyn drove down from Washington, DC. Again, reservations had been made at a motel as base for all of us. The invading party prepared to descend on that unsuspecting Physicist who worked at the Redstone Arsenal. During and after WW II, Will worked with missile and rocket technology in Huntsville. He never shared with anyone what he did. The German rocket scientist,

Norm, Harry, Dick, Peggy, Hope, and Will

Werner von Braun, joined the team in 1960. Will was a middle child and, like me, had a hard time in the family. Beulah always reminded his brothers and sisters that he needed more love than any.

That afternoon, we drove to daughter Ann's house, where Will was repairing her lawnmower. He was in the workshop and didn't hear us approach. Dick and Harrison, entering the shop first, greeted Will. He was flabbergasted! Cautiously, he greeted everyone, wondering what was happening. He asked me whether we were on our way to another place. We all sang "Happy Birthday." He glanced at Betty as if wondering whether she knew what was going on. Soon he relaxed, and reality started to sink in. He was very pleased we had all come to make his day. Dick helped Will finish the repairs, and we enjoyed cool soft drinks on the patio in the shade. Most of the family was together again. It was like old times.

That evening we met at Applebee's for dinner. There was quite a crowd, but extra tables were soon joined. We were treated with real Southern cooking. Each one could order his/her own meal. To our astonishment, the waiters wrote the orders on paper napkins. They were humorous and yet efficient. Peggy and I ordered shrimp dinners, I recall. The food was delicious, the service excellent. You can imagine the rather boisterous conversations, the rapid delivery of jokes, homespun recollections, and recalling previous birthday celebrations. It was as if we were again in Wall Lake at the farm, enjoying their mom's array of her favorite meals, with all the other goodies. How we wished Beulah and Henry were still living in order to join the family festivities.

With pomp and circumstance, the large birthday cake was ceremoniously placed in front of Will, with all the candles lit. After he had blown out the candles, we started to sing the birthday song. But, the head waiter raised his hand for attention and proceeded to lead a group of fellow waiters in the most unique presentation of the song we had ever heard. To begin, some hummed and clapped their hands, others gyrated in a bold display of bodily contortions. Then clapping in rhythm, all sang their rendition of "Happy, Happy Birthday," some in tune, others in harmonious dissonance. How we did laugh and applaud. I have never again heard such a performance!

The cake, ice cream, and coffee were served. Will was shell shocked by such commotion and well wishing. We invited the whole clan to the motel to continue the celebration with gifts, more reminiscing, and humorous exchanges. At one point, Dick brought down the house by saying, "I'm hungry!" Of course he was joking, I think. Gradually, it dawned on us that we had long journeys the next day. Most reluctantly, we had to say our farewells, but all agreed that it had been worth it. Will said, "I can't recall a better birthday!" Neither could we.

Chapter 55

A Wedding, Remembered in a Will, Increased Concern

In the Fall of 1997, while Peggy was taking the final chemotherapy treatments, we received a call from John Hou wondering if we were able to attend his wedding to Anne Ko. Peggy was on the extra extension. Before I could draw a breath, she immediately said, "Yes!" This was an art for her, to sum up a situation in a second and respond. Esther's husband, Joe, once inquired how the Schlorholtz family could so rapidly make decisions. I replied that it was in the genes and by following Peggy's example. It was my disposition to mull things over a bit, as Joe meticulously did. Peggy's quick reaction was based on an emotional virtual reality. She was recalling the close ties we had with the Hou family in Pakistan and in New Jersey after their retirement. I was wondering whether Peggy was well enough to travel that far. In any case, John was delighted and asked me to give a short homily to which I agreed.

To shorten the travel time, we took a plane from Tampa to Newark, rented a car, and drove to the hotel in upper New Jersey. Our reservation had been made by John. The next evening, we drove to a nearby town where the wedding ceremony was to take place at the Presbyterian Church. A full rehearsal was held with a most efficient, proficient, and insistent consultant who had clearly done it all before. Later, we joined the rehearsal dinner at a posh Chinese restaurant. Choosing from innumerable plates of the most delicious foods served on the lazy susan, we joined in the festivities of the evening. We were in the midst of the dearest of friends whom we had known from Lahore days and in Short Hills where they now lived. You can imagine the chatter and joy of the hour. After dinner, friends from MIT, from which both had graduated, and work colleagues started "roasting" John and Anne. Their intent was to embarrass the future bride and groom with a full recital of every humorous reference and joke one can imagine. John got the worst of it. It was a night to remember.

The next evening, the impressive wedding ceremony was conducted by the local Pastor, and I gave that short homily. In the appropriately decorated church filled to capacity, the bride and groom exchanged their vows and joyfully entered into matrimony. Afterwards, we all drove back to the hotel for a superb dinner, the men in tuxedos and the women in flowing gowns, all except Peggy and me. She wore her favorite blue sari, and I wore my black Hart, Schaffner & Marx suit, complete with cummerbund. The parents of the bride and groom sat with the newly wedded couple. I snapped a lot of photos and treasure them to this day. There was a full orchestra and dancing. Everyone had an exhilarating time. Peggy kept going, motivated by the joyous occasion of sharing in our extended family. The next morning, as Peggy and I were taking our leave, we were delayed by having to scrape the ice from our car. We made it safely back to Newark and Florida; however, she had a short relapse after we got home. That trip to New Jersey had been strenuous, but Peggy exclaimed she wouldn't have missed it for the world!

(Author's update.) Nearly every spring, when baseball training begins here in Florida, John, Anne, and their two children, Alexander and Emma, come South for a "breakfast visit." Alex, a loyal Yankee fan, wears their full uniform. He pitches baseball for his school and likes Science, Math, and History the best. Emma, the younger sister, plays soccer. Her nickname is "The Merry Widow." Yes, she has a deadly attack. Her favorite subjects are Science and Math. She added, "And I know all about Math!" We spend two hours over breakfast in the exchange of memories and jokes, contributed by all present. Nothing compares with long-standing friendship and enduring love.

In February of 1998, a letter arrived from the Polking & Sons law office in Carroll, Iowa. It was with a great deal of apprehension that I opened it. Had something gone wrong? The enclosed letter informed me that I was one of forty-eight beneficiaries named by Ethel and Joe Schweer's Estate in their Will. She was my first school teacher. In part it read, "Since Ethel and Joe had no children, the following beneficiaries appear..." Imagine our surprise! They had never mentioned this to us. I experienced a deep humility and gratitude to be remembered in such a way. (See Chapter Six if you care to refresh your memory of my elementary schooling with Ms. Ethel Peters as my teacher for the first five years.) Peggy and I discussed this and agreed since there were forty-eight beneficiaries, we could expect to receive a few hundred dollars. We put it out of our minds, because we had a suspicion that settling an Estate takes a long time. And we were right in this.

I was busily engaged in my work at Northwood Church. Since I had come to know many more members, the visitation load increased. Calling on the cancer patients at Morton Plant Hospital was the most challenging and difficult. I recall one man who spent twenty-eight days with chemotherapy there. He was in isolation. His wife, in a sanitized gown, called to his attention that I was outside the thick glass window praying for him. She stepped out for a few moments at times to report on his treatment and attitude. This I cautiously shared in the Church Bulletin. People always want to know all the details, but I could only tell them that he was doing as well as possible and receiving the best of treatment and care. After a long recuperation and remission, he and his wife invited Peggy and me for dinner one evening. He thanked me for being there for him. Each time I had visited, he could only gaze in my direction, which was for him a ray of hope and an attachment to dear church members who prayed for him daily. His wife, too, was recovering her health. Being a caregiver is not easy.

Visitations were never routine or monotonous. One dear woman in Brier Creek was getting impatient with her bedridden affliction. Her daughter, a Home Health Care nurse, cared for her in a loving faithful way but had daytime duties. She called me to express her concern for her mother, nearing death she thought. I visited her that very morning and could see she was weak and pale. She was a woman of faith, often quoting verses of Scripture. I read portions of John 14: "Let not your heart be troubled..." and then turned to read those vivid descriptions of heaven in the book of Revelation. After listening intently, she quietly said, "My, that is a wonderful place isn't it!" Three days later, her daughter called to say her mom had passed away. She had told her daughter, "Don't worry; I'm on my way to Eternal Glory." My visit had not caused her death. Her faith, hope, and love for Christ had matured to the point her fears had disappeared. It is an ever humbling experience to be a Pastor.

There are visitations which are enjoyable and memorable. Two special members come to mind: Charlie Seaman and Blanche Marshall. I share just two examples, even though there are many more. Charlie collected things from all over the world. His mobile home was literally stuffed with rare first edition books; autographed copies of novels; letters from distinguished people; post cards from Germany with differing scenes of the Cross, the Lord's Prayer, and all twelve Apostles; an illustrated history of England in gold print; rare buttons. You name it, he had it. Born in Nova Scotia, he and his wife became USA citizens. She had been a pianist of fame in New York. The piano stool was filled with sheets of music which she had played before elite audiences. Charlie took delight in showing me his treasures. Without fail there would be questions regarding the interpretation of some difficult passage of Scripture. We debated many. Blanche was a world traveler. At that time, she had toured ninety-six countries and could give you a travelogue of her impressions of cultures, people she had met, and future trips she was planning. Prim and proper but sharply witty and wise, she kept an eagle eye on the notice board in church – it must be neat and up to date! She was also kind and generous, helping the needy wherever they were.

Finally, the letter from the Law Office arrived. The portion reserved for each and every beneficiary was twenty-three thousand dollars! What I had not anticipated was that the Schweer's farm, their spacious house in Arcadia, and all the furnishings, tools, and the like had been sold at auction. The payments were to be distributed over a period of three years while the tax settlement with the State was being finalized. Each December prior to Christmas, we received a check. At the second Christmas, when the whole family was present, we shared a thousand dollars with each one: Stan, Hope, Esther, John, Tanya, Erik, and Arin. We narrated how Ethel and Joe had remembered and given so generously. We related the story of my schooling and experience of attending a rural Iowan, one-room schoolhouse many years before. I led us all in a prayer of thanksgiving and celebration for the lives of Ethel and Joe. The next year, Stan suggested we trade in our old Taurus and get a new one. Since he is an experienced auto salesman and financial expert, we asked him to negotiate the purchase. A week later, he called and gave us the choice of color, told us what it would cost, and asked if we would like a Honda Accord instead. We settled on a blue Honda Accord. Stan had convinced us we should change from green to blue. We had no credit rating as we always had paid by cash. Our financial advisor said we could pay for the car by check, because a five thousand dollar check had been deposited recently. You guessed it – the final installment from the Will. That's how things ought to work, though it doesn't often happen that way. Stan arrived with our new car; we sold him our old one at a low price in appreciation. Peggy was the first to drive it around the pond! Yes, all had been cleared with the I.R.S.

During this time, Peggy's memory test results were getting steadily lower. Occasionally she wandered looking for her mother. Kind neighbors would help her to return home while I was at work. This was an increased concern. I decided to leave the Parish Associate work and devote my full time to caregiving. There was no alternative. In life, priorities must be set and put into action. Peggy was my very dearest, first priority.

Chapter 56

Northwood, Birthdays, Anniversaries, Pakistan Reunion, Boston

In October 1999, I sent my letter of intention to the senior pastor requesting the termination of my work as Parish Associate by the end of the year. There was no response. Assuming my request was being dealt with, I let things ride and continued visitation and my usual duties. The second to last Sunday in December, I reaffirmed orally with the senior pastor that having heard nothing from him the next Sunday would be my last. (He said he had assumed I would continue through Easter.) I was requested to preach on the final Sunday of the year as the senior pastor would be visiting relatives. My sermon was "The Use and Abuse of Life," the account of the Prodigal Son. My main points were: We make choices in life. It is our choice to use well what we have been given. When, like the Prodigal Son, have we also chosen to abuse and waste our birthright? The final note was centered on the Loving Father who is always ready to forgive, celebrate our return, and welcome us back to the right and true path. "But when he was yet a great way off, his father saw him, and had compassion, and ran, and fell on his neck, and kissed him." Luke 15:20. It was most effective. One woman wondered why I had included all as Prodigals. My reply was, "Too often we take pride in thinking we are not like him!" One of the elders presented a farewell check, and I closed in prayer. I was now free to be a full-time caregiver for Peggy.

To consolidate a lot of birthday celebrations, allow me to briefly note some of them. Each March, we celebrated Peggy's birthday. Most of our children came if it was possible. This was always a highlight for her. In March 2000, the whole Hoft clan arrived, except Norm, Will, and Betty. We had two glorious days of celebration. It was Peggy's seventy-fifth birthday. They stayed at the nearby Scottish Inn. We went out for lunches, but for dinner there was that unfailing Boston Market takeout. Again the united family shared the activities and memories of past years. Peggy enjoyed the excitement and joy of family being together. This was repeated in 2005 for her eightieth birthday. All the children came for that monumental affair. Joy Biswas came from Toronto, saying she could not miss such a landmark in Peggy's life. The cake was heavily frosted and had "80th" in large print prominently displayed. We made sure that Peggy had heaps of ice cream with her cake. This was always a favorite of hers. She bore up well. The stimulus of loving children and close family/friends sparked her memory and warmed her heart.

Joy Biswas at Peggy's 80ᵗʰ

Each December, Stan, Jo Ann, Tanya, and Erik visited to celebrate my birthday and to exchange Christmas gifts. We had sent Hope, Esther, and John their Christmas boxes and had received ours. The gifts were neatly arranged around the tree, which we decorated each year on my birthday. Stan and I exchanged copies of the World Almanac, an annual ritual. There were more than enough gifts for/from everyone. All protested that Peggy had given too many gifts, but all understood it was her way to share her love and generous expression of heart.

The same happened for anniversaries. We had always celebrated our and other anniversaries with cards and gifts. Peggy had a special calendar on the wall with the dates of birthdays and anniversaries for family and friends. Those dates she could remember! Since all the children could make it, they arranged a program for our fifty-sixth wedding anniversary in 2002. We invited close friends from the Sunday school class and the whole family to a luncheon at the China Star, our favorite buffet with five long tables filled with Chinese delicacies – from dim sum to green tea ice cream. The manager made available a large banquet room for our thirty-five invited guests. We met at noon. After a word of welcome, Arin placed elaborate garlands around Peggy's and my necks, the same ones used to bid us farewell by the Naulakha Church in Lahore, Pakistan in 1960! From our stored box of treasures, they gave the party an air of oriental flair and tradition. Esther, as mistress of ceremonies, introduced everyone. All were invited to indulge themselves at the serving tables, return to the banquet room, and enjoy the sumptuous goodies. Then the entertainment began. Esther gave Peggy her gift – a plaque stating she was the Woman of the Year! Joe

presented me with a *Time* magazine cover under glass, acclaiming me as the Man of the Year! There were other cards and gifts too numerous to list here. Guests were requested to add their greetings and anecdotes, which they did. It was a gala affair. I had made an arrangement with the manager, whom we well knew from our frequent visits there, to pay for the party. (He deducted ten percent from the bill, because it seemed to him that we

Joanne Rowley and John at our 56ᵗʰ

were a church group.) This caused quite an adverse reaction from our guests, who insisted they wanted to pay. I explained that according to Asian custom, the cost was borne by the one who had invited everyone. It was time for Joe and John to organize the group photo. With the backdrop of colorful Chinese characters and designs, it was a masterpiece. A good time was had by all!

Special Friends and Family at Peggy's 80ᵗʰ

In August of 2000, Peggy and I drove to Pennsylvania, near Allentown, to attend the Pakistan Reunion, where our missionary and AID people who had labored together were to meet. This Reunion was held on alternate years, in some part of the USA. En route, we stopped for two nights at Princeton to nostalgically relive our years there.

Old Friends from Pakistan Get Together Again
(Florida gathering pictured here)

What a blessing and thrill that was. Peggy and I attended worship at Miller Chapel noting that non-USA students were now a strong minority, registered at the Administration building (but missed meeting with the President of the seminary because he was on a lecture tour), sat in a class desk in Old Main, viewed Erdman Library, and wished we could still live at South Hall. None of the Professors with whom I had studied was on the Staff roster. We had all grown older, or were in retirement. Peggy was not feeling too well and tired easily. The next day, we traveled to East Straudsburg to spend Saturday and Sunday with Mary Schlorholtz, Wayne's wife. He had passed away. She entertained us royally. Her son, Tom, got up before dawn to catch enough brown trout to add to the feasts. David, Karen, and Tyler also came to meet us. Tyler and Arin are the same age. We had a great time and attended church together. But, Sunday evening as Peggy and I were getting ready for bed, she delayed for too long coming from the bathroom. I found her suffering severe stiffness, practically unable to move. Half carrying her, I got her into bed and massaged her neck and shoulders. She relaxed and fell asleep. By morning she seemed to be okay. I did not mention this to Mary, not wanting to alarm her.

We drove to the Retreat Center, registered, and were comfortably settled by late afternoon. The Reunion Committee had chosen accommodations well for the one hundred twenty guests. We were surrounded by former colleagues and friends, many of whom were older than I remembered. Dinner was served, and there were welcomes and introductions. We were pleased to see many Pakistani Christians in attendance. Among them were Anwar Samuel and his wife. He had been the athletic director at FC College during our years there. We also recognized nurses from the United Christian Hospital in Lahore. The list of fellow missionaries is too long to record here. I hope they understand. To mention a few: Bob and Rowena Tebbe, Fred and Roberta Ritze, Bob and Gerdine Stanton, Mary Wheeless, Dr. Bob and Ginny Dunlap, George and Anne Tewksberry, the Sagers, Williams, Bowes, and the Pakistan Bible Society secretary. He still carried a gun slug under his shoulder after being shot by two zealots who tried setting fire to the Bible Society library at the entrance to Anarkali Street.

Daily routines of meals, Bible studies, prayer, singing, and discussion groups were enjoyable means of renewing acquaintances and reliving old times in Pakistan. Of course, we had to listen to some who rehearsed their aches and pains, their hobbies, recent incidents of challenge, and slightly exaggerated noble activities. But we did honor the accounts because they came from the heart and soul of dedicated people. Our children's teachers of Murree Hills days were there. We learned about some previously unknown escapades, which we inwardly doubted – our little angels would never have been any trouble to their teachers. Each afternoon, when everyone was exhausted, the presentation programs centered around five spectacular mission field experiences. These slightly embellished accounts helped us recall events and places we had known. Not having asked Peggy and me to present our experiences, they missed what would have been strict objective reporting. The lecture on Islam and present-day issues was well done. All things considered, the Reunion was a success. There is a close feeling of emotional association with those who like us had become brothers and sisters in a common cause. We were an extended family.

Our next stop was Boston to visit Esther, Joe, Arin, and John. Esther had become a senior vice president at her bank and was still busily engaged in affordable housing and community development work. Among numerous projects that Esther was instrumental in creating, one of our favorites was low cost housing for grandparents who by necessity became the primary caregivers for their grandchildren. We enjoyed seeing some of the community investment work she loves so much to do. Brother John has said he is disappointed if he doesn't get invited to an awards banquet for Esther every couple of years. Joe's expertise in public relations had helped him become the Director of Communications for an engineering college. And Arin was an active lad of ten! He entertained us with computer and TV games. Highly competitive, he loved playing a computerized tennis game with Grandma Peggy, also a fierce competitor. By maneuvering a joy stick, one could actually swing a racket. Arin consistently won. Joe finally inquired where the "helps book" was. Arin reluctantly admitted that he kept it in his room (not wanting to give the advantage to an opponent). Grandma had met her match! We were reminded that a few years earlier, while helping them move from Oak Square to their home on Smith Avenue, Grandpa was assigned the task of protecting Arin from getting crushed by the Gentle Giants Moving Van crew. I held him by the hand while heavy objects were being carried out. He had fussed and when Esther asked him what was wrong, he exclaimed, "I'm trying to get away from Grandpa."

John joined us in the evenings for pizza, salads, and hot rolls at Bertucci's – Arin's favorite eating place. John was teaching yoga as a principal instructor at the Harvard Wellness Center and other places. His Ageless Yoga videos were soon to be in production. He also held retreats for his students and was planning tours to India and Nepal. Most importantly, he related the progress he was making teaching Arin all the uncle tricks, like smashing a raw egg on one's head without breaking it, wearing hideous masks at Halloween, and playing April Fool's Day tricks. We had an exciting visit. However, the night before starting back to Florida, Peggy had another attack of stiffness. She made me promise not to let on to Esther and Joe. I didn't – but with a great deal of anxiety. Providentially we arrived safely in Florida and our condo on Whitebridge Drive.

Chapter 57

Not Coping in the Condo, Sale, Packing,
Moving to Mease Manor

The first week of our return, I made an appointment with Peggy's neurologist. He ordered x-rays which he announced gave absolute proof that she had suffered minor strokes. He reassured us that since there had been no evidence of physical aftereffects, Peggy should remain on her prescribed medicines and take it easy. All went well until she began to complain about the pain in her groin later that year. Dr. Baldi referred us to the Helen Ellis Hospital near Tarpon Springs, where there were pain specialists. Two of the doctors started an investigation of possible causes for the pain. Was it a hernia? X-rays could not confirm this. Powerful pain medicines were prescribed, but still the pain persisted. After a few more visits, Peggy was referred to Dr. John Sullivan, a specialist in hip problems. He diagnosed the problem. Peggy needed a hip replacement. There was an open date in two weeks; we made the appointment for surgery.

The hip replacement operation went well. Dr. Sullivan announced that it was state of the art. Hope and Frank drove down from Atlanta to be present the day of surgery on Monday, the day after Palm Sunday. All went well, but there would be two weeks of recuperation at the Health Clinic adjoining the hospital. Peggy had her own private room, good meals, and many rounds of physical therapy. Her therapist was Rhoda, who insisted on a strict schedule of exercises. I stayed each day with Peggy from 8:00 in the morning until 8:30 in the evening, after she was relaxed enough to sleep. This meant a daily round trip of twelve miles. I made my own breakfast to be in time to help Peggy with hers. After she had eaten lunch and the evening meal, I quickly had my meals at the hospital cafeteria. They insisted I keep my distance as she learned to use the walker, pushing that contraption up and down the halls. There was also a series of stretch and balancing exercises. After about ten days, I watched her making good progress on the walker when suddenly another patient asked, "Do you want to race?" An athlete always ready to compete, Peggy elevated her walker and swung it in the path of that very surprised man. Rhoda was furious! She informed her that was dangerous – they would have to talk about the incident in her room. Laughing, Peggy protested, "But he challenged me!" The man didn't mind that she had blocked his way. In fact, in the afternoons while she was taking a nap, he would impishly glance into the room and ask in mock fear, "Is she coming out?" We had a good laugh as I told him he was safe for the moment. Peggy completed the course, and with a new walker in the trunk of the car, we headed for home. She had to continue exercises for many months, but her left hip worked like new.

During that year and the next, Peggy suffered from attacks of Urinary Tract Infections (UTI), panic anxiety attacks, and a gradual decrease in Memory Loss tests. A panic attack is extremely serious. The symptoms are similar to a heart attack, with intense pressure in the chest and severe pain. I recall driving Peggy to the Countryside Hospital one evening to the Emergency Room. The doctor told me I had done the right thing, thinking at that time it was indeed her heart. She was admitted and spent one night there. By the next morning, the doctor had cleared her, stating it was panic anxiety, not a heart attack. You can imagine the stress and strains this caused. While Peggy was able to move about in the condo and walk up and down the sidewalk outside, she was frustrated that she could not circle the pond. It was quite a struggle to attend worship and Bible Studies. Peggy rebelled against using that walker in public, especially at church. I could deal with this, but her daily requests that we drive to Iowa to visit her parents were increasingly insistent. (Both had passed away years before.) There were many other trials, but we carried on.

In May of 2005 toward evening, Peggy in a soft subdued voice made a statement: "Al," she said, "I've been thinking. What would I do if something happens to you? I couldn't manage to take care of all this." I was deeply impressed by her awareness of our situation and her vulnerability. I had assumed I could be her caregiver forever. "We are going to move," I told her and immediately explored and considered the retirement homes in the area. When we discussed this with Esther during her regular Saturday morning call, she remarked, "Why don't you consider Mease Manor in Dunedin? Howie, a co-worker of mine, has recently returned from visiting his parents there. They just love that place. Dunedin is a special town on the Gulf of Mexico with many activities and charming places of interest." She was on to something. Near Highland Lakes there was only one motel and not much to keep visiting family entertained. Peggy and I visited Mease Manor, got the facts and costs, asked about services, and observed the friendly atmosphere. Denise, our contact person in marketing, convinced us we would be most happy and content there. However, there was a six-month waiting list. That sounded ominous to me.

Who would buy our condo? Judy and Fred Churchsmith had visited us and liked our place. I decided to give them a call. Informing them of the situation, I asked if they would like to buy our condo. Without consulting each other, they gave an immediate "Yes!" We reported the good news to Mease Manor and intimated that we would like to move in as soon as possible. At that date there was not one deluxe suite vacant, but they would inform us when one became available. Patience is a virtue!

I began to pack in earnest, gathering cartons from Publix, U-Haul, and the Post Office. In the June, July, and August heat I sorted, wrapped, and packed many, many cartons. These I stacked in the garage. I had never realized how much we had. I was reminded of a friend in Nepal saying, "Pilgrims have to travel light." Too late for that! John was especially concerned that moving might seriously disorient Peggy.

In July, Judy and Fred visited us to finalize a deal. They measured every nook and corner. After being interviewed by the Executive Committee for approval of the sale and terms, we signed an Agreement of Good Faith. We wondered when our suite would be ready. Every week, I called Mease Manor inquiring about vacancies. Not yet! Then, Judy and Fred got a stupendous offer for their property in Minnesota and sold it. Talk about faith! Peggy and I reported this new development to the marketing people at Mease Manor. We were in a squeeze to vacate our condo. Denise said she would see what could be done. Two days later, she called to say we should come and see a possibility. They had joined the paint room on Floor Five to a two-room apartment, creating a full suite. We would have preferred a view of the Gulf, but the one facing New York Avenue was available. We agreed to take it. A tentative date for October 1 was set. We made the down payment and shared the good news with Judy and Fred. I arranged a moving date for September 27, which was accepted by Denise. She was imploring and pressing the maintenance people to complete renovations.

A week before that date, Peggy was weak in the legs with a possible UTI. She responded well to the medicine but still had weakness. The next afternoon, I watched in utter shock and amazement as she literally crawled from the living room to the bathroom. I helped her and then drove straight to the local Health Store to purchase a travel chair. That solved the problem somewhat except it had to be pushed – night and day! Hope called saying she was coming to help. We hired the Welcome Home Location Company to help us move. Pam arrived with the floor plan of our suite. Measuring everything, she studied where things would fit into the new rooms. She did this successfully with two exceptions: the large green sofa and the eight-cup percolator. We affirmed the date of the 27th for moving. Pam said they would arrive early that morning, before 8:00. The closing date was set for the 26th. Judy and Fred had hired our granddaughter Tanya to arrange the closure process at the First American Title and Insurance office where she worked as manager. It went off without a hitch. We hurried over to Mease Manor to give them the full payment and were designated as Lifetime Members.

Hope arrived the 26th evening, ready to help pack, but all was ready. She noticed that night before the move that Peggy became disoriented in the hustle and bustle of last-minute preparations. Seated in her portable chair, she took off her clothes and placed them in the washing machine, then managed to stand and walk a few steps down the hallway toward her Alfred. He said, expressing their deep shared love which had overcome all obstacles, "That's my wife, that's my Peggy." Before 8:00 am, as promised, a large van arrived with six determined packers, plus two trucks. My, what efficiency! They wrapped things and placed them in blue tubs taped to indicate placement in the suite. The furniture was placed in the trucks and much more. While I kept watch over the whole process, Hope pushed Peggy to the verandah of the Club House, a shady place and appropriate viewpoint. By 11:30 the condo was empty. We locked the door and had lunch at Kally K's. The crew had told us that they needed time to unload and put things in the assigned places. They did an excellent job. By 5:00, the in-charge lady invited us into our suite. All was in place – bed, sofa adorned with mirrored pillows from Pakistan, Beulah's paintings safe, dishes, cabinets arranged as before, bookcases, linens. Overwhelmed by the almost exact re-creation of the familiar condo in the unfamiliar setting, Peggy wept with gratitude. The excess cartons were piled in the spacious verandah, a mountain of them. We had not downsized enough.

What a blessing it was to settle into our suite the very same moving day with everything placed as planned. We were weary, but could relax and begin to enjoy our new home. Hope stayed several days to help put the final touches to the repositioning of smaller items the way Peggy wanted them. Those thoughtful movers had even placed fresh milk, bread, butter, fruit, and cold cuts in the fridge. Their service was a bit expensive, but we could never have made that move without their help. The next weekend, John arrived to assist in putting the books and paintings in place. He liked our suite and was pleased to note that his mom had not become as disoriented as he had feared. We took our lunches and dinners in the first-floor dining room, which was large enough to accommodate two hundred seated at tables for two, four, or five diners. Tanya joined us for dinner one evening and marveled how comfy our suite was.

Esther Prepares our First Breakfast on the Verandah

The next weekend, Esther came to help. She, too, was favorably impressed with our suite of three rooms, two bathrooms, a screened verandah off the second bedroom, and a larger verandah off the living/dining room. The only place the dining room table fit was on the large verandah. Early the next morning, Esther had cleared everything off that table, placed a bouquet of flowers in the middle, and had breakfast ready and served in that bright sunny corner. She had opened the sliding windows. The fresh October air was refreshing. We could hardly drink it all in – our move was complete

338

and our future promising. Two weeks later, Stan and Jo Ann came to help move the TV, computer, and other accessories into the second bedroom. From that day, it was referred to as the office or TV room. They, too, were pleased with the place and were glad for us that the move to Mease Manor had gone so well.

Chapter 58

Difficult Times, Decision, Celebration of Life,
Return to Iowa

If you have ever been a one hundred percent/twenty-four hours a day/seven days a week caregiver, you will understand what I am about to write. This is most painful for me, but love, respect, and honor for Peggy must override grief, separation, and "heart trouble." Gradually, Peggy's memory and health deteriorated. I did all I could to refresh that memory, but each morning was like downloading a computer program. We started from nearly blank to recalling family, the elusive dates of the month, the concerns of a strong-willed and insistent Peggy. I prepared the meals, helped her shower, get dressed. She insisted on facing the large mirror to comb her hair, apply color to fading eyebrows, lipstick, and the necklace chosen for the day. She was particular about her appearance and dress. We got to know Dillard's quite well, selecting pantsuits, blouses, and accessories. She never lost her self-esteem and pride of appearance. These were deeply ingrained in her character and lifestyle. I was amazed at the vitality of her subliminal soul alleviating the gaps in her brain.

The travel cart was a godsend. At night, it served as transport, four or five times a night, taking Peggy to the bathroom and back to bed. It was her "chair" for all meals, our walks around the spacious backyard of Mease Manor by the pond and Carolina pines, and all activities everywhere. Pushing that travel cart was good exercise for me. For dinner, we often chose table twenty-four, which was a convenient location for Peggy to remain in her cart. Each evening, during dinner, that dreaded Sundown Syndrome would bring much anxiety and concern. Peggy wanted to know when we were starting out to visit family in Iowa. In her hallucinations, she insisted that Hope and Esther were waiting for us in the foyer. Nothing I said would decrease her pain and worries. Many times she refused to eat, leaving most of her food untouched. I bought compartment trays to take the food home, but she only picked at her food. At times, she would refuse to take her pills – it took a lot of cajoling.

Most Sundays, we placed the cart in the trunk of the car and attended worship at the First Presbyterian Church of Dunedin, where Rev. Victoria Byroade was pastor. Peggy was attentive, sang hymns, and often in a low voice shared her opinion of what was going on that bothered her. One rapid-fire preacher spoke so fast that Peggy turned to me and asked, "Is that Japanese?" Transferring her membership from Northwood, she was received into the Dunedin Church. She was still able to pray out loud and join in our daily reading of scriptures and family prayers. How grateful I was to have moved to Mease Manor. There were lots of helpful, friendly neighbors.

First Presbyterian Church of Dunedin

Incidentally, six months after we sold our condo the housing market crashed. Had we not moved at that time, we would have been trapped in the condo, unable to sell, not able to cope, unable to afford Mease Manor. All our family, including Judy and Fred, arranged to meet for our Sixtieth Wedding Anniversary in 2006 at noon in the small dining room at Mease Manor. Everyone related a memory or anecdote. Judy told the story of how Peggy and I had met at the Hoft farm and how Peggy had thrown an orange at me in High School. The staff did a marvelous job of decorating the room, serving the dinner, and providing the chocolate cake and ice cream. The young server began to cut such large pieces of cake that Esther intervened. She continued to cut large pieces for everyone, but a small one for herself. "Unfair!" all protested. Our children gave us a digital camera and taught their bewildered dad how to operate this new technology. Joe and John, assisted by Arin, had us pose for the family photo. We treasure it, but Peggy looks forlorn in her cart.

In March of 2006, Peggy collapsed in front of the bathroom lavatory. I tried to lift her into the cart but was not able. I called the emergency nurse station. Within four minutes she was there and advised the front desk to call 911. Within ten minutes the

341

Rescue Squad arrived, examined Peggy, and recommended taking her to ER. I followed in our car. Peggy had a severe UTI and was hospitalized for four days. The rules of Mease Manor were that following hospitalization a patient would spend twenty-one days in the Mease Continuing Care (MCC) center adjoining the main buildings. This was a period of rehabilitation, therapies, and nursing care. Meals were served in the room until the patient was able to join others at the dining room, where attendants served and helped whenever necessary. I helped Peggy as much as I could during the day. It kept me running to join her at mealtimes, do the laundry, and comfort her in her room until she was weary enough to respond to her sleeping pill.

On her return home, things went well for some time. Hope and Esther visited us that first weekend. Peggy was glad to see them. At Christmas, the family joined us. Peggy and I enjoyed decorating the tree, shopping for gifts, and celebrating those festive days. All stayed at the Best Western on the Gulf, a fifteen-minute walk from Mease. Then Hope Abigail, Frank, and family stopped for a visit on their way back from Tampa to Atlanta after a seven-day cruise. Peggy hardly recognized them, because she had not seen them for a long time. Hope was saddened by Peggy's lack of response to her questions. It was a short stopover, but most helpful for me. In March of 2007, Peggy had another UTI attack, hospitalization, and

A Warmhearted Visit by Helyn and Harry Hoft

referral to MCC for another twenty-one days. It was the same program and frustration as the earlier one. For Easter, Harrison and Helyn came to see Peggy. I was surprised that Harry and Peggy could talk a "blue streak" about being home on the farm and with their dear family. I arranged for a private dinner served in the fireside room. We had a good time together.

After that, during the summer, Peggy's Alzheimer's and Dementia worsened. I won't go into the details of those most difficult months. Fifty to sixty times a day, Peggy

342

would vehemently demand that we drive to Iowa to see her mom. After lunch, she would lie on the couch and I in the recliner chair. Many times she would waken me by the click of the front door "on her way down to the kitchen where her mom was working," as she told me. It was almost impossible to persuade her not to leave. I admit to having a shorter fuse. Peggy once remarked that I had changed in the last months. She confided to Hope, "I think Dad has slipped a bit." (I'll spare you the details of that most troublesome time.)

On September 4, Peggy and I had appointments with Dr. Dilella who came to the conclusion that for the health of both of us I should no longer try to care for Peggy. The next day, the Director of Nursing at Mease visited us and shared that given our mutual decision with the doctor, the process of moving Peggy to Assisted Living on the third floor of Mease should be speeded up. With a broken heart, I helped Peggy move on September 14. They forbade me to spend the night with her. They would take care of her. But it didn't work. During the night Peggy, separated from her husband, became so overwhelmed and disoriented that her behavior and conduct reached a crisis point. She was transported to ER. The Director said they could handle the situation. Esther called Mease Manor that very day to inquire about her mom's welfare, then called Tanya who came over immediately to inquire what was happening. Tanya and I went to the ER, talked with the Social Worker, and learned that MCC had refused to admit her because they lacked the special care Peggy would need. She suggested The Gardens at Dunedin on Patricia Avenue, because they had a secure ward for Alzheimer's residents and nursing care. Tanya and I got Peggy admitted and brought over her personal things and basic clothing. The wheelchair transport brought her over. She was able to walk, using a cane. With no memory of what had happened during the night and that day, Peggy understood only that Tanya was "giving her a room in her house." This comforted her, and she was grateful for her granddaughter's loving care. We tucked her in, being assured that she would be okay.

The next week at The Gardens went quite well. Then the morning of September 22, they found Peggy lying on the floor, having fallen out of bed. She did not appear to be hurt, but she fell again that evening. Taken to the ER, she was admitted into the hospital where she was treated for UTI, bruises on her back and arms, a sore left rib cage, though no broken bones. She spent four days there. Consulting with Susan of Social Services, we decided that Peggy should return to Mease Continuing Care.

However, they declined to admit her, because she needed more adequate care. We decided to admit her in Manor Care, a nursing home adjacent to the The Gardens on Patricia Avenue. Stan and Jo Ann drove down from Branford to help in getting Peggy admitted there. The Director and Jo Ann had worked together in the Mease Dunedin Hospital years before. Jo Ann, always the compassionate professional, spoke with everyone on our way out, asking them to "Take good care of our mom." Kind and competent personnel gave her the best of care. I visited her every morning from 10:00 to 12:00 and from 3:00 to 6:00 every afternoon.

How We Chose to Remember Peggy

Stan and Jo Ann again came for a visit the third week of October. Hope visited the next weekend and John the following weekend. Esther came on Wednesday. We visited Peggy on Thursday and Friday. Peggy remarked how beautiful Esther's hair was. Hearing me talking, she said, "There's my Al" and asked me to pray. Peggy passed into Glory at 7:20 Saturday morning, November 10, 2007. She had wanted to see the whole family before "relaxing and departing." Esther had also come to help send out the Christmas letter (which John had helped compose). We sent out another letter informing our worldwide family of our loss. Esther stayed with me for two weeks, responding to the myriad calls, emails, and cards of condolence.

On November 23, we all assembled for the Celebration of the Life of Peggy at 10:00 am in the Mease Manor auditorium. Over seventy were in attendance. Rev. Victoria Byroade led the worship. The whole family joined in placing the floral arrangement, portraits of Peggy throughout her life selected and framed by John, and a brass urn for the centerpiece. Joe and John set up the sound system and video projector. After the Prelude, Bach's "Jesu, Joy of Man's Desiring," and Peggy's favorite, "The Old Rugged Cross," there was a reading of scriptures, a film of loving memories prepared by Esther and Joe, and prayers followed by A Family Time of Sharing, when memorable eulogies were given by John, Hope, John Hou (who had come from New Jersey), Joe, Stan, and Esther. The Postlude was Handel's Hallelujah Chorus. Joe, John, and Arin each videotaped the entire ceremony. Later John produced the DVD *Auntie Peggy: Celebration of a Remarkable Life*. (Author's note: After Azam Gill, in France, happened to read online an article on Aunty Peggy in *The St. Petersburg Times*, we were reunited with the dear Gill family from our early days in Kasur, Pakistan forty years before.)

The weather in Iowa is too severe to risk traveling there in winter for an interment. The summers are too hot. We finally agreed on September 20, 2008. I drove to Stan and Jo Ann's, stayed overnight, and next morning early the three of us sped toward Iowa with Stan driving. Guided by the new GPS, we whizzed through Atlanta, Nashville, and had an overnight in Clarksville, Tennessee. We had calculated three days of driving, but the GPS directed us the shortest

The Wheatland Church: Al's Childhood Church

distance through St. Louis at breakneck speed, and on to Carroll, Iowa. We arrived there at 5:00 pm a day earlier than planned. I had made reservations for three nights at the Carrollton Inn. The receptionist informed me there was not a vacant room that night in the whole of Carroll as a dog show was in town. Jo Ann called her sister,

Jean, in Rockwell City and explained our problem. Without hesitation, Jean welcomed me to stay overnight in her home. Stan and Jo Ann were already scheduled to stay there. It was most pleasant to meet Jean, her sister, Mary Lou, and husband,

Larry. I had a comfortable rest. Toward noon the next day, Stan and Jo Ann drove me to Carroll via Rockwell City for lunch. This time they had a room ready for me. John had arrived a week early to take seven hundred representative photos of Western Iowa – farms, prairies, a county fair, churches. Hope drove in from Omaha having flown from Austin. Esther and Joe, Harrison and Helyn, Hope Abigail and Frank all settled in with us at the Carrollton Inn. Arin was in college. We spent Friday visiting Blackhawk Lake, the three cemeteries, and had lunch at the Hay Loft in Wall Lake.

On one of the most pleasant mornings Iowa had during September, our family, relatives from near and far, Peggy's and my high school classmates, former neighbors of ours, and friends of many years met at the Wheatland Presbyterian cemetery. We placed the brass urn and a large portrait of Peggy between bouquets of roses. Rev. Donald Gibson, the Pastor whom we had known for forty years, led us in the burial service. He read the scriptures we had chosen, led us in heartfelt prayers, and gave an

Inscribed on the Back of Our Stone

extraordinary, inspiring sermon. He called to our attention what had been inscribed on the grave stone. On the front side was a large SCHLORHOLTZ and Peggy's and my names, with the appropriate dates. On the back carved in stone was: Presbyterian Church USA in Mission, Pakistan – 1954-1978, Nepal – 1978-1989, By Love Serve One Another, and Philippians 4:4-8. There, in the shade of sturdy poplar trees, Peggy is at Peace where there is no more pain or suffering. What a blessing are enduring

346

love and comfort expressed by those with whom we are knitted together by the Love of God. We greeted one and all.

The women of the Wheatland Church had prepared a luncheon in the dining hall for all who wished to attend. This was the custom. It provided a time to chat and thank all who had made that special effort to share in our grief. Homegrown watermelon

The Wheatland Cemetery: Al's Childhood Farmstead
Stood on the Soft Rise in Background

and tomatoes were delicious. Afterwards, Ray and Kathy Wilhoite opened their hearts and the Hoft family house to us. They had farmed the land since they bought it from Henry and Beulah in 1963. We were all able to return home for Peggy. The next morning, Sunday, our family attended worship in that rural church from which we had come and to which we now returned for this final Benediction.

That evening, those of us who were still there gathered in a small dining room of the Carrollton Inn for a final meal of fellowship and the sharing of loving memories. It was a tender moment of meeting, greeting, and farewells. Monday morning, we all went our separate ways to carry on.

Chapter 59

Carrying On at Mease Manor, Close Friends

After the Celebration of Peggy's life, I was surrounded by our children and their families. There was much to discuss and share. A solid thread binds together grieving and yet also rejoicing over the happy memories and joyous recall of what made Peggy so special to each one of us. We talked of Iowa and the visits made to parents, grandparents, cousins, and friends. Much was serious, but there were lighter moments of the happy times in Pakistan. Many, many instances of "Do you remember when...?" It warmed my heart to hear of their devotion to their mother and what made her special to them. Underneath the banter, I sensed they were trying to comfort me and to blunt the loss, which we all shared deeply.

Inevitably, they had to return to their homes and work. That is when one feels the reality of loneliness settling in. I missed my Peggy. And yet, something I had said to many grieving church members over the years came to mind: "Our sorrow is deeply felt and there is nothing wrong with shedding tears, but life goes on. God is in the midst of one's suffering and His Grace and Love are constant to help carry the burdens of one's soul, heal the broken heart, and fill the void." I reread Peggy's Workable Verses and found comfort and an affinity of spirit as I reflected on those truths and insights of Reality which we shared in faith, hope, and love. I was reminded of the choices confronting me – become bitter and succumb to despair, or give thanks to God for the more than sixty-five years of shared love and life. I resolved to carry on, to honor the privilege that had been mine, and to continue the best possible job of life.

It came as a shock to discover how unwell I was. One doesn't realize while concentrating on caregiving the subtle deterioration and weakening of the body. I was overweight, had Diabetes Two, troubled sleep, and a weakened condition. My doctor helped me plan a schedule of exercising on the cross trainer, walking a mile each day, eating nutritious foods. I started in earnest to do daily John's Yoga Exercises, which he had developed as a principal instructor at the Harvard University Wellness Center. In six months, I lost eighteen pounds, lowered my blood sugar count, and felt a lot better. But, a routine physical examination revealed a heart murmur and abnormal heart rhythm. I was referred to a cardiologist, who has been treating me successfully. Enough of that!

How glad I was to be living at Mease Manor Retirement Community. Every Wednesday morning at 9:00 the housekeeper brings fresh linens and bath towels, cleans the bathroom and kitchen, dusts, and vacuums all the carpets. Whenever there is a need, I call maintenance. Within minutes they put things right. What help and convenience that is. My dad always refused to live in a Home, or Nursing Home. He said it was lining up to die! However, at Mease one is a part of an extended family, a good place to live. Fellow residents are open, friendly, and helpful. After Peggy died, they did not pity me, they showed compassion and concern. Most of them had already traveled the road I was now on. I learned not to inquire, "How are you?" The response was a review of aches and pains, operations, hip replacement, and the like. A simple "Good morning" or "Good evening" with a smile was better. At church one morning, the greeter remarked that I looked a bit sad. I told her about Peggy. "I know," she said, "grief is hell!" Then she carried on about her departed husband and how devastated she was. That is not condolence or expressing sympathy, that is adding to one's sorrows. One learns.

Occasionally, I invited Tanya to dinner at Mease, at noon on Sundays, because she was busy at work during the week. Every two or three weeks she would send an email inviting me to join her and her fiance, John Dunn, for a noon lunch at one of our favorite restaurants in Dunedin. We chatted about many things: family, work, and the latest news and issues of the day. It was great to have her living so close. Stan and Erik installed a new TV and computer. Jo Ann and Tanya visited in the living room while they were teaching me the art of surfing and using new programs. I wanted a manual of instructions, but they insisted I master the "concept" of what a computer can do rather than read about it. I did take notes. They also came for my birthdays. John came for a visit as often as he was able, with a pile of Indian curries. He brought a new scanner, able to scan four slides at a time, rather than only one as my old one did. He also taught me how to use it. I was being inundated with new technology. But it did prove that an old dad can learn new tricks! Esther and Joe visited and often sent boxes filled with rice and curries, videos, paperbacks, and beautiful cards. Esther calls me every Saturday morning at 8:00 sharp. This keeps me abreast of what is going on in Boston. Hope and Stephen visited at Christmas complete with all their camping equipment in their faithful Tundra pickup. Hope calls me Sunday evenings. All of them often send emails – we are a family keeping in touch and up to date. It makes me feel younger that many fellow residents at Mease do not own, want, or use a computer. I am free to do a lot of reading of books long neglected. During 2009, I read the whole Bible from Genesis through Revelation, including all the study notes. With the help and concern of family and friends, I am able to carry on at Mease.

There is no substitute for close friends. I am privileged to have many. The first three tables on the right as one enters the dining room on the first floor are unofficially reserved for us widowers/bachelors. It has become a tradition. Each table has places for five diners. The serving begins at 4:30. Waiters, who are high school students, take our orders from the menu and serve us a three-course meal. There is a six-week schedule of menus and choices with a wide selection of main courses, soups, vegetables, beverages, and desserts. I mention this because it is the setting for my close circle of friends. One can predict which chair will be occupied by whom, like students and churchgoers who regularly attend.

Let me name them: Ted is from Maine, a retired service station owner whose father helped build a long seawall using four-ton blocks of granite. He is our connoisseur of fish. Gus from upstate New York attributes his good health to working hard on a farm – he is ninety-six. Carl B. is a patent lawyer from Ohio who has worked in Washington, DC. Andrew is from Maryland and Virginia where he worked at the Pentagon in personnel. Dick is also from the Nation's Capital, having worked at the Federal Communication Commission. Dr. Ray, a distinguished scholar, taught law at Florida University. George is from Costa Rica, a quiet man very precise in manner and speech. John helped to invent synthetic gasoline – he is an apt businessman. Bob was the Managing Director for Proctor and Gamble in Cincinnati, Ohio. Jim is the golf fan, who at ninety-five still arranges the putting sessions on Mease's putting green. Carl C. from Michigan was a prisoner of the Japanese in World War II, forced to work in a coal mine. Dr. Earl is a psychologist/psychiatrist from Tennessee. Then there is Al. You already know what he did. The range in age is from eighty-six to ninety-six. I am the youngest.

The dinner hour is a special time for relaxation, sharing what is on our mind, and discussions of many current problems and issues. At first, I noticed that every topic was discussed with the exception of religion and politics. I joined this group during the lengthy and turbulent election campaign of 2008. Cautiously, I probed because I had learned that all Parties were represented. Gradually, I shared my views on rather broad issues which helped to break the ice. Finally, we agreed to talk about politics and religion. The rule was that no one try to persuade or force on others a strongly held opinion, but rather agree to work toward the substance of things for a better understanding. Ted said, "That's okay as long as it includes a lot of humor and laughter!" This was my cue to share many of my old jokes and anecdotes. Having lived in Asia for thirty-five years, I shared insights of parallel situations and conditions in Pakistan and Nepal. They were amazed to hear about life abroad and how people of other lands had similar problems, only in a different cultural setting. We also discussed the wars in Iraq and Afghanistan, the Israeli and Palestinian conflict, and what was happening in Pakistan. There were many questions about Islam, what Muslims believe, who were the Taliban, and how people could become suicide bombers. I related that in Pakistan when I was Chaplain at FC College in Lahore there were organized movements in Ichhra, led by Maudoodi and others. We agreed that many times religious and political extremists, convinced that they were driven to take violent action, tried to legitimize their hate and anger, believing they were doing the Will of the Almighty. Behind such militants is a person, group, or cause manipulating and using them. I assured my friends that such people were a small minority. The majority did not condone what was happening, but out of fear or intimidation did not dare to offer opposition. I am convinced that these friends of mine ought to be requested by the Congress to become a Committee on Common Sense and Consensus. Today the USA, tomorrow the entire world!

We do have distractions from the women diners at tables nearby. As we engage in loud laughter and quiet shouting, they wonder what is happening. One of them suspected that we were telling "dirty stories." I shared a strategy to defend our integrity. One evening, Dick joined a table of those dear ladies, where one asked, "What do you men talk about that makes you so noisy?" He replied, "Oh, I suppose the same things you ladies do." "Aren't they awful!" she remarked. One lady developed the habit of greeting us as "Hello, kids!" We innocently retorted, "Why do you call us small goats?" She also wanted to know why we men sat by ourselves instead of joining tables with women. My reply was that we had joined in a defense mechanism to guard against all those beautiful women in the dining hall! "You can't get way with that," she said and gave me a hug! Andy called attention to the fact that I was blushing. I quickly replied that Mark Twain had said, "Man is the only animal that blushes, or needs to." We keep a wary eye on her as she enters the dining room.

Whenever one hears that one of the group is ill or in the hospital, visits are made and get well cards are sent. Rides for errands and appointments are given to those who do not have a car. Why? Ted has the answer, "This is our family!" It is a tremendous blessing to have such close friends.

Chapter 60

Keeping Busy
Prologue

Peggy and I have always been savers of what is important and significant. As we moved from the condo to Mease Manor this became glaringly apparent. There were eight plastic containers filled with documents, letters, and reports. These were stored on the large verandah. Following Peggy's death, there were also piles of condolences, emails, and cards. Not wanting to discard them, Esther helped me get started arranging those treasures in large albums, the kind with acid-free paper savers. These were in addition to the very large albums of photos and letters Esther had assembled for our fiftieth wedding anniversary, the album Hope had done preserving the letters from Peggy to her parents, and Jo Ann's photo album for my eightieth birthday. I filled nine more with family photos, emails, cards, and letters of condolence. This kept me busy and helped me to recall what Peggy and I had experienced and done. It was good healing therapy and tempered the sharp edges of grief.

There were stored in one closet forty-three carousels of slides, plus three large cartons filled with slides dating back to the 1950s. Using the scanner that John had given me, I worked at reducing the eventual total of eleven thousand slides four at a time. John had also found online an eighty-at-a-time slide sorter. This was a great convenience. It enabled me to sort out and file in categories, such as people, places, scenes, cities, family, relatives, excursions, and the like. I filled forty plastic trays complete with tags for identification. Such a process enabled me to put scanned images into computerized categories and folders according to subject. I ended with one hundred sixty-nine folders under My Pictures. What an amazing technology! I also sorted several hundred letters Peggy had sent to her parents and friends. These I placed in paper savers bound in three-inch filing binders. It was no small matter to put them into chronological order by date and context when the postmark was too faint, or the letter was only headed Tuesday, the 12th. Those letters have been a large source of my recall in recording this book of memories. How thankful we are that Peggy's mom saved every one!

Next, I revised a Five Generation Genealogy of the Schlorholtz family. The original had been done by a cousin in Kamrar, Iowa. He sent it to Judy and Fred. Judy made many revisions and sent a complete, revised copy to me. Included were the notes on how, when, and why our ancestors came from Germany to the USA, finally to settle in Iowa. I wanted to preserve this record of our heritage for all seven of our immediate family. That meant a lot of printing. But it was worth it. Each one has a bound copy and an appreciation of the family lineage.

While engaged in these tasks, I was kept busy with the preparation for requested lectures. Dr. Earl suggested to the Chairperson of the Residents Committee representing four hundred members at Mease that I was well versed in the Middle East Conflict focusing on Israel and the Palestinians. He had gathered this from our frequent reviews of that conflict as we dined at our Bachelors' table. In June of 2008, they gave me a twenty-five minute slot on the program. I began by thanking them for giving me two hours! That caused a moan and much laughter after I assured them the twenty-five minute limit was real. John had requested that I videotape the affair. He wanted to make a DVD for the family. So I charged up the camera, which I had not used for awhile, put in a new tape, and tried it out the morning of the lecture in the Mease Auditorium. A big red flag appeared to inform me the battery had to be replaced. I scurried around town to find one. Thanks to Radio Shack I was successful. The lecture went well, since I had limited the scope of history to the last hundred years, tracing the fall of the Ottoman Empire, how the Colonial Powers had carved out the boundaries of the countries in the Middle East, how Jews had populated Palestine and declared the State of Israel in 1948, how the Palestinians reacted, the ensuing wars and attempts to find a solution to the conflict to the present. Carl B. remarked that he recognized the professorial in my presentation. He must have been referring to my manner of delivery, not to any arid presentation. That's what friends are for.

The Men's Club, which meets every third Wednesday of the month, needed a speaker for the September meeting. No one volunteered. I inquired whether they would like a lecture on "International Humor." They laughed and wondered who would present such a program! I admitted that over the years I had collected jokes and anecdotes from many lands and would share some of them if they agreed. This kept me busy for a month. Sorry, I will not share those with you here. However, if you invite me, I'll ask John to send you the DVD, though it is pricey. At the December meeting, I presented "Christmas in Pakistan" and the next spring reported on my experiences as a teacher at FC College, "Learning and Teaching." That is how I was, in part, kept busy at Mease. Attending the First Presbyterian Church of Dunedin for worship on Sundays and related activities was a source of joy and fellowship.

There was a foolish mishap. On February 12, 2009 I suffered a fall. I remember the date well, because it was Carrie's birthday and John was coming that day for a visit. About 10:30 in the morning I was taking my routine walk around the South Lawn of Mease when some birds distracted me. Glancing in their direction, I stumbled and smashed my face against the concrete sidewalk. Profusely bleeding, I tried to get up. A gentle voice told me not to. She said she had called 911 and that help was on the way. Cheryl had been working at the front desk of Mease. Answering a cell phone call, she was sitting on the bench outside when she saw me fall. The Rescue Team arrived and took over. They did what was necessary and transported me to the nearby ER. Mease called Tanya, who immediately came to see me. I spent the entire afternoon there getting x-rays, scans, and seven stitches. At 5:30 John called saying he and Tanya would soon be there to take me home. This they did. I related with embarrassment what had happened. John got me settled for the night, but at 11:00 I noticed the forehead wounds were bleeding. We went back to ER and they applied pressure packs. That worked. During the weekend John cared for me in an excellent way. How thankful I was that he was there to look after me during those first crucial days. Yes, my face turned that ghoulish bruised color. I ate my meals at home. It took over a month for healing, stitches out, and recovery. I am deeply indebted to those Guardian Angels who were there for me and am being extra careful now.

The highlight of February, 2010 was the privilege to conduct the wedding ceremony for grandson Erik and Kristin Muire in Tallahassee. What an honor for an eighty-six year "young" Grandpa! It had been some time since the last wedding. I could not even find a copy of the ceremony. Rev. Vicki Byroade came to my rescue. I adapted her material to fit the occasion, sent it to Kristin and Erik, and accepted their revisions. I also found my black Hart, Schaffner, and Marx suit and my preaching robe and stole. On the 18th, I drove to Stan's and Jo Ann's, stayed overnight, and on the 19th the three of us drove to the motel. At 5:30 the Wedding Rehearsal was held at The Retreat on Bradley's Pond. Everything went well because Kristin and Erik had perfected every detail. Stan and Jo Ann hosted the rehearsal dinner at a posh restaurant, really first class! On the 20th we assembled for the Wedding. Stan was Best Man. How grand were the Groomsmen in their tuxedos! How beautiful the Bride and her seven Bridesmaids, with Tanya among them! The Mothers were seated. Precisely at 6:00 the Bride appeared on the arm of her Father. The ceremony began. All went perfectly without a glitch. One hundred fifty guests attended the reception and enjoyed the catered dinner. There was a time for giving and receiving gifts and cutting the cake, followed by dancing. John, his dear friend, Joanne, and Joe videotaped the ceremony, reception – the whole the joyous celebration. This has become another treasured family DVD. Kristin's parents hosted a delicious brunch the next morning at their home where we had a more quiet visit with the parents, aunts, uncles, and joyful new couple!

Al Blesses a New Generation

Prologue

If you have read, dear reader, all that has been recorded here, you are to be congratulated. It is realized that there are gaps and omissions, but it is hoped you have grasped the nuances and spirit of Something we wanted to Share. Peggy and I are indebted to literally thousands of people from many lands. They have enriched our lives. We are a community of the heart, of the soul, and joy of life amidst the trials and vicissitudes of our human journey. Our love for each other, for our family, and for the lives we were privileged to help will never fade or be lost in obscurity, because all has been recorded on the Eternal Ledger of God's Will and Kingdom. How we pray that increasingly in our world, so torn and violent, there will arise an era of Peace and Goodwill for all. Pray for the Leaders of all countries that they will help their citizens and immigrants, not hurt those striving to attain their potential. Pray for the Peoples of all nations, the privileged as well as those in dire need, that By Love we can Serve one Another.

As I review the contents of this book, I am humbled that so much could be crammed into the storehouse of our experiences and efforts to make the world a mite better than we found it. How grateful I am to have shared more than seventy years with the love of my life, doing what we together were called to do. Peggy's mission lives on in the lives of countless people in many lands, where what she shared and did has taken root in the growth and development of receptive hearts and minds.

Thank you for joining in this Celebration of Life and Outreach! Inevitably, there comes the time for farewells. God Bless! Carry on! Keep the faith, hope, and love alive and thriving!